Economics and Evolution

Economics, Cognition, and Society
This series provides a forum for theoretical and empirical investigations of social phenomena. It promotes works that focus on the interactions among cognitive processes, individual behavior, and social outcomes. It is especially open to interdisciplinary books that are genuinely integrative.

Editor: Timur Kuran

Editorial Board: Ronald Heiner
Sheila Ryan Johansson

Advisory Board: James M. Buchanan
Albert O. Hirschman
Mancur Olson

Economics and Evolution

Bringing Life Back into Economics

Geoffrey M. Hodgson

Ann Arbor
The University of Michigan Press

To Nicholas Georgescu-Roegen and Richard R. Nelson,
and to the memory of George L. S. Shackle,
who moved us from equilibrium
and showed us the way to evolution

Published in the United States of America by
The University of Michigan Press
1996 1995 1994 1993 4 3 2 1

Library of Congress Cataloging-in-Publication Data applied for
ISBN 0–472–10522–1

Printed in Great Britain

Contents

Preface

This book is about the application to economics of evolutionary ideas from biology. It is not, however, about selfish genes, or the alleged determination of our behaviour by the genetic code. It does not establish the superiority by breeding of the English aristocracy, or any other favoured race, gender or social class. The idea of economic evolution endorsed here has much more to do with social culture and has little, if anything, to do with genes. Further, the conception of evolution as progress towards greater and greater perfection, along with the competitive individualism sometimes inferred from the notion of the 'survival of the fittest', are found to be problematic.

Is this, then, a book that relates to biology at all? The trouble is that many popular conceptions of biology are based on nineteenth-century notions of evolution, and often more on ideas such as those of Herbert Spencer rather than those of Charles Darwin. In addition, the reductionist biology of the sociobiologists and the devotees of the selfish gene is now strongly contested by a variety of different views from within biology itself. Indeed, it is not beyond exaggeration to state that the life sciences are undergoing a theoretical revolution which is bound to spill over into other sciences, including the social.

By nature I am a restless person, and thus I have never been enamoured of the neoclassical concept of equilibrium. It is the search for an alternative mode of theorizing to the mechanical, and particular acquaintance with the 'evolutionary' economics of institutionalists such as Thorstein Veblen, that led to this project to explore the past and future relationship between economics and biology.

My *Economics and Institutions* (1988) is a forerunner and companion to the present book. In some respects their primary concerns are similar: to map out the field and to raise the important questions, rather than to provide definitive answers. Their common stem is institutional economics, although the references to that tradition and its philosophical roots are more extensive and self-conscious in the present volume.

Concerning the possibility of progress in economic science, one can find sources of optimism and pessimism in my earlier work. The 1988 book had long sections devoted to the critique of neoclassical theory, but it was also suggested that this mainstream body of thought displayed a trajectory of development which had positive features: particularly the growing uneasiness, even among the mainstream, with neoclassical conceptions of time, information, learning and maximization (Hodgson, 1988, p. 5).

Yet despite this positive trajectory, evidenced in the works of neoclassical avant-garde thinkers such as George Akerlof, Kenneth Arrow, Frank Hahn and Joseph Stiglitz, it is clear that the citadel remains intact, and there are as yet no clear signs of a change of attitude among the neoclassical intellectual rank and file, who monopolize institutions and positions of power within the profession.

Despite this, the present work does not devote as much space to the critique of neoclassical theory. The primary objective is to continue clearing the ground for the task of theoretical reconstruction, and to consider the appropriate tools for this task that lie to hand.

It should be emphasized that there is not a well-rounded 'alternative' theory here, merely signposts to, and modest suggestions for, the economics of the future. Those that look for such an instant 'alternative', perhaps as a condition for giving anything heterodox serious consideration, simply forget the history of their own orthodoxy. Neoclassical economics took the combined efforts of more than a dozen exceptionally gifted minds over a period of more than ninety years – from the 1860s to the 1950s – before it emerged in its modern form. Likewise, the construction of a new economics is a massive task, and this is no more than a small and partial contribution.

Acknowledgements

Much of this work was completed while the author was a research fellow, for six months in 1991, at the Swedish Collegium for Advanced Study in the Social Sciences. SCASSS is located in the ancient town of Uppsala. At its university Carl von Linné (Linnaeus) laid out the taxonomic foundations of modern biology. What he accomplished by first 'organizing species into a coherent plan ... was a vital preliminary to the theory of evolution' (Worster, 1977, p. 32). It is also the city where Anders Celsius, conscious of the depths of the Swedish winter and the heights of its summer, devised the temperature scale which takes his name.

By good fortune, the author enjoyed another three months, during 1992, at the Zentrum für Interdisziplinäre Forschung (Zif) at the University of Bielefeld, Germany, as a member of an interdisciplinary research group of scholars, including philosophers, biologists, economists, sociologists and anthropologists. An early draft of this work was circulated among these colleagues at Zif, and their extensive comments were invaluable.

The author is very grateful for the time and resources provided by SCASSS and by Zif, and for the highly congenial and supportive groups of international colleagues found in both institutions.

Parts of this work have already appeared in print as separate articles. Some brief passages in chapter 1 and elsewhere are taken from the introduction to the book *Rethinking Economics* (Edward Elgar, 1991), edited by myself and Ernesto Screpanti, to whom thanks are due for his agreement to use this material from our joint introduction. Formal acknowledgements for other permissions are given overleaf.

The author is very grateful to many people for stimulating discussions and helpful comments on drafts of this work. They include Esben Sloth Andersen, Stephen Batstone, John Beatty, Stephan Böhm, Robert Boyd, Tom Burns, Dale Bush, Walter Carlsnaes, Lorraine Daston, Mike Dietrich, Kurt Dopfer, Alasdair Dow, Bill Dugger, Bill Durham, Mary Farmer, Peter Galasi, Tony Giddens, John Grahl, Tim Gray, Bo Gustafsson, Frank Hahn, Geoff Harcourt, Sean Hargreaves Heap, Daniel

Hausman, Peter Hejl, Margaret Jones, Elias Khalil, Christian Knudsen, Richard Langlois, Tony Lawson, Mats Lundahl, Uskali Mäki, Maureen McKelvey, Stan Metcalfe, Philip Mirowski, Sandy Mitchell, Joel Mokyr, Tracy Mott, Richard Nelson, Klaus Nielsen, Pavel Pelikan, Jonas Pontusson, Allan Pred, Michel Renault, Peter Richerson, Hilary Rose, Steven Rose, Warren Samuels, Paolo Saviotti, Ernesto Screpanti, Neven Sesardic, Gerald Silverberg, Peter Sloep, Brian Snowdon, Ian Steedman, Brinley Thomas, Marc Tool, Jonathan Turner, Tinne Vammen, Viktor Vanberg, Peter Weingart, Adrian Winnett, Ted Winslow, Sidney Winter, Ulrich Witt, Björn Wittrock, Peter Wynarczyk, Mo Yamin, and several anonymous referees involved with the publications mentioned in the preceding paragraph. Ann Bone provided excellent editorial help at the copy-editing stage.

In particular, the author is moved by the incredible generosity of several people in this list who have taken the time to read the manuscript and to offer insightful suggestions for improvement in plenty. In a small number of cases the author found himself in stubborn disagreement, and not all advice has been followed, but thanks are due nevertheless. In regard to the suggestions and corrections that were accepted, these were so numerous that a decision had to be made not to acknowledge each suggestion at the appropriate point in the text, but to convey the author's profound gratitude through personal communication, rather than in the publication itself.

Despite the benevolence of so many, writing is still an unsociable business, as every author knows. Living with an off-beat economist is one burden, with a recluse another. Yet all the members of my family have shown remarkable tolerance and generosity. Their personal and emotional support is acknowledged with deepest thanks.

The author and publishers are grateful for permission to draw on material by the author previously published elsewhere.

In chapter 3 from 'Economic Evolution: A Preliminary Taxonomy', *The Manchester School*, June 1993.

In chapter 5 from 'Marx, Engels, and Economic Evolution', *International Journal of Social Economics*, vol. 19, 1992.

In chapter 7 from 'The Mecca of Alfred Marshall', *Economic Journal*, March 1993.

In chapter 8 from 'Carl Menger's Theory of the Evolution of Money: Some Problems', *Review of Political Economy*, vol. 4, no. 4, October 1992.

In chapter 9 from 'Thorstein Veblen and Post-Darwinian Economics', *Cambridge Journal of Economics*, vol. 16, no. 3, September 1992.

In chapter 12 from 'Hayek's Theory of Cultural Evolution', *Economics and Philosophy*, April 1991, by permission of Cambridge University Press.

In chapter 13 from 'Economic Evolution: Intervention contra Pangloss', *Journal of Economic Issues*, vol. 25, no. 2, June 1991, by special permission of the copyright holder, the Association for Evolutionary Economics.

In chapter 14 from 'Evolution and Intention in Economic Theory', in *Evolutionary Theories of Economic and Technological Change*, ed. P. Paolo Saviotti and J. Stanley Metcalfe, copyright © Harwood Academic Publishers GmbH, 1991.

In chapter 15 from 'Why the Problem of Reductionism in Biology has Implications for Economics', *World Futures*, vol. 36, 1993, by permission of Gordon and Breach Science Publishers SA.

PART I
Introduction and Conception

Always history is being made: opinions, attitudes, and institutions change, and there is evolution in the nature of capitalism. . . . it is pertinent to call attention to the utter inapplicability to such changes, i.e. to history in the large, of the tendency towards a price equilibrium. Probably we must go further and reject entirely the use of the mechanical analogy, the categories of force, resistance, and movement, in discussing basic historical changes.

Frank Knight, *The Ethics of Competition*

I am pretty certain that the following prediction will prove to be correct: theorising of the 'pure' sort will become both less enjoyable and less and less possible . . . rather radical changes in questions and methods are required . . . the signs are that the subject will return to its Marshallian affinities to biology. . . . Not only will our successors have to be far less concerned with . . . grand unifying theory . . . [but also] less frequently for them the pleasures of theorems and proof. Instead the uncertain embrace of history and sociology and biology.

Frank Hahn, 'The Next Hundred Years'

1

A Brief Diagnosis

There comes a point in the development of a science when its fundamental concepts and propositions, indeed its whole method and approach, become the subject of inextinguishable controversy between the defenders of the faith, the habitual iconoclasts, and the would-be evangelists of the new. This is happening more and more in economics today.

Crisis is now an over-used word. Yet the deepening theoretical problems within economics suggest no other description. Indeed, the proclamation of a 'Crisis in Economic Theory' by Daniel Bell and Irving Kristol in 1981, in a celebrated collection of essays, now seems almost an understatement. The problems at the theoretical core of economics are now seen to be even more serious than they were in 1981.

Once Again on Crisis and Chaos in Economics

For instance, the development of general equilibrium theory has now reached a serious impasse. Quite early on it was realized that the reasonable assumption of potential diversity among individuals threatened the feasibility of the project. Such diversity undermined the mathematical tractability of the whole exercise. Consequently, to overcome this problem, many types of interaction between the individuals have to be ignored. Even with the highly restrictive psychological assumptions of rational behaviour, severe difficulties are faced when the behaviours of a number of actors are aggregated (Katzner, 1991). As a result, leading protagonists of general equilibrium theory have now expressed misgivings concerning the state of the art (Arrow, 1986; Hahn, 1980; Kirman, 1989).

Furthermore, theoretical work in game theory and elsewhere has raised questions about the very meaning of notions such as rationality, which lie at the 'hard core' of the discipline, to use Imre Lakatos's (1970) famous phrase.[1] Even devotees of this theoretical genre such as Robert Sugden (1990, p. 89) are now persuaded that 'game theory may rest on a concept of rationality that is ultimately little more than a convention.' Such quandaries induce critics such as Philip Mirowski (1986a, p. 257) to assert: 'Game theorists have opened the Pandora's Box marked "rationality," and do not know how to close it again.' As a result, general confidence in the postulates of rationality has been undermined:

> There was a time, not long ago, when the foundations of rational-choice theory appeared firm, and when the job of the economic theorist seemed to be one of drawing out the often complex implications of a fairly simple and uncontroversial system of axioms. But it is increasingly becoming clear that these foundations are less secure than we thought, and that they need to be examined and perhaps rebuilt. Economic theorists may have to become as much philosophers as mathematicians. (Sugden, 1991, p. 783)

Even highly neoclassical developments such as the theory of rational expectations have unwittingly undermined much confidence in the postulates of rationality. Whatever its faults and virtues, such a theory raises questions concerning the nature of learning processes in economic systems. This, in turn, has exposed a problem as to what is meant by 'rational learning'. How can agents be said to be rational at a given point in time when they are in the process of learning and acquiring relevant information? The very act of learning means that not all information is possessed and global rationality is ruled out.

Above all, with these core problems concerning the concept of rationality and general equilibrium theory, the attempt by economists, dating from the writings of Bernard Mandeville and Adam Smith, to demonstrate that self-seeking actions can lead to social order and even optimal results seems to have foundered. Thus Arrow (1987, p. 233) has gone so far as to remark: 'People just do not maximize on a selfish basis every minute. In fact, the system would not work if they did. A consequence of that hypothesis would be the end of organized society as we know it.'

The extent to which such fundamental questions concerning mainstream economics are being raised by its leading practitioners is very striking. With such doubts about these hard-core issues, one begins to query the very substance of what is termed 'neoclassical economics'. Consequently, orthodoxy is beginning to lose the ability to police its own boundaries.

The doubts about the concept of rationality that have emerged in the mainstream of economics since the mid-1980s offer an opportunity to reconstruct behavioural postulates on different foundations. It is suggested in chapter 14 below that the emergence of a freestanding concept of rationality in economics, unrelated to any underlying psychology, was tied up with a bifurcation in the whole of social science in the interwar period. For this reason the growth in the substance and

A Brief Diagnosis 5

prestige of experimental economics, where the behaviour of human agents is examined under experimental conditions (Loomes, 1989; Roth, 1988; V. L. Smith, 1982), is welcome, whatever the limitations of the technique. It may well eventually help open the door to a quite different – and more realistic – theorization of behaviour in economics.

Additionally, the intrusion of chaos theory into economics undermines the idea that propositions in this discipline should be judged simply by the criterion of whether or not they generate 'correct predictions'. As discussed further in chapter 14 below, with non-linear models outcomes are oversensitive to initial conditions, making reliable predictions into the outlying future impossible. Perhaps the most dramatic casualty here is the theory of rational expectations. Even if most agents knew the basic structure of the economic model, in general they could not derive reliable predictions of outcomes and thereby form any meaningful 'rational expectations' of the future.

Even more fundamentally, as Marc Lavoie (1992, p. 78) tersely puts it, chaos theory shows that 'one cannot know the whole through the sum of the parts, which leads to a rejection of atomistic individualism.' Furthermore, 'the finding that optimal paths may be chaotic reinforces the complexities inherent to neoclassical optimal behaviour, and justifies the adoption of bounded rationality.'[2]

There are many other problems at the core of economics, from capital theory to monetary analysis, from the theory of the firm to the economics of welfare. Furthermore, there are prominent misgivings concerning the extent to which economics has become overdominated by mathematics (Debreu, 1991; Grubel and Boland, 1986; McCloskey, 1991; Mirowski, 1986b; Novick, 1954; Rotwein, 1966; Woo, 1986) or the extent to which mathematics is abused (Blatt, 1983). The triumph of formalism in economics – dating from the 1940s and 1950s – is now being reassessed.

General misgivings concerning the apparent theoretical victories in economics in the decades of the mid-twentieth century are now voiced in lofty places. For instance, some have noted that, being captivated by formalism, economists are doing much less to improve the empirical grounding of the subject. Consider the following complaints, by two Nobel Laureates. The first is Wassily Leontief (1982, pp. 104–7):

> Page after page of professional economic journals are filled with mathematical formulas leading the reader from sets of more or less plausible but entirely arbitrary assumptions to precisely stated but irrelevant theoretical conclusions. . . . Year after year economic theorists continue to produce scores of mathematical models and to explore in great detail their formal properties; and the econometricians fit algebraic functions of all possible shapes to essentially the same sets of data without being able to advance, in any perceptible way, a systematic understanding of the structure and the operations of a real economic system.

Almost a decade later, Milton Friedman (1991, p. 36) writes:

Again and again, I have read articles written primarily in mathematics, in which the central conclusions and reasoning could readily be restated in English, and the mathematics relegated to an appendix, making the article far more accessible to the reader.

These voices are not alone. There are theoretical as well as empirical queries about the kind of formal theories or modes of theorizing that have become common. One can find critical and ponderous statements in the writings of leading economic theorists such as George Akerlof (1984, 1991), Kenneth Arrow (1982, 1986), Frank Hahn (1991), Amartya Sen (1976–7, 1989) and Joseph Stiglitz (1987), to name a few.

Such a crisis in the subject should not be taken to imply, however, that the orthodox or neoclassical paradigm is about to be overturned. The questions and controversies are so basic and important that the response is often to reassert belief in the fundamentals with renewed vigour, and to attack heresy with increasing force. As Hahn (1991, p. 49) writes: 'After all in other spheres, say religion, one often encounters increased orthodoxy amongst some just when religion is on the decline.'

The existence of a crisis at the core of a science is no guarantee that it will overcome the problems and anomalies and move on to a new and superior theoretical framework. After all, even from an evolutionary perspective there is no inevitability of progress. The reassertions of faith may be so strong as to drown the critical murmurs; the faithful may be so well placed in academia as to deny the critics sufficient outlet or resources.

And as every modern evolutionist knows, there are cases of lock-in with positive feedback which prevent progressive change. As Peter Allen and M. Lesser (1991, p. 166) have wittily suggested, the evolution of economics as an academic profession is a case of lock-in comparable to the evolution of the peacock's tail. Sets of genes producing the beautiful tail in the male, and making it sexually attractive for the female, are mutually reinforcing, and become selected because of the greater progeny involved. However, there is no useful function performed: no enhancement of fitness in terms of finding food or escaping predators.

Likewise, the cultural evolution of norms and institutions can lead to the emergence and reinforcement of non-functional modes of behaviour. Just as the beautiful tail evolves with the peacock, economics has evolved an ever more intricate and beautiful mathematical formalism, similarly with little or no functional advantage for the development of economic policy. The developers of abstract theorems and proofs are awarded with prestige and resources, although there is an increasing suspicion by those on the outside that economics has less and less to do with real economies. Scientific practice in academia is not immune to the functionally redundant ceremonies and routines found in other communities and cultures.[3]

Intellectual Monopoly versus Theoretical Pluralism

Faced with these problems there is no instant solution. Neither is there an adequate and well-formed heterodoxy waiting in the wings. Austrian economics, Post Keynesian economics, Marxian economics, institutional economics: they are all afflicted with deep internal theoretical problems of their own. We have to be candid about the limitations of even our most favoured approach in economics, whatever it may be. In this, we can do no better than follow the example of the self-avowed 'neoclassical' economist Hahn (1984, pp. 7–8):

> The most strongly held of my views . . . is that neither is there a single best way for understanding in economics nor is it possible to hold any conclusions, other than purely logical deductions, with certainty. I have since my earliest days in the subject been astonished that this view is not widely shared. Indeed, we are encompassed by passionately held beliefs. . . . In fact all these 'certainties' and all the 'schools' which they spawn are a sure sign of our ignorance . . . we do not possess much certain knowledge about the economic world and . . . our best chance of gaining more is to try in all sorts of directions and by all sorts of means. This will not be furthered by strident commitments of faith.

Hahn's welcome comment seems to endorse a theoretical pluralism, embracing both neoclassical and non-neoclassical approaches. This pluralism contrasts with the prevailing view that economics is defined in terms of a single, and neoclassical, method or approach. Particularly since the famous essay by Lionel Robbins (1935), among economists the prevailing practice has been to regard this subject as being defined by a single type of method or analysis, with an associated set of core assumptions. If the subject is defined in this way then not much theoretical pluralism within economics is possible; we are stuck with a single type of theory or approach.

Elsewhere, however, a science is normally defined as the study of a particular aspect of objective reality: physics is about the nature and properties of matter and energy, biology about living things, psychology about the psyche, and so on. For many economists, in contrast, their subject is defined in terms of a single methodology and core theory, not as the varied study of a real object – the economy.

Of course, any science is likely to have a ruling paradigm and will sometimes eschew contesting approaches. But the point is whether the science is itself defined by the core theoretical elements of the ruling paradigm or by the real object of study. In the former case contested approaches are excluded by mere definition of the boundaries of the subject, not by other, more suitable, criteria.

This neoclassical monopoly in economics denies space and legitimacy for 'all sorts of directions' and 'all sorts of means'. It provides a convenient mechanism for dealing with dissidents. Anyone who does not accept these core assumptions and methods is then regarded as simply not being an economist. It is not a question of whether they are right or wrong; those that disagree are simply sent into exile, into the sociology department or elsewhere.

Furthermore, such a definition of economics rebuts criticism and potential change at the hard core. If the subject is defined by its basic methods and core assumptions it thereby becomes inert. While many examples of partiality and intellectual monopoly can be found in the history of other sciences, if they had more closely followed the Robbinsian example then it would still be taught that the earth was at the centre of the universe and that the material world consisted simply of the four elements of earth, water, air and fire.

Apart from being a recipe for intolerance, the current definition of economics elevates formalism and axiomatics to unwarranted heights. At the outset, core assumptions are taken as unquestionable and given. Agents must maximize because economists assume they do, and so on. For the theoretical economist the game becomes one of simply drawing logical conclusions from a combination of preordained assumptions at the core, and more malleable, secondary assumptions at the periphery. Attempts to address the real world, or to evaluate basic assumptions on the basis of the conceptualizations of such a reality, are thus downgraded.

This present work is informed by the pluralistic sentiment that economics should not be constituted by fixed methods or assumptions. Defined loosely, economics should be the study of the social relations and processes governing the production, distribution and exchange of the requisites of human life. Economics is thus an attempt to address aspects of the real world.

This is not a rigid definition and it is not intended to be. Economic reality is necessarily embedded within broader social relations, culture and institutions, and the real boundaries between the 'economy', and 'society' and 'polity' are fuzzy and unclear. The looseness of the definition is at least in one respect an advantage. There is a need for a more tolerant and permissive atmosphere, and for genuine, scientific competition between several rival paradigms in our discipline. Economics should retain its standards of rigour but be more open and pluralistic in terms of the compass and administration of the discipline.

Above all, intellectual monopoly poses a threat to science. Economists may advocate free competition, but often do not practise it in the marketplace of ideas. A new spirit of pluralism in economics is required, involving critical conversation and tolerant communication between different approaches. Such pluralism should not undermine the standards of rigour; an economics that requires itself to face all the arguments will be a more, not a less, rigorous science.[4]

The Transcendence of Modernism

Here we embark on a small attempt to help to redirect and enhance the processes of theoretical development of economics. At the outset it must be noted that the strategy proposed here has no guarantee of success. In the very spirit of theoretical pluralism it should be supplemented by other additional attempts to diagnose and rectify the malaise afflicting our subject. The present approach can then be compared to others in academic debate.

Why are many economists intolerant of different approaches? Why is there such resistance to theoretical innovation and change at the hard core of the subject? Why is mathematics raised to unwarranted heights? Why are the attempts to engage with empirical reality so limited? It is the contention of this book that we may find some of the answers to these questions by examining the most fundamental philosophical presuppositions of modern economists, and the kinds of metaphors employed.

At the philosophical level the proposal herein may thus be more radical than others; it is to question the very roots of modernist science, as applied to economics, in the philosophy of René Descartes and as exemplified by the mechanistic tradition of physics founded by Galileo Galilei and Sir Isaac Newton. This is indeed a tall order, but the challenge has parallels in the 'postmodernist' trend in contemporary thought (Amariglio, 1990; Brown, 1991; Dow, 1991a, 1991b), along with the invocation of a postwar 'turning point' in science and culture (Capra, 1982).

Despite its installation at the foundations of modern thought, there have since been many challenges to Cartesianism. As early as the seventeenth century, Blaise Pascal rebelled against its strictures. Contrary to his fellow Frenchman, Pascal argued that reason could not find all truth and there had to be a place for intuition, even a degree of faith.

The principal modern European philosophers who broke substantially from Cartesianism on key points include Henri Bergson, Martin Heidegger, Edmund Husserl, Friedrich Nietzsche, Alfred North Whitehead, and the Ludwig Wittgenstein of his later writings. The main American dissenters to Cartesianism are located in the pragmatist tradition of Charles Sanders Peirce, William James and John Dewey. Peirce, for instance, revolted against the Cartesian and Newtonian views of science, and rejected in particular their mechanical determinism. For this reason, he and the later pragmatists were attracted to Darwinism because it seemed to recognize the randomness, creativity and spontaneity in the universe (Wiener, 1949; Russett, 1976). Likewise, Dewey (1929, p. 97) saw the negative side of the Galilean intellectual revolution, after which all that 'counted for science became mechanical properties formulated in mathematical terms'.

None of the above thinkers can be discussed in any depth. Due to limitations of space, our excursion here into philosophical fundamentals must be highly constrained. The remaining part of this chapter addresses some of the fundamental philosophical issues involved. The reader should be forewarned that the sketch is a highly rudimentary one. The objective is to identify some of the philosophical issues at the roots of economic theory, and fill in the philosophical background to the present work, but without the full and rigorous presentation of a philosophical system. Furthermore, an important link is made to the important topic of metaphor which is discussed more extensively in the next chapter.

Clearly, the philosophical issues raised here would themselves require full-length book treatment. After all, philosophical discussion is notoriously boundless and open ended. As Brian Barry (1970, p. 166) suggests, the 'higher methodology' may be compared to that 'undiscovered country' mentioned by Shakespeare's Prince Hamlet, 'from whose bourn no traveller returns'. Several of my colleagues have set out for that land in search of the philosophical elixir to transform economics, later sending back splendid messages of intellectual adventure, but alas never to return to and settle upon the more oppressive territory of the dismal science. I may join them one day, for on all reports it seems an attractive place to spend one's later years, but the concerns of the present volume are somewhat different. Consequently, the reader must be provided with a brief travelogue rather than an extensive and detailed exploration.

Realism, Pragmatism and Organicism

Consider some of the philosophical influences relevant for the project in hand. The first is the tradition of sophisticated modern realism which now has some sway, even within economics. The realists emphasize the existence of an external world apart from our thoughts, about which we can obtain some knowledge. In this manner an alternative to 'as if' reasoning is asserted, reclaiming the importance of the pursuit of truth, rather than mere predictive instrumentalism in economic science.[5]

There is also the influence of American pragmatism, particularly Peirce. Peirce is also sometimes described as a realist (Boler, 1963). However, his definition of reality as 'the dynamical reaction of certain forms upon the mind of the community' (Peirce, 1935, pp. 433–4) would not be acceptable to many realists.[6] His work has a strong hermeneutical quality, and the reconciliation of Peircian hermeneutics with modern realism remains an open question. Nevertheless, there is a prima facie case for the incorporation of some of Peirce's ontological and other insights within a realist perspective.[7]

One of the strong arguments linking the pragmatists such as Peirce and Dewey to modern realists such as Roy Bhaskar (1979) is their attempts to formulate a sophisticated naturalism as an alternative to Cartesian dualism. A realist cannot support the proposition that either human society or human ideas are completely separable from their foundation in nature. Yet much of social science today proceeds as if this proposition was true. In contrast, both naturalists and realists agree that nature, matter and mind are all real, and not divided by any Cartesian boundary. However, this does not imply a single-level explanation, or a reductionist dissolution of one into the other. In particular, the naturalistic philosophy of Whitehead is notable for its rejection of both dualism and reductionism, positing a multilevelled ontological hierarchy.

Indeed, Whitehead provides an important linkage between some of the aforementioned philosophers. In one of his works he acknowledged an intellectual debt both to 'English and American Realists' and also to Bergson, James, and Dewey (Whitehead, 1929a, p. vii). The pragmatist philosophers James and Dewey were the principal followers of Peirce, and pragmatism as a whole is the philosophical foundation of American institutional economics.[8] In addition, both the pragmatists and the institutionalists were strongly impressed by evolutionary ideas in general and Darwinism in particular.[9]

Whitehead's philosophy is also of great intrinsic significance, for a number of reasons which shall become evident later in this present work. He too was influenced by biology and theories of evolution. At present, his intellectual connection with two relevant and important economists shall be noted. First, the leading institutionalist John Commons (1934, pp. 17, 96) referred to Whitehead and seems to have been strongly influenced by his organicism.[10] Second, there is a personal and intellectual connection between Whitehead and John Maynard Keynes. Keynes came under the influence of Whitehead in Cambridge in the first decade of the twentieth century, before Whitehead's transfer to London in 1910 and his emigration to the United States in 1924. As well as his ventures into logic and mathematics, Whitehead promoted an organicist philosophy. A number of writers including Allan Gruchy (1948) and Edward Winslow (1986, 1989) have noted the organicist thinking in Keynes's *General Theory*, and it is reasonable to suggest that Whitehead is partly responsible for this feature.[11]

In an organicist ontology, relations between entities are internal rather than external, and the essential characteristics of any element are outcomes of relations with other entities. This relates to the central question in social theory as to whether or not structure may be represented simply as the property of the interactions between given individuals. Organicism denies that individuals may be treated as elemental or immutable building blocks of analysis. Just as society cannot exist without individuals, the individual does not exist prior to the social reality. Individuals both constitute, and are constituted by, society. We often hear the truism that society is composed of individuals. The organicist does not deny this, but insists that individuality is itself a social phenomenon.

Since Keynes, however, Whitehead has had a negligible influence on economics, reflecting the resurgence of the mechanistic and atomistic view in the postwar period. An explicit exception, however, is the work of Nicholas Georgescu-Roegen (1971), particularly in regard to such concepts as purpose and time. With his idea of the hierarchic ordering of the real world, Whitehead also had a strong personal influence on pioneering systems theorists such as James Miller (1978).[12]

The postwar resurgence of atomistic and mechanistic thought in economics is not an isolated event. Indeed, ever since Adam Smith, economists have most frequently adopted an atomist rather than an organicist ontology. But names such as Karl Marx stand out as important exceptions. Marx held the view that economic motivations are moulded or formed by social circumstances and institutions. In the *Grundrisse*, for instance, Marx argued that the standpoint 'of the isolated individual' was not a general or eternal truth, but a product of the particular historical epoch associated with the rise of modern capitalism (1973, p. 84). Consequently, we cannot take maximizing or self-interested economic behaviour for granted. These are specific historical phenomena, formed in specific cultural milieux.

Related views were expressed by one of the few English economists who could reasonably be described as an institutionalist, namely John A. Hobson, a person who interchanged ideas with both Veblen and Keynes. Hobson (1929, p. 32) wrote: 'An organized unity, or whole, cannot be explained adequately by an analysis of its constituent parts: its wholeness is a new product, with attributes not ascertainable in its parts, though in a sense derived from them.' However, despite his links with Marxism, institutionalism and Keynesianism, Hobson has not had a strong or enduring influence on economic thought.[13]

A final brief mention is reserved for a more recent figure: neither an economist nor strictly a professional philosopher, but a writer of significance on organic systems and on the history of science. The writings of Arthur Koestler (1964, 1967, 1978, 1980) have several features in common with those of Peirce and Whitehead. In all of them is found a rejection of Cartesianism, a critique of philosophical materialism, a stress on the indeterminism of creativity and novelty, and a complex and differentiated conception of human consciousness. Although several of his scientific speculations are highly questionable and have been widely rejected, much of Koestler's work was an attempt to overcome the narrowness and rigidity of modern science, imposed by the straitjackets of Cartesian and Newtonian thought.

Accordingly, from Peirce to the present day, there seems to be a fascinating intellectual network involving, among others, American institutional economics, Keynes's economics, realist philosophy, American pragmatism, and the organicism and systems thinking of Whitehead and Koestler. It is from these trends that we may discover the means of surpassing Cartesianism and mechanistic materialism. Further, they provide a basis for a fruitful theoretical development in economics, involving elements of institutionalism, and also the theories of Keynes and the modern Post Keynesians.

Challenging Cartesianism

To illustrate some of the polarities of thought that are involved in this venture, a brief discussion of some features of Cartesian philosophy follows. On the whole, these are transcended in the writings of several modern philosophers such as Peirce and Whitehead. Peirce's critique of Cartesianism is a major feature of his work (Scheffler, 1974, pp. 42–57). Whitehead (1926, p. 82) indicted Cartesian epistemology as the source of those 'quite unbelievable' abstractions by which 'modern philosophy has been ruined'.

For Descartes, the source of all knowledge was the critical, rational and reflexive mind. This implied a concept of an undivided consciousness in which all thought activity was deemed to be at one level, in contrast to the Aristotelian tradition which offered a differentiated picture of our mental behaviour and capacities. Descartes saw a clear division between the mental and the material worlds, and this dualism has a number of ontological, epistemological and methodological consequences. A discussion of the ontological aspect is found in Whitehead's work. He points out that for Descartes

there are material substances with spatial relations, and mental substances. The mental substances are external to the material substances. Neither type requires the other type for the completion of its essence. Their unexplained interrelations are unnecessary for their respective existencies. In truth, this formulation of the problem in terms of minds and matter is unfortunate. It omits the lower forms of life, such as vegetation and the lower animal types. These forms touch upon human mentality at their highest, and upon inorganic nature at their lowest. The effect of this sharp division between nature and life has poisoned all subsequent philosophy. . . . there is no proper fusion of the two in most modern schools of thought. For some, nature is mere appearance and mind is the sole reality. For others, physical nature is the sole reality and nature is the epiphenomenon. (Whitehead, 1938, pp. 204–5)

Whitehead argues that Cartesian dualism should be replaced by an organicist view where physical nature and life are fused together in a hierarchic order. Central to this concept are the ideas of creativity, purposefulness and emergence with which modernist, Cartesian science has been unable to reconcile itself.[14] As Whitehead (1938, p. 211) writes: 'Science can find no aim in nature: Science can find no creativity in nature; it finds mere rules of succession. . . . The disastrous separation of body and mind which has been fixed on European thought by Descartes is responsible for this blindness of Science.'

Concerning epistemology, Descartes argued that through rational reflection and introspection we may come to know truth. For him, appearances and sense-data are to be mistrusted; we know our own thought better than we can know the world. As Piero Mini (1974, p. 285) stresses: *'The logic of Cartesianism drives all thought . . . toward fabricating a world in accordance with our own mathematical ideas of it.'* The knowledge of such truth develops through the exchange and accumulation of consistent, rational thought; the process is ostensibly cumulative and open to all who are capable of reason.

Accordingly, Descartes believed that the supposedly rational foundation of thought is more important than the historical investigation into the actual thought processes leading to novelty or discovery. Descartes 'ignored the actual process of thought-formation, inventing, instead, an all-rational ego as the creator of theories' (Mini, 1974, p. 222). The historical development and creation of ideas thus became irrelevant to those ideas themselves. As a result, there is deemed to be 'an unbridgeable gulf between the philosophy of science and the history of science' (Mirowski, 1987b, p. 1005).[15] The context of discovery is thus quarantined from the context of justification. Science is seen as mechanical and impersonal, subject to enduring rules of scientific method.

In contrast, the view that theories stand by themselves and are independent of their history and context is rejected here. To comprehend scientific progress, and indeed science itself, an understanding of the origin and historical development of ideas is important. As the modern philosopher Larry Laudan argues, the appraisal of any theory should be on the basis of its progressiveness in problem solving and the effectiveness of the research tradition with which it is associated. Consequently, intellectual history is an essential constituent of any such appraisal. He emphatically concludes, therefore, that *'no sensible rational appraisal can be made of any doctrine without a rich knowledge of its historical development'* (Laudan, 1977, p. 193). It is in this spirit that this present attempt to help develop an evolutionary economics contains a substantial discourse in the history of ideas. It is a necessary condition of the reform of economics that it looks again at its own history.

In his epistemology, Descartes was a rationalist. Further, his dualistic schema created a dichotomy between rationalism and empiricism. The philosophical empiricists of the seventeenth and eighteenth centuries revolted against Cartesian rationalism, attributing all knowledge to sense experience. But in this view they exaggerated the role of sensation, seeing knowledge as a passive reflection of outside reality. In fact, the empiricists offered little more than the other side of the Cartesian coin, sustaining the same division between the mental and material worlds. Both rationalism and empiricism downplayed the roles of habit, action and intuition in the sustenance and development of ideas. For much of philosophy subsequent to Descartes the process of enquiry was divided into 'induction' and 'deduction'. Empiricists stressed the value of the former, rationalists the latter. However, philosophers such as Bergson, Peirce and Whitehead helped to transcend this dichotomy, attempting to provide a systematic alternative to both empiricism and rationalism.

The anti-Cartesian thrust of pragmatism is no where clearer or more sustained than in the works of its founder, Peirce himself, and this fact accounts for much of the renewed interest in this previously neglected philosopher (Apel, 1981; Bernstein, 1983; Mirowski, 1987b; Rorty, 1979, 1982). Peirce dissolved the antimonies of rationalism and empiricism seemingly at a stroke, making 'Habit and Custom, instead of intellect and sensations, the foundation of all science' (Commons, 1934, p. 150). Instead of Descartes's emphasis on rational doubt, Peirce stresses belief. For Peirce belief is not mere thought – it is connected with action. Over two centuries before, Pascal (1932, p. 73) had written against the same Cartesian rationalism: 'Custom is the source of our strongest and most believed proofs.' Peirce (1878, p. 294, and 1934, pp. 255–6) goes even further: habit does not merely reinforce belief, the 'essence of belief is the establishment of habit'.[16]

Contrary to Descartes, we 'cannot begin from complete doubt. We must begin with all the prejudices which we actually have' (Peirce, 1934, p. 156). Given that some predispositions are unavoidable, the final perfection of truth can never be attained. Nevertheless, the search for knowledge is not in vain. Furthermore, it is a social endeavour, in which we inevitably rely on both the recent work of others and on the undesigned, mysterious and sometimes unsatisfactory conventions of usage and meaning that have been built up over centuries.

Peirce argued that scientific knowledge was grounded neither in discrete 'facts' nor in self-contained logical propositions. Descartes was in error because 'all cognitions are expressed in signs and so implicitly refer to others and are fallible' (Scheffler, 1974, p. 53). In contrast to Descartes, Peirce concentrates on the role of the shared tradition of enquiry by a scientific community, both as the thread of continuity and the locus of evaluation in the process of scientific enquiry. This hermeneutic quality of Peirce's thinking involves an attempt to steer a course between objectivism and relativism (Bernstein, 1983).

Abduction and Scientific Creativity

As asserted above, one problem with modern mainstream economics is its overemphasis on mathematical formalism. Concern over the limitations of mathematical and deductive reasoning was expressed long ago by Pascal (1932, p. 2): 'mathematicians wish to treat matters of intuition mathematically, and make themselves ridiculous, wishing to begin with definitions and then with axioms, which is not the way to proceed with this kind of reasoning. Not that the mind does not do so, but it does it tacitly, naturally, and without technical rules.'

Likewise, the founder of pragmatism believed that both deduction and induction had a limited role in science. Although he was a highly competent mathematician, Peirce saw the limits of the mathematical mode of reasoning. He argued that through mere deduction no theoretical novelty or real progress could be attained, as the logical conclusion was already contained in the premises (Peirce, 1958, pp. 123–5). Like Pascal, Peirce stressed the limitations of deduction and the creative role of intuition.[17]

Mathematics can be useful, and its discovery inventive, but its application involves logical syllogism rather than real theoretical novelty. Furthermore, by focusing attention on the formalistic chain of reasoning, rather than implicit categories or fundamental assumptions, mathematics encourages theoretical conservatism rather than innovation, despite any gains that may be made in terms of elegance and precision.

In exceptional cases, however, mathematics may encourage theoretical change. For instance, developments in game theory in the 1980s eventually led to the much wider acceptance and utilization of Herbert Simon's (1955, 1957, 1959a) concept of bounded rationality.[18] Nevertheless, the creation of this concept was not itself due to mathematics, and without the prior publication of Simon's idea – in a 'rhetorical' form – the game theorists would not have been able to use it.

However, contrary to some critics of economic orthodoxy, recognition of the limits of formalism does not mean that we must wallow in empiricism. Although Peirce put some weight on induction in the development of science, he observed that experiment and observation actually played a minor role in the genesis of many scientific theories.[19] Furthermore – and contrary to naive Popperian falsificationism – it is unreasonable to abandon a hypothesis immediately when it is contradicted by empirical results; good theories are often surrounded by a penumbra of contradictory facts (Peirce, 1958, pp. 54, 60). Here Peirce's position is echoed today by the physicist J. M. Ziman (1978, pp. 39–40) and by the economist Brian Loasby (1976, pp. 19–20; 1991, pp. 5–6), who both argue that it is reasonable in some cases to ignore a few facts which could do fatal damage to a theory.

Peirce thus added a third category to the traditional dichotomy of induction and deduction. This he termed 'abduction', and it concerned the creative process of forming an explanatory hypothesis. According to Peirce (1934, p. 90), induction 'never can originate any idea whatever. No more can deduction. All the ideas of science come to it by the way of abduction.' Hence abduction alone could account for creativity and progress in science: 'Abduction is the process of forming an explanatory hypothesis. It is the only logical operation which introduces any new idea; for induction does nothing but determine a value, and deduction merely evolves the necessary consequences of a pure hypothesis' (p. 106). For Peirce (p. 121), pragmatism was 'nothing else than the question of the logic of abduction': the genuinely creative element in scientific enquiry.

By abduction, Peirce seems to have in mind the spark of intellectual creativity or intuition, kindled in the tinder of assimilated facts.[20] He writes:

> The abductive suggestion comes to us like a flash. It is an act of *insight*, although of extremely fallible insight. It is true that the different elements of the hypothesis were in our minds before; but it is the idea of putting together what we had never before dreamed of putting together which flashes the new suggestion before our contemplation. (Peirce, 1934, p. 113)

This Peircean notion of abduction finds a strong resonance in subsequent philosophy of science, sometimes under the term 'retroduction' (Hanson, 1958; McMullin, 1984), occasionally as 'retrodiction' (Bhaskar, 1975), and at least once as 'ontological imputation' (Quine, 1953). To this list should be added Gilbert Harman's (1965) closely related discussion of 'the inference to the best explanation'. One of the clearest recent attempts to elucidate the notion of abduction, in a realist philosophical framework which is specifically related to economics, is by Tony Lawson (1989, pp. 68–73).

For Peirce, an important source of creativity in science was the 'abductive' transfer of metaphor from one scientific discourse to another. The 'abduction' of metaphor enables us to put together 'what we had never before dreamed of putting together'. It is to this creative function of metaphor that we turn in the following chapter, as it is a major theme of this present book.

By raising the question of the source of creativity and innovation in science, rather than the static analytic structure of its existing theories, Peirce shows the limitations of both empiricism and mathematical formalism. Also, more positively, he identifies the key matter of metaphor. We may thus learn something about modern mainstream economics by examining the metaphors at its core, and help to explain its theoretical conservatism. As a result we shall be impelled to search for more fruitful replacement metaphors, in the hope that they may lead to future theoretical creativity and practical results.[21]

2
On Mechanistic and Biological Metaphors

The latter part of the preceding chapter focused on Charles Sanders Peirce's concept of 'abduction'. Being different from, and supplementary to, induction and deduction, this concept transcends both empiricism and Cartesian rationalism. Peirce saw that the 'abductive' transfer of metaphor from one discipline to another was an important source of novelty and creativity in science. In this chapter I focus on the role of metaphor in general, and evaluate in particular both the mechanistic and biological metaphors in economics.

The Role of Metaphor in Science

Practising scientists often regard metaphors as mere literary ornaments. It is sometimes suggested that they should be removed to reveal the essential theory below. Recourse to mathematical modes of expression is often motivated in part by a desire to remove all such 'literary frills'. However, modern philosophers of science take a very different view. Mary Hesse (1980, p. 111) complains that: 'It is still unfortunately necessary to argue that metaphor is more than a decorative literary device, and that it has cognitive implications whose nature is a proper subject of philosophic discussion.' Similarly, Max Black (1962, p. 237) concludes in a substantial study of metaphor and analogy in science: 'Metaphorical thought is a distinctive mode of achieving insight, not to be construed as an ornamental substitute for plain thought.'

Aristotle wrote of the ability to use metaphor as a 'sign of genius'. He defined it in his *Poetics* as 'the application to one thing of a name belonging to another thing'. It is with the rise of modern science, from the seventeenth century, that metaphor gets a bad name. Clearly, for a formalist or a nominalist the use of metaphor is a superficial matter, even a distraction: a confusing renaming of entities which can have nothing to do with their essence. Prominent philosophers such as Thomas Hobbes and John Locke dismissed the use of metaphor as a superfluous distraction in intellectual endeavour. But this kind of response is challenged by modern philosophers.

Metaphors may lead or mislead. By their nature, they are never complete, precise or literal mappings. If they were precise representations they would not be metaphors, and the juxtaposition of similar but different conceptual frameworks would be lost. This juxtaposition, involving a degree of similarity and dissimilarity, can have both creative and damaging effects.

Metaphors are more than similes. In fact, as George Lakoff (1987) argues extensively, metaphors are central to reason (Lakoff and Johnson, 1980). To take an apposite example, to describe the economy as 'evolving' is not simply to state that the economy develops like an organism or a species in the natural world. It may also prompt the investigator to consider the many meanings and ambiguities in the term 'evolve' and the many extensions and facets of the implicit analogy between the natural and the social world. As Black (1962) argues, the use of metaphor involves interaction, by invoking and filtering different but associated conceptual systems. The interaction generates a novel semantic context, and goes beyond the literal meaning of the terms of the metaphor itself. The upshot of Black's argument is to conceive of metaphor as more than semantics, involving beliefs about reality and not simply the meanings of the words themselves.

In an analysis which differs from that of Hesse and Black, Donald Davidson (1980) argues that there is no such thing as metaphorical meaning other than the literal meanings of the words themselves. Nevertheless, metaphors are still important, because they have the power to jolt us into new ways of thinking. The metaphor does not convey any propositional content, other than in its literal interpretation, and there is thus no question of the truth or falsehood of the metaphor as a whole. According to Davidson, the importance of metaphors is psychological: they can help generate responses leading to novel and creative results.

With particular regard to the transposition of the biological analogy, John Maynard Smith (1972, pp. 36–43) and Michael Ruse (1986, pp. 32–5) distinguish between the heuristic and the justificatory roles of an analogy. An analogy-as-heuristic suggests ways of approaching the study of a phenomenon without implying the same kind of causal relationships. The stronger idea of analogy-as-justification involves a transfer of claims of truth from one domain to another. However, the distinction between these two types of analogy is not as clear in practice, as all theories involve the dogmatic adoption of hard-core assumptions, and even heuristic analogies will dispose the theorist to make untested assumptions of one kind rather than another.

Whatever the precise analysis, analogy and metaphor are indispensable in both philosophy and science, despite pretensions to the contrary. Richard Rorty (1979, p. 12) writes: 'It is pictures rather than propositions, metaphors rather than statements, which determine most of our philosophical convictions.' Science in general is infused with analogy, and as the examples given by Black (1962) and Hesse (1966) show, it often proceeds by importing metaphor from other domains. To use a metaphor to describe metaphor itself; it involves the sexual recombination of structured groups of ideas from different sources. Such a process of sexual recombination, as in genetics, is perhaps the main source of novelty in the development of science.[1]

As noted in chapter 4 below, the Darwinian revolution was no exception. Darwin's ability to transfer metaphor from one intellectual discipline to another is widely noted.[2] Edward Manier (1978), for example, refers to the studies by Black and Hesse on the role of metaphor in science and argues that many important aspects of Darwin's theory could not have been expressed without metaphors. Key Darwinian terms such as the 'struggle for life' concealed a multitude of different meanings.[3]

Such metaphors create interlocking chains of ideas. Darwin's metaphors, in particular, were 'not only non-mechanistic and non-reductionist, they were thoroughly anthropomorphic and moralistic' (Manier, 1978, p. 159). These metaphors helped Darwin to free himself from previous and questionable ideas and theories in biology. Hence the Darwinian revolution was created in part by the use of metaphor.

Despite the evidence and arguments cited above, many scientists eschew metaphor and try to remove it from their work. But this strategy has its own pitfalls. All scientists are forced to use language and concepts, even if their presentations are in largely mathematical terms. Accordingly, there is the near certainty that metaphor will always sneak in by the back door. This creates the possibility of confusion and ambiguity at a fundamental theoretical level. As shown in chapter 10 below, the work of the economist Joseph Schumpeter involved an attempt to avoid metaphor which led to such problems.

The triumph of formalism has done nothing to limit the extensive use of metaphor in economics: with terms such as 'human capital', 'market forces', 'consumer sovereignty' and 'natural rates of unemployment'. The use of metaphor affects not merely the phrasing, but the structure and substance of the discipline (Samuels, 1990). Yet the metaphorical references may be partially obscured by the progress of formalism in economics. As mathematical symbols replace words, the analogies may seem to disappear. Yet this is an illusion. As Donald McCloskey (1985, p. 74) puts it: 'Noneconomists find it easier to see the metaphors than do economists, habituated as the economists are by daily use to the idea that of course production comes from a "function" and of course business moves in "cycles".' Furthermore, mathematics itself is riddled with metaphors and analogies: 'groups', 'sets', 'mappings' and 'matrices', to name but a few.

As long ago as 1882, Peirce (1958, p. 46) wrote:

> But the higher places in science in the coming years are for those who succeed in adapting the methods of one science to the investigation of another. That is what the greatest progress of the passing generation has

consisted in. Darwin adapted biology to the methods of Malthus and the economists; Maxwell adapted to the theory of gases the methods of the doctrines of chances, and to electricity the methods of hydrodynamics. Wundt adapts to psychology the methods of physiology; Galton adapts to the same study the methods of the theory of errors; Morgan adapted to history a method from biology; Cournot adapted to political economy the calculus of variations.

It is thus argued that a source of creativity in science is through the juxtaposition of two different frames of reference, so that already existing but previously separate ideas can cross-fertilize. Larry Laudan (1977, p. 103) argues that the amalgamation of different research traditions may produce a sum greater than the constituent parts. Arthur Koestler (1964, 1978, 1980) has coined the term 'bisociation' to describe the kind of adjoining of different ideas which occurs both in the act of scientific creation and in so many kinds of humour. Metaphor itself is an important example. As I. A. Richards (1936, pp. 93–4) wrote, metaphor is 'two thoughts of different things active together . . . whose meaning is a result of their interaction . . . a borrowing between and intercourse of thoughts, a transaction between contexts.'

Thomas Kuhn (1970, p. 85) points out that the transition from a paradigm in crisis to a new and progressive one is far from a cumulative process, rather 'it is a reconstruction of the field from new fundamentals.' Hence if the fundamentals of mainstream economics involve the metaphor of the machine, then it is from outside this mode of thought that materials for the construction of a new economics could be found.

The Mechanistic Metaphor in Economics

Even at the foundation of modern economic science, Adam Smith appealed specifically to metaphor in his essay on *The Principles which Lead and Direct Philosophical Enquiries: Illustrated by the History of Astronomy* (Smith, 1980). Smith (1983, pp. 145–6) himself makes his commitment to the Newtonian scientific method clear. As Loasby (1989, pp. 1–5, and 1991, pp. 6–8) points out, Smith used Newtonian astronomy as primarily a set of 'connecting principles'. These made sense of his experience and were fitting for his own theoretical work. However, Smith recognized that such principles were invented, and potentially false. Whatever their truth in the cosmological sphere, for him they were also applicable to other domains of enquiry, including economics.

The mechanistic metaphor still dominates mainstream economics today. A number of authors – including John Casti (1991), David Hamilton (1991), Bruno Ingrao and Giorgio Israel (1990), Philip Mirowski (1988a, 1989b), Richard Norgaard (1987) and Michael Rothschild (1992) – have emphasized the extent to which mainstream economics has been influenced by premodern physics, and particularly mechanistic ideas. Indeed, it is clear that modern economics has forgotten the source of the crucial metaphor from which it gained so much inspiration during the eighteenth and nineteenth centuries. With its present focus on mathematical form rather than conceptual substance, attention is shifted away from the nature and origin of core assumptions in economics.

There is another reason why these fundamental issues have been neglected. Economics, even as a proud and often insular discipline, has never been uninfluenced by the changing landscape of other sciences around it. But nowadays it is typical for the queen of the social sciences to enter foreign territory to impose her own rule, and to repress rather than assimilate any alien notions. Self-confident in its own presuppositions, 'economic imperialism' has now become the mode. The aim has been to show that theoretical tools of economics are applicable to every social and political, and even biological, problem. In regard to the imposition of ideas from economics on to biology, this development will be critically examined below.

'Economic imperialism' suggests a one-way transfer of ideas from economics into other disciplines. Past incursions by economists, however, have sometimes been of a more modest and reciprocal kind. There have been many exchanges of ideas with other sciences, including those addressing the natural and physical worlds. Indeed, the smuggling of ideas in both directions, between economics and other disciplines, has been more extensive than often imagined.

For example, the ideologies of atomistic individualism, spawned by the development of capitalism in the sixteenth and seventeenth centuries, inspired an atomistic ontology in physics. In the other direction, and to take another case, the leaders of the 'marginal revolution' in economics in the 1870s based their formal expositions on a 'field theory of value' derived from the now obsolete branch of nineteenth-century physics known as energetics (Mirowski, 1988a, 1989b).

The deficiencies of the metaphor taken from classical mechanics have been discussed at length elsewhere.[4] There are a number of perennial problems involved, all relating to the limitations of Cartesian philosophy and Newtonian principles. For instance, movement is reversible in the 'conserved system' of Newtonian mechanics; there is no arrow of time. 'Classical mechanics only knows motion, whereas at the same time the processes of motion are completely reversible and in no way give rise to any qualitative changes' (Thoben, 1982, p. 293). Although in some non-conserved, mechanistic theoretical systems the possibility of irreversibility emerges – such as with the addition of friction – the reasons are quite different from those in more complex systems. Above all, with mechanistic presuppositions, cause and effect can be mirrored by logical syllogism, and logical replaces historical time (Robinson, 1974).

However, the economic system involves agents, not mere particles who mutually interact with each other according to Newtonian laws. Economic agents have knowledge and purpose. For this reason it is not possible to separate completely the observer from the object of observation. Observation and knowledge of the economic system reacts upon the system itself. As Kenneth Boulding (1970, p. 121) points out, 'knowledge of the social sciences is an essential part of the social system itself; hence objectivity in the sense of investigating a world which is unchanged by the investigation of it is an absurdity.' In contrast to classical mechanics, this reminds us of the quantum theory and the Heisenberg uncertainty principle.[5]

There is the general difficulty of incorporating information and knowledge in a mechanistic scheme. In classical mechanics there is no place for thoughts and ideas: all is mere matter, subject to Newtonian laws. However, choice, as George Shackle (1972, p. 355) has argued extensively, is more than 'a mere part of the machine of determinate conduct'. Further, what is involved is more than the indeterminacy of stochastic variation that is associated with the Heisenberg principle. The reality of human choice and purpose requires a notion of teleology or finalism rather than merely efficient cause. The explanation of economic phenomena requires reference to intentions, and not simply stochastic outcomes or mechanical cause and effect.

It is easy to trace the derivation of the ideas of rationality and equilibria, the core concepts of neoclassical economics, from the inheritance of mechanistic thought: 'Classical mechanics considers a system of material points upon which directional forces operate at a distance according to calculable laws of motion. The choice of paths is governed by the principle of least action, which may be termed the economic principle if we take the term in its widest sense as denoting a maximum-minimum principle' (Sebba, 1953, p. 269). Hence, subject to a combination of forces, economic agents optimize to the point of equilibrium as if they were mere particles obeying mechanical laws.

The Cartesian ideal of the rational individual is one guided by logical and consistent thought. In modern neoclassical economics, rather than the acceptance of real chance and spontaneity, an 'error term' is added, as a kind of stochastic apology for the unknown forces that have not been included (Mirowski, 1989a). There are no systematic mistakes, no human misunderstandings, no blind passions, no surprises (Shackle, 1972).

It is not proposed here that the use of mechanistic thinking in economics has been entirely without value. Nevertheless, as we have seen, the limitations are severe. In sum, the mechanistic metaphor excludes knowledge, choice, purpose and qualitative change of a more complex and irreversible kind. Clearly much is missing here. The strength of the alternative, biological, metaphor is that a place can be found for all these important features of economic life, although as shown in chapter 14 it is outside mainstream biology that we must find places for purpose and choice.

It should also be noted that modern physics does not exemplify the kinds of problems identified here. In fact, it now embraces organicist ideas and modes of thought which are quite compatible with similar strains of thought in biology (Bohm, 1980; Brooks and Wiley, 1988; Capek, 1961; Capra, 1975, 1982; Faber and Proops, 1991; Georgescu-Roegen, 1971). It could thus be suggested that the source of reforming metaphor for economics could be from modern physics rather than biology, but it is far beyond the scope of the present work to examine this alternative source of metaphor. Crucially, although some modern physicists have adopted an organicist ontology, the question of purposeful behaviour and the nature of living things is addressed more directly, although still not adequately, in biology. Furthermore, biology, like economics, deals with phenomena at a far more complex level of organization.

Taking recourse to biology is not simply a tactic. The advantages over the mechanistic metaphor are obvious. Clearly, real world economic phenomena have much more in common with biological organisms and processes than with the mechanistic world of billiard balls and planets. After all, the economy involves living human beings, not merely particles, forces and energy. The appropriation of ideas from biology portends considerable improvement for economic science.

But biology is not a panacea. The primary reason for turning in its direction is the recognition that economies are made up of living, human beings, and are part of ecosystems containing other forms of life. The aim is to bring back life into economics, not to worship another science. Nevertheless, the biotic world cannot be understood without biology.

Transaction Costs in the Trade with Biology

The strategy in this work is to attempt to use biology both to help counter the mechanistic metaphor and to provide some basis for the future development of economic science.[6] There are risks involved; biology has been often abused by social scientists in the past, sometimes with horrendous social and political consequences. There was the episode of 'Social Darwinism' and lamentable former associations of biological thought with sundry pro-aristocratic, racist or sexist ideologies. Hence for some the idea of evolution has a very limited appeal.[7] As Donald Campbell (1965, p. 21) rightly suggests, a major reason why evolutionary theory has lain fallow in the social sciences for much of the postwar period is 'the early contamination of the evolutionary perspective with the reactionary political viewpoints of the privileged classes and racial supremacist apologists for colonialism'.

This raises the question of the kind of policy conclusions that modern biology is supposed to support. It is still widely assumed that evolutionary thinking involves the rejection of any kind of state meddling, subsidy or intervention, and the support for laissez-faire on the basis of the idea of 'survival of the fittest'. Depending on your point of view, this may become a reason to either endorse or eschew the adoption of the evolutionary metaphor in economic science.

It shall be shown in this book, however, that it is wrong to assume that evolutionary theorizing always points to the optimality of competitive outcomes, or to laws of evolutionary 'progress', or to the sagacity of laissez-faire. According to modern theory, evolutionary processes do not necessarily lead to – by any reasonable definition – optimal consequences. Similar arguments apply in the economic as well as the biotic context. The possibility of some form of non-comprehensive yet proficient state intervention in economic life – be it an industrial policy, some form of indicative planning, or whatever – is thus highlighted by modern evolutionary theory.

Moreover, it should be emphasized that biology has internal problems of its own. Indeed, biology is not itself free of mechanistic metaphor and reductionist methods. Although arguably his work began to transcend mechanistic thought, Darwin idolized Newton. Even today, a large number of biologists are committed to reductionism, even concerned to explain biological phenomena in physical and mechanistic terms. The use of optimization techniques in biology, many appropriated directly from neoclassical economics, is widespread. There is even an explicit Cartesian strand within modern biology (Ghiselin, 1974, 1975). Within its boundaries, however, there are also pronounced attempts to transcend this modernist strain of thought.

A prejudice must be admitted here. An economist who turns to biology to search out an alternative to the mechanistic metaphor is hardly likely to be greatly attracted to the mechanistic and reductionist strands of biological thought, whatever their contemporary importance. Much greater attention is given to the alternatives.[8]

To some extent it is possible to pick and choose. Internally, biology is refreshingly controversial and lacking in consensus on some key issues. However, the lack of consensus in biology will mean that no claim can be made for majority endorsement for favoured ideas from that scientific community. Indeed, there is the likelihood that the kinds of authorities invoked (or criticized) here will not always be those finding (or denied) approval by the majority of biologists.

Clearly, it is not possible to go into all the interpretations and illuminating debates between different schools of thought within that science. Notably, however, important trends within the discipline point to an organicist ontology, a more pluralistic methodology, and the transcendence of Cartesian dualism. The principle guiding such a choice is that such theoretical attributes are much more relevant for the highly complex, living system of the human economy.

Leading mainstream biologists such as Theodosius Dobzhansky

(1968) and Ernst Mayr (1972, 1985a), as well as more heterodox scientists such as Niles Eldredge (1985a) and Stephen Jay Gould (1982a), along with historians of biology such as Manier (1978), voice the view that the Darwinist legacy provides the seeds of an alternative to the 'Cartesian' or 'reductionist' approach. The view taken in the present work is that recourse to biological analogies, while they need to be handled with great care, is probably the best strategy for moving economics out of its restrictive and mechanistic patterns of thought, and providing a basis for fruitful development at the fundamental level.

However, a preeminent problem with the biological analogy relates to the conceptualization of the human agent and his or her role in the evolutionary processes of economic life. The main dilemma can be stated thus: if economic development is determined by some process of natural selection, with something analogous to genetic replication and to random variation or mutation, then what role remains for intentionality, purposefulness or choice, which have been central to economic discourse for well over a hundred years? Can there be intention or purpose if the analogue to the genetic code has already predetermined all, except the additional random variations caused by nature's anonymous dice?

As with many 'hard-core' metaphors, their transposition from one science to another may open up problems in their source as well as their destination. Despite the facade of modernist science, the problem of 'vitalism', involving choice, will, teleology and purpose, has been persistent within biology. Although 'vitalism' is now out of fashion, it raises real issues of importance, even if the notion is shunned by present-day biologists who confine themselves to causal rather than intentional explanations. Dissenters from strict Darwinism, including Arthur Koestler (1967, 1971, 1978, 1980), have tried to instate concepts of will and purpose in the science, but with limited effect. This whole problem should not be ignored or underestimated, and it is addressed at length in chapter 14.

Naturalism and the 'Economy of Nature'

Natural metaphors have already played a prominent and sometimes troublesome role in the development of social science. Even the dominance of mainstream economics by the mechanistic metaphor has not debarred appeals to 'natural' circumstances to endorse economic arguments, and the use of relatively safe and convenient ideas from biology. Take the term 'natural', as in the 'natural prices' of the classical economists, or in the so-called 'natural rate of unemployment' today. This key word is more complex than may appear at first sight. It has changed its meaning over the centuries, and is still ambiguous and elusive. 'Nature', Raymond Williams (1976, p. 184) writes, 'is perhaps the most complex word in the language.'

When the classical economists referred to 'natural prices' they meant prices in accord with economic laws which had the same status as laws of nature. Like the supposed laws of physics, such laws were seen to be eternal and independent of the particular kind of socioeconomic system under investigation. Thus the classical economists claimed to discover nature's social-economic laws, just as Sir Isaac Newton and others had previously discovered its laws for the physical world.[9] Even today, economists write of the 'natural rate of unemployment' with this same and persistent meaning.

Behind this adoption of the term 'natural' there is often a hidden ideological agenda. What is assumed to be natural is also assumed to be good: even God-given for some. Whether the formulation is secular or religious, the result is often to suggest that many kinds of economic intervention must disrupt the 'natural' progress towards the good. The choice to interfere is thus denied. Other than to aid and promote the natural order there is no policy discretion. Clearly, these imputations are highly questionable.

In this present volume the appeal to the metaphors of nature is on quite different grounds. Long gone from modern biology is the Panglossian idea that nature provides 'the best of all possible worlds'. Long gone from modern biology is the idea of general or developmental laws. The invocation of that science is not to confirm universal propositions within economics, but to admit the possibility of a quite different programme of study that can help to solve key problems.

Another past instance of the appropriation of biological metaphors into economics is Armen Alchian's (1950, 1953) use of the idea of 'natural selection' in theory of the behaviour of firms. This was subsequently developed by Stephen Enke (1951) and Milton Friedman (1953) in an effort to support the neoclassical hypothesis of profit maximization. Later, Oliver Williamson (1975, 1985) appealed to the idea of competitive 'natural selection' in an attempt to support his notion that survival means efficiency. As discussed in later chapters, the use of some vague idea of 'natural selection' from biology to support such conclusions is highly questionable. In addition, other than arguments of this type, the appeal to biological metaphor by modern economists is relatively unusual. Furthermore, modern mainstream economists do not make use of the ideas from biology which may help economics to overcome the limitations of its more prominent mechanistic metaphors. On the contrary, the 'natural selection' ideas of Friedman, Williamson and others are a case of the importing of ill-formed ideas from biology to bolster rather than replace a fundamentally mechanistic paradigm.

Arguably, the influence of economics on biology in the postwar period has been more significant than the influence of biology on economics. For instance, some biologists refer to Herbert Simon's works and his concept of satisficing (Arnold and Fristrup, 1982; Wimsatt, 1980).[10] In other cases there has been a transfer and incorporation of mathematical techniques. The use made by biologists of game theory, originally developed in economics by John von Neumann and Oskar Morgenstein (1944), by John Maynard Smith (1982) and others working on population genetics, has been a particularly important instance. In fact, after developing the concept of an evolutionary stable strategy within game theory, this concept was then transferred back to economics in the work of Robert Sugden (1986).

There is also Michael Ghiselin's (1974) adoption in a biological framework of the notion of 'methodological individualism' – developed originally by economists – along with yet another metaphorical reference to 'nature's economy' in the biotic sphere. In a more formal vein, the biologists David Rapport and James Turner (1977) analyse food selection, 'predator switching' and other biological phenomena using indifference curves and other analytical tools taken from economics. Note also the appropriation of constrained optimization models by sociobiologists.[11]

Yet these instances, important as they are, should not delude us into thinking that the conceptual intercourse between economics and biology has been substantial. Particularly in the cases cited in the preceding paragraph, what has been involved is partly a continuance of the export from economics of individualistic ideas and notions of optimization which were originally taken from economics in a less refined and less formalized mould long ago by Charles Darwin, but which contrast with the organicist and non-reductionist strains in modern biology.

The Case of 'Economic Imperialism'

Alfred Marshall (1949, p. 637) saw economics as 'a branch of biology broadly interpreted'. A school of postwar neoclassical economists, including Gary Becker, Jack Hirshleifer and Gordon Tullock, are fond of quoting this phrase, yet they reverse Marshall's meaning, and try to make biology 'a branch of economics narrowly interpreted'.[12]

The ideas and models developed by Becker, Hirshleifer and Tullock are of considerable interest to the evolutionary economist. What concerns us here, however, is their self-proclaimed 'economic imperialism' and some of its underlying assumptions. They argue that common 'economic' principles are supposed to bind biology to economics: 'All aspects of life are ultimately governed by the scarcity of resources' (Hirshleifer, 1982, p. 52). 'Competition is the all-pervasive law of natural-economy interactions' (Hirshleifer, 1978, p. 322). Furthermore, 'the evolutionary approach suggests that self-interest is ultimately the prime motivator of human as of all life' (Hirshleifer, 1982, p. 52). In sum: 'Fundamental concepts like scarcity, competition, equilibrium, and specialization play similar roles in both spheres of inquiry' (Hirshleifer, 1977, p. 2).

Thus economics and biology are seen as addressing common root problems which are soluble with similar or identical concepts and toolkit theories. Hence the basis for: '"Economic imperialism" – the use of economic analytical models to study all forms of social relations rather than only the market interactions of "rational" decision makers' (Hirshleifer, 1982, p. 52). What is the end result of this invasion? Hirshleifer (1977, pp. 3–4) writes: 'As economics "imperialistically" employs its tools of analysis over a wide range of social issues, it will *become* sociology and anthropology and political science. But correspondingly, as these other disciplines grow increasingly rigorous, they will not merely resemble but will *be* economics.' Hence the case for the conquest of other social sciences and biology by the 'economic imperialists' rests on the presumed universality of such ideas as scarcity, competition and self-interest.

The inspiration drawn from sociobiology is that the process of natural selection should result in the emergence of something like 'rational economic man', providing the bridgehead for the maximizing postulates of economics across to biology and other sciences. Like the sociobiology it emulates, the Becker-Hirshleifer-Tullock school assumes that fitness is ordinally measurable. The 'ordinalist fallacy' has long been challenged in economics (Armstrong, 1958; Georgescu-Roegen, 1954). Accordingly, the presumption of absolute fitness maximization is questioned by critics of sociobiology.

One problem with the maximization idea is that it fits uneasily into an ongoing evolutionary framework. Global maximization is a concept fitting to an unreal and transparent eternity, not the incremental and imperfect adjustments in an evolutionary process (Cooper, 1989; Goldberg, 1975). Accordingly, rather than unrelenting competition and improvement, organisms 'satisfice' rather than maximize: they find niches to protect themselves from competition.

In many ways the Becker-Hirshleifer-Tullock arguments are redolent of the Social Darwinists. Many of the earlier criticisms of this current still apply. For instance, Lester Ward (1893) drew a distinction between the economy of nature and economics, noting that nature exhibited massive waste rather than stewardly economy. Instead of flowing straight, rivers waste energy in their meanderings; many species lay thousands of eggs, of which only a few will reach maturity. Instead of tolerating this inefficiency, humans intervene in nature, ploughing, hoeing and weeding, to improve agricultural productivity.

The Social Darwinists often drew parallels between the competition in the natural and the social worlds. Yet even Herbert Spencer frequently stressed the reality of cooperation. Peter Kropotkin (1842–1921) drew on his own field experience to publish *Mutual Aid* in 1902 (Kropotkin, 1972), showing plentiful evidence from biology that competition and scarcity are neither universal nor natural laws.[13] Likewise, the philosophers John Dewey and James Tufts (1908, pp. 368–75) countered the dogmas of the inevitability of rivalry, competition and self-interest in the social sphere. In addition, Herman Reinheimer (1913) rejected the universality of competition in both the social and the natural spheres.[14] Since then, many subsequent studies attest to the view that there are plentiful cases of cooperation in both nature and human society, and relatively limited instances of direct competition over scarce resources.[15] Alfred North Whitehead (1926, p. 256) argued the case well when he wrote:

> The watchwords of the nineteenth century have been, struggle for existence, competition, class warfare, commercial antagonism between nations, military warfare. The struggle for existence has been construed into the gospel of hate. The full conclusion to be drawn from a philosophy of evolution is fortunately of a more balanced character. Successful organisms modify their environment. Those organisms are successful which modify their environment so as to assist each other. This is exemplified by nature on a vast scale.

Even the modern theoretical concept of natural selection does not imply universal or intense competition. As the philosopher of biology Elliott Sober (1981, p. 100) has elaborated:

> competition is a familiar way of thinking about natural selection; yet, curiously, the familiar cases of natural selection that serve as textbook examples do not involve competition. The evolution of industrial melanism and of immunity to DDT do not involve there being a common resource in short supply. Competition is a special case, not a defining characteristic, of natural selection.

Likewise, Richard Lewontin (1978, 1980) argues that competition for limited resources is not necessary for natural selection.

In claiming to find such universal 'economic' principles in nature, Becker, Hirshleifer and Tullock turn to the sociobiology of Edward Wilson (1975, 1978) and others. A problem here, however, is that in Wilson's sociobiology there is only a thin and limited concept of culture, placed within genetic constraints. As Wilson (1978, p. 167) himself argues: 'genes hold culture on a leash.' He thus suggests that culture is ultimately determined and driven by genes alone.

In contrast, anthropologists such as Robert Boyd and Peter Richerson (1985), Luigi Cavalli-Sforza and Marcus Feldman (1981) and William Durham (1991) argue for a 'dual inheritance' model where 'information' can be conveyed at the cultural level as well as the genetic. Although they interact, each tier has its own autonomy. It is thus argued that sociobiology of the Wilson type does not include culture in its full sense.[16] A consequence for Becker, Hirshleifer and Tullock is that by attempting to fuse economics with such sociobiology they are removing culture from economics and thereby even undermining its status as a social science.

Indeed, the 'dual inheritance' model challenges some of the neoclassical assumptions in economics. As Boyd and Richerson (1980, p. 110) demonstrate, the adoption of a model with cultural as well as genetic transmission means that 'one should be cautious about the assumption of economic man even within the economic sphere, since the explicit inclusion of cultural transmission in models of human behavior may create rather different kinds of behavior.'

As Elias Khalil (1992) has argued, the kind of biology which attracts Becker, Hirshleifer and Tullock has attracted similar criticisms from heterodox biologists which are strikingly similar to prominent criticisms of neoclassical economics by heterodox economists. Becker, Hirshleifer and Tullock attempt to build a bridge between a biology and an economics which have parallel defects: both are reductionist, both exclude teleology, both have an essentially programmed or passive conception of the agent or organisms, both take the selector (nature or preferences), factors of production (nutrients or inputs) and information (genotypes or technology) all as given. The arguments presented in part IV of the present book draw on quite different traditions in biology, establishing a process orientated and historical mode of analysis that is quite different from the economics and biology embraced by the 'economic imperialists'.

There are parallels between the natural and the human worlds, but they have to be drawn with care. One of the biggest errors, committed by the Social Darwinists long ago, was to see the individualism and greed of modern competitive capitalism as universal in both spheres. By seeing capitalism in nature, the capitalist system was thus deemed to be 'natural'. It was hence regarded as both inevitable and superior to all other systems. It is this same ideological error which is at the root of 'economic imperialism', yet abundant evidence both from biology and human anthropology cries out against it.[17]

However, we should not draw the conclusion from examination of the case of neoclassical 'economic imperialism' that economics and biology should be kept well apart. Instead, the need for a reform of economics itself is indicated. Ironically, it is probably the severance of the links between the two subject areas in the decades since the 1920s that has enabled the resurgence of arguments of the Becker-Hirshleifer-Tullock type. Economists have become ignorant of the earlier criticisms of Social Darwinism and given passive audience to its resuscitation. A more informed attempt to draw parallels between economics and biology would not have proceeded from the fallacious 'universal laws' laid down by Hirshleifer and his colleagues.

The Value of the Biological Metaphor

Despite all the problems and dangers, it is suggested here that modern biology provides a rich source of ideas and approaches from which the new economics may draw. But this is little more than a hunch – we cannot demonstrate the value of a particular set of ideas for the development or reconstruction of a science unless the task is completed. And we are at the beginning of this task, rather than at its completion. Consequently, the utilization of biology has to be based on expectation and conjecture rather than demonstrable cash value.

Some may regard the appeal in this present book to biological ideas as irrelevant – even a mistaken appeal to the authority of another science. Yes, there has been a deliberate attempt here to show directly the relevance of work in biology and elsewhere for the venture at hand. To the formalist or apriorist these appeals may seem out of place. But to some extent they are unavoidable. Either we openly invoke the ideas and metaphors of others, or we rest on the anonymous testimony of unquoted words, each tangled in a web of meanings from which it can never be free, and in which the Holy Grail of purity and unambiguity can never be found.

In all, the application of an evolutionary approach to economics seems to involve a number of advantages and improvements over the orthodox and mechanistic paradigm.[18] For instance, it enhances a concern with irreversible and ongoing processes in time,[19] with long-run development rather than short-run marginal adjustments, with qualitative as well as quantitative change, with variation and diversity, with non-equilibrium as well as equilibrium situations, and with the possibility of persistent and systematic error-making and thereby non-optimizing behaviour. In short, an evolutionary paradigm provides an alternative to the neoclassical 'hard core' idea of mechanistic maximization under static constraints. The theory of rational choice at the core of mainstream economics relies on static assumptions, the notion of an eventually constant decision environment, and the idea of global rationality, all of which are challenged in evolutionary theory (Cooper, 1989; Goldberg, 1975).

Another extremely important reason why ideas from biology are of relevance to economics is that both economic and biotic systems are highly complex. They encompass tangled structures and causalities, involve continuous change and embrace huge variety. Partly for this reason, there is the problem of degrees of inclusiveness and complexity, and the corresponding tiers of abstraction and units of analysis. This has been faced up to and debated by a number of prominent biologists, but far less attention has been given to this vital issue in economics. The adoption of biological metaphors may help to redress the balance.

It may be suggested that the adoption of an evolutionary metaphor taken from biology means the loss of the capacity to predict that is associated with mechanistic modelling. This is not strictly true because in some cases, such as Conrad Waddington's (1957, 1969, 1972) idea of channelled, 'chreodic' development – discussed later in chapter 13 – some kind of limited prediction is possible in biology. Furthermore, it should be emphasized that if a mechanistic system has nonlinear properties – such as in the three-body problem – the mathematical result may be chaos and there still may be unpredictability. Prediction may not be viable, even in a mechanistic world. The loss of some capacity to predict is real, but in any case the greater weight in the science of complex systems should be on explanation rather than prediction (Scriven, 1959).

Notably, in biology there is a discourse not only concerning reductionism and the appropriate units of evolutionary selection, but also over the viability of further reduction from genetics down to molecular biology, and even below to chemistry and physics (Sober, 1984b). In contrast, confident in the Newtonian metaphor of the indivisible, 'individual' particle, mainstream economics traditionally proscribes discussion of the psychological or social foundations of individual purposes and preferences as being beyond the bounds of the subject.

In contrast, and partly because of the acknowledged complexity of the phenomena which it attempts to analyse, biological science exhibits a theoretical pluralism (Gould and Lewontin, 1979; Mayr, 1985b). This applies to both the variety of competing approaches within the subject as a whole, and the acceptance by individual theorists of a set of possible alternative explanations of given phenomena. Consider an example of the latter: in addition to the idea of natural selection, Darwin allowed also for Lamarckian use and disuse and even for the direct influence of the environment. He argued that natural selection was the 'main, but not the exclusive means of modification' (Gould and Lewontin, 1979, p. 589).

Here there is a similarity between the implicit scientific method of Darwin and that of Thomas Robert Malthus, as Anthony Flew (1959, 1963, 1978) has pointed out. In their approach there is a rigorous deductive core, but it is deemed to prove little on its own and it is thus placed in the context of a mass of empirical material (Hull, 1973, pp. 3–36). Hence there are deductive arguments combined with contingent empirical premises and conclusions. Likewise, in modern biology, a number of theories and explanations typically compete not necessarily for overall supremacy or intellectual monopoly, but in their claims to identify the main, rather than the exclusive, cause in given real circumstances. Fortunately, biology does not present the near monopoly of methods and approaches that stifles economics today. In contrast, classical physics has typically stressed parsimony and exclusiveness in theoretical explanation.

There is another reason why the turn to biology is of value and significance. As Fritjof Capra (1982) and others have argued, the Cartesian and Newtonian world-views have sanctioned habits of thought which involve an ultimately untenable conceptual division between humankind and the remainder of the natural world. Human beings are regarded as thinking, allocating, legislating, consuming and producing, and the mental dilemmas involved in this human-centred view have become the main subject matter of all the social sciences. Yet humans are living beings alongside others in a natural environment. Accordingly, in material terms at least, there are limits to the natural resources available and to the tolerances of the ecosystems on the planet. The invocation of the biological metaphor surely helps remind us of these vital issues for the twenty-first century.[20]

Furthermore, some reassurance is found in the fact that some of the greatest economic theorists, even some from the mainstream, have stated a belief that biology is a most fruitful source for further development in economics. Such a view was held by Alfred Marshall and by Thorstein Veblen, among others, and two separate chapters examine the nature and role of the biological metaphor in their works. This does not mean that these theorists were successful in infusing economics with ideas from biology: their success was minimal at most. Some of the reasons for this failure have been discussed in this work.

Despite the failure, the expression of the potential value of biological thinking for economics has been repeated at periodic intervals ever since: importantly by János Kornai (1971), with great finesse by Nicholas Georgescu-Roegen (1971), misleadingly and one-sidedly by Becker, Hirshleifer and Tullock (discussed above), with the clarity of a popularizer by Kenneth Boulding (1981), and briefly and surprisingly by Frank Hahn (1991, p. 50).

Another source of reassurance is the burgeoning literature on economic evolution and technical change.[21] However, there is relatively little attention here to the deeper conceptual and methodological questions involved, e.g. units of selection, causality in evolution, reductionism. Taking these ideas on board involves greater reference to and deliberation upon biology and evolutionary theory. Several close and useful analogies between the biological and economic spheres have already been demonstrated in this area.

Furthermore, there are clear signs of a revival of evolutionary thinking in anthropology and sociology (Barkow, 1989; Durham, 1990, 1991; Hallpike, 1986; Schmid and Wuketits, 1987). Ideas from biology have also found their way into sociology, particularly with the work of Niklas Luhmann (1984, 1986). It is clear that evolutionary ideas are presently having an impact in a number of the social sciences.[22]

The Aim of the Present Work

It is not a straightforward matter to build up a science with use of the biological metaphor. It would be unwise simply to pillage biology uncritically of its ideas. Even if such a reckless approach was generally viable, biology itself does not present a consensus of ideas or methods: it is developing rapidly and contains a diversity of sometimes conflicting views. Consequently, any attempt to examine the utility of the biological metaphor must take a careful look at the internal controversies within biology itself.

Furthermore, the reconstruction of economics is far from being an easy matter, and it cannot be achieved in a single book, nor by one person. The task here is more modest: to clear away the undergrowth of dangers and misconceptions, and to till the soil of fundamental concepts, so that the seeds of a future evolutionary economics may be germinated.

The aim here is not to construct a universalistic theoretical framework, partly borrowed from biology, in which the specific and historically conditioned circumstances of economic development are overshadowed. On the contrary, the aim is to use theoretical tools to identify the specific nature and dynamics of different structures and institutions. However, absolute relativism is logically impossible. Even Marx, in his construction of a theory specifically related to the capitalist mode of production, had to use universal concepts – time, labour, production, mode of production itself – to address specific historic phenomena. His work invokes metaphors and – often mechanistic – modes of reasoning which are disconnected from the specific historical object under investigation. To emphasize: the use of the biological metaphor in the present work is not itself a universal theory, but more a metatheoretic guide to understanding the specific.

It is judged that one of the best ways of addressing some of the key problems involved in this enterprise is to explore the extent to which evolutionary and biological ideas have been used by economists in the past. A primary purpose of parts II and III is thus to trace the extent and nature of this interchange of ideas. In general, with one or two exceptions, the theorists are examined in chronological order of their birth.

The works of a number of economic theorists are examined, from the birth of economic science in the eighteenth century to the arbitrary cut-off date of 1980. The principal theorists discussed here all developed their ideas in this period.[23] They include Bernard Mandeville (1670–1733), Adam Smith (1723–1790), Thomas Robert Malthus (1766–1834), Charles Babbage (1792–1871), Karl Marx (1818–1883), Frederick Engels (1820–1895), Carl Menger (1840–1921), Alfred Marshall (1842–1924), Thorstein Veblen (1857–1929), Joseph Schumpeter (1883–1950) and Friedrich Hayek (1899–1992). Herbert Spencer (1820–1903) is added to the list because of his important (but now almost forgotten) nineteenth-century influence on conceptions of socioeconomic evolution in general, and on the economics of Marshall and Veblen in particular. The struggles of these theorists with the evolutionary metaphor are particularly illuminating, because they show the pitfalls and blind alleys, as well as the open vistas, which the journey into biology can bring.

Much of the book may appear as an excursion into the history of economic thought. However, it is history of thought with a difference. The purpose is not simply to disclose and dissect the meaning of each chosen author's work. There is an important additional aim: to illuminate modern conceptions and controversies associated with the notion of evolution. The project is not simply to understand past ideas but to examine the viability of different formulations of economic evolution.

The disadvantage of this mode of presentation is that we shall sometimes evaluate the writings of economists from the past by means of seemingly anachronistic concepts taken from modern biology. However, this is not as reprehensible as it may seem, as all history, by its very nature, involves the probing of materials from the past with the concepts of the present.

The advantage is that this work may provide much more than a history of economic thought, perhaps a guide to the future reconstruction of our subject with the scientific materials of the present.

Ideas of evolution in economic thought thus appear as a mosaic. We may take the picture as a whole and evaluate its overall merit and form. Or we may examine each piece for its detail and the precision of its craftsmanship. Or we may use the surface of each piece to mirror, perhaps in a different hue, the related ideas from elsewhere in the pattern, or even to reflect the illumination from the science of biology. It is partly because we are dealing not with economic thought as an isolated entity but with the complex relationship between economics and biology that all three approaches are adopted here.

The succession of historical personages in this volume proffers convenient receptacles for the discussion of specific topics. The chapter on the Darwinian revolution thus provides a forum for the introduction of the distinction between ontogeny and phylogeny, the chapter on Herbert Spencer an opportunity to outline Lamarckism, the discussion of Thorstein Veblen prompts a passage on cumulative causation, a chapter on Friedrich Hayek is an obvious place to raise the question of group selection, and so on.

The final part of the work examines some remaining key concepts and theories, but within a structure not based on the historical development of the ideas themselves. Instead, the focus is on the restoration of key concepts and ideas in the fabric of economics: the rebirth of life in our science.

3
Economic Evolution:
A Preliminary Taxonomy

Evolutionary ideas in economics have enjoyed a remarkable revival in the 1980s, particularly following the work of Richard Nelson and Sidney Winter (1982). Nevertheless – and with the latter work as a clear exception – the use of the term 'evolutionary' by economists is often vague and imprecise. A problem with many disputes over the application of evolutionary ideas to social science is that often the very notion of 'evolution' is not defined with sufficient clarity, or is even used in different senses.

Jacques Monod is reported to have stated in a lecture that: 'Another curious aspect of the theory of evolution is that everybody thinks that he understands it!' (Dawkins, 1976, p. 19). Such common thoughts belittle the complexity of the theory and the enormity of Darwin's achievement. One of the problems is that the word 'evolution' is itself highly ambiguous.

The term 'evolution', like the word 'development', derives from the Latin verb *volvere*. This means 'to roll' but it is often used in Latin in a broader sense to refer to the general idea of motion. The companion verbs *evolvere* and *revolvere* are more explicit, respectively denoting forward and backward motion, as in the unrolling and rolling-up of a scroll. The word 'evolution' therefore derives from the Latin word associated with a specifically directional and predestined activity; the scroll is unrolled to reveal that which is immanent and already within.

It was in this spirit that the word 'evolution' was first applied systematically to biological phenomena by the German biologist Albrecht von Haller in 1744.[1] Haller applied it to the preformationist notion that all major structures of the adult are already preformed in the sex cell, and that ontogeny is the unfolding or 'evolution' of this pre-built complexity. Subsequently in the eighteenth century it was generally associated with ontogeny: the growth and development of a single organism.

It is not widely appreciated that the great theorists of 'evolution' such as Jean Baptiste de Lamarck and Charles Darwin generally avoided the term. It was Herbert Spencer, not Darwin, who popularized the term 'evolution' in the nineteenth century. Darwin did not introduce the word until the sixth edition of the *Origin of Species*, and then he used it only sparingly.

The modern association of the word with the Darwinian theory of natural selection is very different from the conception of Haller, or even of Spencer. For Haller, given that the entity was preformed at the start of the 'evolutionary' process, no structural or major organic development was implied, other than the unfolding of the organism. Although Spencer embraced a notion of more complex organic change, it is argued below in chapter 6 that it was nevertheless still very close to ontogenetic development, and gave no prominence to natural or competitive selection.

Another sense in which 'evolution' is used in common parlance is in opposition to 'revolution' in the political or social sphere. However, these two words share the same Latin root, and originally 'revolution' meant precisely to roll or revolve, in the sense of a circular movement in return to an original or 'natural' state of affairs. Despite their opposing use in political discourse, the two terms both used to imply an unrolling or revolving motion.

Despite this deep ambiguity with the term 'evolution', the term is still used casually in public and academic circles, vaguely connoting 'development' and often with the unwarranted confidence and assurance that everyone knows what it means. Nothing is more guaranteed to generate confusion and to stultify intellectual progress than to raise such a muddled term to the centrepiece of economic research, while simultaneously suggesting that a clear and well-defined approach to scientific enquiry is implied. The term can be used to describe a varied group of approaches in economics, perhaps in contrast to the exclusive focus on equilibrium in neoclassical theory, but it does not indicate a well-defined type of analysis. Given the profound ambiguity, it is necessary to make clear whether, for instance, an analogy to natural selection or to ontogeny is implied. The identification of the different types of evolutionary theory in economics is a major theme of this book.

Some of the misconceptions and mislabelling that have occurred in 'evolutionary economics' are due to the inadequate exploration of biological theory. The latter has developed very rapidly since the Second World War, further undermining many popular misconceptions of the evolutionary process. It has been noted in the preceding chapter, for instance, that the association of evolutionary selection with optimization and efficiency is one important idea that is now rejected by many biologists. Likewise, other theorists have argued that biological outcomes are not necessarily 'the best of all possible worlds'.

As there are many recent cases of economists adopting such ideas in their work, it is especially important to disentangle the many different meanings of the term 'evolutionary' in this context. This is the principal aim of this chapter. A taxonomy is proposed, with reference to examples discussed in more detail later. Finally, a particular class of evolutionary economic theory is examined in more detail: the one corresponding to natural selection or 'descent with modification' in a Darwinian or Lamarckian sense. It is suggested here and in a later chapter that the work of Thorstein Veblen provides the best example of this case.

A Taxonomy

As with all taxonomies, some items are difficult to classify. This is particularly the case with economic theorists, whose work is complex and sometimes even contradictory. Nevertheless, the taxonomy is not in vain, mainly because it raises important questions of substance and demarcation to categorize the different theories. A multitude of meanings of 'economic evolution' is possible, as shown in the diagram.

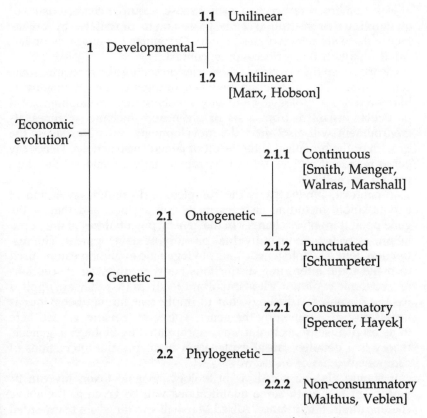

'Economic evolution': a taxonomy of meanings

This taxonomy is not exhaustive, but covers the major cases to be discussed here. Types 2.2.1 and 2.2.2 in particular have a huge multiplicity of further subdivisions, related to questions such as: What is (are) the unit(s) of selection? What is the source of variation? Is there a place for creativity; if so to what extent and of what type? Does the conception of evolution involve perfectibility or inevitable progress? Many of these further subdivisions are not discussed here because of lack of space.

Type 2.2 could be subdivided in a different manner, for instance between Lamarckian and Darwinian conceptions of (phylogenetic) evolution. Lamarckism differs from strict Darwinism mainly because it admits the possibility of the inheritance of acquired characters. Darwin himself flirted with Lamarckian ideas but he did not adopt the whole Lamarckian explanation of variety and its sources, or the Lamarckian teleology of purposeful behaviour. Today, Lamarckism is generally rejected by biologists because no mechanism has been widely accepted as an explanation of how an acquired character would be encoded in the genes and thus passed on to future progeny. However, it is widely accepted that socioeconomic evolution can be Lamarckian, at least in a broad rather than a strict sense; acquired characteristics of an individual or institution can be passed on to, or imitated by, others. Hence there are no advocates of strict Darwinian evolution, as understood today, in the socioeconomic context.

Clearly, even the taxonomic categories presented above require some clarification. The distinction between ontogeny and phylogeny is borrowed from biology.[2] Ontogeny involves the development of a particular organism from a set of given and unchanging genes. Its environment will also affect this development, but nevertheless the growth of the organism is the result of genetic instructions. Hence the genes represent a given set of (environmentally dependent) developmental possibilities.

In contrast, phylogeny is the complete and ongoing evolution of a population, including changes in its composition and that of the gene pool. It involves changes in the genetic potentialities of the population, as well as their individual phenotypic development. The distinction between ontogenetic and phylogenetic evolution can be used to make some interesting distinctions between differing conceptions of 'economic evolution'. It is important to stress that they are applied for the purposes of analogy, not to imply that human behaviour is necessarily determined by the genes. The term 'genetic' is used here in its original sense, before it was appropriated by biology; a 'genetic' theory is a detailed causal explanation involving the interactions of component units of a system.

It should also be noted, as in biology, that no taxonomy can be perfect. In this work some qualifications will be given to the above classifications. For instance, Alfred Marshall's writings are many-sided and full of nuances and qualifications. Likewise, in the works of Léon

Walras there are passages where he proposed a version of evolution close to type 2.1.2 rather than type 2.1.1. Nevertheless, it is maintained that the taxonomy is of some analytic use.

Examples of Type 1

To illustrate the taxonomy with some examples: the developmental notion of evolution, type 1, can be considered first. One example of type 1 evolution would be the Marxian idea that history is progressing – whether 'deterministically' or not – through a series of stages, from 'primitive communism', through classical antiquity, feudalism and capitalism, to socialism and communism in the future. This 'stages' theory of evolution involves no detailed reference to the constituent elements that drive the evolutionary process. Instead, the driving force has a holistic quality, as if development was in accord with a pre-ordained plan.

Marx mentions Darwin in a few places in *Capital*, but on close examination there is much in the Marxian theoretical system that is antagonistic to Darwinian evolutionary ideas. Marx did not assimilate Darwinian theory in his social science partly because it was incompatible with the mechanistic world-view within which he was still entrapped. For instance, for Marx, the socioeconomic system moves from revolution towards the equilibrium of a classless society, in which the sources of fluctuations and struggle are eliminated.

In contrast, when historical movement is made to proceed in terms of Darwin's biological principles it is impossible to predict the character and form of social change. On the basis of Darwinism, change would occur as the result of chance variations; these are a source of unpredictability, and deny evolution any predetermined goal. The idea of change resulting from a process of natural selection among a population of individual entities exhibiting great diversity and variety is markedly different from the conception of history as the clash of collectives engaged in class struggle.[3]

Some, but not all, of Joseph Schumpeter's accounts of economic development could also fall into this type 1 category, particularly when in various passages he discusses the broad span of historical development, in general terms very similar to that of Marx (Schumpeter, 1976, first published 1942). John A. Hobson's *Evolution of Modern Capitalism* (1926) could also be mentioned in this context.

Much work by evolutionary sociologists and social anthropologists is also of this 'developmentalist' type. Accordingly, critics of evolutionism in the social sciences such as Anthony Giddens (1984, pp. 228–43) and Robert Holton (1985) have identified social 'evolution' exclusively with theories of the 'unfolding' or developmentalist type. Thus Giddens reflects the views of many sociologists when he sees evolution as 'social change as *the progressive emergence of traits that a particular type of society is presumed to have within itself from its inception'* (1979, p. 233, emphasis in the original).

A crucial issue here is the lack of a detailed mechanism to explain development or change; in its place is the view of history 'unfolding', or passing 'inevitably' through stages. While 'analytical Marxists' such as John Roemer (1981, 1988) and Jon Elster (1985) may attempt to rescue Marxism here, the 'developmentalist' label applies to typical works in the Marxian tradition hitherto. In general, this conception of history has much more in common with *evolvere*, or unrolling, than with Darwinian natural selection.

In addition, type 1 could be subdivided into 'unilinear' or 'multilinear' cases. Notably, some Marxists have considered the possibility of multiple pathways to the future, involving different sequences of historical stages.

Examples of Type 2.1

The 'genetic' label for type 2 notions of economic evolution need not be taken to imply explanations in terms of biological genes, although sociobiologists such as Edward Wilson (1975) and economists such as Jack Hirshleifer (1977, 1978) do seem to accept the idea that social phenomena are determined by, and explicable in terms of, the DNA. Here, however, a broad and general meaning is implied by the word. A 'genetic' evolutionary process is one which derives in some way from a set of fairly durable human entities. The biological genes are one possibility, but alternatives include: human habits, human individuals, organizational routines, social institutions, even entire economic systems. Their 'genetic' quality is best approached through illustration.

It is said that there is a theory of economic evolution in the writings of Adam Smith.[4] Smith starts from the idea of a set of individuals with given predispositions, motives or sentiments. By analogy, these individuals could be taken as the 'genes' in his theory. On this basis he examines the development of an economic system, including its prices and allocations. The outcome is unintentional: the result of an 'invisible hand'.

In this case the 'organism' in question is the economic system. Because the motivated individuals are taken as given for the purposes of his analysis, they have an enduring and thereby a 'genetic' quality. This is ontogenetic evolution, because the development of an 'organism' (the economy) is explained from the 'genetic material' (motivated individuals). It is not phylogenetic, because there is not necessarily a process of evolutionary selection or genetic drift among a population of different organisms, nor does there need to be any change in the 'genetic material' for the purposes of the theory. Smith's evolutionary theory is thus an example of type 2.1. The reason why Smith is placed in the subcategory 2.1.1 and not 2.1.2 will become clear later.

Other examples of this 'ontogenetic' type are found in Carl Menger's account of the evolution of money and in the key texts of both Marshall and Walras. These are discussed, respectively, in chapters 8, 7 and 10. Of course, grouping these theories together under the 'ontogenetic' label does not mean that they are identical in other respects. For instance, the theories of Smith and Walras are very different in terms of the degree and type of dynamism assumed.

Although Schumpeter is often associated with the new wave of evolutionary theorizing since the 1980s, he explicitly rejected the employment of the biological analogy in economics, concluding that 'no appeal to biology would be of the slightest use' (Schumpeter, 1954, p. 789). Throughout his works, Schumpeter most frequently employs the term 'evolution' in a developmental sense, but excluding a Lamarckian or Darwinian process of evolutionary selection.

The closest that Schumpeter gets to a 'genetic' account of the evolutionary process is his analysis of the microeconomics of entrepreneurial activity. But without a selection process this account is more ontogenetic than phylogenetic. Other than allusions to the competitive process, no analogy with natural selection appears in Schumpeter's work. Indeed, he rejected such analogies.

In chapter 10 it is argued that Schumpeter adopted a conception of 'economic evolution', often close to type 1, but sometimes having the attributes of type 2.1. But if his theory is of the latter kind then it is 'punctuated ontogeny', that is, dynamics in a given setting punctuated by revolutionary leaps in which one ontogenetic process is displaced by another. It is thus a unique example of type 2.1.2.

Examples of Type 2.2

Contrast these examples of ontogeny with the implicit idea of evolution in the writings of Thomas Robert Malthus. He considers a population of individuals and their competitive struggle for the means of livelihood. Unlike the examples of ontogeny, there is a *selection* process, in which some individuals prosper and procreate, while others, with their progeny, are less fortunate.

For Malthus the object of evolutionary analysis is an aggregated population of individuals, rather than a socioeconomic system. Furthermore, he considers the evolutionary process of selection within, and development of, such a population. Close to the Darwinian idea of 'natural selection', the population changes through differential birth and death.

We may devise a Malthusian 'thought experiment' in which individuals are again analogous to the genes. The composition of the 'gene pool', that is of the population, changes as a result of the process of selection. This, precisely, is phylogeny: an example of type 2.2. It is thus, perhaps, no accident that the influence of Malthus on Darwin was as important as that of Smith; this issue is discussed in more detail in the next chapter.

Phylogenetic evolution involves the development of different genetic rules through some cumulative process of feedback, and the subsequent effects. This could simply involve changes in the composition of the human population, as in the Malthusian case, or changes in habits, routines, institutions or systems, or combinations of these. But in phylogenetic evolution there is not necessarily a final outcome, a state of equilibrium or rest. It would thus seem reasonable to consider Malthus's exposition as a tentative example of type 2.2.2.

Veblen was one of the first to adopt the explicit image of a Darwinian process of selection. He argued that economics should be an 'evolutionary science', where instincts, habits and institutions are taken as analogous to genes. Veblen observed that habits and routines have a stable and inert quality, and often sustain their important characteristics through time. The 'natural selection of institutions' (Veblen, 1899, p. 188) then becomes the pivot. Veblen advanced a phylogenetic conception of evolution, in which all elements may change in a process of cumulative causation.

Notably, Veblen argued against the idea of finality or consummation in economic evolution. For Veblen (1919, p. 436) evolution 'is a scheme of blindly cumulative causation, in which there is no trend, no final term, no consummation'. In part, Veblen took this view because he recognized the role of creativity and novelty in the evolutionary process; he had an explanation of the sources of variety in social evolution.

This emphasis on the ongoing creation of variety, ensuring that evolution has no final consummation, puts Veblen's theory in category 2.2.2. Overall, Veblen's conception of evolutionary economics contrasts not only with that of Smith, Marx and Menger, but also with that of Marshall and of Schumpeter.

The new wave of evolutionary modelling that started in the 1980s also has a phylogenetic quality, typically involving a selection process with a population of firms. In the models of Nelson and Winter (1982), for example, the firm's inbuilt routines are treated as analogous to the genes. Selection goes on as ill-adapted routines fall out of use and ones associated with higher profit levels are adopted. Similar ideas have been incorporated in later evolutionary simulations. In some key respects, therefore, the 'new wave' is closer to the ideas of Veblen rather than to those of Schumpeter.

However, although the new wave involves evolutionary models of a phylogenetic character, sometimes they gravitate towards an equilibrium. Under the initial conditions there is a variety of evolutionary entities, and a selection process takes place. There may be further sources of variety in the system, typically through some randomized parameters, but they are often not sufficient to disturb the overall progress towards equilibrium. As Richard Lewontin (1982, p. 151) writes: 'selection is like a fire that consumes its own fuel ... unless variation is renewed periodically, evolution would come to a stop almost at its inception.'

For example, the simulations published by Nelson and Winter (1982) and others are strictly phylogenetic, but asymptotic to an ontogenetic form in which an equilibrium is obtained. Although qualitative changes occur, they are limited. However, the intention of Nelson and Winter is to show that it takes a rather elaborate set of assumptions to get a model that converges on such an equilibrium. While their selected simulations have a consummatory quality, their general argument is that even if equilibrium exists it is normally a moving target. Consequently, their theory is in general of a non-consummatory type.[5]

In Friedrich Hayek's work (1988) evolutionary selection operates upon rules, their success or otherwise being demonstrated by the viability of the group with which they are associated. However, despite Hayek's emphasis on entrepreneurial creativity, the system is deemed to gravitate towards some kind of equilibrium: the so-called 'spontaneous order'. The resemblance of this evolutionary conception with the invisible hand of Adam Smith is widely recognized. However, whilst Smith's invisible hand is ontogenetic, Hayek's evolution of a spontaneous order is phylogenetic with an ontogenetic asymptote. Hayek's emphasis, furthermore, is on the emergence of order, not on the possibility of instability or of 'spontaneous disorder'. In full, phylogenetic evolution, variety may be not only the source of order, but also of disruption and crisis.

Reasons have thus been given for placing Hayek's evolutionary theory in the 'consummatory' category of phylogeny. Also it is argued in chapter 6 that Herbert Spencer's conception of evolution fits here too. However, it should be noted that the distinction between type 2.2.1 and type 2.2.2 rests on the degree of creativity and variety in the system and its effect on any consummatory progress towards order or equilibrium. Hayek's theoretical system could be reconstructed to put equal emphasis on spontaneous disorder as well as order. Such a reconstruction would be perfectly in accord with the stress on novelty and creativity found in the writings of Hayek and other members of the Austrian School.

This usefully focuses our attention on the role of novelty and creativity in evolution. While in the biotic sphere the primary sources of variety are genetic mutation and recombination, in the socioeconomic system variety is often the fruit of human creativity. In phylogenetic evolution of type 2.2.2, such creativity and ongoing variety is sufficient to ensure that no equilibrium is permanent. Qualitative change is of greater and wider scope. Even if there is equilibrium it may be 'punctuated' or disrupted.[6]

Phylogenetic Evolution: Some Elaborations

In the context of economic theory, we have seen that ontogeny is a means by which the concept of equilibrium can be smuggled back into an evolutionary frame. In contrast, phylogenetic evolution encompasses natural selection, where equilibrium is far from inevitable. In the case of phylogenetic evolution of type 2.2.2, where creativity and variety are not ultimately constrained, equilibrium here may be a temporary outcome. It is the purpose of the remainder of this chapter to examine the analogy with phylogenetic evolution in more detail.

Stephen Jay Gould and E. S. Vrba distinguish between 'sorting' and 'selection' (Gould, 1985; Gould and Vrba, 1982; Vrba and Gould, 1986). Sorting is defined as the broader term, merely meaning differential survival rates. However, differential survival rates can occur for many reasons, including chance. It does not imply any particular causal mechanism. The term selection, on the other hand, implies causality: an organism survives because it has greater fitness in a given context.

Strictly, phylogenetic evolution covers all cases of sorting, and not just selection. Furthermore, modern biological theory is putting increasing emphasis on other sorting mechanisms, other than natural selection (Depew and Weber, 1985a, p. 227; Kauffman, 1985). Here, however, the focus will be on natural selection and its analogues. Several component principles are involved. First, there must be sustained variation among the members of a species or population. Variations may be blind, random or purposive in character, but without them, as Darwin insisted, natural selection cannot operate.

Second, there must be some principle of heredity or continuity through which offspring have to resemble their parents more than they resemble other members of their species. In other words, there has to be some mechanism through which individual characteristics are passed on through the generations.

Third, natural selection itself operates either because better-adapted organisms leave increased numbers of offspring, or because the variations or gene combinations that are preserved are those bestowing advantage in struggling to survive. This is the principle of the struggle for existence. It is important to note that evolutionary selection in biology occurs by both differential rates of death and differential rates of birth; it is a matter of procreation as well as destruction.

The application of the metaphor of natural selection to economics must be on the basis of analogous principles. Arguably, the units of selection in economic evolution can be individuals, routines, institutions or systems. A methodological individualist, however, would almost certainly insist that the only appropriate unit of selection is the individual.[7] We now consider each of these principles in turn, with an eye to the economic analogue.

The Principle of Variation

The principle of variation emphasizes the essential, developmental role of variety and diversity.[8] The biologist Ernst Mayr establishes the importance of 'population thinking' in which variety and diversity are paramount. This 'population thinking' contrasts with the Platonic notion of 'typological essentialism' in which entities are regarded as identifiable in terms of a few distinct characteristics which represent their essential qualities.[9]

In typological thinking, species are regarded as identifiable in terms of a few distinct characteristics which represent their essence. Accordingly, all variations around the ideal type are regarded as accidental aberrations. By contrast, in population thinking, species are described in terms of a distribution of characteristics. Whereas in typological thinking variation is a classificatory nuisance, in population thinking it is of paramount interest because it is precisely the variety of the system that fuels the evolutionary process.[10]

The relevance of 'population thinking' to economics has been stressed by J. Stanley Metcalfe (1988) and others.[11] It suggests the importance of the examination of frequencies and their distribution, rather than ideal cases. How does variation arise and how is it retained? In biological evolution the principal mechanisms here are first, mutation, and second, sexual recombination along Mendelian lines. In the theory of the firm developed by Nelson and Winter (1982), there is an analogue to mutation. In some cases, for example, when a firm's profit levels become intolerably low, it is forced to search for a new technology.

Arguably, mutation in an economic context can include both the planned reorganization of, and unintended changes within, institutions. It is thus much more frequent and pervasive than mutation in biology. Other than the direct merger of institutions and firms, however, there is no obvious analogue to sexual recombination or Mendelian genetics in the socioeconomic sphere.

The fact that socioeconomic evolution is Lamarckian – involving both purposeful behaviour and the inheritance of acquired characters – is also relevant here. In the biotic sphere, and especially in small populations, stochastic mutations can accumulate and cause 'genetic drift'.[12] In socioeconomic systems much more rapid drift is possible, through the succession of imitation, improvement and acquired character inheritance. Given that socioeconomic behaviour is purposeful, systems of values, visions of the future, economic expectations, can all guide and accelerate such a process. This is still phylogenetic evolution, because the nature of the 'genetic' material – the institutions and routines – is changing. Yet it is a kind of phylogenetic evolution where purpose and drift are relatively more important than selection.[13]

As noted above, a key question concerning any theory or model of economic evolution is whether or not it encompasses a renewable source of variety and change. In a landmark work on the evolution of organizations, W. McKelvey (1982, p. 77) uses terms from biology to make a useful distinction between two sources of variation. Autogenic variation is self-generated or caused by forces within an institution. Allogenic variation is caused by forces outside an institution.

Importantly, the maintenance of variety involves constant error-making, as well as continuous selection of the more adapted forms. For selection to work there must be rejection, and the process must thus involve ceaseless mistakes as well as refinements.

However, in economic evolution the source of variation is not simply error. Phylogenetic evolution occurs in open systems which can import variety from other systems, or generate it through the creative acts of agents themselves. In the economic context this means not simply quantitative economic growth, but technological innovation, the development of new products, the building of new structures and institutions, all with new dimensions and linkages. Evolution, in this sense at least, is qualitative as well as quantitative.

The Principles of Heredity, Selection and Struggle

The principle of heredity suggests that the units of selection in economic evolution must have some durability and resilience, even if they are not as permanent as the DNA. Furthermore, there must be some mechanism through which characteristics are 'passed on' to other units.

Writers such as Veblen (1919) and Nelson and Winter (1982) argue that habits and routines have a stable and inert quality, and often sustain their important characteristics through time. While these are more malleable and do not mutate in the same way as their analogue in biology, habits and routines do have a sufficient degree of durability to regard them as having quasi-genetic qualities.

The principles of natural selection and struggle for existence posit some selection mechanism in which better-adapted types of unit can increase their numbers, either relatively or absolutely. Veblen and others propose that the units of selection in socioeconomic evolution are institutions, suggesting that some institutions become extinct because they are not well adapted to their general socioeconomic environment.

However, there is a possibility that a strict analogy with natural selection might break down here. Such a selection process requires some degree of stability in the institutions themselves and in the nature of the selection process. Also the latter must operate over a sufficient period of time. Otherwise selection cannot establish a consistent result.

We must also consider the possibility that some institutions are less likely than others to pass on their characteristics and thus 'procreate' through imitation. The natural selection of institutions is not simply a matter of relative death rates of different types of institution but also the probability that institutions of different types will be established in the first place.

As in the case of biological evolution, the selection of some entities and the extinction of others does not necessarily imply that the favoured entities are morally just, or that they are superior in an absolute sense. One reason for this is that selection always operates relative to a given environment. The dinosaurs prospered for millions of years. Relative to the environment of that period they were highly successful. They were probably wiped out because of a sudden and cataclysmic environmental change, caused by a large meteorite or whatever.

Contrary to many presentations,[14] it should also be pointed out that just as there are no true markets in the non-human biotic world, selection in economic systems does not necessarily involve markets. Leaving aside whether or not markets are, or are not, more efficient in providing mechanisms for the selection and development of different technologies and innovations, there are other possible mechanisms of selection. However imperfect, selection also occurs in centrally planned systems, and in economies where activities are determined and resources allocated on the basis of custom. Furthermore, markets themselves are institutions (Hodgson, 1988, ch. 8). As socioeconomic evolution involves the selection of institutions, markets themselves are objects of evolutionary selection as well as being the context of further selection – at a lower level – upon their establishment. (This point is discussed further in chapter 12 below.)

The Concepts of Fitness and Adaptation

In biology the concepts of adaptation, fitness and evolutionary success have been controversial and problematic, and only recently have adequate definitions emerged (Arnold and Fristrup, 1982). Evolutionary *success* is a retrospective measure of the relative increase or decrease in the descendants of a lineage, as a fraction of a specified population over a specified time interval. In contrast, *fitness* refers to the propensity of a unit to be successful in those terms (Mills and Beatty, 1979). *Adaptation* refers to any heritable character that increases the fitness of an entity within a given set of environments, or the evolutionary process resulting in the establishment of such a character in the population of entities.

Clearly, there is an important difference here between fitness and survival. The modern definition of fitness as a 'propensity' implies an expectation of success: not simply the actuality of survival at the current time.[15] Notably, with these terms defined in this way, the idea of 'the survival of the fittest' is not a tautology: fitness is not the same as survival. Also the idea is false: it is possible for units with greater fitness to be unsuccessful.[16]

If the general unit of selection in economic evolution is the institution, it is not appropriate to consider evolutionary success simply in terms of the number of such institutions. Addressing economic evolution in the context of a capitalist economy, a better measure of the success of an institution within that system would be the growth rate of its assets, valued through the market in money terms.

On this basis, Metcalfe's (1988) definition of the 'fitness' of an economic institution can be adopted. This is defined as the 'propensity to accumulate'. Usefully, this connects some notion of economic efficiency with that of economic growth. An adaptable institution is one which possesses characteristics which give it a greater propensity to invest or accumulate, such as higher profits and a tendency to plough back much of that profit into investment.

Concluding Remarks

The intention in this chapter has been to sketch out a preliminary taxonomy for the concept of economic evolution. In concentrating on the 'phylogenetic' type, attention has been paid to the applicability of appropriate concepts from biology.

The incomplete and exploratory character of this analysis should be emphasized. It is clear, for instance, that there are many types of Darwinian and Lamarckian evolution which have not been examined. Phenomena such as evolutionary 'drift' – a stochastic process rather than one of evolutionary selection – further complicate the picture.

Furthermore, some overlap of the principal categories is possible. This is especially true in the case of economic evolution when multiple levels of selection are considered.[17] In these terms it is possible for evolution of one type to occur at one level and another type at another. For instance, ontogenetic evolution of specific institutions may be occurring with given individuals as 'genes'. But simultaneously, there may be struggle between, and phylogenetic 'natural selection' of, those same institutions.

It would be no problem in principle to modify the above taxonomy so that the more complex cases could be included. Above all, this exercise is designed to help eliminate the vagueness and ambiguity that currently surrounds much of the literature in this area, and to encourage the employment of analogies with the appropriate biological theory with more care and precision. Such an outcome can only assist a more rigorous approach to evolutionary theory and modelling in economic science.

PART II
Evolution in Economics? From Mandeville to Marshall

The history of economic thought is irrepressible. It would survive even if it were banned ... Many economists denigrate the history of economics as mere antiquarianism but, in fact, they have deluded ideas about the history of their own subject. After all, whenever anyone has a new idea in economics, whenever anyone hankers to start a new movement or school of thought, what is the first thing he or she does? Why, it is to rummage the attic of past ideas to establish an appropriate pedigree for the new departure. All the great economists of yesterday did exactly that: Smith, Ricardo, Marx, Marshall and Keynes all drew on the history of economics to show that they had predecessors and forerunners; even Milton Friedman, when he launched the monetarist counterrevolution against Keynes, could not resist the temptation to quote David Hume over and again. The history of economic thought cannot be abolished and, were its study declared illegal, it would be studied in basements behind locked doors.

Mark Blaug, Introduction, *Historiography of Economics*

and organs necessary for its subsistence: some new order or economy must be tried and so on, without intermission; till at last some order which can support and maintain itself, is fallen upon' (Hume, 1886, vol. 2, p. 429). Reflecting on this, C. Bay (1958, p. 33) goes so far as to describe Hume's account as 'a doctrine of the survival of the fittest among human conventions – fittest not in terms of good teeth but in terms of maximum social utility'.

However, it would be wrong to jump to the conclusion that Hume has discovered natural selection, because his statement is incomplete and unclear, in several respects. In particular, it is not clear whether the process described by Hume is pragmatic bumbling, intentional behaviour involving trial and error, or something closer to Darwinian natural selection.

Thus there is no difficulty in interpreting Hume's passage in the sense of the development of a single organism, rather than a process of natural selection. After all, all organisms in their development appear to have mechanisms that allow them to vary their phenotype adaptively in response to environmental contingencies. Some have sophisticated trial-and-error learning mechanisms of the type to which Hume alludes.

Indeed, in Hume's words, the process 'at last' reaches a final state, as if it were the consummation of the growth of an organism at its maturity. This is ontogeny. It is not a phylogenetic process of natural selection in which the genetic material changes and in which – in an open system – a final state is never reached.

Influences on Darwin

In view of the above conclusion, it is necessary to assess the view of Hayek that

> the idea of cultural evolution is undoubtedly older than the biological concept of evolution. It is even probable that its application by Charles Darwin to biology was, through his grandfather Erasmus, derived from the cultural evolution concept of Bernard Mandeville and David Hume, if not more directly from the contemporary historical schools of law and language. (1982, vol. 3, p. 154)

There is no denying that the influence of Mandeville and the Scottish School on Darwin was of great significance.[2] Unfortunately, Hayek's account of the emergence of evolutionary ideas – an influential one for economists – is one-sided to the extreme. Hayek repeats his account of the supposed influence of Bernard Mandeville, David Hume and Adam Smith on Darwin many times, to the unfortunate extent that Thomas Robert Malthus, and several others of significance, lose all mention and credit.[3]

It is not entirely clear how such a grave error can be explained, yet it should be noted that the Malthusian account was that social development would lead to the disaster of scarcity and famine unless it was checked. Hence, while Malthus saw disorder and chaos coming out of this evolution, Hayek always wishes to side with Mandeville and Smith, and stress the emergence of unintended spontaneous order rather than Malthusian catastrophe. Malthus did not have Hayek's degree of faith in the efficacy of the market, and he rejected the stability or finality of any social equilibrium or order.[4]

Darwin's notebooks (Gruber, 1974; Vorzimmer, 1977) show that in 1838 and 1839 Darwin read a number of Smith's works, including his *Theory of Moral Sentiments*. But although Darwin read Dugald Stewart's summary and discussion of *The Wealth of Nations*, no record has come to light of him actually reading the latter work. Furthermore, Smith and the Scottish School cannot be given exclusive responsibility. It is also clear that in 1838, when Darwin was on the verge of his theoretical breakthrough, he also read Malthus's famous *Essay*, along with a highly influential review of a work by Auguste Comte (Schweber, 1977; Hodge and Kohn, 1985), beside the works of several other scientific authors.[5] While the influence on Darwin of Mandeville and the Scottish School should not be underestimated, it is wrong that the equally important influence of Malthus should be overshadowed or denied.[6] Schweber (1985, p. 36) puts it neatly: 'the *Origin* is the embodiment of Darwin's own intellectual upbringing: the synthesis of the great Cambridge and Edinburgh traditions,' the respective habitats of Malthus and of the Scottish School.

There is a number of scholarly works that consider the varied influences on Darwin's thought, as evidenced in his notebooks and elsewhere.[7] The overall picture is both complex and controversial. It is generally agreed, however, that the Scottish School bolstered Darwin's belief that complex phenomena could arise as an unintended consequence of the actions of many individuals. Thus Silvan Schweber suggests that the reading of Adam Smith and Dugald Stewart reinforced Darwin's 'focus on the *individual* as the central element and unit in his theory and led him to accept the Scottish view of trying to understand the whole in terms of the individual parts and their interactions' (Schweber, 1977, p. 233, and also pp. 277–8). Essentially, Smith and the Scottish School gave Darwin the idea of order and regularity being based on a chaotic multitude of individual units, and emerging without common intention or conscious design.

Notably, Smith writes often of the 'oeconomy of nature', particularly in *The Theory of Moral Sentiments* of 1759 (see, for instance, Smith, 1976a, p. 77). This is indeed a resonant phrase, and it was in use long before Smith, as Theodore Brown (1981) has shown. One of its major and influential uses was in the tract *The Oeconomy of Nature*, published in Latin by Carl Linnaeus in 1751. Both Smith and Darwin were disciples of Linnaeus, and it is probably from him that they both got the term. But when Smith marvels at the 'oeconomy of nature' he is extolling the virtues of an outcome which is unintended, but seems to be the creation of an intelligent agent, as if endowed with the will of God. There is no sense here of Darwinian natural selection, which has no purpose, equilibrium or end, and does not necessarily economize on natural resources.

To take another topic in Smith's work, in one essay he discusses the formation of languages (Smith, 1983, pp. 201–26). Yet there is no recognition here of a selection process, of different sounds competing for common usage and currency. He does not spell out the details and mechanisms of the emergence of words or language with anything like the precision and detail associated with the – even then brief – account of the development of such institutions in the work of Carl Menger. The search for a sophisticated idea of evolution or anything clearly resembling natural selection in Smith's writings is in vain. Hence, while Smith's influence on Darwin is important, it does not involve the crucial ingredient of natural selection.

Variety and the Division of Labour

But natural selection is merely one of the several vital components of Darwin's theory. Another is the principle of variation and divergence, upon which natural selection must operate. There is an obvious resonance here with the Mandeville–Smith idea of the division of labour.

However, the Smithian idea does not proceed from the assumption of the initial diversity of talent or skill. Both Smith and Hume presume that each human being at birth is broadly similar in ability. Smith assumes that variations in skill arise from learning-by-doing in the process of production itself. As Smith himself writes in the *Wealth of Nations*: 'the difference between the most dissimilar characters, between a philosopher and a common street porter for example, seems to arise not so much from nature as from habit, custom, and education' (1976b, pp. 28–9). Consequently, skill differences are not 'so much the cause as the effect of the division of labour'. For Smith it is the division of labour that alters character, not character that determines the allocation of tasks.

Although the division of labour is seen by Smith to yield huge increases in productivity, its energy is not derived from the organization of workers with dissimilar skills into different tasks. Instead, the impetus to this subdivision is 'the extent of the market' which opens up increasing opportunities for specialization. And it is the subdivision itself which contributes to the development of particular skills. Hence the riches of industrial organization are seen to flow ultimately from market relations, not preexisting diversity. This is in marked contrast to Darwin's theory of natural selection, where *ex ante* differences in character are the evolutionary fuel.

Schweber (1980, p. 270) proposes that one other 'likely source that introduced Darwin to the concepts of the division of labor was Charles Babbage's influential book *On the Economy of Machinery and Manufactures'* which was first published in 1832. Darwin certainly knew Babbage well, and they were part of the same scientific and social circles in London.[8]

There is a key difference between the concepts of the division of labour in the writings of Babbage and Smith. Babbage (1846, pp. 175–6) placed emphasis on the fact that each individual is endowed with different degrees of skill and strength. He argued that clear advantages arose from allocating workers to tasks for which they had just sufficient muscle or ability, without wasting skilled workers on inferior tasks, and without giving work to those with inadequate skill or strength.[9]

Thus, for Babbage, in contrast to Smith, the division of labour is *founded* on different types and degrees of skill; such variety is its origin not its result. Smith considers differences in skills to be a consequence rather than a cause of the division of labour, whereas for Babbage it is the other way round. As Ugo Pagano (1991, p. 319) puts it:

> Babbage and Gioia say that the division of labour increases productivity because it minimises the amount of learning which is required for doing. Smith says that the division of labour increases productivity because it maximises the amount of learning acquired by doing. Or, to put it another way, for Babbage and Gioia the learning necessary for the doing is minimised whereas for Smith the learning due to the doing is minimised.

Accordingly, for Babbage, the motive force of production and growth is not simply the market, it is also human diversity at the point of production itself. In so far as the notion of the division of labour bequeathed to Darwin the idea of variation and diversity as the *preexisting* basis of organization and growth, its genesis is more likely to have been from Babbage than from Mandeville or Smith.

The Nature of Evolution: From Mandeville to Smith

In particular, it is important to stress that while Mandeville, Ferguson, Hume and Smith all helped to foment the Darwinian revolution in theoretical biology, their metaphors were related more to mechanistic rather than evolutionary or living systems. They presumed equilibria or stationary states, rather than ongoing processes. They sought out 'laws of motion' of economic systems akin to the laws of Newtonian physics. They saw the economy as a kind of 'microcosm of the celestial arena' (Clark and Juma, 1988, p. 200) in which the invisible hand balanced the forces of supply and demand emanating from individual self-interest.

To summarize the ideas that emerged in this period. There is first the proposition that the order and integrity of the social or natural world is not necessarily due to design, either of human agents or of God. The great contribution of Mandeville and the Scottish School is their conception of a complex order arising as an unintended consequence of the interactions of even conflicting or self-interested individual units. Coordination and eventual prosperity can thus be achieved on the basis of specialization and a division of labour. This helps prepare the ground for the idea of natural selection but it does not itself provide it.

On the whole, these writers suggest that the spontaneous social order emerges as a harmonious steady state: as a social equilibrium within which tension and conflict can eventually be largely if not wholly contained. There is a clear note of finality in their conception which contrasts, as we shall see below, with the Malthusian struggle for survival and the unending processes of Darwinian evolution.

Let us pursue the analogy drawn from modern biology. The object of evolutionary analysis for Mandeville and the Scottish School is the socioeconomic system. Thus it is appropriate to assume that the socioeconomic system is analogous to a given organism, and the individuals within it are analogous to the genes.

Mandeville and the Scottish School typically write as if this 'genetic' material – that is the set of individuals themselves, not the biological genes – is given. They examine the development of the socioeconomic structure as it emerges unintentionally from the combined actions of all the individual 'genes'. Again this is analogous to the biological notion of ontogeny – the development of the organism from the coding in its given genetic material.

In pursuing their objectives, and in relation to their general environment, individuals develop habits, dispositions or behavioural rules. This is analogous to the emergence of the phenotype from the genotype. Note that ontogeny does pay due regard to the environment of the organism, as the same genotype may have different phenotypical results in different environments. However, the key point is that the genetic material remains constant. When Mandeville writes of the development of social order from the interaction of greedy individuals, and Smith claims to expose the origin of economic order and the mechanisms of growth, they are both taking, for the purposes of their analyses, the population of individuals with their various propensities as given.

The above arguments have their place, and may go some way to help to explain the origins of social order and the springs of economic growth. However, a broader conception of socioeconomic evolution is possible. For the Scottish School, habits and rules may change, but changes in individual preferences and propensities are not crucial for their argument. Accordingly, what these authors do not contemplate is the development of different individual goals and purposes, or even a different population of individuals, through some cumulative process of feedback.

Consequently an analogue to phylogeny is not considered: the evolutionary processes of selection or genetic drift among a whole population of individuals. If individuals and their propensities are analogous to the biological genes, then the arguments of Mandeville and the Scottish School are confined to ontogeny. If phylogeny were to be studied then changes in the pool of individual propensities would be addressed. This could occur either through the Darwinian 'natural selection' of different individuals, or through a quasi-Lamarckian process in which the characteristics of individuals may change, or even through some equivalent of near-random 'genetic drift'. In contrast, the emphasis is on the development of a single 'organism' from its 'genetic' material, rather than a cumulative process of development in which dispositions and purposes may be subject to major change.

There is a policy stance that emanates from the individualistic outlook of these classical economic thinkers. It relates to so many past attempts to apply evolutionary thinking to the social or economic spheres. Once mechanisms that help generate an unintended and undesigned natural and social order are discovered, once competition and the struggle for survival are seen to yield some evolutionary benefits, and once social diversity and division are likewise endorsed as functional, then it is one easy step to giving them a positive moral sign. It is another stride of no greater difficulty to embrace policy conclusions of a Panglossian kind. Although the above thinkers were often cautious in drawing such policy conclusions, many of their followers and interpreters have been less so.

Clearly, the *Fable of the Bees* is an attempt to reveal the hidden benefits of self-interest, acquisitiveness and the haggling of exchange, and Mandeville's sympathies were towards *laissez-faire*.[10] Smith, likewise, saw ample gains coming from the channelling of self-interest into commerce and productive activity. With some important qualifications, he is also noted for his advocacy of free trade and his opposition to the protectionist policy of the mercantilists.[11]

The Malthusian Inspiration

In a famous passage, Darwin (1904, p. 120) explains how his own theory was inspired by the picture of 'the struggle for existence' in the

Essay on the Principle of Population by Malthus. This autobiographical statement has proved to be controversial, and has been belittled by some, particularly those with an allergy to Malthus. However, a detailed examination of Darwin's notebooks confirms that the biologist found crucial stimulation in Malthus's *Essay*, even if some of the elements in Darwin's thinking had already been formed (Jones, 1989). The Malthusian population theory provided a general vision of 'crowding and struggle' and enabled Darwin to 'identify an agent for natural selection' (Gould, 1978, p. 22). Malthus thus hinted at some of the driving forces behind selection which were to be combined with the other elements of Darwin's theory (Herbert, 1971, 1977; Kohn 1980; Schweber, 1977, 1985).

It is interesting to note that Alfred Russell Wallace has described in his autobiography (1905) how Malthus also exerted a similar influence on him. Using the same inspiration, Wallace developed a theory of natural selection independently of Darwin and prior to the appearance of the *Origin of Species*, although there are significant differences between the two theories (Kottler, 1985; Nicholson, 1960). In fact, it was the knowledge that Wallace had independently formulated the principle of natural selection and was about to announce it to the world that prompted Darwin to rush the *Origin of Species* into print (Gould, 1980a, pp. 43–4). The spur of competition proved true for Darwin himself! The point to be emphasized here, however, is that both authors found crucial stimulation in the work of Malthus.

It is suggested here that Malthus's role in Darwin's theoretical revolution is no less than that of Mandeville and the Scottish School, and that an aversion to Malthusian propositions has often led subsequent theorists up a wrong trail. It is curious, for instance, that Joseph Schumpeter (1954, pp. 445–6) simply denies that Malthus had a significant influence on Darwin.[12] Although the precise extent of Malthus's influence is open to dispute, it is rash and relatively rare to ignore it entirely. Other writers have attempted to diminish Malthus's role in the development in evolutionary theory, and some of these are effectively countered by Robert Young (1969) and later by Lamar Jones (1989). Although the intensity and nature of Malthus's influence is disputed, many interpreters of Darwin's notebooks agree that the author of the *Principle of Population* provided at least a vivid picture of crowding and struggle, and thus a force behind the ongoing process of natural selection.[13]

Nevertheless, despite his importance, Malthus himself was not a 'first cause'. He too was influenced by visions of the natural world. On the first page of his *Essay* he observed the 'crowding and interfering with each other's means of subsistence' among plants and animals. Malthus's thoughts about nature thus influenced his theology and his political economy. It is thus appropriate to suggest that some proto-evolutionary ideas travelled from biology to the social sciences, to later return and influence biology in a refined form. The early development of the natural sciences and of economics thereby involved substantial interdisciplinary dialogue.

It is important that we should not be tempted to portray such dialogues simply as 'influences' from one individual to another. Smith, Malthus, Darwin, and all the others, were part of the social and intellectual culture of their age. Furthermore, it was an age of rapid social, political, industrial and economic transformation. As Adrian Desmond and James Moore (1991) have shown, Darwin was far from unaffected by this cultural and political context. For this reason we should be cautious of 'looking deeper and deeper and in greater and greater detail into the minutiae of Darwin's notes and thought processes,' as Young (1985b, p. 633) argues.[14]

Indeed, the danger in this empiricist procedure is not simply that the cultural context is ignored, but that individuals may be ignored too. The reason is that intellectual history is 'overdetermined' (Young, 1985b, p. 634). It may be possible to find sufficient factors to explain the origin and development of Darwin's theory in his notebooks without appealing to Malthus. But this does not rule out the Malthusian inspiration. The reason being that we are dealing with a complex web of plural causes, all located in a cultural context. It is from this perspective that the contribution of Malthus should be examined.

Malthusian Natural Theology

In one respect, Malthus's theory of population offered Darwin yet another mechanistic picture, this time including whole populations rather than mere elements. Malthus offered a model of exponential population growth. Accordingly, Darwin made lots of calculations of growing populations, observing the effects on crowding. Such work led later in the history of biology to the application of the logistic curve and to the Lotka-Volterra equations of interacting populations.

Yet there was much more to Malthus than mere mechanism. As Malthus (1798, p. 364) put it in the first edition of his *Essay*: 'Had population and food increased in the same ratio, it is probable that man might never have emerged from the savage state.' Hence the principle of population was more than the divergence of an arithmetic and a geometric series; it provided the spur to constructive activity and development.

There is a strong overtone of theology here. As David Kohn (1980) and John Pullen (1981) suggest, to understand Malthus's contribution both to political economy and to the Darwinian revolution it is necessary to examine the natural theology that permeates his famous *Essay*. Contrary to Scott Gordon (1989), it is not simply a matter of 'economics', narrowly defined. Malthus addresses a key problem faced by all believers: why should a wise and caring God plan or allow the existence of such wickedness and suffering in the world? Malthus's answer is that the intended role of evil is to energize us for the struggle for good.

Compare this viewpoint with that of Mandeville. For him, vice is both indispensable and socially useful, in that it leads to the greater good. But this is a harmonious outcome, and one furthermore in which vice is cynically accepted. This sentiment contrasts with that of the restless reverend in two crucial respects. First, for Malthus, there was no ultimate harmony. Second, he held the view that evil should not be tolerated in any degree or form. Malthus simply explained the existence of such sufferings and wrongs in terms of their function in arousing humanity to strive unceasingly for virtuous ends. For him, all this was part of God's plan.

Malthus's argument has been widely misinterpreted as an apologia for the immorality of an imperfect world. Instead, it is a warning that without evil to struggle against, the virtuous may become complacent or inert. Contrary to the simplistic misinterpretation that Malthus condoned the ills of the world, for Malthus evil remains something to be fought. But at the same time he recognizes its paradoxical function.[15]

A similar argument applies to the existence of diversity, suboptimality, error and struggle in the natural sphere. Malthus (1798, p. 379) saw 'the infinite variety of nature' which 'cannot exist without inferior parts, or apparent blemishes'. This ontological diversity was seen as having an essential and ultimately beneficial role in God's creation. The function of such diversity and struggle was to enable the development of improved forms. Without such a contest, no species would be impelled to improve itself. Without the test of struggle, and the failure or even death of some, there would be no successful development of the population as a whole. Dov Ospovat (1979) and others have identified the Malthusian inspiration in such terms. Darwin (1859, p. 490) himself wrote: 'From the war of nature, from famine and death, the most exalted object which we are capable of conceiving, namely the production of the higher animals, directly follows.'

As a by-product of his natural theology Malthus thus challenged both Platonic essentialism and logical dualism. For him, good is invigorated by evil and life is replenished through death. At the philosophical level, this challenge was neither sophisticated nor entirely self-conscious, and it did not expunge Cartesianism and mechanistic thinking from Darwinism or other subsequent biology. But its relevance and significance should not be overlooked.

To recapitulate, there are two vital ideas here. Although they both have a theological origin, they can be reconstructed in the kind of scientific terms that were acceptable to Darwin. First, Malthus hints at the essential, dynamic function of diversity and variety. As we have seen, a similar hint comes from the work of Babbage, but with Malthus it takes a different form. The existence of diversity, with its included blemishes and impurities, is seen as essential to the vitality of the whole. Second, for Malthus, natural development found a contribution not only from life but also from death: birth and extinction were functionally and inextricably bound together in the struggle for existence.

Accordingly, one of the main reasons why Malthus wrote his work on population was to counter radical and utopian ideas concerning the perfectibility of society. Indeed, the full title of the first edition is *An Essay on the Principle of Population, as it Affects the Future Improvement of Society, with Remarks on the Speculations of Mr. Godwin, M. Condorcet, and other Writers*. That is why two rationalistic utopians are mentioned so prominently, and singled out for criticism.[16]

It is untrue that Malthus believed that the world was incapable of improvement. Instead, he accepted some reforms but upheld that the creation of a perfect social order was impossible. Furthermore, as well as offering no solace for radicals such as William Godwin, there was no comfort in the *Essay* for Panglossian conservatives such as William Paley either. In opposition to Malthus, both the conservatives and the radical utopians believed in harmony and perfectibility; they simply differed in their idea of perfection.

Malthus's conception of endless struggle, diversity and impurity within a population ruled out any such optimal outcomes. By implication, according to any chosen value system, optimality was unattainable. As a counterblast to unblemished optimism and theological complacency, the *Essay* became one of the most disputed and widely discussed books of the first decades of the nineteenth century.

Malthus's doctrine of the imperfectibility of the world thus had two important by-products, of enduring significance for economic science. First, no kind of economic mechanism, including the market, could ever bring about an optimal order. Second, given that no optimum was possible, and that every result necessarily contained bad elements in opposition to the good, then no means or outcome should be denied moral evaluation. The utilitarian device of disregarding the morality of the means, by assuming that they served clear and specified ends, did not work for Malthus. Neither ends nor means could be entirely cleansed of evil, and both were thus subject to moral vigilance and scrutiny. His utilitarianism was thus qualified, and his ideas were in contrast to the more pronounced utilitarian drift of much subsequent economic theory; he provided a place for ethical assessment of both policies and outcomes.[17]

It is necessary to appraise Malthus's ethical theory without conflating it with his specific policy pronouncements. The latter, of course, bear all the reactionary hallmarks of a nineteenth-century cleric. Malthus opposed welfare handouts to the poor, on the supposed grounds that they added to the upward pressures on both prices and population and thereby exacerbated the very conditions that they were meant to relieve. However, he was not a thoroughgoing free-marketeer, as shown by his support for the protectionist Corn Laws. Even his theory of population was not fatalistic; he advocated the limitation of the birth rate. In his *Principles of Political Economy* he wrote that 'it is impossible for a government strictly to let things take their natural course' (Malthus, 1820, p. 16). Further, his theory of gluts involved a denial of the existence of effective equilibrating mechanisms and pointed to some limitations of the free market. Consequently, for Malthus, neither self interest nor the invisible hand had unqualified virtue.

Lyell, Paley and the Malthusian Breakthrough

Before Malthus, one major influence on Darwin was the work of the great geologist Sir Charles Lyell (Hull, 1985, pp. 790–1; Kohn, 1980; Young, 1969, pp. 129–31). Darwin took a copy of Lyell's *Principles of Geology* with him on his voyage on the *Beagle*. In general, Lyell's work was important for several reasons, including its attempted and influential refutation of Lamarckian theory. Lyell directed attention at the question of the precise mechanisms of evolutionary change, even suggesting possible upheaval and disequilibrium in nature. In this respect he went beyond Linnaeus and those others who saw nothing in nature but harmony and order (Worster, 1977, pp. 142–3). But while Lyell emphasized the struggle for existence, he did not go so far as Malthus, to suggest the crucial idea that the less fit may not survive and thereby a process of selection occurs.

In the protracted theological and scientific controversy around Malthus's ideas, some of them were distorted by his sympathizers as well as by his opponents (K. Smith, 1951). Participants in this debate such as William Paley tried to render Malthus's message more palatable. As Young (1969, p. 116) puts it, Paley saw the Malthusian process as 'a means for periodically re-establishing the harmony of nature'; far from being a mechanism for change, Paley saw the Malthusian doctrine as a 'defence of the *status quo* both in nature and society'. Paley's blunted and more comfortable version of Malthus's theory often prevailed.

As an undergraduate, Darwin read Paley at Cambridge.[18] In particular, Darwin was influenced by Paley's notion that 'the functions of an organism are to be explained in terms of its own good – not in terms of the desires or needs of other species, man not excepted' (Hardin, 1960, p. 57). Although this idea is a rebuttal of explanations of natural phenomena based on their supposed utility either for man or for God, its harmonious overtones are questionable. From our present vantage point we can see some similarities between Paley's argument and functionalist sociology, and with what Stephen Jay Gould and Richard Lewontin (1979) have described as the adaptationist doctrine in biology.

Furthermore, Paley's harmonious and functionalist view prevented Darwin for some years from seeing the full significance of conflict in nature. As Young (1969, p. 118) argues: 'Paley and Malthus influenced Darwin in very different ways. Paley stresses perfect adaptation; Malthus stresses conflict. These were, at one level, antithetical. Darwin synthesizes them. Struggle both *explains and produces* adaptation.'

Against both Lyell and Paley, who viewed species adaptation as the harmonious process of 'fitting round pegs into a neatly preordained round hole' (Kohn, 1980, pp. 145–6), Malthus led Darwin to view nature in a very different way. Darwin jotted down his thoughts in his 1838 'D' notebook as he was reading Malthus's words: 'there is a force like a hundred thousand wedges trying [to] force every kind of adapted structure into the gaps in the oeconomy of nature, or rather forming gaps by thrusting out weaker ones.'[19]

This tension between, on the one hand, a harmonious and perfectionist view of evolution and, on the other, a view based on imperfections and contradictions, in which neither equilibrium nor an optimum may necessarily be attained, survives to this day. For instance, as we have seen, the positive functions of diversity and variety, in the form of specialization and a division of labour, were suggested by Mandeville and the Scottish School, and later by Babbage. Darwin follows Malthus to make one further leap. But it is a leap across the abyss, separating the peaceful meadows of harmony and perfectibility from the rocky land of impurity, struggle and change. While the classical division of labour involves parts fitting together in a seamless whole, for Malthus and Darwin even imperfection and disharmony play a positive and energizing part in the system, driving it onwards in endless transformation.[20]

Malthus's emphasis on the developmental role of variety and diversity is seen by the biologist Ernst Mayr (1964) as the instigation, through Darwin, of modern 'population thinking' in biology, in which variety and diversity are all-important. Recognition of variety and diversity is not only acknowledgement of the complexity of the real world, it is a vital component of the modern theory of evolution. As noted in the preceding chapter, such 'population thinking' contrasts with 'typological essentialism' in which entities are regarded as identifiable in terms of a few distinct characteristics which represent their essential qualities; in population thinking, species are described in terms of a distribution of characteristics. Whereas in typological thinking variation is a classificatory nuisance, in population thinking such variety is seen to fuel the evolutionary process. As Elliott Sober (1985, p. 885) argues: 'The concept of natural selection requires a novel kind of population thinking.'

The key idea of population diversity or variety demarcates Darwin's theory from the essentialist mechanics of Newton. It is abundantly clear, however, that Darwin, like Smith, came from a Newtonian starting point. For instance, natural selection was seen as analogous to a 'force'. Yet while this force operated on the 'mass' of variety in the natural world, variety is quite different from mass in the Newtonian scheme. Hence, as Schweber (1985, pp. 48–9) points out:

> Darwin abandoned the Newtonian model of dynamical explanations in important respects and came to a novel conceptualization of dynamics for biological systems. . . . One could not describe the dynamics of a community of organisms simply from the pairwise interaction of the organisms and from interaction of the organisms with the environment. Living systems were infinitely more complicated than Newton's planetary system. Biological 'elements' had characteristics that were changing in time: they had a history. All the interactions of organisms whether with one another or with the environment were non-additive, non-instantaneous and exhibited memory. It was the ahistorical nature of the objects with which physics dealt that gave the Newtonian scheme the possibility of a simple, mathematical description. It was precisely the *historical* character of living objects which gave biological phenomena their unique and complex features.

We may suggest that if Mayr is right in his assertion that Malthus suggested the idea of 'population thinking' to Darwin, along with the role of variety in natural selection, then Malthus can be credited with providing Darwin with a means of surpassing Newtonian thinking, even if the ideas of both Malthus and Darwin remained mechanistic in other respects.

There are other crucial features in Malthus's work. In particular, Malthus's *Essay* shifted Darwin's attention from competition among different species to rivalry between more similar individuals (Ghiselin, 1969, p. 59). 'Through the reading of Malthus, Darwin suddenly came to realize that the most intense "struggle for existence", so often referred to in the literature of the preceding 200 years, was amongst individuals of a single species' (Mayr, 1985b, p. 767). With his notion of super-fecundity, of a perpetual existence of a reproductive surplus, Malthus suggested to Darwin that the struggle for existence was not so much among different species but among individuals of the same species.

Schweber (1985, pp. 50–1) even suggests that from the familiar Malthusian principle of increasing numbers, Darwin derives a 'maximalization principle', meaning 'the strongest tendency to increase' for 'every single organism'. Hence Darwin takes an idea from Malthus and turns it into a principle of individual maximization, before it had become clearly stipulated and widely adopted in economics.

In at least one vital respect, Malthus turned the view of Mandeville and the Scottish School upside down. While Mandeville had argued that from individual 'defects' such as greed and vice, a healthy economic system could arise, Malthus saw that healthy individuals can create catastrophic results. Hence, as Catherine Gallagher (1987, p. 83) argues, with Malthus, 'the social and economic significance of the vigorous body was radically reconceptualized.' Malthus thus offered the spectacle of healthy procreation leading to overcrowding and death, rather than the more comforting picture of the public benefits of vice that had been drawn by Mandeville, and the vision of harmony and economic growth arising from individual acquisitiveness described by Smith. Darwin's revolution involved the Malthusian synthesis of both apparently contradictory viewpoints into a dynamic whole, where death and vitality played host to each other.

However, unlike Mandeville and the Scottish School, for Malthus the object of evolutionary analysis is merely an aggregated population of individuals, rather than a socioeconomic system. Furthermore, he considers the evolutionary process of selection within, and development of, such a population. Thus, close to the Darwinian idea of 'natural selection' the population changes through differential birth and death, rather than, for instance, some Lamarckian process in which the characteristics of individuals may alter.

Malthus was primarily concerned with overall numbers, and not the selection of different individuals, or changes in the frequency of characteristics in a population. Nevertheless, through the idea of change resulting from contest and struggle, he hints at the idea of natural selection and phylogenetic evolution, rather than the ontogeny of the emergence of a given system.[21]

The Contributions of Malthus and Classical Political Economy

In sum, the view taken here is that the inspiration of Malthus for the Darwinian revolution should certainly not be rated below that of Mandeville and Smith, and some, like Sandra Herbert (1971, 1977), have argued that he was the most important single influence. However, it has been suggested above that Darwin's intuitive insight may have been derived as much from Malthus's natural theology as his political economy. To use the words of Howard Gruber (1985, p. 31): 'Darwin abstracted one key idea out of context and turned it upside down – from the scourge of humanity to the motor of evolution.'

While to the modern reader Malthus's social and economic policies are reactionary and conservative, they should be put into the context of his time. Most economists of this period tolerated no more than limited social engineering and economic intervention, excepting some relatively minor intercessions deemed to enhance competition, to clear the way for the market, or to promote growth. Such proclivities were given a later shift when Darwin's theory, which both Smith and Malthus had helped to inspire, was wrongly adopted by some subsequent social theorists as the refutation of all kinds of planned economic intervention and as the vindication of market competition.

However, the apparent parallels between competition in the capitalist and the natural worlds have misled some writers into suggesting that Darwin's *Origin of Species* was simply the political economy of nineteenth-century industrial capitalism transferred to the natural domain. It was not as simple as that. There was a transfer of ideas from political economy to biology, but it was as much to do with Malthusian natural theology as with, say, classical theories of value and price. And the transfer itself was inspirational and creative.

Indeed, Gordon has over-reacted against the simplistic transfer thesis by suggesting that 'no substantial support can be provided for the thesis that the Darwinian theory of evolution drew significantly upon ideas in contemporary Political Economy' (1989, pp. 456–7). To reach his novel conclusion, he presents us with a sanitized version of classical political economy, free of metaphor, of ideology or of links with other sciences.

In attempting to establish his conclusion, Gordon points out that Darwin did not read a great deal of political economy. He argues, further, that the 'perfect competition' of classical economics contrasts with competition in the natural world. In the former 'there is no rivalry at all' (ibid., p. 455) since there is a multitude of firms all able to produce and sell at the current market price, whereas competition in nature involves rivalry and the 'struggle for existence'.

The latter point is easily dispensed with. Malthus's theory of population was different from the conception of competition in any kind of political economy – classical or otherwise – which stresses equilibrium outcomes.[22] In contrast, Malthusian population theory did involve rivalry and a struggle for existence. Gordon's account is defective for several other reasons. First, he neglects the general influence of Adam Smith on the contemporary intellectual climate, and particularly the individualistic mode of explanation championed by Smith. Second, he neglects the theological dimension of Malthus's ideas, which helped Darwin to look death in the face and to give it a role in his theory of natural selection. Third, Gordon ignores the personal relationship between Babbage and Darwin, and the influence of Babbage's ideas in political economy on the biologist. Fourth, at the time when Darwin was developing his theory, political economy enjoyed a high scientific status and was a widely popular subject for discussion (Berg, 1980, pp. 32ff). Even if Darwin did not read all the major texts in political economy, as an intellectual moving in the scientific circles of Britain's capital city it is inconceivable that he was not relatively knowledgeable about, and affected by, such ideas at the time.

We are thus able to conclude that there was a transfer of ideas from political economy to Darwin's biology, but it was more to do with the spark of inspiration than the careful transfer of theorem and proof.

Furthermore, although Darwin was clearly influenced by the political climate of his time (Desmond, 1990; Desmond and Moore, 1991), it would be a mistake to caricature Darwin's theory simply as the import of bourgeois ideology into the natural world. This thesis is easily rejected:

> If it were true that ... the theory was the inevitable consequence of the Zeitgeist of early nineteenth-century Britain, of the industrial revolution, of Adam Smith and the various ideologies of the period, one would think that the theory of natural selection would have been embraced at once by almost everybody. Exactly the opposite is true: the theory was almost universally rejected. (Mayr, 1985b, p. 769)

Accordingly, Antonello La Vergata (1985, p. 913) writes that 'nowhere is the tendency to resort to easy formulas more evident than in the frequency with which Darwin's view is linked to the British competitive ideology.'

In sum, Darwin was neither immune from the cultural and political influences of his time, nor did his theory amount to a straightforward transfer of bourgeois ideology to science. Instead, to use Peircean terms, it is better described as a classic case of 'abduction', where sparks of scientific creativity, generated in part from Darwin's knowledge of classical political economy and Malthusian natural theology, were transferred to biology. Michael Ghiselin (1969, p. 16) and Antonello La Vergata (1985, p. 939), for instance, express a widespread opinion when they write of Darwin's ability to transfer methodologies and theoretical points of view across disciplinary boundaries. It was a clear case of abduction or intellectual recombination. Such transferable metaphors helped Darwin free himself from the traditional perspectives of his time (Manier, 1978; Young, 1985a). The displacement of metaphor from one scientific discourse to another thus helped create a truly novel result.

We should not expect to find the theory of natural selection in the writings of Smith or Malthus, but this does not rule out the role of their ideas in providing crucial insights for the father of modern biology. And recognition of the abductive sparks moving from political economy to biology does not, of course, deny the importance of the medium of the cultural and political environment at the time. Indeed, the oxygen is as vital as the spark itself.

5

Revolutionary Evolution:
Karl Marx and
Frederick Engels

In the preceding chapter we have discussed the extent to which Darwin was influenced by social theorists from Mandeville to Malthus. Several of the succeeding chapters in this book evaluate the extent to which economists have used Darwinian or other evolutionary ideas from biology.

Karl Marx (1818–1883) and Charles Darwin (1809–1882) were close contemporaries. Their paths must have crossed frequently in London, but apparently they never met (Colp, 1974). It is well known that Marx was impressed by Darwin's *Origin of Species*, although the idea that he went so far as to ask permission from Darwin to dedicate a volume of *Capital* to him turns out to be a myth.[1] While praising Darwin's theory as 'a natural-scientific basis for the class struggle in history', Marx also hinted, as early as 1862, at the possibility of apologetic and pro-capitalist interpretations: 'It is remarkable how Darwin recognises among beasts and plants his English society with its division of labour, competition, opening-up of new markets, "inventions" and the Malthusian "struggle for existence"' (1977, pp. 525–6). Thus Marx correctly foresaw the ideological uses to which Darwinism would later be put.[2]

Arguably, Marx and Engels were primarily attracted by Darwin's covert materialism, his rebuttal of creationism and his implicit dethronement of God (Gould, 1978, pp. 23–8). There could have also been tactical reasons: a desire to associate their own theories with a revolutionary breakthrough in natural science (Urena, 1977). What is clear from a close examination of their writings is that Marx and Engels did not actually take Darwin's theory of natural selection on board. If their theory of socioeconomic change is evolutionary, it is not so in a Darwinian sense.

Marx and Engels after Malthus

While Marx and Engels admired Darwin they abhorred Malthus, seeing his population theory as 'a libel against the human race'. For them, Malthus was a plagiarist, a bought advocate and a shameless sycophant of the ruling classes (Marx and Engels, 1953, pp. 22–3). Wishing to associate their theory with the Darwinian scientific revolution, they attempted to prize Darwin and Malthus apart, professing the view that Darwinism would be more scientific without its Malthusian content.[3]

Marx mentions Darwin in a few places in *Capital*, but normally he left his friend Frederick Engels (1820–1895) to deal with controversies in the natural sciences. The most extensive treatment of Darwin and Darwinism by Marx or Engels is in the latter's *Dialectics of Nature*. Therein Engels mentions Darwinism in passing about a dozen times, to devote no more than three additional pages to a critical discussion of the notion of the 'struggle for existence' or 'struggle for life' (Engels, 1964, pp. 311–14). This notion is associated with Malthus and rejected as a weak ideological buttress for capitalist competition.

However, in this brief but energetic endeavour the Darwinian baby is thrown out together with the Malthusian bathwater. Engels (p. 312) makes the amazing statement that Ernst Haeckel's idea of '"adaptation and heredity" can bring about the whole process of evolution, without need for selection and Malthusianism.' What Engels ignores here, however, is that Haeckel was a prominent follower of Darwin who had adopted natural selection as part of the Darwinian package. Crucially, there has to be some kind of driving force behind the natural selection process to make it work. Darwin (1904, p. 120) claimed that Malthus had provided him with this idea. In any case, whatever the rebuttal of any kind of selection is meant to do for Malthus it is enough to dispense with Darwin too.

Furthermore, although Engels's *Dialectics of Nature* is not without its merits, the reader will search there in vain for a clear and adequate account of Darwin's theory of natural selection. Engels is, for instance, perceptive enough to recognize in the Darwinian theory an 'inner connection between necessity and chance' (1964, p. 311). But beyond this, and without a sufficient explanation of the theory in their writings, we can only surmise whether or not Marx or Engels had the barest understanding of the essentials of Darwinian biology.

It is also ironic to note that Engels attempted to dispense with Malthus – and implicitly Darwin too – by using the writings of Haeckel.[4] This was hardly an appropriate authority for an egalitarian such as Engels. Haeckel (1834–1919) was not only a professor of biology at Jena but also a great popularizer of Darwin and the founder of a nationalist and highly racist strain of Social Darwinism (Gould, 1978, pp. 210–17). He depicted the black African races at an intermediate stage of evolution between white humans and the apes. One wonders why it was necessary or admissible to use such a racist instrument to wage such an all-out struggle against the 'reactionary' Malthus.[5]

On close examination there is much in the Marxian theoretical system that is antagonistic to Darwinian evolutionary ideas. The idea of change resulting from a process of natural selection among a population of individual entities exhibiting great diversity and variety is markedly different from the conception of history as the clash of collectives engaged in class struggle. In fact, Engels (1964, p. 314) saw the view of history based on the struggle of social classes as much richer in content than the 'weakly distinguished phases of the struggle for existence'.

The Conception of Evolution in Marx's Economics

In Marx's economics it is assumed that value calculations pertain to the most profitable technique that has become established at a given time. Value quantities thereby relate to the amount of 'socially necessary' labour time involved with this technique. By this theoretical device the essential function of variety in the economic process is expunged. Without ever-present variety there is no raw material for natural selection. It is significant that Marx, along with both the classical and the neoclassical economic theorists, focuses on the emergence and eventual dominance of a single technology.

Some commentators have highlighted the famous footnote in *Capital* where Marx relates technological development to Darwin's account of 'the formation of the organs in plants and animals' (Marx, 1976, p. 493n). The temptation is to assume that Marx is drawing a direct analogy between technological and biological evolution. The footnote should be read carefully: Marx does no such thing. His reference to Darwin is simply to make the point that the history and development of technology should not be regarded solely as the inspirations of single individuals, and accordingly the real history should be studied, just as Darwin had produced 'the history of natural technology'. Neither the concept nor the words 'natural selection' can be discovered in this footnote.

One of the few references to 'natural selection' in Marxian writings is in another footnote in *Capital* (Marx, 1976, p. 461n). Here, however, the phrase appears within a direct quotation from the *Origin of Species*, where Darwin makes the point that a set of parts which has to perform 'diversified work' may retain its variety and diversity under natural selection. Darwin argues that once functions become more specialized, then selection will tend to preserve one type only: the type that is most efficient in relation to that specific work. Although natural selection is mentioned, this quotation does not reveal the full mechanism.

Indeed, the quoted words are not incompatible with Marx's general suggestion that specialization will prevail, leading to the diminution of variety and the emergence of the 'socially necessary' technique. Marx seems to be employing Darwin's words to make this point. However, this is a misleading interpretation because Darwin is addressing a special case, whereas Marx is making a general point about technological evolution under capitalism. If the particular point were made general it would remove variety and the Darwinian motive forces of technological evolution from the picture.

Although Marx's extensive discussion of machinery and technological change remains unparalleled among economists, the mechanisms leading to the expansion and development of the productive forces are not sufficiently clear. There is an incomplete picture of the way individual inspiration and purpose interact with social and cultural conditioning. Thus a prominent and celebrated feature of Marx's analysis is the idea of the 'forces of production' straining against and eventually breaking the 'relations of production' in some revolutionary convulsion. Whatever the veracity of such a vision, it leaves the nature of those very 'productive forces' and the energies impelling them to be explained. Although he made a major contribution to the theory of technological change, the account of how productive forces themselves evolve is left vague. Marx, however, was neither the first nor the last social theorist to have vague evolutionary intuitions without a clear conception of the evolutionary processes of change.

Revolutionary Evolution

The Marxian conception of history has much more in common with evolution's Latin etymology as *evolvere*, or unrolling, than with Darwinian natural selection. However, a clear limitation of the analogy with the unrolling of a parchment is that it does not encompass a key idea that Marx inherited from Hegel, of internal contradiction and conflict leading to disruptive change. For Marx and Engels, of course, the class struggle is the motor of history, with change occurring in leaps of a revolutionary and possibly violent nature.

Also, like Hegel before, Marx and Engels regard history as a series of developmental stages. For them, historical progress is represented by a sequence of social formations, from 'primitive communism', through feudalism and capitalism to communism in the 'higher' form. It remains controversial whether or not this interpretation of history is deterministic, and whether or not there are different routes to the classless utopia; the developmental process could be unilinear or multilinear. What is clear is that for Marx and Engels it was possible to rank these stages, and that the final stage was the 'inevitable' outcome of socioeconomic forces being played out through history. Society was deemed to be perfectible, in the communist form.

Note first, with the supposed development from 'primitive' to 'full' communism there is precisely a suggestion of a revolving movement, returning to the original position but at a 'higher' level. Clearly the Marxian view of history is more revolutionary, in that sense, than evolutionary.

Second, and more importantly, communism refers to a unified social order in a state of harmony. Not only is the basis and actuality of social struggle presumed to have disappeared, but also there is no variety in the forms of ownership and of productive institutions. It is assumed that under communism there is neither conflict between classes nor a diversity of material interests and socioeconomic forms. Marx and Engels suggest that such a system could be technologically dynamic, but in so far as human motivation depends on some degree of social variety and disruption, in such a system there is no fuel for further change.

Karl Marx and Herbert Spencer are regarded as being at the opposite ends of the political spectrum, the former believing in common ownership, the latter in markets and laissez-faire. However, they both believed in the perfectibility of society, and both on the basis of a single and ubiquitous type of economic arrangement. In this respect at least, Marx's evolutionism has more in common with Spencer's ideas than with the Darwinian emphasis on variety.

Arguably, a uniform, integrated and supposedly harmonious society would be very vulnerable to external shocks, such as unforeseen kinds of natural disaster, or to major internal changes, such as those resulting from major developments in technology. Without internal variety, such a system could be highly unadaptable, and could suffer profound and painful crises as a result of the consequent disruptions.

It has been noted in the preceding chapter that Malthus had opposed the idea of the perfectibility of society. He saw diversity and struggle as part of the development of improved forms. And one of the main reasons why Malthus wrote his work on population was to counter radical and utopian ideas concerning the perfectibility of society. Although Marx and Engels were not rationalistic utopians, they did believe in the possibility of a harmonious society, and in a communist mould.

It is not necessary to support any 'Malthusian' praise of famine and death. The key point is the significance of diversity and pluralism in modern society. In this vein a Malthusian critique of perfectibility applies to the modern proponents of a 'pure' economic system based entirely on markets and private property, just as it does to advocates of 100 per cent central planning.[6]

Marx and Darwin Contrasted

In a pioneering comparison of institutional and Marxian conceptions of economic evolution, Abram Harris (1934, p. 56) makes a perceptive assessment of the differences between Marxian and Darwinian theory:

> It is not strange that Marx and Engels, preoccupied with the arduous labours of propagating heterodox ideas in a hostile intellectual environment, overlooked the stark differences between their own preconceptions and those of Darwin. Except for superficial resemblances in terminology, there is hardly any connection between class conflict and Darwin's principles of 'struggle for existence' and 'natural selection.' For when the dialectics of historical movement is made to proceed in terms of Darwin's biological principles it is impossible to predict the character and form of social change. On the basis of Darwinism change would occur as chance variations, unpredictable phenomena, highly uncertain in outcome, and tending to no predetermined goal.

As Joseph Schumpeter (1954, p. 445) remarks: 'Marx may have experienced satisfaction at the emergence of Darwinist evolutionism. But his own had nothing whatever to do with it, and neither lends any support to the other.' An identical conclusion is reached by Enrique Urena (1977) in his study of the many references by Marx and Engels to Darwin. In a similar vein, Anthony Giddens (1984, p. 243) notes that 'in Marx there is an inverted Hegelian dialectic, tortured into a particular developmental shape, that has no direct analogue in more orthodox evolutionary theories.' It is not to belittle Marx's great contribution to economics to discover that he did not take on board much of Darwin's theoretical revolution in biology.

Marx and Engels did not assimilate Darwinian theory in their social science because there it was incompatible with the mechanistic zeitgeist within which they were still entrapped. To escape, much of their theoretical system would have had to change. As Norman Clark and Calestous Juma (1987, p. 48) argue:

> The main problem with Marx is that he recognized the significance of evolutionary factors but returned to a classical Newtonian world-view, especially in his prognosis for future social systems. In Marx's world, the socioeconomic system tends to move from moments of extreme fluctuations, of class struggles, towards social equilibria governed by socialist principles – classless societies in which the sources of fluctuations and struggle are eliminated. Like Newton's cosmology, society settles into an equilibrium, as the underlying social laws that Marx sought to lay bare, prevail over individual action.

Although Darwin's *Origin of Species* shattered many ancient ideas concerning the creation of species in general and humanity in particular, the full scientific force of his theory was not widely appreciated until much later. Indeed, the ontological and methodological implications of Darwinian biology have yet to be spun out in full. As described in later chapters, there are also other economists, alongside Marx and Engels, whose idea of evolution was markedly inadequate or vague.[7]

6
Herbert Spencer:
The Lost Satellite

Darwin's reputation has had many ups and downs since the publication of the *Origin of Species*. Not only did his scientific esteem reach a low ebb around 1900,[1] but also, for much of the nineteenth century, Charles Darwin was rivalled in standing by Herbert Spencer. Trained in physics and mathematics, and being a brilliant polymath and synthesizer, Spencer made a significant contribution to biology and extended evolutionary ideas to ethics and social science. In his own day, he became 'a towering figure in the world of learning' (Carneiro, 1968, p. 124). He was particularly popular in the United States of America, where from 1860 to 1903 over 386,000 of his books were sold (Hofstadter, 1959, p. 34). Although Spencer is largely rebutted and ignored today as a social theorist, and is much overshadowed by Darwin in biology, the examination of Spencer's ideas is important because of their overt and covert influence on past social scientists, including many economists.

Indeed, the writings of economists as prominent as Thorstein Veblen and Alfred Marshall cannot be properly understood without an appreciation of Spencer's influence. Even where the influence of Spencer is not explicit, as in the case of Friedrich Hayek for example, several similarities with the ideas of the influential Victorian have been discovered (Gray, 1984, pp. 103–10).

Even so, it still may be questioned why Spencer is considered here at some length. Even discounting the fact that he was for five years a subeditor of the *Economist*, he himself is not usually described by that title. He wrote a three-volume work on *The Principles of Sociology*, but no comparable work on economics. It is indeed unfortunate that modern mainstream economists hold sociology in such low esteem, in small part because it requires us to make a case for the devotion of one chapter to Spencer's widely persuasive ideas on socioeconomic evolution.[2]

There are at least four important reasons for considering Spencer in this context. First, the extent of his past influence on the subject of economics, either direct or indirect, makes his inclusion necessary.

Second, for many decades Spencer's influence as a biologist was almost as great as that of Darwin, raising the question as to whether political economy was affected by Spencer, just as Spencer may have been influenced by political economy. Third, unlike Darwin's, Spencer's writings cover both the biological and the social sciences. Indeed, he proposed a unified system of science, spanning both natural and social phenomena, in which the economy was certainly a part. Fourth, although he ignored several key topics in economic theory, he clearly formulated economic policies, albeit of a simplistic and laissez-faire kind.

Notably, Spencer developed a conception of evolution and published a version of it in 1852, a few years before the appearance of Darwin's *Origin of Species*. However, as discussed below, Spencer's theory is inferior to the idea of natural selection developed by Charles Darwin and Alfred Russell Wallace, and lacks an adequate explanation of the evolutionary process and its transmission mechanisms.

Nevertheless, Spencer's output of works established him as one of the most influential scientists and philosophers of the Victorian era. His thinking was shaped by the laissez–faire principles of the time. Early in adult life he was influenced by the politics of the Godwinian anarchist, Thomas Hodgskin (1787–1869). Partly from Samuel Taylor Coleridge (1772–1834) he derived the general idea of a universal pattern of evolution. The principle of the conservation of energy, formulated by James Joule (1818–1889) and others in the 1840s, also became a core assumption in his theoretical system. Some of his other fundamental ideas were taken from the works of the biologist Jean Baptiste de Lamarck (1744–1829) and the embryologist Karl Ernst von Baer (1792–1857). Although many of his basic concepts were derived from others, Spencer had the ability and resolution to bind dispersed ideas together into a systemic whole, spanning physics, biology, psychology, sociology and ethics. In part it was this all-embracing and synthetic quality of his work that accounted for its popularity.

Crucially, it was Spencer, not Darwin, who popularized the term 'evolution'. It is possible, as Stephen Toulmin (1972, pp. 330–1) has argued, that Darwin resisted the term because he objected to its association with teleological notions of progress and development. Likewise, Ernst Mayr (1992) has cautioned against the association of Darwin with the kind of Victorian progressivism that Spencer championed in the last half of the nineteenth century.[3] Whatever the substance of these arguments, it is a fact that Darwin did not introduce the word until the sixth edition of the *Origin of Species*, and then only sparingly. On the whole, Darwin preferred phrases like 'descent with modification' to 'evolution'.

Furthermore, it was Spencer, not Darwin, who invented the slogan 'survival of the fittest'. It was not until 1866, after the first edition of the *Origin of Species* had appeared, that Darwin was persuaded by his friend Wallace to use Spencer's 'survival of the fittest' phrase, rather than 'natural selection', in key passages in that work (Waters, 1986, pp. 207–8). The word 'selection', Wallace argued, implied the existence of an agent doing the selecting, and some could take this agent to be God. Wallace was clearly more concerned at the time to deny the deity a role in the evolution of non-human[4] species than to rebut the Panglossian ideas that were associated with Spencer's famous phrase. Some of the unfortunate consequences of Spencer's promotion of the term are discussed later in this chapter.

Influences on Spencer

While Spencer drew some inspiration from Malthus, the latter's influence on Spencer has been overstressed by writers such as John Burrow (1966), Scott Gordon (1991, p. 425) and Marvin Harris (1968). Robert Young (1969) points out that Spencer gave Malthus only a slight mention in the two 1852 essays in which a sketchy notion of evolution appears.[5] There is a vague allusion therein to natural selection, but its application is confined to human society and the precise mechanism of selection is not entirely clear. Spencer's associated discussion of fertility and population growth in these essays reflects a general concern with these issues at that time, much stimulated by Malthus's own provocative work, but not necessarily the ideas of Malthus himself. It is thus likely that Malthus did not provide the same kind of influence as he did in the case of Wallace and Darwin.

A much more important influence on Spencer was the theory of epigenesis, or development, formulated by von Baer.[6] The embryological development of a single organism was conceived by von Baer as a process of successive differentiations leading to increasing structural complexity: 'There is gradually taking place a transition from something homogeneous and general to something heterogeneous and special' (quoted in Mayr, 1982, p. 473).

Accordingly, Spencer (1892, p. 10) defined evolution as 'a change from an indefinite, incoherent homogeneity, to a definite, coherent heterogeneity through continuous differentiations'. Evolution, for Spencer, involves progress; he argued that complexity is generally associated with fitter and more adaptable forms.

Although, since Spencer, many other writers have repeated the latter idea, it should be noted that the definition of complexity is not at all straightforward. In the first place, complexity must be distinguished from variety (Saviotti, 1991, p. 177). Complexity requires variety, but means more, involving some kind of structured interaction between the varied elements (Nicolis, 1987, p. 163; Stent, 1985, pp. 215–16).[7]

Note also that Spencer's definition of evolution involves a universal directional movement from one state (homogeneity) to another (heterogeneity). The definition is thus quite close to the etymology of the word 'evolution' as a predetermined and progressive unrolling or unfolding; it is not the same as a definition in terms of some kind of Darwinian process of natural selection.

Furthermore, there are other major substantive differences between Spencer's and Darwin's ideas. For instance, while Spencer, like Darwin, saw diversity and variety as part of evolution, these concepts played different roles in their theories. For Darwin, diversity was the essential fuel for the process of natural selection.[8] Although Spencer also saw selection at work, for him, as for von Baer, diversity was more significant as the teleological result of the evolutionary process, rather than its essential starting point. Furthermore, Spencer saw evolution as leading to equilibrium and greater harmony, a process he described as 'equilibration'. He wrote: 'the changes which evolution presents cannot end until equilibrium is reached, and that equilibrium must at last be reached' (Spencer, 1890, p. 524). For him, diversity did not mean antagonism; antagonism was seen to lead to disintegration and decay. In contrast, diversity in Darwin's theory can sometimes be beneficial, even if it involves fierce antagonism and competition.

Following von Baer, Spencer formulated two significant principles which recurred in his writings. The first, the 'change from the homogeneous to the heterogeneous, is displayed equally in the progress of civilization as a whole, and in the progress of every tribe or nation; and is still going on with increasing rapidity' (Spencer, 1890, pp. 342–3). The second concerned a simultaneous tendency towards integration: 'In every more or less separate part of every aggregate, integration has been, or is, in progress' (ibid., p. 307). The teleological character of both these formulations is self-evident.

In suggesting that evolution meant a tendency towards increasing specialization and differentiation, combined with sufficient functional integration to ensure the coherence of the system, Spencer proposed two general principles that were applied to both natural and socioeconomic evolution. These ideas are of some enduring significance, and it is notable that they have frequently recurred in the writings of others, well into the twentieth century, and often without reference to, or apparent knowledge of, their precedent. The twentieth century has been marked by the periodic and 'unknowing rediscovery of Spencer' as Jonathan Turner (1985, pp. 7–8) puts it.

Thus, for example, Spencer can be regarded as one of the early architects of general systems theory (Turner, 1985). Also there are close parallels between Spencer's ideas and the work of Ilya Prigogine and his associates, with their emphasis on 'increasing complexity' and the move from the undifferentiated to the differentiated state in evolving systems (Corning, 1983, pp. 73–5).

As noted above, the Lamarckian influence on Spencer was also highly significant. In *Zoological Philosophy* of 1809, Lamarck argued that environmental circumstances lead to the differential use and disuse of organs (Lamarck, 1963; Burkhardt, 1977). High levels of use encourage the strengthening and development of the organ, while low levels lead to deterioration and eventual disappearance. In addition, characters which are thus developed by use can be inherited by offspring.

Lamarck proposed that in the case of organisms with nervous systems, habits constitute a key intervening variable between the organism in question and its changing environment. Alterations in the environment lead to the creation of new habits which, in turn, exercise organs differently. Greater use thereby leads to changes in organic structures, and these can be inherited. Consequently, habits determine form, and not vice versa. It is environmental changes rather than genetic variety which drive Lamarckian evolution. Organisms and species are mutable and constantly changing. They adjust continuously as if attempting to reach harmony with their environment.

Again the contrast here with Darwin is clear. Lamarck argued that variation was a function of the environment, but for Darwin 'variation was present first, and the ordering activity of the environment ("natural selection") followed afterwards' (Mayr, 1982, p. 354). For Lamarck, the environment was the key agent of change. In contrast, Darwin inclined more to the view that change resulted from a combination of variation and environmental selection. Although Darwin sometimes regarded evolution as teleological and progressive, these views were even more prominent in the writings of Lamarck.

Spencer defended Lamarckian ideas, even after sustained criticism by other theoretical biologists. For instance, he did not accept Charles Lyell's alleged refutation of the principle of the inheritance of acquired characteristics. Spencer was a Lamarckian with only minor modifications. He recognized natural selection, but gave it a secondary role.

In contrast to the biotic world, it is now widely recognized that cultural and economic evolution are Lamarckian in the sense that acquired characteristics may be inherited in these spheres. But even cultural and economic evolution does not exclude some kind of selection process. Nevertheless, in Spencer's theory the idea of natural selection was not primary. Even in the biotic sphere, Spencer put much greater stress than Darwin on functional modification through 'use and disuse'. This was seen as the essence of progressive evolution, rather than the cause of deviations from its main course.

True to his Lamarckian principles, Spencer shifted the meaning of the word 'evolution' from the old idea of development unfolding from within (Gould, 1977, p. 31). But he did not go so far as to invest it fully with its modern selectionist meaning. Instead, Spencerian 'evolution' was centred on the Lamarckian kind of organism–environment interactions, rather than on a process where natural selection had a primary role.

Lamarckian Teleology

With his teleological belief in progress, Spencer (1855, p. 492) proposed that 'life attains more and more perfect forms', and that humans were no exception to this rule. Progress was conceived in epigenetic or ontogenetic terms. He thus wrote: 'Progress, therefore, is not an accident, it is a part of nature; all of a piece with the development of the embryo or the unfolding of a flower' (Spencer, 1851, p. 65). For him, evolution meant increasing progress and efficiency in the direction of the ideal state. The evolutionary process was seen as a beneficent journey from the lower to the higher form of organization or life, and from the inferior to the superior.

True, in the *First Principles* and elsewhere, Spencer recognizes the possibility of systemic dissolution. Socioeconomic systems may fail to coordinate, and thus break down and regress. Nevertheless, and in his writings as a whole, by far the greater weight is put on his law of progress: the transformation from the homogeneous to the heterogeneous.

It should be emphasized that within modern biology such progressionist themes are now widely disputed (Dupré, 1987; Nitecki, 1988). Evolution is not necessarily a grand or natural road leading generally towards perfection. Even the idea of increasing diversity in nature has been challenged (Mani, 1991).[9] In evolution, change can be idiosyncratic, error can be reproduced genetically, and an obscure or tortuous path to improvement can elude discovery. Evolution thus does not provide us with a supreme moral arbiter.[10]

In fact, Spencer's view of the perfectibility of society clinches the argument in favour of a minimal influence of Malthus on Spencer. As Young (1969, p. 137) argues:

> Far from being an application of Malthus, the sanguine belief in inexorable evolutionary progress which was characteristic of Spencer was more reminiscent of the doctrines that prompted Malthus to write the polemical first edition of his *Essay on the Principle of Population*. Spencer's *laissez faire* optimism is far closer to Rousseau, Condorcet and Godwin than to Malthus. True, Spencer had a place for struggle, but it basked in the light of Progress. This must be the real source of nature's energy. Thus Spencer's evolutionary theory provides a negative case: it was fundamentally anti-Malthusian.

Admittedly, some selection processes appear in Spencer's writings, such as his recognition that different social systems may be 'selected' through war. Yet the concept of selection is not at the core of his evolutionary thought, and lacks a full exposition. Instead there is the supreme law of progress, the transformation 'from homogeneity to heterogeneity' and the evolution to ever more complex systems. Spencer mentions struggle, but he gives it no special stress. He sees evolution as producing heterogeneity but always in the context of increasing harmony and movement towards equilibrium. Spencer (1890, p. 525) thus writes of 'a gradual advance towards harmony between man's mental nature and the conditions of his existence'. His conception of heterogeneity specifically excludes antagonism and strife. While for Malthus antagonism is creative, for Spencer it leads to destruction.

Although Spencer accepts that Malthusian selection might operate in certain circumstances, progress in the Malthusian model is regarded as too indirect and too slow. Instead the chief factor, in the social context at least, is the Lamarckian idea of 'use and disuse'. As Young (1969, p. 135) argues: 'The main feature of Spencer's explanation was not population pressure but progress itself.' Being a part of Victorian intellectual culture it was not difficult for Spencer to place the Lamarckian conception of evolutionary progress at the apex of his theory and to enhance it with teleological supremacy (Hirst, 1976).

The 'Persistence of Force' and Neoclassical Economics

One of Spencer's 'first principles' is the 'persistence of force'. He preferred this phrase to the 'conservation of energy', but it is with those latter words that this general principle is familiar to us today. In fact, Spencer was one of the major popularizers of the nineteenth-century brand of physics known as energetics, in which this principle was the centrepiece (Capek, 1961, p. 102). Furthermore, Spencer shifted biology away from the nascent organicism and population thinking established by Darwin, translating biology back 'into the language of physics' (Bannister, 1979, p. 19).

As Philip Mirowski (1989b) has shown, the formal and substantial metaphors of the energetics school were adopted wholesale by pioneering neoclassical thinkers such as William Stanley Jevons and Léon Walras. Notably, the energetics metaphor involves the attainment of equilibrium through optimization under constraint: a core idea of mainstream theory to this day. Spencer thus influenced neoclassical economics by being one of the main proselytizers of energetics.

In his early work on social theory, Spencer synthesized Lamarckism with a version of utilitarianism, seeing changes that directly or indirectly maximized human happiness as progressive. The 'persistence of force' is thus transposed into the social realm into the individual maximization of utility. Accordingly, society is perfectible, attaining this blissful equilibrium state when humanity has fully adapted in accordance with its environment.

This is further confirmation of Spencer's conception of evolution having its outcome in perfect equilibrium and harmony. Change comes about as units adapt to the pressures of their environment. Motion ceases in the state of equilibrium when each unit has reached the most satisfactory possible state. Theo Suranyi-Unger (1931, p. 25) has thus suggested that this Spencerian conception was instrumental in stimulating Léon Walras to develop his formal theory of general equilibrium. The even more obvious and explicit influence of Spencer on Alfred Marshall is discussed extensively in the next chapter.

However, Valerie Haines (1988, p. 1208) states that Spencer moved away from strict utilitarianism. Indeed, he came to reject utilitarian comparisons of interpersonal utility based on the assumption of the uniformity of human nature. The reason for this rejection, however, was not the same as that advanced by many modern neoclassical economists. Primarily, such uniformity conflicted with Spencer's supposition of variety and diversity. But Haines is wrong to imply that Spencer entirely abandoned a utilitarian evaluation of evolutionary progress. Further, as modern neoclassical economics shows, the rejection of interpersonal utility comparisons does not imply the rejection of a utilitarian calculus. In fact, Spencer (1904, p. 88) wrote late in his life:

> I have never regarded myself as Anti-utilitarian. My dissent from the doctrine of Utility as commonly understood concerns not the object to be reached by men, but the method of reaching it. While I admit that happiness is the ultimate end to be contemplated, I do not think that it should be the proximate end.

As John Gray (1984, p. 104) notes, Spencer's moral theory, like that of Friedrich Hayek, is a species of 'indirect utilitarianism' in which all states of affairs are somehow evaluated by reference to the utility they contain, for instance in regard to their utility for an anonymous individual. According to this view, attempts to aggregate individual utilities are regarded as unsound, and strategies of direct utility maximization are condemned as self-defeating.

What does occur in Spencer's theory is a shift from the exclusive emphasis on the pursuit of happiness or utility by multiple individuals as both the engine of change and the criterion of progress. The engine of change becomes vaguely subsumed under his Law of Evolution – the move towards increasing differentiation and progress. He puts greater and greater emphasis on the progressive development of organisms and societies from homogeneity to heterogeneity. While the maximization of individual utility provided some causal mechanism for the activity and supposed adaptation of individuals, this was lacking in the vague teleological idea of movement towards greater heterogeneity and complexity.

Atomism and Individualism

Some authors have described Spencer's ontological standpoint as organicist (Paul, 1988, p. 269). However, mere recognition of the interconnections between entities is not sufficient to qualify as organicism.

After all, integration and interconnection can be depicted in a purely mechanical model. Consider, for example, modern general equilibrium theory in economics. Its metaphor is mechanistic, and each part – the individual – is an atomistic and self-contained unit. It is 'organic' only in the limited sense that everything may impinge on everything else – like billiard balls on a table or gas molecules in a jar.

It is true that Spencer frequently compared society to a living organism. Again, the use of an analogy between society and a living thing is not sufficient to qualify as organicism. An atomist conceives of a living thing in terms of its discrete parts and their interactions. So did Spencer. Importantly, in an organicist ontology, relations between entities are internal rather than external, and the essential characteristics of any element are outcomes of relations with other entities. In contrast, in an atomist ontology, entities possess qualities independently of their relations with other entities.

An individualistic and atomist outlook does not necessarily involve the rejection of the concept of society or the denial of significant human interaction. Many atomists go so far as to accept that the individual is partially formed by his or her environment. However, the interaction is seen as one between atomic entities. Regarding society as whole, the atomist sees in society only a limited kind of unity. Society is addressed in mechanistic terms. It is regarded as no more than the interplay of self-contained individuals pursuing their own ends, plus the social arrangements connecting them. The social system is seen as the complex interplay of atoms rather than as an organic whole.

With the above qualifications, there is no problem in describing Spencer's ontology as atomist. Although Spencer stressed both individual entities and their relations with each other, social and biological objects were seen to possess qualities independently of these relations. In sum, Spencer's theory fitted more neatly into the atomist rather than the organicist conception.

Spencer's thought belongs to the nineteenth century, where scientific prestige belonged to the mechanistic kind of thought, and accordingly, as Alfred North Whitehead (1926, p. 128) put it, biology aped 'the manners of physics'. Accordingly, Spencer's deployment of nineteenth-century energetics as one of the foundation stones of his theoretical system should also be noted in this context (Capek, 1961, pp. 101–3). For Spencer, evolution involved the continuous redistribution of matter and motion. Like the ancient atomists, he upholds the constancy of matter and the indestructibility of motion.

Nevertheless, within this atomist ontology Spencer had a conception of society as a structure which inspired subsequent sociology. Where Spencer did not have a clear idea of the mechanism of evolution, and Darwin provided one, Darwin's theory focused on the natural selection of individual organisms without much regard to the biotic system as a structured whole. Whereas Darwin and Spencer were both atomists, there were important differences. Comparing the two, Spencer's conception of an interrelated system was the richer, but his idea of the mechanism of evolution the poorer.

Built on these atomistic ontological foundations, and combined with a lingering utilitarianism, Spencer's view of socioeconomic evolution was both deterministic and individualistic. Although he believed that both regress and progress were possible, for Spencer every event had an efficient cause. Furthermore, his system of causality encompassed both the natural and the social world: 'Spencer's belief in the universality of natural causation was, together with his *laissez faire* political creed, the bedrock of his thinking' (Burrow, 1966, p. 205).

Along with many other nineteenth-century theorists, Spencer's notion of natural causation meant that explanations of social phenomena were not reduced simply to individual but to individual-biological terms. Spencer did not make the modern distinction between biological evolution, involving the transmission of genetic information, and social or cultural evolution, in which information is transmitted by imitation and learning. His conception of natural selection operated on biological characters. Hence, in modern terms, Spencer was a biological reductionist.

Consequently, the pace of social evolution, like biological evolution, depended on 'the rate of organic modification in human beings' (Spencer, 1880, p. 366). Even if culture and institutions changed, according to Spencer social evolution occurred only in so far as the biological characteristics of human beings were altered. Social evolution involved the adaptation of human biology to changes in the surrounding conditions.

Spencer's Failure

However, in his quest for a unified science, Spencer failed to give sufficient attention to key differences between biological and social evolution, even accepting evolution in Lamarckian terms. Lamarckian biological evolution is animated by environmental change, rather than mutation and selection acting on variety, and this environment is very much external to the species involved. Much, although not all, environmental change is strictly exogenous, involving changes in climate or the populations of competing species, for example. Spencer adopted this idea and insisted on the importance of environmental change.

In contrast, in the case of human social evolution, environmental disturbances of this type are secondary. Without denying the impingement of nature on human existence, more frequently in human society environmental changes are due to the activity of humans themselves. The general idea of the relative importance of endogenous sources of socioeconomic change has been widely accepted by social scientists, at least since the abandonment of the Jevonsian idea that business cycles were driven by sunspot activity.

Consequently, the sources of variety and change are quite different in the social and biological domains. Under the biological firmament, endless and exogenous change from the natural environment can bring about continuous adaptation. In contrast, in the restricted zone of society, there is no obvious reason why change from the environment external to the socioeconomic system should be sufficiently dramatic or rapid to provide adequate variety.

As in the biological world, the adaptation of one unit vitally affects the environment of others, but in society this feedback mechanism is much more important – at least in Lamarckian terms – because of the relative unimportance of additional, exogenous changes. It is thus quite possible for human social adaptation to converge on an equilibrium where no further adaptation is required. The only further evolution would, in Spencer's terms, result from the biological evolution of human beings themselves.

We know today that the convergence properties of such cybernetic feedback mechanisms cannot be assured, especially when non-linearities are involved. But probably Spencer would not have been happy with a chaotic or explosively divergent outcome; it would have conflicted with his faith in harmony, progress and order. In the case of convergence the problem remains that there is no continuing source of variety in the system. In modern Darwinian theory variety is continuously created by Mendelian sexual recombination and by genetic mutation, as well as by environmental disturbances. Spencer's Lamarckian theory of social evolution focused on increasing complexity and heterogeneity but lacked an adequate explanation of its source and renewal.

We may now address this question: Is Spencer's theory of social evolution ontogenetic or phylogenetic? Against earlier critics of Spencer, Robert Perrin (1976, pp. 1353–6) asserts that Spencer's theory involves phylogenesis, but he does not define this and identifies it with a vague notion of speciation. This begs the question of the mechanism of speciation, and it is more useful to identify phylogenesis explicitly with some idea of selection or genetic drift through time on a thereby changing 'genetic' material. Haines (1988) stresses the 'evolutionary' quality of Spencer's theory, without mentioning phylogenesis but suggesting something closer to this true meaning.

It can be accepted that Spencer's theory does have a phylogenetic quality. However, both Perrin and Haines fail to note the inadequate revelation of renewed variety. In Spencer's theory the burden of explanation is on determination by prior conditions. Without novelty and renewed variety, the theory may still be phylogenetic, but with an outcome that converges to a stable equilibrium. According to Spencer (1890, p. 496): 'Evolution has an impassable limit.'

Thus social evolution ends after the change due to initial variety has occurred, unless the biological evolution of humans themselves provides further basis for social change. However, given that human biological evolution is much slower than the social, this further source of variety is insignificant, and we can presume a final and stable result. Furthermore, Spencer's deterministic scheme ruled out human novelty and creativity. For such reasons the pragmatist philosopher William James had been persuaded by Charles Sanders Peirce's critical interpretation of Spencer and wrote of Spencer's theory as 'an absolute anachronism reverting to a pre-Darwinian type of thought' (James, 1880, p. 459).[11]

Such convergence on the stable state narrows the gap between phylogeny and ontogeny. With no further source of renewal or variety the former converges on the latter. In other words, Spencerian socioeconomic evolution, while strictly phylogenetic, is asymptotic to ontogeny as the source of variety progressively dries up. Spencerian evolutionary development is not only like the ontogeny of the social 'organism'; as Stephen Jay Gould (1977, p. 31) notes, in defining evolution as progressive change towards increasing complexity, Spencer is actually using an 'ontogenetic metaphor'.

Among other things, Ernst Haeckel is remembered for his doctrine that 'ontogeny recapitulates phylogeny.' In other words, the story of the growth and development of a single organism seems to spell out the tale of evolution as a whole, just as the human being grows from a few cells, through a fishlike embryo, to *homo sapiens*. Spencer unwittingly reverses and transforms Haeckel's controversial law. For him, 'phylogeny approaches ontogeny.' As systems supposedly evolve from simplicity to complexity, they are deemed to recapitulate the general ontogenetic story of development as related by von Baer. Although it could be interpreted as phylogenetic, Spencer's theory of evolution reduces essentially to ontogenetic metaphor and form.[12]

It should be noted that phylogenetic evolution, at least in the Darwinian sense, does not necessarily involve optimization and progress. Strictly, an evolutionary process involving Darwinian selection cannot be an optimizing one because for such evolution to work there must always be a variety of forms from which to select. For selection to work there must be rejection, and the process must thus involve ceaseless error-making as well. Above all, optimization implies finality and eventual stasis; in contrast, Darwinian evolution means change, process and a conception of continuously unfolding time.

It has been pointed out by several critics that Spencer failed to specify an adequate evolutionary mechanism. This was the problem with much evolutionary thinking, even after Darwin. Likewise, Spencer's Lamarckian theory lacked full explication, and he was thus forced to fall back on to the mystical notion of a universal and unknowable motive force, an 'inaccessible Ultimate Cause' (Wiltshire, 1978, p. 207), working generally in the direction of 'progress'.

However, Spencer did try to identify such a mechanism. From the idea of the 'persistence of force', Spencer infers that its different effects on various parts will generate divergences and heterogeneity. Hence the closest that Spencer gets in developing any such a general mechanism is his argument that homogeneous systems are inherently unstable, and thus the transition from the homogeneous to the heterogeneous must be universal in all integrated systems.

Many critics, however, have pointed to problems in these ideas.[13] For instance, Spencer regards antagonistic systems as also unstable. Without clear criteria to distinguish between the complex and the antagonistic, and indeed between homogeneous and heterogeneous entities, Spencer's later theory remains vague and highly problematic. There is a lack of a clear evolutionary mechanism in his theory except for the mysterious workings of a superordinate energizing force.

Indeed, there is an internal problem in Lamarckian theory which Spencer failed to address and solve; where do the rules that guide the variation in the Lamarckian system come from? The improving rule that promotes new variety in response to the environment has to come from somewhere. Indeed, it has been suggested by Donald Campbell (1965, 1975) that this is a problem of potentially infinite regress, and may even at bottom require a Darwinian explanation. Whatever the answer, it is evident that Spencer does not have a clear or adequate picture of the evolutionary mechanisms involved.

Although Spencer shifted the meaning of the word 'evolution' and gave it a particular form, in some respects his theory still has similarities with the developmentalist idea of *evolvere*, rather than a genetic theory of selection. Furthermore, it was a developmentalist notion without adequate specification of its mechanisms: falling back on the vague and problematic notion of the 'persistence of force'.

In sum, the inadequacies and ambiguities in Spencer's theory defy its precise classification. At best he offers a Lamarckian version of phylogeny, but one reaching perfectibility and equilibrium, and for this reason it is not unlike ontogeny.

It is significant, but not widely known, that Spencer in his later years came out as a vehement critic of Darwinism. As Peter Bowler (1988) has argued, it was the vague notion of evolution rather than the details of Darwin's theory that had become widely accepted in the 1860s and the 1870s. But by the 1880s, Darwinism was in eclipse (Bowler, 1983). Spencer (1887, 1893) cashed in on the mood of the times, describing the idea of natural selection as an inflexible dogma: a mere matter of faith for the scientific community. Although he himself had previously accepted a limited role for selection, his Lamarckism remained the core of his theory. Even the long discussion of 'evolution' in his *Principles of Biology* was in developmentalist terms, no more than hinting at the idea of natural selection. His ideas had never been evolutionary in a truly Darwinian sense.

Spencer and Laissez-Faire

Spencer's combination of individualism with an optimism in progress gave his writings a distinctly Panglossian tone. He thus was one of the ever-growing band of writers to utilize the biological analogy to sustain a non-interventionist policy in economic and social affairs.

However, unlike later Social Darwinists such as William Graham Sumner, Spencer hesitated to take the principle of the 'survival of the fittest' as an unqualified justification of competition between humans to the point of the extinction of the unfit, and as grounds for the rebuttal of charitable social policy (Peel, 1971, p. 20). In fact, Spencer held the view that Darwinian processes of natural selection were of lesser significance in the evolution of humanity. The more significant processes were believed to be Lamarckian, whereby individuals adapted to their environment and passed on beneficial acquired characters to their offspring.

Spencer's primary justification of laissez-faire was more to do with these Lamarckian principles than the selective mortality of the maladapted. For him, the important factor was to provide an environment which would promote the Lamarckian processes of adaptation and assimilation so that the fittest could emerge, rather than a process necessarily leading to the demise of the unfit. Unrestricted and market-based competition between individuals and firms was believed to supply such a context, in which technological, social and economic advance could take place. In contrast, state provision was deemed to be deficient because it reduced the environmental pressure, thereby cosseting individuals and averting change. Accordingly, Spencer took the commonplace view that state regulation led to economic sclerosis and stagnation.

However, while the justification of laissez-faire was in terms of its supposedly dynamic consequences, Spencer advocated a static outcome in structural economic terms. The state of perfection towards which he thought socioeconomic evolution was leading was a market system based on voluntary and contractual cooperation between individuals. However, this advocacy of market liberalism based on the legal foundations of individual, private property seems to contradict Spencer's definition of evolution in terms of progress towards heterogeneity and diversity. For him, the goal of heterogeneity applied to the plurality of atomic units, but not to that of economic structures.

At the inception of his career, Spencer was celebrated as a radical, endorsing industrial dynamism and opposing the rigidities of the British aristocracy. By the end, he appeared as a conservative defender of laissez-faire, opposed to many social reforms and fearing the growth of concentrated state power associated with the potential growth of an increasingly regulated capitalism. It is indeed remarkable that the evolutionary doctrine that seemed at its inception to threaten the established religion and the reigning conception of the social and natural order was by some transformed into a weapon to be used against economic interventionism or egalitarianism. While making an important and original contribution, Spencer was one of the first to put evolutionary theory to such apologetic purposes and his influence still pervades popular conceptions of evolution today.

It is testimony to the enduring influence of people like Spencer and Sumner that advocates of laissez-faire still often appeal to biological evolution to justify their creed. It is demonstrated in this present volume, however, that evolutionary ideas from biology do not properly support such a philosophy. Whether one may draw radical or conservative ideas from evolutionary biology often depends on the relative emphases on variety, mutability or stasis. Just as advocates of racism, sexism, nationalism and imperialism have all claimed to find succour in biology, so too have devotees of mutual aid, pacifism, communism, socialism, Fabianism and anarchism (Himmelfarb, 1959).

Although Spencer's popularity declined markedly in his later years, it was not principally because he saw society in biological terms. The widespread conceptual separation between the social and the natural sciences came later, in the early decades of the twentieth century, particularly with the influence of Max Weber (Hennis, 1988), and after Spencer was long gone.

Spencer's Legacy: 'The Survival of the Fittest'

Partly due to Darwin's endorsement, but also to Spencer's immense popularity in the nineteenth century, the idea of the 'survival of the fittest' became an unfortunate general characterization of the very notion of evolution. Spencer used this term to refer to competition both within and between species. Although the emphasis in his sociological writings was on competition between rather than within societies, his depiction of struggle among both individuals and groups has had a wider and enduring influence. Some of the problems in this portrayal are now briefly discussed.

For instance, as Theodosius Dobzhansky et al. (1977, p. 98) point out, natural selection does not lead to the superlative fittest, only the tolerably fit. Further, as Herbert Simon (1983, p. 69) argues, although the fitter may survive, there is no reason to presume that they are the fittest in any absolute sense. This clearly suggests evolution is 'satisficing' in regard to fitness rather than 'maximizing'.

Clearly, a process of natural selection cannot be an optimizing one, at least in the strict sense, because for evolution to work there must always be a variety of forms from which to select. Indeed, without variety there would be no evolution. Furthermore, for selection to work there must be rejection, and the process must thus involve cease-less error-making as well. In a Darwinian evolutionary process, error is more than a stochastic perturbation, it is the very source of evol-utionary change. In contrast, in Lamarckian evolution it is the processes of perfection and learning, rather than error-making, that are given the central role.

'Survival of the fittest' is additionally an ill-conceived slogan be-cause the mechanism of 'natural selection' in modern biology does not even necessarily lead to survival. In other words, 'survival' and 'fitness' are not necessarily connected.

Consider the evolution of tendencies to either 'selfish' or 'altruistic' behaviour. While universal altruism may be most beneficial for all members of the species, the possible existence of a 'prisoner's dilemma' – where individual selfishness is the best one-off individual response to prevailing cooperation – can lead to the breakdown of the arrange-ment of universal altruism with its advantages for all. There is not necessarily any universal mechanism 'by which natural selection tends to favour the survival of the species or the population. The population, in fact, may "improve itself to extinction"' (Elster, 1983, p. 54).[14]

Thus the mere fact of survival, even to a numerous and sustained extent, need not always imply fitness. The conclusion here concurs with that of Elliott Sober (1981, p. 99): 'The so-called tautology of the survival of the fittest is no tautology at all; the fitter do *not* always turn out to be more successful.' Likewise, Anthony Arnold and Kurt Fristrup (1982, p. 117) argue that the 'concept of natural selection is sometimes clouded by the equation of fitness with survival – a popular miscon-ception that is reinforced by the phrase "survival of the fittest".'

The linking of 'survival' with 'fitness' is thus found to be problem-atic. There are two further reasons why the Spencerian slogan of 'survival of the fittest' is misleadingly one-sided. The first relates to the focus on the word 'survival', and the second on the term 'the fittest'.

Taking the word 'survival' first. The emphasis on this term implies that there are some who do not survive. In the context, therefore, the word thus implies a process of extinction as well as the fact of endur-ance. However, as Gould (1982b, p. 101) has noted, Darwinian natural selection does not simply operate by differential death but also by differential birth. The issue of fecundity is thus of key importance. As Mayr (1985b, p. 768) puts it: 'Selection is not merely mortality selec-tion as reflected in the slogan "survival of the fittest", but "success in leaving progeny", as Darwin saw quite clearly and mentioned specifi-cally as part of natural selection.' Accordingly, the idea of 'success in leaving progeny' is just as important in Darwinian natural selection as 'survival of the fittest'. It is significant that one phrase was promoted by Spencer and widely adopted, but not the other.[15]

Second, the concept of 'the fittest' is often interpreted in an absolute sense, without regard for the fact that any concept of fitness must always be relative to a given environment. In general, organism behaviour is not simply a result of environmental change but also in part its cause. The philosopher Alfred North Whitehead (1926, p. 140) put this point well. He argued:

> There are thus two sides to the machinery involved in the development of nature. On one side, there is a given environment with organisms adapting themselves to it. The scientific materialism of the [nineteenth century] epoch emphasized this aspect. From this point of view, there is a given amount of material, and only a limited number of organisms can take advantage of it. The givenness of the environment dominates everything. Accordingly, the last words of science appeared to be the Struggle for Existence, and Natural Selection. Darwin's own writings are for all time a model of refusal to go beyond the direct evidence, and of careful retention of every possible hypothesis. But those virtues were not so conspicuous in his followers, and still less in his camp-followers.

In contrast:

> The other side of the evolutionary machinery, the neglected side, is expressed by the word *creativeness*. The organisms can create their own environment. For this purpose, the single organism is almost helpless. The adequate forces require societies of co-operating organisms. But with such co-operation and in proportion to effort put forward, the environment has a plasticity which alters the whole ethical aspect of evolution. (ibid.)

The fact that fitness is environment dependent, and that the environment includes other organisms as well as the climate and soil, means that the very idea of an absolute or independent concept of fitness is highly problematic.

Some of these issues will be raised again in later chapters. The purpose here has simply been to suggest that by popularizing the phrase 'survival of the fittest' Spencer did not offer evolutionary science a great service. In sum, the phrase overemphasized the attributes of the atomistic organism, without sufficient regard to its relations with others and its general environment; it highlighted the function of success rather than that of error; it stressed fitness and struggle rather than fecundity and reproduction; it emphasized strife rather than cooperation. We still live with the adverse legacy of Spencer's questionable term to this day. In an attempt to escape from its multifarious problems, there is thus a strong argument in modern biology that the idea of the 'survival of the fittest' can and should be abandoned (Waters, 1986).

Spencer: Decline but Survival

During the final decades of the nineteenth century, Spencer's scientific views suffered damaging attacks from the scientific community. It was the pragmatist philosopher Peirce (1923, pp. 162–3, and 1935, pp. 15–16) who saw the deepest inconsistency in Spencer's ideas, emanating from his flawed attempt to combine the principle of the conservation of energy with a notion of evolution.

Peirce pointed out that the energy conservation principle was equivalent to the proposition that all operations by mechanical laws can be reversed. In contrast, biological evolution normally involves irreversibility. Hence even Spencer's idea of evolution, of progress from homogeneity to heterogeneity, cannot be explained in terms of reversible mechanical laws. Spencer's theoretical conception was thus internally inconsistent. Despite all the bold proclamations, the internal structure of his evolutionism was weak. It was built on the anomalous, mechanistic principle of the conservation of energy: a tragic case of mixed metaphors.

Furthermore, Spencer was not able to reconcile his principle of increasing heterogeneity with the rising thermodynamics in the latter decades of the nineteenth century. The entropy law in thermodynamics implies that heterogeneity should diminish through time, in apparent conflict with Spencerian evolutionary progress. There is a way out of this problem but Spencer did not find it. It is only more recently that evolution and entropy have been reconciled.[16] However, they can only be reconciled on the basis of a recognition that living and social systems are in a 'far from equilibrium' state, and in an open system (Laszlo, 1987, pp. 21–2; Prigogine and Stengers, 1984). This contrasts with Spencer's emphasis on the emergence of equilibrium.

The reconciliation between evolution and entropy sees evolution as a temporary and countervailing trend to the entropy law. Complex organization and order become locally possible in an open system, but only with the result that overall entropy is greater. The ultimate cost of evolution is greater waste and accelerated disorder. The entropy law is thus not negated; the eventual outcome must be the homogeneity of the chaotic state. This is in direct contradiction to Spencer. The entropy law implies that complexity and heterogeneity are unstable in that they must eventually lead to disorder. Spencer's view is the opposite: he believed that homogeneity was the unstable condition.

Furthermore, with the development of biological theory, Lamarckism came under increasing attack. Scientists such as August Weismann (1893) were effectively clearing the ground for the later synthesis between Darwinian natural selection and genetics. Spencer himself got the worst of a heated debate over the mechanisms of evolution with Weismann in the 1890s (Peel, 1971, p. 20).

Finally, as we have noted, Spencer's biological reductionism rapidly became unpopular in the early decades of the twentieth century, particularly with the growing reaction against Social Darwinism. Racist and other obnoxious misinterpretations of biological theory eventually led to a strong reaction within social science, even at the cost of cutting it loose from its biological foundation. Spencer's work was a severe casualty of this reaction, becoming entirely ignored despite its importance and preceding influence.

Consequently, for both ideological and scientific reasons, Spencer's views quickly fell out of favour. But his enduring influence should not be underestimated. Unfortunately, there are many cases, with an example or two in later chapters, where he has been entirely forgotten even by respected historians of late nineteenth-century social and economic thought.

As argued elsewhere in this work, it is evolutionary ideas of a Spencerian kind that are typically echoed by economists, rather than the more subtle alternatives. In many cases the exponents are seemingly unaware of the resemblance of their ideas to those of Spencer, but his orbiting presence is no less significant for that.

7
The Mecca of Alfred Marshall

It is appropriate today that Alfred Marshall retains his reputation as a highly innovative and perceptive economic theorist. As well as being a foremost architect of neoclassical theory, he explored the boundaries of this paradigm and considered the possibility of a more dynamic economic science. Among other noted facets of his work is his appeal to more dynamic ideas from biology. In an appendix to his *Principles*, Marshall (1949, p. 637) wrote that 'economics, like biology, deals with a matter, of which the inner nature and constitution, as well as the outer form, are constantly changing', thus economics 'is a branch of biology broadly interpreted'. However, as argued below, this fusion of the two sciences is not actually achieved in Marshall's work.

Alfred Marshall is often quoted for his statement that 'the Mecca of the economist lies in economic biology rather than in economic dynamics' but we are less often reminded of what immediately follows: 'But biological conceptions are more complex than those of mechanics; a volume on Foundations must therefore give a relatively large place to mechanical analogies; and frequent use is made of the term "equilibrium," which suggests something of a statical analogy' (Marshall, 1949, p. xii).

Marshall's Ambivalence

The fact that Marshall was ambivalent towards the biological metaphor is supported by insightful examination of the texts by Brinley Thomas (1991). Marshall saw the limitations of mechanical reasoning, and turned to biology in his search for inspiration and metaphor. However, the science was young and the mechanisms of evolution were not fully understood. At the time, many biologists were questioning the Darwinian approach. Furthermore, in substance it was not Darwin's theory that dominated evolutionism at the time. As Peter Bowler (1988, p. 5) argues: 'Darwin's theory should be seen not as the central theme in nineteenth-century evolutionism but as a catalyst that helped bring about the transition to an evolutionary viewpoint within an essentially non-Darwinian conceptual framework.'

In fact, there was an alternative and bolder synthesis to Darwinism on offer. For Marshall, as for many of his contemporaries, 'the writings of Herbert Spencer were even more significant than those of Darwin' (Thomas, 1991, p. 3). Marshall (1975, vol. 1, p. 109) recollected how 'a saying of Spencer sent the blood rushing through the veins of those who a generation ago looked eagerly for each volume of his as it issued from the press.' John Maynard Keynes (1924, p. 13) quoted Mary Marshall's account of how her husband would read volumes of Spencer on their walking holidays in the Alps. In the preface to the first edition of the *Principles* Marshall (1949, p. viii) emphasized the notion of continuity in regard to development and singled out the writings of Spencer and Hegel, because they had 'affected more than any other the substance of the views expressed in the present book.' After Spencer's death, Marshall (1904) wrote: 'There is probably no one who gave as strong a stimulus to the thoughts of the younger Cambridge graduates thirty or forty years ago as he. He opened a new world of promise.' It is clear that the Spencerian influence on Marshall was as great as any economist and certainly should not be ignored. Furthermore, it is argued in this chapter that while Marshall saw the value of the biological metaphor for economics, in part the Spencerian influence thwarted the development of an adequate evolutionary analysis.

Nevertheless, unlike many of his contemporaries, and even to some extent Spencer himself, Marshall was acutely aware of the need to address the actual mechanisms of evolutionary change. By modern standards, even biologists did not understand them well at the time.

Early on in his career Marshall began to see the limitations of mechanistic reasoning in economics. In particular, in his investigations of increasing returns, it became clear to him that a movement up or down the long-period supply curve is irreversible. Marshall's intellectual honesty was such that he did not assume away even grave problems of this kind.[1] Indeed, he became ever more convinced that increasing returns was a real and unavoidable phenomenon of contemporary capitalism. Furthermore, as Martin Currie and Ian Steedman (1990, p. 30) emphasize, Marshall's argument concerning time irreversibility has a wider application than the case of increasing returns. He was nagged by the problems of increasing returns and time irreversibility for the remainder of his life.

The *Principles* deals primarily with economic statics. Marshall planned another volume to deal with dynamics and the elusive element of time (Whitaker, 1990a). This companion work was to address irreversible changes and organic development, drawing its inspiration more from biology than from physics. Some of these issues are briefly addressed in the *Principles*, but they are not integrated into his analysis in a systematic way. Although that work is peppered with the occasional biological metaphor, the essence of the analysis is mechanical, addressing equilibrium outcomes, as Marshall himself admits.

The Organical Analogy

Kenneth Boulding (1981, p. 17), David Reisman (1987, pp. 338–57), Neil Niman (1991) and others have noted the extent to which Marshall depicts economic development as being 'organic' in quality. However, this does not necessarily imply an organicist ontology, in which relations between entities are internal rather than external, and the essential characteristics of any element are outcomes of relations with other entities. Such organicism is incompatible with the metaphor of nineteenth-century mechanics.

The acknowledged influence of Hegel on Marshall would seem to provide a prima facie case for imputing to the economist an organicist view. This does not, however, stand up to closer examination. The influence of Hegel, at least on Marshall's mature writings, is rather limited (Groenewegen, 1990; Whitaker, 1977) and does not seem to extend to ontology. As Talcott Parsons (1932, p. 219) put it: 'He took from Hegel only what suited his own preconceptions, and used it only to round off the sharp edges of his own tradition – as in his idea of the "organic" nature of social change.'

Although Marshall often discussed the way in which an economic entity may depend on its relations with others, he was unable to proceed in his *Principles* without considering each element as an atomistic unit. In fact, despite his richer intuitions, Marshall's conception of the 'organic' nature of reality came to little more than the knowledge that everything depends upon everything else. As noted above in the case of Herbert Spencer, such a notion is perfectly compatible with an atomistic ontology. The 'organic' reasoning in the *Principles* was indeed of a limited and Spencerian kind, impoverished in comparison with the richer organicism of philosophers such as Alfred North Whitehead (1926).

Consider Marshall's treatment of the 'representative firm'. Although he associates this notion with a vague idea of 'organic development', it is essentially a theoretical device to deal with organic variety by entrapping and ignoring it, rather than by encompassing diversity within an idea of an ongoing process of competition and change. This largely heuristic concept deals with the varied population of firms by identifying a single set of distinct characteristics which are deemed to represent the essential qualities of the population, i.e. the industry, as a whole. It is not a single firm, or even a typical firm; it is an imaginary firm which exhibits, in microcosm, the 'representative' features of the entire industry. The perception of conflict and diversity within that domain are thus diminished by the concept of the representative firm.

The predominant conceptualization of the representative firm in Marshall's work is more an example of 'typological essentialism' than 'population thinking': a distinction which has been introduced in chapters 3 and 4 above. In 'population thinking' variety and diversity are all-important: 'There is no "typical" individual' (Mayr, 1982, p. 46).

As already noted, in typological thinking species are regarded as identifiable in terms of a few distinct characteristics which represent their essence. Accordingly, all variations around the ideal type are regarded as accidental aberrations. By contrast, in population thinking, species are described in terms of a distribution of characteristics. 'The heart of population thinking', Elliott Sober (1985, p. 880) writes, 'consists in the idea that theories may be stated relating the interactions of population properties and magnitudes.' It is precisely these population and relational properties that the concept of the representative firm ignores.

Not only is the substance of the 'representative firm' inorganic, its application is mechanical. It is a reductive method of depicting a long-period equilibrium for the industry as a whole, by means of a theory of the firm. As Thomas (1991, p. 7) remarks: 'If the "representative firm" is a biological concept, is it not strange that two-thirds of the references to it in the *Principles* are in Book 5 which is devoted to mechanical equilibrium analysis?' Although Marshall's use of such analysis was careful and highly qualified, he had no developed alternative on offer.

However, Marshall does not quite go all the way to reduce the 'representative firm' to an atomistic unit and typological item; that was done later, by Arthur Pigou, Edward Chamberlin, Joan Robinson and others. The hint of organicism in Marshall's concept – and it is no more than that – is that the representative firm represents the whole industry, rather than a single firm. As a concept it is thus Janus-faced: it looks one way into the misty future of bio-economics, and another into the then-clearer mechanistic world of equilibrium theory. Unfortunately, the mechanistic vision prevails, even in Marshall's own work and especially in the hands of later interpreters.

Elsewhere too the faces of Janus may be found. For instance, although Marshall's mode of reasoning in regard to the industry diminishes the role of variety, he occasionally recognizes its function elsewhere, for instance in terms of entrepreneurial activity leading to variations in organization and innovation. He writes: 'The tendency to variation is a chief cause of progress' (Marshall, 1949, p. 295). Here variety becomes a cause as well as an outcome. He also considers some kind of selection for profitability in the competitive process, but without any extended reference to the Darwinian metaphor. These important insights represent signposts to a truly evolutionary economics; they hint of the concerns that would have been raised in the projected second volume, but they are overshadowed in the *Principles* by the mechanical concept of equilibrium and the representative firm.

The Biological Blueprint

The most penetrating and analytical remarks from Marshall concerning the application of biological ideas to economics are in chapter 8 of book 4 of the *Principles*, which 'reads like a blueprint of a book on economic biology' (Thomas, 1991, pp. 8–9). Its eight pages indicate substantial appreciation and understanding both of the biology of his time, and some of the difficulties that would be faced if the full volume on economic dynamics were ever to be written.

In the chapter Marshall sees an analogy between the subdivision of functions and organic differentiation in nature and similar phenomena in industry. Here the influence of Spencer is abundantly clear. For instance, Marshall (1949, pp. 200–1) postulates

> a fundamental unity of action between the laws of nature in the physical and in the moral world. This central unity is set forth in the general rule, to which there are not very many exceptions, that the development of the organism, whether social or physical, involves an increasing subdivision of functions between its separate parts on the one hand, and on the other a more intimate connection between them.[2]

Marshall is clearly evoking Spencer's central idea that evolutionary progress involves a combination of differentiation and integration, and he repeats and illustrates the same notion in a subsequent paragraph. Like Spencer and Adam Smith, but unlike Charles Darwin, variety is seen as a result of social, economic or biological development, not its major cause. Furthermore, Marshall is clearly replicating Spencer's idea of the unity of the natural and the social sciences.

It is striking that, in an otherwise excellent discussion of Marshall, Brian Loasby (1978, p. 6) quotes the very same words as above from the *Principles*, but sees therein a connection with Adam Smith alone, failing to give Spencer any mention anywhere in his essay.[3] With knowledge of Spencer's writings, his influence on Marshall can hardly be ignored.

However, unlike Spencer, and rather than taking some vague mechanism of natural selection for granted, Marshall (1949, p. 201) immediately and carefully remarks that the 'doctrine that those organisms which are most highly developed ... are those most likely to survive in the struggle for existence, is itself in process of development. It is not yet completely thought out either in its biological or its economic relations.'

He perceptively suggests that the 'law' of the 'survival of the fittest' addresses survival not in an absolute sense but in relation to the environment. He considers the possibility of selection processes which are injurious to that environment, or to other species. The implication, which Marshall does not draw out explicitly, is that in some cases evolutionary selection can actually lead to extinction, or to a dead end. What is clear, however, is that Marshall recognizes organism–environment interactions, of relevance to both biologists and economists, which are even today neglected in much evolutionary theory.

Further, Marshall (1949, p. 201) resists the temptation to paint the evolutionary analogy in Panglossian tones: 'the struggle for survival may fail to bring into existence organisms that would be highly beneficial.' He argues that for a worthwhile innovation to be adopted in the economic sphere it must bring higher profits. He argues that many socially beneficial but unprofitable arrangements may not actually appear in the struggle for existence.

But such a 'hard truth' offends Marshall's moral sensibilities. So he then spends a page or so presenting an unsatisfactory theory of altruistic group selection in support of the proposition that 'the struggle for existence causes in the long run those races of men to survive in which the individual is most willing to sacrifice himself for the benefit of those around him; and which are consequently the best adapted collectively to make use of their environment' (ibid., pp. 202–3).

As in many other theories of group selection, the limitation of this argument is that Marshall does not give an adequate reason why altruistic behaviour should sustain itself. Admittedly, the groups with altruists may be fitter in terms of their capacity to prosper, conquer or grow in numbers. But the non-altruistic, free-riding individuals within any such group will be at an advantage in relation to the altruists. There is no explanation of the necessary selection or survival of altruists within an altruistic group. Without such a sustaining mechanism, altruism may simply disappear, despite the comparative fitness of the altruistic group as a whole. It is shown elsewhere in this work that the notion of group selection is indeed viable, but it should not be taken for granted.

Despite his vagueness on the question of group selection, in places Marshall clearly recognizes that the mechanisms of evolution have to be specified rather than assumed. He identifies the essential notion of heritable fitness in the context of races or groups, and finds the appropriate analogue in the institutional sphere: 'This influence of heredity shows itself nowhere more markedly than in social organization. For that must necessarily be a slow growth, the product of many generations: it must be based on those customs and aptitudes of the great mass of the people which are incapable of quick change' (Marshall, 1949, p. 203).

As we shall see later in the present work, this apparent reference to the quasi-genetic function of 'customs' is reminiscent of the institutional economists.[4] In the work of Thorstein Veblen, for instance, institutions are both replicators and the units of selection in economic evolution. But unlike the institutionalists, Marshall emphasized his belief that evolutionary change was always gradual. Indeed he adopted the motto of Leibniz: 'the maxim that "nature does not willingly make a jump" (*Natura abhorret saltum*) is specially applicable to economic developments' (Marshall, 1919, p. 6).[5]

The final tribute made here to Marshall's understanding of biology in this chapter of the *Principles* concerns the following passage:

> Adam Smith, while insisting on the general advantages of that minute division of labour and of that subtle industrial organization which were being developed with unexampled rapidity in his time, was yet careful to indicate many points in which the system failed, and many incidental evils which it involved. But many of his followers with less philosophic insight, and in some cases with less real knowledge of the world, argued boldly that whatever is, is right. . . . This doctrine of natural organization contains more truth of the highest importance to humanity than almost any other . . . But its exaggeration worked much harm, especially to those who delighted most in it. For it prevented them from seeing and removing the evil that was intertwined with the good in the changes that were going on around them. It hindered them from inquiring whether many even of the broader features of modern industry might not be transitional. (Marshall, 1949, p. 205)

Clearly, this is a spirited rebuttal of Panglossian interpretations of Smithian industrial evolution. But it is more, as hinted in the last sentence quoted above. In fact it is not only an elliptic critique of the classical stationary state, but also a rebuttal of Spencer's idea that society moves towards a more perfect equilibrium. The equilibrium of the stationary state is questioned by the suggestion of the possibility of potentially disruptive development within a spontaneous social order. Thus while accepting Spencer's account of progress towards greater complexity, Marshall sees the possibility of it leading to disruption rather than integration of the economic system. Marshall goes on to make the important point that

> the doctrine took no account of the manner in which organs are strengthened by being used. Herbert Spencer has insisted with much force on the rule that, if any physical or mental exercise gives pleasure and is therefore frequent, those physical or mental organs which are used in it are likely to grow rapidly. (ibid.)

This is a clear recognition of the significance of a Lamarckian doctrine of evolutionary change, as the reader may confirm by examining the subsequent paragraphs in the *Principles*. Lamarck argued that environmental circumstances lead to the differential use and disuse of organs (Burkhardt, 1977). High levels of use encourage the strengthening and development of the organ, while low levels lead to deterioration and eventual disappearance. Such Lamarckian ideas were adopted by Spencer wholesale, and through him they found their way to Marshall.

Thus on this one cited page of the *Principles* are pieces of Spencer, Lamarck and Hegel, wrapped into one, forming a potential weapon against the classical economists' conception of the stationary state.[6] Similarly, Marshall elsewhere argues that activities may give rise to new wants, just as wants may give rise to new activities.[7] Marshall's instinctive gradualism can be challenged on the basis of an extension of these dynamic arguments, as will become clear in the discussion of Thorstein Veblen later in this work.

Marshall's prescient chapter on industrial organization then skips through the then-fashionable topic of eugenics, and reaches a conclusion. But in subsequent chapters, apart from the occasional organic metaphor, we journey through a static and mechanical world, leaving the dynamic promises of biology long behind.

Promise Unfulfilled

However, with his dynamic, Lamarckian notion of 'development through use', Marshall had unwittingly begun to undermine the mechanistic foundations of his static analysis, and these ideas seemed to play on his mind for the remainder of his life. In one place he emphasizes the distinction between the evolutionary and the mechanistic approach, by reference to qualitative as well as to quantitative change:

> [The] catastrophes of mechanics are caused by changes in the quantity and not in the character of the forces at work: whereas in life their character changes also. 'Progress' or 'evolution', industrial and social, is not mere increase or decrease. It is organic growth, chastened and confined and occasionally reversed by the decay of innumerable factors, each of which influences and is influenced by those around it; and every such mutual influence varies with the stages which the respective factors have already reached in their growth. In this vital respect all sciences of life are akin to one another, and are unlike physical sciences. And therefore in the later stages of economics, when we are approaching nearly to the conditions of life, biological analogies are to be preferred to the mechanical, other things being equal. (Marshall, 1898, pp. 42–3)

By 1902, the implications of this line of argument had been further developed in Marshall's thought. In a letter of that year to John Bates Clark, he expressed further disillusionment with static analysis based on competitive equilibrium. Reflecting on the time around 1870 when he was working out his theory of value, he wrote:

> I then believed it was possible to have a coherent though abstract doctrine of economics in which competition was the only dominant force; and I then defined 'normal' as that which the undisturbed play of competition

would bring about: and I now regard that position as untenable from an abstract as well as from a practical point of view. (Marshall, 1961, vol. 2, p. 67)

In the preface to the eighth edition of the *Principles* Marshall (1949, p. xiii) saw that: 'The main concern of economics is thus with human beings who are impelled, for good and evil, to change and progress. . . . The central idea of economics, even when its Foundations alone are under discussion, must be that of living force and movement.' He saw with increasing clarity the relevance of biological analogies for this project. Yet, as Thomas (1991, p. 11) regretfully concludes: 'Economic biology remained promise rather than substance.'

Marshall bestows great gifts with his rigour, but tantalizes us with his intellectual honesty to the extent that, while in reality enriched, we feel all the poorer for want of explanation, almost as if it were better that we had remained in ignorance.

Marshall repeated his qualified sentence on 'the Mecca of the economist' in every preface to the *Principles* from the fifth edition on. However, as Thomas (1991) and Whitaker (1990) show, he delayed and procrastinated over the planned volume on economic dynamics. In effect, Marshall's statements in the prefaces and the chapter on industrial organization were together a farewell to the biological analogy for mainstream economic science, for most of his followers did not share his reservations concerning mechanical modelling, or his concern still to turn to the Mecca for occasional inspiration and guidance.

Ironically, far from instigating an interdisciplinary research programme on economic dynamics, Marshall's insights from biology were subsequently ignored. As Nicolai Foss (1991) and Neil Niman (1991, p. 32) point out, later Marshallians neglected the biological aspects of Marshall's thinking, and abandoned any attempt to recast economics along biological or evolutionary lines. Thus, for instance, Marshall's influential follower Pigou (1922) turned instead to physics for inspiration, and in his hands the representative firm became the firm in mechanical equilibrium (Pigou, 1928). Furthermore, as Scott Moss (1984) shows, equilibrium concepts were developed that were no longer consistent with non-homogeneous economic agents. The ease with which biology was later purged from the Marshallian system, to be replaced by a fortified metaphor from mechanics, suggests the highly limited degree to which truly Darwinian evolutionary ideas had been originally implanted by Marshall in his *Principles*.

By the time of Marshall's death in 1924, the dialogue between economics and biology had virtually ceased. It lived on in the United States, but only with the periodic recitation of Thorstein Veblen's contribution by a minority of economists. Despite the theoretical revolution of John Maynard Keynes, the metaphor of economics remained mechanistic, and the subject became even more formalistic in method.

In his famous article on Marshall on the centenary of his birth, Shove (1942, p. 323) noted 'a return to the mechanical as against the biological approach' in mainstream economics. Despite its Marshallian pedigree, the theory of the firm in the postwar microeconomic textbooks showed little trace of biology (Gee, 1983; Newman, 1960). Partly as a result of these developments, interdisciplinary work became less fashionable. Biology no longer claimed much intercourse with economics, and the evocation of biology by economists was left to a small number of mavericks. As noted elsewhere in this work, it was not until the 1950s that orthodoxy rediscovered the evolutionary analogy, but then only in an inferior, half-hearted and equilibrium orientated form.

Accordingly, biology was virtually excluded from economics from the late 1920s until the middle of the century. Yet it is ironic that 1926 to1939 were 'the years of high theory' (Shackle, 1967). This may suggest that the Keynesian revolution involved an ejection of biological thinking. More plausibly, the Keynesian aspects of that revolution were limited and, rather than by Keynes, the revolution was won by a mathematical formalism emulating physics. Hence it was mainly this 'formalistic revolution' and the construction of the neoclassical synthesis by Paul Samuelson, Sir John Hicks and others that banished biological thinking to the fringes of economic science.[8]

With current developments in evolutionary economics, at last it may be possible to bring Marshall's Mecca into sight. But such a journey can be completed only if the historical context of past efforts in evolutionary economic thinking are scrutinized and modifications made where necessary. We help prepare for future theoretical development partly by reducing our ignorance of the past.

8

Carl Menger and
the Evolution of Money

Carl Menger was born in 1840, two years before Marshall. However, Marshall has been considered in the preceding chapter, and immediately after Spencer, because of the importance of the connection between the two British theorists. Furthermore, there are interesting points of comparison between Menger and Veblen, and the latter theorist will be considered in the succeeding chapter.

The principal reason for the inclusion of a discussion of Menger here is his 'evolutionary' theory of the origin of money. This exemplifies a more general utilization by the Austrian School of economists of an 'evolutionary' metaphor, as applied to the analysis of the emergence of social institutions. The Austrian School's adoption of such evolutionary ideas is discussed elsewhere in the present work, particularly in relation to the work of Friedrich Hayek. Accordingly, there are aspects of Menger's life and work which are not addressed here, such as his important controversy with the German Historical School. The focus on Menger's view of the evolution of money does highlight several questions and issues, some of which appear again later in the discussion of Hayek.

Money as an 'Organic' Institution

Menger (1892, 1963, 1981) viewed money as a paradigmatic 'organic' social institution, alongside language or common law. By 'organic' he did not mean natural or biological, or even the quality of being structurally interconnected with the environment. For Menger, an 'organic' social institution is one which, although the product of human action, is not the product of human design.

In particular, money is seen to arise out of the combination and interaction of individual decisions, although no one may have intended the outcome. Accordingly, this view differs from the 'state theory of money' or 'monetary nominalism' of the institutionalist Georg Knapp (1924), which has roots in the works of Aristotle and has been endorsed by some monetarists.[1] In opposition to the latter viewpoint, for Menger and the Austrian School the emergence and continuance of a monetary system of exchange does not necessarily require the legislation and backing of the state.

Menger, in *Problems of Economics and Sociology* of 1883, accepts that 'history actually offers us examples that certain wares have been declared money by law' (see Menger, 1963, p. 153). But these declarations are often seen to be 'the acknowledgement of an item which had already become money'. Although cases of the emergence of money by agreement or legislation are important, Menger argues that: 'the origin of money can truly be brought to our full understanding only by our learning to understand the *social* institution discussed here as the unintended result, as the unplanned outcome of specifically *individual* efforts of members of society' (ibid., p. 155). An account of the supposed evolutionary process through which money could emerge is found in his 1871 *Principles of Economics*:

> As *each* economizing individual becomes increasingly more aware of his economic interest, he is led by this *interest, without any agreement, without legislative compulsion*, and *even without regard to the public interest*, to give his commodities in exchange for other, more saleable, commodities, even if he does not need them for any immediate consumption purpose. With economic progress, therefore, we can everywhere observe the phenomenon of a certain number of goods, especially those that are most easily saleable at a given time and place, becoming, under the influence of *custom*, acceptable to everyone in trade, and thus capable of being given in exchange for any other commodity. (Menger, 1981, p. 260, emphasis in the original)

Clearly a trader may hold a stock of a commodity for reasons other than the purpose of direct personal consumption. In this case, and in a market economy, the commodity may be held with a view to future trade. However, for various reasons discussed by Menger (1892, pp. 246–7), commodities will differ in their saleability. Some commodities will be widely accepted in exchange, others less so. A commodity that is seen to be accepted in exchange will have its saleability enhanced as individuals act on the basis of such a perception.

Hence the process begins on the basis of subjective evaluations, and becomes progressively reinforced through action and the perception of this action by other individuals. Furthermore, as Menger suggests in *Problems*, specific commodities may become more acceptable in exchange through the establishment or influence of custom:

> nothing may have favored the genesis of money as much as the receiving of eminently marketable goods for all other goods, which had been practiced for quite a long time on the part of the most perspicacious and ablest economic subjects for their own economic advantage. Thus practice and custom have certainly contributed not a little to making the temporarily most marketable wares the ones which are received in exchange

for their wares not only by many economic individuals, but ultimately by all. (Menger, 1963, p. 155)

Money thus emerges as a result of some kind of evolutionary pro-cess. Apart from the attribute of being 'most marketable', which is a culmination and consequence of individual perceptions and choices, Menger suggests that the good that emerges as money may be 'the most easily transported, the most durable, the most easily divisible' (1963, p. 154). Consequently, over time, a single commodity or group of commodities will emerge as money.[2]

Evolution and the Invisible Hand

As Gerald O'Driscoll and Mario Rizzo (1985, p. 192) remark, Menger's theory of money 'is reminiscent of Adam Smith's invisible hand rea-soning'. Indeed, there is a direct lineage in the approach to evolution-ary theory from Smith through to the Austrian School. In the discussion of Smithian evolutionary theory in a preceding chapter it was noted that it had a number of features, including first, an emphasis on the spontaneous and unintended emergence of a social order, an 'invisible hand'; second, a process of evolution which normally reaches a har-monious steady state, rather than being continuously disrupted and undermined; and third, a disposition towards a non-interventionist policy based on the belief that such complex evolutionary processes cannot be readily out-designed, or easily improved upon.

Menger goes further than Smith, however, in examining this pro-cess in more detail. For example, he shows how the initial emergence of a convention or social institution such as money may be largely accidental. Subsequent to its tentative emergence in a given locality, it becomes better established through a process of continuous feedback. The initial and local emergence of a convention is thus progressively reinforced by the positive feedback of perceptions and actions in ac-cord with the convention.

Clearly, money is 'selected' here, in a sense. But it would be wrong to conclude that it is analogous to natural selection. What is 'selected' is the convention, or potential monetary unit, itself. However, as argued below, this is not the selection of what is analogous to the 'genetic' elements driving the system.

Interestingly, Menger uses the very term 'genetic' in his argument, asserting that every economic theory 'has primarily the task of teach-ing us to understand the concrete phenomena of the real world as exemplifications of a certain regularity in the succession of phenom-ena, i.e. genetically. . . . *This genetic element is inseparable from the idea of theoretical science*' (1963, p. 94, emphasis in the original).

Of course, Menger did not use the term 'genetic' with the modern, biological meaning. He was writing well before a Mendelian definition of the gene had been proposed by the Danish biologist Wilhelm Johannsen in 1909, and before it had become widely accepted in its modern biological sense.[3] Menger seems to use the term 'genetic' in the sense of regular and durable causal connection at the basic and elemental level. A 'genetic' explanation thus involves tracing out detailed causal connections, rather than, for instance, constructing the conditions for equilibrium.[4]

Nevertheless, although the convention or monetary unit has durable qualities, there are still further reasons why its 'genetic' composition is not at all like the gene in modern biology. Such a unit survives not because its genetically programmed qualities are well adapted in a given environmental context. The monetary unit is wanted because it is wanted; the convention is followed because it is followed. Such reciprocating causation means that cause becomes effect just as effect becomes cause.[5]

The Mengerian evolutionary process is Smithian in character, in that it posits the end state at which a given type of money (Menger) or the social order (Smith) has become widely accepted, established and thereby stabilized. For both Darwin and Lamarck, however, there was no such end-point to an evolutionary process. The Mengerian evolution of money certainly looks like ontogeny rather than phylogeny.

Clearly, the object of evolutionary analysis is an emerging monetary unit and the focus is on the cumulative reinforcement of a given unit. The 'genetic material' is the individuals with their given preferences and goals. Importantly, this 'genetic material' does not change during the emergence of money. There is not necessarily even a process of evolutionary selection between rival monetary units, nor is there a consideration of the changes in individual goals or preferences. The medium of exchange is 'selected', but through cumulative reinforcement, and not necessarily through the sifting and winnowing of competing alternatives. It involves the 'selection' of a path of ontogenetic development, as a plant responds to external stimuli by growing one way rather than another. It is not the full 'natural selection' observed in phylogeny. Indeed, we are confined to ontogeny.[6]

Path Dependency

Robert Jones's (1976) analysis of the Mengerian model raises some important issues. Jones suggests that 'a very common good would emerge as a first commodity money' (p. 775). Consequently, commonness or salience is more important than physical characteristics. However, local salience may vary from market to market. For this reason, and because of the existence of 'transaction costs', a single money commodity may not emerge. Indeed 'there may be several stable equilibrium levels of monetization of trade. Even for a single given distribution of ultimate exchanges, direct barter, full monetization, and intermediate mixes may all be locally stable situations' (p. 773).

Given that there is not a single, determinate equilibrium outcome, the evolution of the monetary unit is a case of path dependency. Under certain plausible assumptions, not only is a mix of money and barter possible, but also mixes of different monetary units. Indeed, the selection process may also depend on a combination of accidents or initial perceptions. As long as the commodity is reasonably durable and not too cumbersome then it can serve as a medium of exchange. In this case the initial 'accidents' leading to the emergence of one rather than another commodity determine whether money is to be coins, cows or cowrie shells. This path dependency undermines the sanctity of any *de facto* evolutionary outcome.[7]

This undermines Menger's belief that the evolutionary selection process tends to favour and replicate the outcomes of actions 'of the most perspicacious and ablest economic subjects' (1963, p. 155). With strong path-dependency, the initial salience of an inferior outcome may lead to a result in which the outcomes of actions of *less* perspicacious and *less* able agents are favoured. This is one of the many cases where evolutionary outcomes are not necessarily the most efficient in such respects.

The 'Legal Restrictions' Debate

The debate over whether it is possible to remove the state largely or entirely from involvement in the monetary system has simmered on in recent years, with most contributions favouring various proposals for the 'denationalization' of money.[8]

However, attempts to point to historical precedents for such a system of 'free banking' in modern times, particularly in Scotland up to 1848 and in New York State from 1836 to 1863, are not entirely convincing (Checkland, 1975; King, 1983; White, 1984a). In the Scottish case only note issue, not coinage, was unregulated. The notes were denominated in pounds sterling and thus had the backing of the English state across the border. In the New York case private bank notes had to be denominated in dollars, and dollars in turn were backed by a gold standard. The New York State authority printed and registered the notes, and the banks were required to hold specie reserves against circulating notes. The failure of the 'free banking' theorists to point to a convincing precedent raises serious questions about the viability of their proposal.

In his attempt to show that 'legal restriction' is not necessary for the emergence of an accepted medium of exchange, Karl Wärneryd (1989, 1990) shows that the selection of money does not depend on the characteristics or efficiency of the commodity in question. Indeed, a type of unit that bears a higher rate of interest may not be selected. Wärneryd shows that the evolutionary selection of money has attributes of the kind of 'coordination game' discussed by Edna Ullmann-Margalit (1977). Once a unit begins to emerge, it establishes a 'convention' with strong 'network externalities'. Like other such conventions, such as language, or driving on the same side of the road, the network externality effect is that we are impelled to use or do something because it is used or done by others.

However, while Wärneryd supports the proposition that state intervention is not necessary for emergence of money, we are entitled to draw the conclusion from his analysis that the legal establishment of money by the state may sometimes be necessary to establish a more satisfactory outcome, or to maintain a given outcome in the face of disturbance or threat. State activity is not necessarily the best way of doing this, but at least such eventualities and their potential solutions should be considered.

The Problem of Quality Variation

In Menger's theory, the emerging monetary unit is homogeneous and invariant. Although not all persons may recognize (say) gold as the emerging monetary substance, Menger assumes that they all know 24 carat gold when they see it. But even gold can be melted down and alloyed with inferior metals. As in modern biology, there is no single, pure, typological item. In contrast, Menger's analysis is a case of 'typological thinking'. There is a preexisting variety in the set of commodity types. But within each type the possibility of quality variation is not considered.

As noted elsewhere in this work, such 'typological essentialism' is an essentially Platonic idea in which entities are regarded as identifiable in terms of a few distinct characteristics which represent their essential qualities. This differs from the notion identified by Ernst Mayr of 'population thinking' in which variety and diversity are all-important. In typological thinking, species are regarded as identifiable in terms of a few distinct characteristics which represent their essence. Accordingly, all variations around the ideal type are regarded as accidental aberrations. By contrast, in population thinking, species are described in terms of a distribution of characteristics. Whereas in typological thinking variation is a classificatory annoyance, in Darwinian evolution the idea of variation encapsulated in population thinking is of paramount interest because it is upon variety that selection operates.

With potential quality variation, the purity and value of the emerging monetary unit may be in doubt. Some actors may notice the high frequency of the trade in a particular commodity, but in contrast to their associates, regard the commodity in question as unreliable and thereby avoid it as a medium of exchange. Such information problems, arising from potential quality variation, could subvert the evolution of the monetary unit. Despite the noted emphasis of the Austrian School on subjectivity and divergences of perceptions, this problem of information and knowledge is ignored in Menger's theory.

In at least one passage, Menger raises the question of potential quality variation. But he immediately dismisses the problem, saying that money is likely to take the form of precious metals, and these are 'easily controlled as to their quality and weight' (Menger, 1892, p. 255).

It is not suggested that Menger generally ignores problems of information and uncertainty; it is well established that he was one of the first major economists to give them precedence. However, the particular problem of quality variation is sidestepped by his implicit assumption that the emerging monetary substance is invariant, and recognizable by all agents. Despite the obvious problem of the debasement of coinage, the implications in terms of the Mengerian story of the emergence of money have not been fully explored.[9]

In general, it is normally assumed by economists that each commodity is homogeneous and well defined. One nineteenth-century exception is found in the work *On the Economy of Machinery and Manufactures* by Charles Babbage. Pointing to a widespread problem of potential adulteration and debasement of commodities, Babbage (1846, p. 134) argues that while in 'some cases the goodness of an article is evident on mere inspection,' in others, like tea and flour, the commodity can be easily adulterated without ready detection.[10]

Furthermore, 'the difficulty and expense of verification are, in some instances, so great as to justify the deviation from well-established principles.' Babbage thus suggests that it is necessary for the government to step in, 'to verify each sack of purchased flour, and to employ persons in devising methods of detecting the new modes of adulteration which might be continually resorted to' (p. 135). In recognizing the possibility of adulteration and debasement, Babbage has put his finger on a possible reason for state intervention.[11] Such problems of quality variation and verification are neglected in Menger's theory of money.

Babbage's argument resembles the later and famous paper by George Akerlof (1970) in which he identifies the problem of information asymmetry in the exchange commodities of uncertain quality. Akerlof implies that the solution to this problem is some system of guarantees or 'quality arbitrage'. There is a related discussion of 'brand name capital' in the free banking literature. The argument is that there is some quality check through the market valuation of competing reputations.

But, to each single observer, 'reputation' is even more elusive, in quality terms, than the carat value of gold. While it is possible that well-functioning markets may help to evaluate the soundness and reputation of financial institutions, it is not convincingly demonstrated that this mechanism is generally reliable, or how the persistent and serious information problems can be overcome. There are cases of self-regulation by banks, but against this there are many cases of fraud and deception being uncovered by state authority. Without such central regulation, the problems of quality variation seem to be even further compounded.

Even if self-regulation is regarded as generally viable, cases where it has worked depend on the initiative of a small number of strong, oligopolistic banking institutions, rather than a more competitive market. This seems to undermine the argument that money will emerge and become trusted and accepted without some such strong institutional verification. The issue is not clear-cut, but it is difficult to see how the reputation of quality-ensuring authorities could be sustained without some overarching regulatory authority: either the state or a group of strong private institutions.

Philip Mirowski (1990b, 1991) makes a relevant and related point when he argues that money is 'a socially constructed institution'. However, 'precisely because it is socially instituted, its invariance cannot be predicated on any "natural" ground, and must continually be shored up and reconstituted by further social institutions, such as accountants and banks and governments' (1990b, p. 712). In other words, the 'value' of money is continually under threat from many devices and stratagems, from coin-clipping to the modern expansion of debt.

In sum, with the emergence of a monetary unit when perceived potential quality variation is a problem, a kind of Gresham's Law[12] may be in operation, when the evolution of any 'good' universal equivalent is continually undermined by the perceived problem of the 'bad'. Given this informational and cognitive problem, the emergence of a monetary unit may be much assisted by strong institutions committed to policing its quality and protecting it from debasement. The further legitimation of a given monetary unit by the state, and its endowment with symbolic significance and grandeur, is also advantageous in facilitating its emergence and stability.

While each individual trader has an incentive to trade in the inferior and debased unit, only large institutions, encompassing the common interest in a sound currency, have an incentive to maintain its value and deter forgery and debasement. Clearly the state is a strong candidate to take on this role.

Of course, the disadvantage in the modern era of paper money is that governments may be tempted to print more cash and allow banks to over-expand their credit. This is a problem of which we are often reminded, and one which motivates the proponents of the 'denationalization' of money. It may or may not be possible to devise institutional safeguards. If it is not, then the state may generally devalue the currency by fuelling inflation, despite validating the monetary equivalent in individual transactions.

However, debasement by inflation is not the same phenomenon as debasement by (say) forgery or coin-clipping. The state can still act to guarantee the equivalence of every single unit of money while acting to undermine its general and common value. Forgery introduces a bad unit alongside the good, while inflation simultaneously undermines the general exchange value of all monetary units. Forgery or debasement create a problem for current exchanges, even if their sustained effects may also be inflationary. Inflation primarily affects the holding of money, intertemporal choices, and long-term contracts. These are different problems, and the state may play a role which is less positive in one rather than the other. The case for a monetary system based on the state must consider both the merits and demerits, and not assume that the state plays an unambiguously negative (or wholly positive) role.

Furthermore, the point being made here is that the Mengerian story of the supposedly spontaneous emergence of money is faulty, and strong encompassing institutions such as the state or central banks are essential to the creation and survival of a viable monetary unit, even if the state (or central bank) may bring associated problems.

Money, Law and Language: Some Key Differences

It is argued above that with potential quality variation individual agents have an obvious incentive to use a less costly or poor quality version of the medium of exchange in preferment to the good. Similar incentives to debase social norms exist in the case of many laws. Laws restricting behaviour, and where there are perceived advantages to transgression, are the ones that require the most policing. Hence people frequently evade tax payments or break speed limits. Without some policing activity the law itself is likely to be debased or 'brought into disrepute'.

In the case of a few other laws, however, people have a direct incentive to conform. For example, there are obvious incentives to drive on the same side of the road as others and to stop at traffic lights. Although infringements will occur, these laws are largely self-policing.

Language also can be self-regulating, because individuals have an incentive to make their words clear. Although meaning – the signified – may be ambiguous, the coding itself – the signifier – must be unmistakable. In communication we are impelled to use words and sounds in a way that conforms as closely as possible to the perceived norm. Language is another example of a convention or standard which exhibits 'lock-in' (Arthur, 1988, 1989, 1990) due to the fact that once it becomes widely used then others have an incentive to do the same. In a similar manner, there are technological conventions, from railway gauges to computer software, which reproduce themselves because of 'network externalities' (Katz and Shapiro, 1985, 1986) and widespread use.

With language, our inbuilt drives to imitate are used to the full, and we have no incentive to bar their operation. Although languages do change through time, there are incentives to conform to and thus reinforce the linguistic norms in the given region or context. Linguistic norms are thus almost wholly self-policing, unlike currency values and most laws.[13] The argument for the intervention of the state is thus much stronger in the case of law and money than in the case of language.[14]

Notably, the argument about potential quality variation applies to most exchangeables, as well as to money. Babbage's argument applied to all commodities where quality variation may exist and is not immediately and fully discernible by the purchaser. He suggests that the state has an important role in establishing and policing standards, using the means of regular inspection and even direct intervention in production. Accordingly, if the state is to regulate production and trade in this way, then it must act as a taxonomist, establishing definitions of each type of commodity so that particular rules in each case may apply. This is another important reason, to add to others I have discussed elsewhere (Hodgson, 1988, pp. 172–94), why modern markets are not aggregates of atomistic traders but institutions in their own right. Such an institution, furthermore, is necessarily supported by networks of other institutions, including the state.

Menger and Institutional Economics

As Andrew Schotter (1981, p. 5) and others have recognized, there is a strong similarity between Menger's account of the emergence of money and social institutions and elements of the burgeoning 'new institutional economics', such as his own game-theoretic analysis of the emergence of conventions and rules. Notably, however, Schotter (1990) explicitly draws the conclusion that some form of state intervention in such processes may often be desirable.

There are also similarities between Menger's account of the emergence of institutions and that of the 'old' institutionalists such as Thorstein Veblen, John Commons and Wesley Clair Mitchell, despite the fact that Veblen depicts Menger as an adversary.[15] There are, nevertheless, important theoretical differences, in addition to the differences of policy which are not our prime concern here.

First, an institutionalist account of the factors involved in the emergence of a monetary economy, such as those sketched by Mitchell (1937, pp. 175–6, 305–6), suggests that this event cannot be explained simply because it reduced costs or made life easier for traders. The penetration of money exchange into social life altered the very configurations of rationality, involving the particular conceptions of abstraction, measurement, quantification and calculative intent. It was thus a transformation of individuals rather than simply the emergence of institutions and rules.

Second, Menger sees the process of evolution he describes as reaching an end state in which the monetary unit is established. In contrast, because the 'old' institutionalists such as Veblen (1919) see evolution as an unending process, their focus is not simply on the emergence of, for instance, custom and habit as a by-product and fixed part of the causal chain; in the Veblenian process of cumulative causation, habits and institutions are both causes and effects, in a sequence of reciprocity.

In fact, there are problems with both the start and the end-point of the Mengerian evolutionary sequence. Here Alexander Field's (1979, 1981, 1984) discussion and critique of elements of some of the new institutional economics is relevant. He points out that to examine the evolution of a given structure from a given starting point, the rules and structural characteristics at that origin have to be assumed.

Thus Schotter's game-theoretic and Mengerian study of the emergence of institutions assumes the 'rules of the game' at the outset, without considering their emergence. Likewise, to take Field's prime example, the theory of the rise of capitalism proposed by Douglass North and Robert Thomas (1973) must assume given structures and rules to account for the very institutions it purports to explain. And as noted above, markets are themselves social institutions, and by implication these too have to be explained. In sum, we can never reach a primary, institution-free state from which explanation in the 'new institutionalist' vein can begin. There is thus an intractable problem of infinite regress.

Arguably, a Veblenian theory also must take a starting point, even if the end-point or 'consummation' is not assumed. However, the difference with the Mengerian evolutionary conception would be that the starting point would not be regarded as an institution-free 'state of nature'.

It is interesting to note that, in fact, Menger initially developed his theory by observing the prices of goods. He noted that some goods do not have a unique price, but different buying and selling prices. These differences are possible because of transaction costs. In contrast, money, being the most liquid commodity, has a unique price. However, this argument assumes the existence not only of markets and their associated institutions and rules, but also of the prices of commodities.

Conclusion

In conclusion, therefore, Menger's evolutionary explanation of the emergence of money and similar institutions is important and valuable. However, it does not provide us with a complete evolutionary perspective of a phylogenetic kind, nor explain all the things that have to be explained. It would be mistaken, therefore, to use it as an exclusive guide to monetary theory and policy.

The main problem with Menger's theory is that, given potential quality variation, the spontaneous process of evolution of the monetary unit may break down, possibly requiring the intervention of the state or central bank to maintain the currency unit. In sum, there are good reasons to assume that money will be – to use Menger's terminology – a 'pragmatic' rather than a purely 'organic' institution.

PART III
Evolution in Economics? Three Twentieth-Century Theorists

No science has been criticized by its own servants as openly and constantly as economics. The motives of dissatisfaction are many, but the most important pertains to *homo oeconomicus*. The complaint is that this fiction strips man's behavior of every cultural propensity, which is tantamount to saying that in his economic life man acts mechanically.

Nicholas Georgescu-Roegen, *The Entropy Law and the Economic Process*

9

Thorstein Veblen and Post-Darwinian Economics

In a famous article originally published in 1898, Thorstein Veblen (1919, p. 56) asked: 'Why is economics not an evolutionary science?' The term 'evolutionary' was subsequently adopted by institutional economists, but often in broad or developmentalist terms, and with only slight attention to the more precise mechanisms of natural selection as developed in biology. Veblen's knowledge of biological science was remarkably up-to-date, yet evolutionary theory has developed enormously since his death, leaving many of his institutionalist followers well behind. Veblen made a direct appeal to biological science for inspiration; but subsequently, and until very recently, this example has rarely been replicated. Accordingly there has been remarkably little detailed exploration, informed by biology, of what Veblen precisely meant by an 'evolutionary' science, and of the character of the 'post-Darwinian' economics that he attempted to build.[1]

Like Alfred Marshall, Thorstein Veblen saw that the appropriate metaphor for economics was to be found in biology. In particular, Veblen saw the evolutionary metaphor as crucial to the understanding of the processes of technological development in a capitalist economy. But unlike his English colleague, he did not care to develop a static, equilibrium analysis as a prelude to the dynamic. He characterized his own economics as post-Darwinian, and argued that economics should embrace the metaphor of evolution and change, rather than the static ideas of equilibrium that had been borrowed by the neoclassical economists from physics.

However, after rebutting a mechanical prelude to economic dynamics, Veblen was faced with a biology at a stage of development at which the mechanisms of evolution were only partly understood. Consequently, and given his own personal aversion to intellectual 'symmetry and system-making' (Veblen, 1919, p. 68), there was little chance that Veblen would be able to build an economic theory on the Marshallian scale.

Instead, he leaves us with plentiful hints and insights, many brilliant, several contradictory. He writes in a style which is often dazzling and illuminating, but also sometimes evasive or unclear. Partly for the latter reason, and partly because he did not provide us with a systematic theoretical legacy, his significance for evolutionary economics in particular, and economics in general, still remains underestimated to this day.

Importantly, Veblen had a keen and perceptive understanding of the relationships and connections between the social and the physical sciences. In this chapter it will be shown that Veblen had two primary reasons for the adoption of a Darwinian and evolutionary metaphor. One relates to the idea of cumulative causation and an opposition to depictions of the economic process that are consummated in equilibrium. The other is based on the formation of analogies to both the gene and the processes of natural selection in the social world.

As noted in chapter 3, Darwinian natural selection involves several component principles. First, there must be sustained variation among the members of a species or population. Without such variation, natural selection cannot operate. Second, there must be some principle of heredity or continuity, through which offspring resemble their parents more than they resemble other members of their species, due to some mechanism by which individual characteristics are passed on from one generation to the next. Third, natural selection operates either because better-adapted organisms leave increased numbers of offspring, or because the genotypes that are preserved bestow advantage in struggling to survive. The latter is the principle of the struggle for existence. The application of the metaphor of natural selection to economics should be on the basis of analogous principles. It is argued here that Veblen was relatively successful in this regard.

The Early Influence of Evolutionary Ideas

As a student at Yale University, Veblen came under the influence of William Graham Sumner, the Social Darwinist (Dorfman, 1934, pp. 43–6; Riesman, 1963, p. 19). In addition, Veblen read widely, including biology, psychology and philosophy, as well as the social sciences. Significantly, the second article that Veblen published, in 1892, was on Herbert Spencer, and was 'offered in the spirit of the disciple' (Veblen, 1919, p. 387). As a result of these important influences, Veblen became immersed in evolutionary theory, and clear, enduring traces of both Darwin and Spencer can be found in his thought.[2]

Veblen's awareness of developments in evolutionary biology was sufficiently up to date for him to refer to principles of Mendelian genetics in his work (Veblen, 1914, pp. 21–5; 1915, pp. 277–8; 1919, pp. 457–73). This was only shortly after they were beginning to be accepted by some biologists as a possible explanation of variation and heredity in evolutionary theory, and decades before the flowering of the neo-Darwinian hybrid formed by growing Mendelian genetics on a Darwinian stem.[3] He was also acquainted with the mutation theory of Hugo de Vries (Veblen, 1919, pp. 462–7).

It appears that under the sway of these thinkers, as well as leading pragmatist philosophers such as Charles Sanders Peirce and William James, Veblen attempted to develop a theory of socioeconomic evolution. Presuming that human behaviour is dominated by habits of thought, Veblen enquired as to the causes of these habits. Being influenced by the instinct theory in Spencer's *Principles of Psychology* (1855), as well as the later *Introduction to Social Psychology* by William McDougall (1908), Veblen took the view that habits were partly rooted in such instincts. As in Spencer's work, they were seen to represent evolutionary adaptations to changing environmental conditions. However, Veblen identified instincts of both a progressive and regressive kind, and stressed the conflict between them in the modern world.

Instincts and Institutions

From the concept of habits of thought, it was a short step for Veblen to a definition of institutions. According to him, institutions are 'settled habits of thought common to the generality of men' (Veblen, 1919, p. 239). In other words, they are seen as an outgrowth of the routinized thought processes that are shared by a number of persons in a given society.[4]

Crucially, the presumed nature and origin of the different features of instincts and habits in Veblen's work is unclear. In many places he seems to regard their diversity as having racial origins. In others he hints at a sophisticated idea of a conflict between dissimilar institutional developments, each one locked in to separate tracks. But, as we have noted, this lack of sufficient explanation, alongside brilliant insight, is one of the frustrating and characteristic features of Veblen's writing.

As Donald Walker (1977) contends, Veblen's account of the relationship between instincts, habits of thought and social institutions is not entirely coherent. In response, Malcolm Rutherford argues that Veblen started from a genetic research programme with reductive aspects:

> He attempted to follow a causal chain from a pre-institutional state of affairs to the America of the twentieth century, and to do so he required some non-institutional, exogenously determined human drives with which to start the analysis. However, given the rejection of orthodox psychologism, he also had to argue that these instinctive drives could easily be overturned or contaminated in the course of institutional development. (Rutherford, 1984, p. 333)

Veblen may have originally entertained a reductionist position in which explanations of human behaviour can be reduced to instinctive drives. However, he quickly moved away from it when he realized that institutions could be seen as not only being formed by, but formative of, such elements.

This development and change in his thought accounts for some of its contradictory aspects. Veblen often repeats that habits of thought are moulded or even inculcated by culture, practice or technology. For example: 'What the discipline of the machine industry inculcates . . . in the habits of life and thought of the workman, is regularity of sequence and mechanical precision' (1904, p. 309). More generally: 'A habitual line of action constitutes a habitual line of thought, and gives the point of view from which facts and events are apprehended and reduced to a body of knowledge' (1934, p. 88). Thus, for Veblen, habits of thought are founded not simply on the instincts but on human culture and habitual action.

Furthermore, in at least one place, and especially in his later works, Veblen (1914, pp. 2, 7) made it clear that instincts are not purely biological. Indeed, not only were instincts seen to give rise to habits of thought but they were sometimes described as being formed by them. Instinct is thereby 'a matter of tradition out of the past, a legacy of habits of thought accumulated through the experience of past generations.' It 'falls into conventional lines, acquires the consistency of custom and prescription, and so takes on an institutional character and force' (ibid., p. 7).

Notwithstanding this, and as Charles Leathers (1990, p. 166) notes, Veblen still failed to explain how instincts 'became and remain heredity elements of human nature'. Although Darwin, Spencer and Sumner put Veblen on this path, his 'use of instinct theory declined markedly in his later work, and for most of his positive theory of institutions and institutional change his instinct theory has only minor significance' (Rutherford, 1984, p. 313).

Nevertheless, the incomplete move against biological or genetic reductionism in Veblen's work is of enormous importance. It distinguishes him from the prevailing biologism of the late nineteenth century as well as from the ubiquitous evolutionary theory of Herbert Spencer. Veblen (1899, p. 188) clearly saw institutions as well as individuals as units of evolutionary selection. With modern hindsight, this suggests the notion that the information transmitted through learning or imitation to institutions or individuals was analogous, but different from, the transmission of genetic information in the process of biological evolution. Consequently, institutions are both replicators and the units of selection in socioeconomic evolution. In any case, Veblen's adoption of institutions as units of selection clearly demarcates his theory from that of Spencer.

Veblen and Spencer

Veblen noted several criticisms of Spencer's theory in his works.[5] Other objections, like the final point in the last paragraph, were implicit. While Spencer anticipated a capitalist system in which peaceful industrial activity excluded militarism and war, Veblen, in contrast, regarded the pecuniary activities of the 'absentee owners', or shareholders, as essentially dysfunctional and predatory in character. For Veblen, as for Marx, capitalism would always have inner conflicts and imperfections. Accordingly, Veblen argued, first, that Spencer's typology of social systems was not exhaustive and that the missing option of socialism provided an escape from its false alternatives (Veblen, 1919, pp. 402–5).

Second, Veblen had a much more adequate explanation of the sources of creativity and variety in socioeconomic evolution. In some passages Veblen relied on biological mutation. In these instances he shared Spencer's biological reductionism but his theory contrasted with that of Spencer by incorporating the ideas of Johann Gregor Mendel. Elsewhere, Veblen (1914, pp. 86–9) devised the concept of 'idle curiosity' and this can serve as a genesis for diversity and variation. He suggested that the human tendency towards experimentation and creative innovation could generate novelty in an ongoing manner.[6] This could lead to new and improved ways of thinking and doing, and consequently the generation of the greater variety upon which evolutionary selection would operate. For Veblen, 'idle curiosity' is a major source of technological change. In other passages the principle of cumulative causation was itself relied on to explain cumulative divergence, potential instability and novelty.

Third, as in his criticisms of Marx, Veblen rejected the notion of the perfectibility of society. Being more a Darwinian than Spencer, Veblen inclined to the Malthusian critique of the notion that society could be perfected or human happiness could be optimized. As Robert Young (1969, p. 137) argues, Spencer's belief in progress and perfectibility was more reminiscent of the very utopians such as Godwin and Condorcet that Malthus had chosen to attack, rather than of Malthus himself. Spencer's evolutionary theory was fundamentally anti-Malthusian, at least in this respect. Although Veblen had socialist leanings, he argued against the idea of finality or consummation in economic development. Variety and cumulative causation mean that history has 'no final term' (Veblen, 1919, p. 37). In Marxism 'the final term was socialism or the classless society. Veblen rejected the teleological concept of a final goal as pre-Darwinian' (Hill, 1958, p. 138).

As discussed in chapter 4, Malthus saw diversity as both initial to change and renewed through time, and hinted at a process of selection that was to inspire Darwin. Like Lamarck, Spencer saw the source of variety in the adaptation of individuals to their environment (Burkhardt, 1977). Organisms adjust continuously as if attempting to reach harmony with their surroundings. For Lamarck and Spencer, the environment was the key agent of change. It was for Darwin too, but for him 'variation was present first, and the ordering activity of the environment ("natural selection") followed afterwards' (Mayr, 1982, p. 354). For Darwin, change resulted from a combination of variation and environmental selection. It was this insight – which Darwin had taken and modified from Malthus – that Veblen followed. Hence the fourth major difference is that Veblen and Spencer had different conceptions of the place and function of variety in the evolutionary process. Lamarck and Spencer saw the pressure of adaptation by individual organisms to their environment as the main source of variety and change. In contrast, for Darwin and Veblen, change also resulted from selection upon preexisting variety in a population.

Fifth, Veblen (1919, pp. 148–230) rejected Spencer's rationalistic and hedonistic psychology:

> Spencer is both evolutionist and hedonist, but it is only by recourse to other factors, alien to the rational hedonistic scheme, such as habit, delusions, use and disuse, sporadic variation, environmental forces, that he is able to achieve anything in the way of genetic science, since it is only by this recourse that he is enabled to enter the field of cumulative change within which the modern post-Darwinian sciences live and move and have their being. (p. 192n)

Accordingly, there is a considerable divergence between the ideas of Veblen and Spencer.

Veblen, Darwinism and Cumulative Change

The significance of the last quotation given above needs to be elaborated, for it contains a key to Veblen's adoption of a 'post-Darwinian' approach.[7] Veblen argues that pre-Darwinian science was 'taxonomic', and centred on the notion of natural laws which

> formulated the immutable relations in which things 'naturally' stood to one another before causal disturbance took place between them, the orderly unfolding of the complement of causes involved in the transition over this interval of transient activity, and the settled relations that would supervene when the disturbance had passed and the transition from cause to effect had been consummated, – the emphasis falling on the consummation. (1919, p. 37)

In opposition to this 'taxonomic' view, Veblen sees that with 'post-Darwinian' science the 'process of causation' has come to take the first place in the enquiry, 'instead of that consummation in which causal effect was once presumed to come to rest ... modern science is becoming substantially a theory of the process of consecutive change, realized to be self-continuing or self-propagating and to have no final term' (ibid.).

It should be noted, however, that for Veblen post-Darwinian biology does not transcend mechanical analogies:

> in the Darwinian scheme of thought, the continuity sought in and imputed to the facts is a continuity of cause and effect. It is a scheme of blindly cumulative causation, in which there is no trend, no final term, no consummation. The sequence is controlled by nothing but the *vis a tergo* of brute causation, and is essentially mechanical. (Veblen, 1919, p. 436)

Thus for Veblen a key attraction of Darwinian ideas is more to do with the examination of causal processes, of a never-ending and cumulative nature, never reaching a state of equilibrium or rest. Their lure is not to do with any supposed alternative to mechanistic theory.

Limitations of Orthodox Economic Theory

The emphasis on cumulative change is a persistent theme in Veblen's work, signalling a source of fundamental divergence between his type of thinking and the equilibria orientated conceptions of both neoclassical economics and Spencerian theory. Criticisms in this vein are raised, for example, against the work of Marshall, whose theorems 'indicate the conditions of survival to which any innovation is subject, supposing the innovation to have taken place, not the conditions of variational growth' (Veblen, 1919, pp. 176–7).

Similarly, Veblen criticizes the economics of Carl Menger and the Austrian School who 'struck out on a theory of process, but presently came to a full stop because the process about which they busied themselves was not, in their apprehension of it, a cumulative or unfolding sequence' (1919, p. 70).

In both English and Continental economic theory, Veblen argues, the process stops for a simple reason: a 'faulty conception of human nature'. He elaborates: 'the human material with which the inquiry is concerned is conceived in hedonistic terms; that is to say, in terms of a passive and substantially inert and immutably given human nature' (p. 73). Hence the cumulative quality of evolutionary thinking rests precisely on the fact that it does not take human nature or preference functions as given or for granted.[8] Both the circumstances and temperament of an individual are part of the cumulative processes of change: 'They are the products of his hereditary traits and his past experience, cumulatively wrought out under a given body of traditions, conventionalities, and material circumstances; and they afford the point of departure for the next step in the process' (p. 74).

Veblen goes on to recognize, most perceptively, that both the individual and the environment, in which selection takes place, are affected by these unceasing developments: 'The economic life history of the individual is a cumulative process of adaptation of means to ends that cumulatively change as the process goes on, both the agent and his environment being at any point the outcome of the last process' (pp. 74–5). Clearly, marginalist theory is limited in this respect. For any scientist interested in economic phenomena:

> the chain of cause and effect in which any given phase of human culture is involved, as well as the cumulative changes wrought in the fabric of human conduct itself by the habitual activity of mankind, are matters of more engrossing and more abiding interest than the method of inference by which an individual is presumed invariably to balance pleasure and pain under given conditions that are presumed to be normal and invariable. (p. 240)

What Veblen was seeking was precisely a theory as to why change and transformation takes place, not a theory which muses over equilibrium conditions after individual preferences and technological possibilities are established. 'The question', he wrote, 'is not how things stabilize themselves in a "static state", but how they endlessly grow and change' (1934, p. 8). In sum, as Veblen (1919, p. 77) asserts: 'an evolutionary economics must be a theory of a process of cultural growth as determined by the economic interest, a theory of a cumulative sequence of economic institutions stated in terms of the process itself.'

This passage, originally published in 1898, is one of many where Veblen presents the idea of cumulative causation. Veblen's work in this area is thus an important precursor to that of Allyn Young (1928), Gunnar Myrdal (1939, 1944, 1957), Nicholas Kaldor (1972) and K. William Kapp (1976). Despite Veblen's earlier discussion, the idea of cumulative causation is more frequently associated with Myrdal and Kaldor.

A brief discussion of these Veblen–Myrdal and Veblen–Kaldor connections is appropriate. Myrdal originally took the idea of cumulative causation from the monetary economics of Knut Wicksell, coming to regard himself as an institutionalist later, in the 1940s.[9] However, Kaldor was taught and inspired by Young, and it is almost certain that Young, in turn, was prompted by Veblen's repeated use of the 'cumulative causation' idea when he associated it with the particular phenomenon of increasing returns (Young, 1928). Young, 'a friend of Mitchell and admirer of Veblen' (Dorfman, 1964, p. xlviii) taught Kaldor, and hence there is a clear – but hitherto unexplored – link between the Veblenian and Kaldorian schools of thought. This complements the acknowledged influence of Myrdal on Kaldor.

Institutional Inertia

It is suggested that cumulative causation can occur at all levels of social evolution, from the formation of institutions to macroeconomic development. Thus Veblen (1919, p. 241) argues that: 'institutions are an outgrowth of habit. The growth of culture is a cumulative sequence of habituation, and the ways and means of it are the habitual response of human nature to exigencies that vary incontinently, cumulatively, but with something of a consistent sequence in the cumulative variations that so go forward.'

The cumulative, self-reinforcing aspect of routinized behaviour and social institutions is highlighted in a work as early as *The Theory of the Leisure Class*:

> The situation of today shapes the institutions of tomorrow through a selective, coercive process, by acting upon men's habitual view of things, and so altering or fortifying a point of view or a mental attitude handed down from the past. . . . At the same time, men's present habits of thought tend to persist indefinitely, except as circumstances enforce a change. These institutions which have so been handed down, these habits of thought, points of view, mental attitudes and aptitudes, or what not, are therefore themselves a conservative factor. This is the factor of social inertia, psychological inertia, conservatism. (Veblen, 1899, pp. 190–1)

It would seem that the cumulative and self-reinforcing aspect of institutions and routines relates to some kind of process of positive feedback. In this respect there is another contrast with orthodox economics, in which the formation of equilibrium relies on negative feedback processes, such as diminishing returns to scale. Rather than equilibrium, positive feedback can engender such phenomena as lock-in (to use the modern parlance), where outcomes become frozen because of their self-reinforcing attributes (Arthur, 1983, 1988, 1989, 1990). Such locked-in phenomena can thus be regarded as sufficiently stable units of selection in an evolutionary process.

However, cumulative reinforcement of a number of parallel institutions can eventually lead to conflict and disruption. Stephen Edgell (1975, pp. 272–3) summarizes Veblen's view in these terms: 'institutions that emerge during one era may persist into another and the resulting cultural lag is likely to give rise to "friction" between the habits of thought generated by the new material conditions and the habits and institutions more appropriate to an earlier period of cultural development.' The processes underlying institutional change can be likened to strata shifting slowly at different rates, but occasionally causing seismic disturbance and discontinuities.

Institutions as Units of Selection

Furthermore, by recognizing the durable character of institutions, Veblen thus discovered an equivalent to the gene in the socioeconomic world. This is the second main reason for his adoption of the metaphor of Darwinian evolution. Socioeconomic evolution is regarded as a selection process, working on institutions as units of selection, combined with the simultaneous processes of adaptation of both individuals and institutions to their mutual environment:[10]

> The life of man in society, just as the life of other species, is a struggle for existence, and therefore it is a process of selective adaptation. The evolution of social structure has been a process of natural selection of institutions. The progress which has been and is being made in human institutions and in human character may be set down, broadly, to a natural selection of the fittest habits of thought and to a process of enforced adaptation of individuals to an environment which has progressively changed with the growth of community and with the changing institutions under which men have lived. Institutions are not only themselves the result of a selective and adaptive process which shapes the prevailing or dominant types of spiritual attitude and aptitudes; they are at the same time special methods of life and human relations, and are therefore in their turn efficient factors of selection. So that the changing institutions in their turn make for a further selection of individuals endowed with the fittest temperament, and a further adaptation of individual temperament and habits to the changing environment through the formation of new institutions. (Veblen, 1899, p. 188)

There are many interesting facets of this passage. We may briefly comment on the appearance in it of the word 'progress'. Veblen does sometimes seem to equate evolution with progress, as Lamar Jones (1986, p. 1053) has noted. However, this was the almost universal disposition of both biological and social evolutionary thinkers until quite recently (Nitecki, 1988). And further, Veblen seems to take a different view when he later criticizes adepts of evolutionary thought for infusing their science with a 'beneficent trend; so that "evolution" is conceived to mean amelioration or "improvement"' (1919, p. 55). He also considers 'spectacular instances of the triumph of imbecile institutions over life and culture' (1914, p. 25).

What is most interesting is Veblen's suggestion that institutions and habits of thought are units of selection in an evolutionary process. While these are more malleable and do not mutate in the same way as their analogue in biology, institutions and settled habits do have a sufficient degree of durability to regard them as having quasi-genetic qualities. However, Veblen specifies neither the precise mechanisms nor the criteria of the institutional selection process. His capacity for great insight, such as into the causal explication of human behaviour, is matched by a vagueness on some other matters of theoretical detail.

Veblen implied that biology and economics were on different onto-logical levels, but united by some broad and common evolutionary themes. Not only does this idea provide Veblen with a biological metaphor. It also becomes a basis for analysis of fundamental econ-omic activities. Work, for instance, is seen as involving a degree of practical knowledge or know-how which is both acquired and routinized over time. Indeed, the industrial skill of a nation consists of a set of relevant habits, acquired over a long time, widely dispersed through the employable workforce, reflective of its culture and deeply embedded in its practices (Veblen, 1914; Dyer, 1984). In the last quarter of the twentieth century this idea has been rediscovered by Richard Nelson and Sidney Winter (1982) and applied to their evolution-ary theory of the firm. For this reason, as Curtis Eaton (1984) has pointed out, the work of Nelson and Winter is as much 'Veblenian' as 'Schumpeterian'.

Veblen turns his conception of the quasi-genetic quality of habits of thought into a 'Darwinian' theory of the relationship between ideas and vested interests. This clearly demarcates him from all major al-ternative streams of economic thought. As the following quotation shows, he breaks explicitly from Marx on this point:

> Under the Darwinian norm it must be held that men's reasoning is largely controlled by other than logical, intellectual forces; that the con-clusion reached by public or class opinion is as much, or more, a matter of sentiment than of logical inference; and that the sentiment which animates men, singly or collectively, is as much, or more, an outcome of habit and native propensity as of calculated material interest. There is, for instance, no warrant in the Darwinian scheme of things for as-serting *a priori* that the class interest of the working class will bring them to take a stand against the propertied class. (Veblen, 1919, p. 441)

Note that there is also here clear implicit contrast with optimizing rationalism of neoclassical economics, and a rebuttal of the kind of faith in persuasion and reason to be later found in the writings of John Maynard Keynes.[11]

Veblen suggests that while Marx saw the importance of human ac-tion, its assumed basis of its motivation reduced to the problematic notion of 'class interest'. This ignores the processes through which perceptions of circumstances are *interpreted* and thereby transformed into human drives and purposes. Veblen saw institutions and 'habits of thought' as providing the framework for such a cognitive interpre-tation. In general, Veblen's adherence to a 'Darwinian' theory involved a meticulous examination of the causal mechanisms involved in hu-man behaviour, rather than assumptions of either ad hoc maximizing propensities or vague 'social forces'.

Purposeful Behaviour and Lamarckism

It is sometimes alleged that Veblen 'teeters between free will and determinism' (Seckler, 1975, p. 56), and entertained a conception of science from which purpose and intentionality were excluded (Commons, 1934, p. 654). Nevertheless, Veblen's emphasis on human purposefulness is repeated and significant: 'Economic action is teleological, in the sense that men always and everywhere seek to do something' (Veblen, 1919, p. 75).

Veblen (1934, p. 80) saw human purposeful behaviour itself as the result of natural selection. Regarding 'man':

> Like other species, he is a creature of habit and propensity. But in a higher degree than other species, man mentally digests the content of habits under whose guidance he acts, and appreciates the trend of these habits and propensities. . . . By selective necessity he is endowed with a proclivity for purposeful action.

Nevertheless, the nature and definition of what is meant by 'purposeful action' is not always clear, and this is perhaps one source of controversy over Veblen's line of thought (Seckler, 1975; Langlois, 1989). However, Veblen's emphasis on 'idle curiosity', for instance, as well as many of his own explicit statements, would seem to retain a crucial role for human agency in his theory. On the other hand, Veblen held on to a traditional, nineteenth-century view of science which rejected all purpose in the investigation of the facts.

Whatever the appropriate interpretation, any explicit emphasis on purposeful behaviour creates a problem for a strictly 'Darwinian' account of socioeconomic evolution. Purposeful behaviour is more often associated with evolution of a Lamarckian kind, although some biologists, and philosophers such as Karl Popper (1972, p. 229; Popper and Eccles, 1977, pp. 12–13), have argued for an 'active Darwinism' in which purposeful behaviour is admitted.

In contrast, mainstream science has an exclusive emphasis on deterministic causality. Consequently there are difficulties in accommodating the concept of purposive behaviour in its traditional mode of thought. If purpose has a cause, then the cause alone is seen as relevant. The idea of an uncaused purpose is either regarded as an impossibility, or it is ignored because such spontaneity is taken to mean that there is no mechanism to be explained. Even if we regard this aspect of modern science as limited and inapplicable to social science, it still applies to the Darwinian idea of evolution through natural selection. Therein the existence of units or characteristics is explained by direct or indirect reference to survival values. If organisms have plans or intentions then they are not recognized; individual choices and purposes have no place in the explanation.

There is some truth in Veblen's depiction of the 'Darwinian scheme of thought' in terms of 'a continuity of cause and effect' (1919, p. 436). However, he does not seem to wish to deal with the apparent exclusion of purposeful behaviour from such a 'mechanical' scheme. He is not led to adopt explicitly a more Lamarckian view of evolution, in which some notion of purposeful behaviour is admitted. Unlike Spencer, Veblen described himself as a Darwinian, partly because he puts greater stress on the selection process through which some institutions prosper and others became extinct.

Nevertheless, he simultaneously adopted the Lamarckian principle of the inheritance of acquired characters. Indeed, in one passage, writing after a discussion of the fixing of certain social traits, he seems indifferent between a Lamarckian and a Darwinian view of evolution: 'The point is not seriously affected by any question as to whether it was a process of habituation in the old-fashioned sense of the word or a process of selective adaptation of the race' (Veblen, 1899, p. 221).

Again there is insufficient clarity in Veblen's writing. There is a basis for limited mitigation, however. First, as Stephen Edgell and Rick Tilman (1989, p. 1009) point out, Lamarckian theory was still widely accepted, long after the publication of Darwin's *Origin of Species*. Second, the scientific account of the mechanisms of the evolutionary process was not altogether clear in Veblen's time, and around 1900 the Darwinians were somewhat in disarray (Bowler, 1983; Mayr, 1980; Provine, 1985). Third, even Darwin himself had flirted with elements of Lamarckism. As Peter Bowler (1988, p. 98) puts it: 'Darwin himself did not deny a limited role for the inheritance of acquired characters, and he was thus able to admit that the learning of new habits by the animals themselves can play a role.'

However, Darwin dallied with Lamarckism mainly in regard to the acceptance of the possibility of the inheritance of acquired characters. He did not adopt the whole Lamarckian explanation of variety and its sources, or the central causal role of intentionality and purposeful behaviour. Veblen accepted the possibility of the inheritance of acquired characters, and without much else of the Lamarckian baggage, but made explicit reference to purposeful behaviour. In any case, the full-blooded Lamarckism of the sort adopted and developed by Spencer was alien to Veblen's 'post-Darwinian' thought.

The Veblenian Legacy

To some extent, the degree of imprecision in the terms in which Veblen's evolutionary ideas were expressed became an impediment to their theoretical development. In part, this imprecision and incompleteness stems from the limited development of evolutionary theory in biology at his time. But this cannot explain all the vagaries and omissions.

Compared with the integrated theoretical constructions of, say, Marx or Marshall, there is not a comparably systematic theory of industry, technology or the macro-economy in Veblen's work. Consequently, the institutionalists had to look elsewhere for a basis for their policy recommendations. It is partly because Veblen addressed economic systems in such complex and dynamic terms that he fails to provide a systemic theory. To some extent, his achievement is limited by ambition itself.

However, despite some problems and inadequacies, on the whole Veblen was relatively successful in establishing the basis of a Darwinian economics. First, the principle of 'idle curiosity' became the ongoing source of variety or mutation in the evolutionary process. Second, the institution became the unit of relative stability and continuity through time, ensuring that much of the pattern and variety is passed on from one period to the next, so that selection has relatively stable units upon which to operate. Third, mechanisms are identified through which well-adapted institutions are imitated and replicated, and the less adapted become extinct: analogous to the 'struggle for existence'.

Hence a principal component of this achievement is its embodiment of the idea of the cumulatively self-reinforcing institution as a unit of evolutionary selection, to be subject to the procedures of mutation and selection. For Veblen, the objects of economic evolution and selection are institutions and routines. Their fundamental genetic component is habits and instincts.

The nature of the evolutionary process governing these elements is selective rather than purely developmental, and phylogenetic rather than simply ontogenetic. Veblenian economic evolution, in other words, is not confined to the development of the organism from its genetic rules.[12] It is phylogenetic in that the ongoing processes of selection and development of the whole population of institutions are considered. His evolutionary theory is thus more extensive than that of Adam Smith or Carl Menger, and it does not share the exclusive biological reductionism to be found in the works of Spencer. Hence, despite their limitations, Veblen's writings stand out as the most successful attempts, at least until the 1970s, to incorporate post-Darwinian biological thinking into economics and social science.

A particular relevance of Veblen's evolutionary theory is his analysis of science and technology in modern capitalism. It is clear from Veblen's writings that he regarded science and technology as one of the major motors of economic and social advance. The relevance of evolutionary principles from biology to the theory of technological change has again been recognized in recent years, with the consequence that many of Veblen's insights are being repeated and rediscovered, often without recognition of their precedent.[13]

It is also apparent that Veblen kept largely up to date with developments in theoretical biology and was keen to apply relevant insights to economics and social science. There have been enormous developments in biology since his day, but economists have largely neglected his example and failed to attempt to incorporate the appropriate insights. We act in the spirit, if not the letter, of no greater economist than Veblen in attempting to draw inspiration from the science of life.

Veblen fathered American institutionalism but, probably owing to the limited development of biology in the early decades of the twentieth century, in fact this tradition drew little directly from biology after Veblen. John Commons (1934, p. 45), for instance, clearly perceived institutional evolution in Veblenian terms.[14] However, his prime metaphor for his own core idea of a 'transaction' as a fundamental 'unit of activity' – his alternative to the abstract individual of neoclassical economics – was found not in biology but in quantum physics. The quantum was seen as a non-atomistic and analogous 'unit of activity' in which matter and energy, being and becoming, are all combined (ibid., pp. 55–6). Generally, after Veblen, the biological metaphor lies fallow for many years, somewhat neglected even by the American institutionalists, used often in some loose sense where evolution is identified simply with development.[15]

Other major institutionalist writers, such as Clarence E. Ayres, also became excited by Darwinism and its potential application to social science.[16] Prompted by Veblen's matter-of-fact view of science and technology, Ayres invested Veblen's concept of 'idle curiosity' with the full merits of human intelligence and technological progress (Rutherford, 1981). In contrast, incongruously distinguished from technology and science, institutional behaviour was regarded as ossified and 'ceremonial' by Ayres. One was given a positive charge, the other a negative (McFarland, 1986; Waller, 1982).

Apart from the problematic nature of the theoretical distinction between institutions and technology (Dosi, 1988b; Samuels, 1977), and the empiricist view of knowledge and science (Mirowski, 1987b), Ayres failed to note the positive and enabling functions of institutional rigidity (Giddens, 1984; Hodgson, 1988).[17] In this respect he differs from Commons (1934, p. 73), who clearly saw institutions as a liberating as well as a constraining force. Furthermore, it should be stressed that modern evolutionary theory cannot assign an unambiguous negative sign to either error or rigidity, just as it cannot always regard even a hopeful mutation as positive. Evolution proceeds, not in a mechanical manner, of force against resistance, but through the *combination* of rigid and durable entities – genes or institutions – with unceasing selection and change.

Despite its limitations, Veblen's understanding of the nature of evolution was more acute and his ambitions for an evolutionary economics were more substantial. Richard Hofstadter's (1959, pp. 152–5) remarks here are appropriate:

Veblen's conception of the uses of Darwinism in economics was not the most representative of his generation, but in the long run it may be the most enduring. . . . Where other economists had found in Darwinian science merely a source of plausible analogies or a fresh rhetoric to substantiate traditional postulates and precepts, Veblen saw it as a loom upon which the whole fabric of economic thinking could be rewoven.

In his relative success with the evolutionary metaphor, Veblen speaks more loudly and clearly than Marx, although his theoretical system as a whole lacked the latter's symphonic grandeur. It will be argued in the next chapter, with an equivalent degree of heresy, that Veblen's use of evolutionary thinking from biology was much more extensive than that of Schumpeter. Veblen should thus be placed among the founding figures of modern evolutionary economics.

10
Joseph Schumpeter and the Evolutionary Process

Joseph Schumpeter is celebrated today as a great mentor of evolutionary economics. Although the economics of both Karl Marx and Thorstein Veblen retain significant numbers of followers, it is notable that at the present time the name of Schumpeter retains the most explicit connection with developments in evolutionary modelling within this discipline.[1]

Although he did not build up a comprehensive theoretical system, and he wished that no school of economics be founded in his name, Schumpeter was generally a careful and perceptive theorist, and one of enduring significance. He admired Darwin and appreciated the importance of Darwinian biology for science. Notably, Schumpeter's (1976, p. 82) own adoption of an evolutionary metaphor was particularly enthusiastic and sustained: 'The essential point to grasp is that in dealing with capitalism we are dealing with an evolutionary process. It may seem strange that anyone can fail to see so obvious a fact which moreover was long ago emphasized by Karl Marx.'

So it may be a surprise for the reader to discover that Schumpeter's own notion of economic evolution is distanced explicitly from evolution of a biological kind, and excludes any suggestion of a Darwinian or a Lamarckian process of selection. Schumpeter was aware that Marx's evolutionism had nothing whatever to do with Darwinism. Thus when he praised Marx's conception of capitalist development as an evolutionary process, he was knowingly employing the word 'evolutionary' in a sense much closer to Marx than to either Darwin or Lamarck. The case has been stated, now let it be proven.

There are two main aspects to the following argument. The first involves a demonstration that Schumpeter's theory is more close to that of Léon Walras than is often perceived, and that Walras's theory has multiple dynamic aspects which are often ignored. The second involves an examination of Schumpeter's own definition of economic evolution and his rejection of any evolutionary analogue from biology.

Walrasian Wiles

Schumpeter's ideas on 'economic evolution' are scattered through a number of his works including his *Theory of Economic Development*, his *Business Cycles*, his *History of Economic Analysis* and his *Capitalism, Socialism and Democracy*. What gives his theory an apparently schizophrenic quality is his simultaneous admiration for the general equilibrium analysis of Walras. Today, Walras is widely regarded as the antithesis of a fully dynamic or 'evolutionary' approach in economics. Not so for Schumpeter. He wrote:

> so far as pure theory is concerned, Walras is in my opinion the greatest of all economists. His system of economic equilibrium, uniting, as it does, the quality of 'revolutionary' creativeness with the quality of classic synthesis, is the only work by an economist that will stand comparison with the achievements of theoretical physics. (Schumpeter, 1954, p. 827)

This was not a theoretical lapse or a bout of infatuation with formalism. Neither is it correct to follow Allen Oakley (1990, p. 19) and describe Schumpeter's admiration for Walras's general equilibrium model, at least without substantial qualification, as 'a blind-spot in Schumpeter's intellectual make-up'. Not only is the homage to the neoclassical theorist repeated elsewhere (Schumpeter, 1952, pp. 76, 79), but also these words were written in Schumpeter's mature years, and they lead us directly to the core of his economic analysis.

It is argued below that it is highly misleading to assert, as Horst Hanusch (1988, p. 1) does, that Schumpeter 'is not at all interested in optimization and pure equilibrium economics'.[2] Indeed, the contrasting statement of Ludwig von Mises (1978, p. 37) that 'Schumpeter's *Theory of Economic Development* is a typical product of the equilibrium theory' is also an exaggeration but indeed closer to the truth. It shall also be shown that Schumpeter's work derived directly and immediately from the theory of Walras. But rather than it being a 'typical product', it is an extraordinary and ultimately unsuccessful attempt to reconcile statics with dynamics.

Schumpeter's attitude to neoclassical orthodoxy and to the 'marginal revolution' in economic theory led by Walras, Jevons and others was far from outright dismissal. Nevertheless, he consistently pointed to a problem in Walrasian theory concerning its portrayal of the entrepreneur. In the circular-flow model of general equilibrium theory, perfect competition means that entrepreneurs 'operate without profit' (Schumpeter in 1912, see 1934, p. 31). Accordingly, Schumpeter introduced a pertinent discussion of Walras's model:

> In most minds, the idea of economic evolution will call up the associated idea of enterprise. Here again analytic advance, though substantial, proceeded mainly along the old lines . . . the source of entrepreneurs' profits was the fact that things do not work out as planned, and persistence of

positive profits in a firm was due to better-than-normal judgement . . .
the obvious common sense of this explanation may easily cover up its
inadequacy. Walras's contribution was important though negative. He
introduced into his system the figure of the entrepreneur who neither
makes nor loses. . . . And since this system is essentially a static theory
. . . he thereby indicated a belief to the effect that entrepreneurs' profits
can arise only in conditions that fail to fulfil the requirements of static
equilibrium and that, with perfect competition prevailing, firms would
break even in an equilibrium state – the proposition from which one
starts all clear thinking on profits. (Schumpeter, 1954, p. 893)

Thus, for Schumpeter and Alfred Marshall alike, the excursion into
economic dynamics started from a static system of economic equilibrium. Furthermore, in the case of both authors, the one was seen to
complement rather than to negate the other. The 'theoretical norm' of
general equilibrium, 'however distant it may be from actual life, is
what renders to the theorist the service which to the businessman is
rendered by the idea of a normal business situation' (Schumpeter,
1939, vol. 1, p. 45). Having his feet on this apparently firm ground,
Schumpeter went on to consider dynamics. As Norman Clark and
Calestous Juma (1987, p. 57) put it, he starts 'his analysis by assuming
an equilibrium state but devotes much time to the analysis of the
manner in which the equilibrium is destabilized'.[3]

Walrasian Dynamics

Clearly, for Schumpeter, the theoretical norm or starting point is
provided by the general equilibrium system of Walras. This is not
quite as anomalous as it might sound, for Walras's conception of reality is that of 'a process in which there are equilibriating forces at
work but where the attainment of equilibrium is invariably frustrated
by both endogenous changes and exogenous disturbances' (Currie and
Steedman, 1990, p. 69).

Indeed, as Michio Morishima and George Catephores (1988, pp. 37–
8n) point out, 'it is not unreasonable to suggest that Schumpeter's
view of the development of the capitalist economy might have been
suggested by Walras's descriptions.' In support of this interpretation
they quote the following passage from Walras's *Elements* of 1874:

Such is the continuous market, which is perpetually tending towards
equilibrium without ever actually attaining it, because the market has
no other way of approaching equilibrium except by groping, and, before the goal is reached, it has to renew its efforts and start over again,
all the basic data . . . [including] the utilities of goods and services, [and]
the technical coefficients . . . having changed in the meanwhile. . . . For,
just as a lake is, at times, stirred to its very depths by a storm, so also
the market is sometimes thrown into violent confusion by *crises*, which
are sudden and general disturbances of equilibrium. (Walras, 1954, pp.
380–1)

Here Walras went beyond the bounds of much of mainstream neoclassical theory by considering changes in technology. Although, there is, for example, a neoclassical literature on technical change, it is rarely integrated into a Walrasian general equilibrium model. Note also the particular mention by Walras of crises and technological change, and the similarity with some of Schumpeter's statements, a few cited below. For instance, in Walras, as well as in Schumpeter (1934, p. 64), there is the conception of 'change arising from within the system which so displaces its equilibrium point that the new one cannot be reached from the old one by infinitesimal steps' [emphasis removed]. In Walras, as well as in Schumpeter (1939, vol. 1, p. 64), we find a discussion of changing consumer tastes.

With further textual backing from Walras's *Elements,* Morishima and Catephores (1988, pp. 41–2) thus assert: 'It is generally believed that Schumpeter's hallmarks were the terms "entrepreneur," "innovation," and "new combination." However, . . . these phrases were incorporated in an idea that had already been strongly emphasized by Walras and were, if anything, a direct extension of Walrasian concerns with the importance of the entrepreneur.'

A number of other studies have confirmed this appraisal of the relationship between Walras and Schumpeter.[4] Thus Bertram Schefold (1986) identifies the indispensable Walrasian starting point of Schumpeter's analysis. Donald Walker (1986) notes Schumpeter's indebtedness to Walras for his conception of the entrepreneur. Yuichi Shionoya (1986) insists that Schumpeter's admiration for Walras was no mere affectation or passing phase, but was an integral part of his entire theory, as it developed over his life. And Enrico Santarelli and Enzo Pesciarelli (1990, p. 680) argue convincingly that 'the homage paid by Schumpeter to general equilibrium theory is far from being lip service and that it is not entirely due to his admiration for the formal coherence of the theory'. Indeed, Schumpeter was far from hostile to equilibrium analysis. His hallmark is the idea of innovation; like Walras he thought that this could be developed in an equilibriating system.

This does not mean that Schumpeter was entirely satisfied with Walras's theory. Neither did he adopt it wholesale. For instance, his conception of the source of entrepreneurial profit was different from that of Walras. It is known that when Schumpeter met his ageing mentor in Switzerland in 1909, he was told by Walras that the theory of the stationary process constitutes the whole of theoretical economics and economists cannot say anything about historical changes. Schumpeter was profoundly dissatisfied with this remark (Swedberg, 1991, pp. 22, 31–2). Yet throughout the remainder of his life, and in his lectures to students, 'again and again he talked about the need to dynamize the Walrasian system' (März, 1991, p. 167). His dissatisfaction with Walras was not sufficient to lead him to adopt a quite different starting point.

From the Walrasian system, which evidently does contain a kind of limited dynamism, Schumpeter indeed took his cue. He wrote: 'What matters to us is precisely the presence or absence of an actual tendency in the system to move toward a state of equilibrium.' Furthermore, 'this mechanism for establishing or reestablishing equilibrium is not a figment devised as an exercise in the pure logic of economics but actually operative in the reality around us' (Schumpeter, 1939, vol. 1, p. 47).

The Doomed Marriage of Statics and Dynamics

Schumpeter repeatedly emphasized Walras's point that entrepreneurial profit can arise only out of equilibrium. Thus he argued that equilibrium conditions provide 'a limiting state: if this limiting state should occur in practice, the entrepreneur might still hope for more than that since reality is never stationary' (Schumpeter, 1954, p. 893n).

In retrospect, of course, this is all a terrible mess. A regular Walrasian equilibrium depends precisely on the entrepreneur expecting the continuance of that equilibrium. If the entrepreneur expects otherwise, it will cease to be an equilibrium. Hence if the entrepreneur is then to hope for more, this hope must be passive and play no part in perturbing the attained state of rest; it must be hope as if in dreams. There may be 'rational expectations', but again these are only tractable if the system gravitates to an equilibrium; and in any case Schumpeter does not seem to have this modern idea in mind.

By 'statics' Schumpeter (1934, p. 83n) generally means the 'theory of the circular flow', and by 'dynamics' he means economic development in the full, qualitative sense. But the combination of these two quite different modes of reasoning is highly problematic. This can be illustrated by considering the role of the entrepreneur. As both Stephan Böhm and Richard Day have independently remarked, Schumpeter did not show why the entrepreneur should intrude into or emerge from the 'limiting state' of the smooth circular flow. These writers point out that the entrepreneurs thrive in a disequilibrium 'with the fundamental function of *creating* the mechanisms that allow the economy to work' (Day, 1984, p. 73). Consequently: 'Instead of regarding entrepreneurship as an exogenous push thrust upon the economy, it should be seen as part and parcel of the market process' (Böhm, 1990, p. 230).

Given the time at which he wrote, when developments in both the presentation and the criticism of the Walrasian approach were at an early stage, Schumpeter was understandably unaware of all the difficulties involved in attempting to 'dynamize' that system. For instance, he paid no heed to the fact that Walras excluded out-of-equilibrium trading from his model, and that its inclusion leads to severe problems such as path dependency (Bertrand, 1883; Fisher, 1983).

Furthermore, Schumpeter made great play of innovation and the introduction of new products. But subsequent attempts to encompass such 'future' phenomena within the general equilibrium model, by Gerard Debreu (1959) and his followers, have run into severe difficulties. We now know that it is impossible to specify a full list of futures markets, partly because of the escalating complexity and information problems that are involved (Radner, 1968). As Kenneth Arrow (1986, p. S393) sums it up: 'A complete general equilibrium system . . . requires markets for all contingencies in all future periods. Such a system could not exist.'

Despite these problems, Schumpeter continuously tried to reconcile the equilibriating or static with the dynamic theoretical schema. On the one hand is his idea of a stationary state. This refers to 'an economic process that goes on at even rates or, more precisely, an economic process that merely reproduces itself'. This, being 'nothing but a methodological fiction', nevertheless gives us an insight into which real phenomena 'are lacking' (Schumpeter, 1954, p. 964). But Schumpeter did not tell us how we can identify what is missing from a picture without a more adequate depiction with which to compare.

The static thus leads us to the dynamic. Schumpeter summed up this juxtaposition in a passage from another work, where he outlined 'three corresponding pairs of opposites':

> First, . . . the opposition of two real processes: the circular flow or tendency towards equilibrium on the one hand, a change in the channels of economic routine or a spontaneous change in the economic data arising from within the system on the other. Secondly, . . . the opposition of two theoretical *apparatuses*: statics and dynamics. Thirdly, . . . the opposition of two types of conduct, which, following reality, we can picture as two types of individuals: mere managers and entrepreneurs. (Schumpeter, 1934, pp. 82–3)

The problem, however, with this splendidly 'dialectical' reasoning is that it could easily involve contradictory assumptions and lead to other logical inconsistencies. This may not be an immediate and absolute disaster, and indeed Schumpeter was not the first great theorist whose work encompassed tensions and inconsistencies. However, contradictions still have to be resolved, for without appropriate rectification the theoretical system can easily degenerate into nonsense.

Schumpeter was never able to remove the inconsistencies involved in his juxtaposition of equilibriating and disequilibriating mechanisms. As Christopher Freeman (1990a, p. 28) observes:

> It is, of course, essential in any theory of cycles to account for the 'glue' that holds the system together and keeps it on a growth path despite its fluctuations. It *is* essential to account for continuities as well as discontinuities. Walrasian equilibrium theory explains neither, and it

was Schumpeter's misfortune that he attempted to marry it with his own theory of dynamic destabilizing entrepreneurship.[5]

Schumpeter's Definition of Economic Evolution

We now move on to consider Schumpeter's definition of economic evolution. In one place he defined it as 'changes in the economic process brought about by innovation, together with all their effects, and the responses to them by the economic system' (Schumpeter, 1939, vol. 1, p. 86). In a later work this spacious definition was broadened still further:

> The term evolution may be used in a wider and in a narrower sense. In the wider sense it comprises all the phenomena that make an economic process non-stationary. In the narrower sense it comprises these phenomena minus those that may be described in terms of continuous variations of rates within an unchanging framework of institutions, tastes, or technological horizons, and will be included in the concept of growth. (Schumpeter, 1954, p. 964)

Thus for Schumpeter 'evolution' in the broader sense meant little more than general 'change'. In the narrower – but still spacious – sense it was equivalent to the richer notion of economic development.

Development, for Schumpeter, is distinguished from aggregative growth. He wrote in 1912 that if 'the phenomenon that we call economic development is in practice simply founded upon the fact that the data changed and that the economy continuously adapts itself to them, then we shall say that there is *no* economic development.' In contrast, the true development of an economy involves 'changes in economic life as are not forced upon it from without but arise by its own initiative, from within' (Schumpeter, 1934, p. 63).

Although this idea of development clearly embraces structural, qualitative and cultural change, it is too vague to give the concept of evolution a sharp or precise meaning. Throughout his works, Schumpeter most frequently employed the term 'evolution' in this broad, developmental sense, but excluding a Lamarckian or Darwinian process of evolutionary selection.

Significantly, when considering past 'evolutionary' theories in social science, Schumpeter (1954, pp. 442–3) went so far as to associate the name of Condorcet with a variety of 'social evolutionism'. Schumpeter overlooked the point that Condorcet was a believer in the perfectibility of society, and an object of Malthus's attack in his *Essay*. It has been shown in chapter 4 above that this *Essay* was inspirational for an entirely different definition and conception of an evolutionary process. Darwin and Condorcet are poles apart. To associate the word evolution with one, if it has simultaneous linkage with the other, is to confuse its meaning.

Schumpeter's Exclusion of Biology

In accord with his generally tolerant and liberal standpoint, Schumpeter (1954, p. 788) rightly reacted against the biased and improper ideological uses to which the analogy of social with biological evolution had been put. But from this commendable stand he immediately went on to belittle the value of biological theory for social science:

> it may be ... that certain aspects of the individual-enterprise system are correctly described as a struggle for existence, and that a concept of survival of the fittest in this struggle can be defined in a non-tautological manner. But if this be so, then these aspects would have to be analyzed with reference to economic facts alone and no appeal to biology would be of the slightest use. (p. 789)

The slight concession which follows the above passage is the vague admission that a 'genuine appeal to biological facts and theories' may be appropriate 'whenever the question of inheritance of physical or mental qualities of the human material is brought in' (ibid.). But Schumpeter here seems to be referring to 'human material' simply in a biological sense. In any case neither this nor any plausibly related notion of 'inheritance' plays any significant part in his work. For example, there is no inheritance of information or structure through learning or imitation. In sum, it appears that while Schumpeter conceived of 'economic evolution' in a wide and developmental sense, it was not sufficiently wide to incorporate an analogy with natural selection.

Creative Destruction

Although Schumpeter's employment of the notion of 'economic evolution' is often connected with the illuminating phraseology of 'creative destruction', this has a greater affinity with the 'dialectical' and developmental evolutionism of Marx (Elliot, 1980) than with Darwinian or Lamarckian biology. For Schumpeter (1939, vol. 1, p. 102): 'evolution is lopsided, discontinuous, disharmonious by nature ... evolution is a disturbance of existing structures and more like a series of explosions than a gentle, though incessant, transformation.' The saltationist elements in Schumpeter's thinking contrast with the gradualism of Marshall (Metcalfe, 1988, p. 65). Even more importantly, they contrast with the widespread conception of biological evolution at the time. Schumpeter wrote before the emergence of the theory of 'punctuated equilibria' and – with the exception of Richard Goldschmidt's (1940) heretical work – at a time when Darwinism was associated with little else but gradual change. This observation reinforces the point that

Schumpeter's conception of evolution was closer to that of Hegel and Marx, rather than to Darwin or Lamarck.

Economic development, as Schumpeter often emphasized, is 'development from within' (1934, p. 63), the dynamic role of the entrepreneur being one example. There is a sense of innovation and the rational spirit being pitted against rigid institutions and the established order. Capitalism, for him,

> can never be stationary. And this evolutionary character of the capitalist process is not merely due to the fact that economic life goes on in a social and natural environment which changes and by its change alters the data of economic action ... The fundamental impulse that acts and keeps the capitalist engine in motion comes from the new consumers' goods, the new methods of production or transportation, the new markets, the new forms of industrial organization that capitalist enterprise creates. (Schumpeter, 1976, pp. 82–3)

For Schumpeter, evolution meant the denial that equilibrium can be attained as a permanent state of rest, and the assertion of unceasing novelty and change. Entrepreneurial activity and technological transformations meant that theory should treat the economy as a process: as ever changing in historical time. In one place he tentatively brought the Darwinian evolutionary concept of mutation into his analysis:

> The opening up of new markets, foreign or domestic, and the organizational development from the craft shop and factory to such concerns as US Steel illustrate the same process of industrial mutation – if I may use that biological term – that incessantly revolutionizes the economic structure from within, incessantly destroying the old one, incessantly creating a new one. (ibid., p. 83)

But this was no more than a cautious and passing reference to a single concept from biology, placed within his developmentalist scheme rather than in a selectionist theory. In another passage Schumpeter (1939, vol. 1, p. 37) wrote that economics should look to 'physiology and zoology – and not to mechanics' for inspiration on a particular matter. This could be taken as commendable, for the reasons suggested by Marshall in his wider invocation of biology. But, unlike Marshall, Schumpeter did not look to biology as a major source of theoretical inspiration for economic science. In fact, he turns away and looks elsewhere, always steadfastly keen to relate his analysis to the mechanistic system that Walras had borrowed from physics (Mirowski, 1989b).

Sure enough, he implicitly broke the bonds of the Walrasian system in many ways. For instance, his endless emphasis on leaps and discontinuities is an anathema to any true marginalist. However, he did not perceive the damage that his dynamics had done to the Walrasian conception, and he remained true to the Lausanne gentleman to the last.

Reconciling Schumpeter and Walras

This important facet of Schumpeter's writing is not difficult to explain. He certainly admired the detailed, disaggregated and systematic quality of Walras's work, in which an attempt was made to break down social phenomena and explain them in terms of the interactions of constituent parts. Schumpeter probably inherited this reductionist outlook from his days with the economists of the Austrian School in Vienna. It should not be forgotten that Schumpeter is alleged to have been the first to coin the term 'methodological individualism' (1908, ch. 6).[6] In this work Schumpeter (pp. 64–8, 77–9, 85–7, 154–5, 261, 541–7) embraces the Walrasian formal analysis, and significantly he denies that the economist should have any business discussing the psychological processes behind individual preference functions. We may thus concur with Richard Goodwin that Schumpeter had recognizable motives for his supreme assessment of Walras:

> Because in Walras he found the most profound formulation of the basic, unitary conception of the meaning and explanation of separate markets and of their interdependent functioning as a whole ... an idealized market solution that simultaneously yielded the behavior of very many individual markets tightly embedded in a single, whole economy. (Goodwin, 1990, p. 39)

It seems that, for Schumpeter, Walras appeared to explain the functioning of the whole in terms of the atomistic and individual components of the system. On this basis, both Walras's formal achievement and his method were the consistent objects of Schumpeter's admiration.[7]

In contrast, for Keynes, the Walrasian system was part of the faulty orthodox tradition, involving the assumption of Say's Law and the prediction that the system can generally reach a full-employment equilibrium. As Goodwin (1990, p. 41) observes: 'In order to destroy the absurd implicit assumption of full employment, Keynes stated his theory in terms of aggregates. Given his commitment to Walrasian analysis, Schumpeter was bound to reject aggregate analysis ... [which] misses the essential shifts in relative prices and outputs.' Thus Schumpeter's antipathy to Keynes and his praise for Walras are both simultaneously explained by the reductionist outlook and his 'methodological individualism'.

In addition, as Freeman (1990a, p. 19) has noted, Schumpeter 'believed in the self-adjusting mechanism of the market over the long term in a way which Keynes did not'. Accordingly, 'his commitment to Walrasian general equilibrium theory was not simply a mode of exposition or a way of making his ideas more palatable to his colleagues ... but remained a central part of his theoretical apparatus throughout his life despite its apparent inconsistency with his theories of innovation and development.' With this faith in the resilience of the economy, Schumpeter 'continued to stress the "natural" equilibriating tendencies of the system' (ibid., p. 28) even to the detriment of the analysis of institutional, cultural or technological change.[8]

For Schumpeter, the Walrasian theoretical system showed how the market could grope towards equilibrium as a result of individual interactions and price flexibility, even if, for both Walras and Schumpeter, the process was periodically disrupted by innovation and other entrepreneurial activity. For Schumpeter, as for Walras, the general equilibrium analysis involved dynamic gravitation towards equilibrium, as well as the static equilibrium itself. Walras's theory is much more dynamic than often perceived, just as the equilibriating elements in Schumpeter's theory are often ignored. Indeed, as Shionoya (1990, p. 321) has argued, Schumpeter believed that 'dynamic theory cannot stand alone without the support of static theory.'

At the time that Schumpeter was writing, the formal difficulties in the Walrasian system were not well known or well understood. He wrote before the development of non-linear dynamics (Goodwin, 1990, p. 49) and the distinction of Ilya Prigogine (1976, 1980) between 'in equilibrium', 'near to equilibrium' and 'far from equilibrium' systems. Hence Schumpeter was able to regard a system as fully dynamic, even if we now know that its dynamism is of a highly limited type.

Schumpeterian Illusions

In conclusion, the invocation of Schumpeter's name by the new wave of evolutionary theorists in the 1980s and 1990s is both misleading and mistaken. Note for instance the evolutionary modelling in the vein of Iwai (1984a, 1984b), Nelson and Winter (1982), Rahmeyer (1989), Silverberg (1988) and Silverberg et al. (1988). These authors make repeated claims that their work is in a 'Schumpeterian' or 'neo-Schumpeterian' mould. There are superficial similarities, such as an emphasis in common with Schumpeter on invention and innovation, and perhaps even on imitation. But at a deeper theoretical level there is a complete divergence.

In contrast to Schumpeter, the work of the new evolutionary modellers is based on a 'natural selection' analogy, of a Darwinian or of a Lamarckian kind. Nelson and Winter (1982), for example, see routines in firms as being analogous to genes, adopt the idea from Lamarckian biology of the inheritance of acquired characters, draw an analogy to mutation in economic systems, and set up selection mechanisms in their evolutionary models.

Yet, as shown above, Schumpeter eschewed the natural selection analogy for economics and adopted an entirely different conception of evolution in social science. If there is an implicit 'natural selection' analogy in Schumpeter's writings, in the process of competition for instance, then it enters only by the backdoor. It is contrary to Schumpeter's explicit intention.

Despite their current diplomatic convenience and positive ambience, the 'Schumpeterian' or 'neo-Schumpeterian' (Nelson and Winter, 1982, p. 39) labels are thus inappropriate for theoretical work of this type.

In fact, Schumpeter's own conception of evolution was less selectionist and much more Marxian in character: more *evolvere* than natural selection; more economic revolution than economic evolution. It also forms an adjunct of Walrasian equilibrium, and represents an ostensible but ultimately unsatisfactory attempt to reconcile general equilibrium theory with notions of variety and change.

Instead, the exciting evolutionary ideas that have emerged with the 'new wave' have much more to do with Veblen and the 'old' institutionalism than with Schumpeter himself.[9] Using the microcomputer, they have brought rigour and benefit to a version of evolutionary economics, but one more in the spirit of the 'post-Darwinian' economics of the Veblenians. But, as yet, the closer resemblance of this work with that of Veblen rather than Schumpeter has not clearly surfaced either in the academic journals or in the proceedings of the academic associations.

Schumpeter's name is also widely invoked not only as the spiritual symbol of selectionist evolutionary modelling in economics, but also as the father of a theoretical school addressing technological change, despite the fact that he had very little to say about the latter in his work. Indeed, as Arnold Heertje (1988, p. 82) concludes, 'technical change, in the strict sense of the development of new technical knowledge and possibilities, and the diffusion of knowledge are almost wholly absent from his exposition.'

The question should be raised as to why the name of Schumpeter has become associated with the new wave of modelling in evolutionary economics since the 1980s. It should not be denied that there is abundant inspiration for this genre in his work, including his insistence that capitalism is not stable but the source of a never-ending stream of disruptive innovations. But there is more to the adoption of his name than this. It is partly because he seems to offer a bridge between Walrasian equilibrium and a more dynamic theory that he has become the inspiration for a breakaway from the very orthodoxy that he continued to admire. It has been argued here that this rickety bridge is theoretically unsafe, but nevertheless it has offered the means of escape for a significant number of economic theorists. A complete answer to the question would involve an excursion into the sociology of the economics profession, but at the theoretical level both the richness and the ambiguity of his work provide a clue.

Schumpeter was not as aware as Marshall of the possible inconsistencies and logical problems in his own attempt to marry statics with dynamics. He did not have the aptitude to develop or mimic Walras along formalistic lines. He did not create a comprehensive theoretical system of the stature of that of Marx. He did not go as far as Veblen or von Mises to entirely reject static or equilibrium-based theorizing. However, like Veblen, the greatness of his work is in its flashes of illumination, rather than in its systematic rigour.

Perhaps it is fortunate that Schumpeter was not adept at formal or mathematical reasoning. He lived at a time when an economist could still gain tenure and acclaim without such capabilities. If he had had greater mathematical competence then he would probably have wasted his entire life in a largely fruitless attempt to dynamize fully the Walrasian theory – something that has still not been achieved to this day – probably to become forgotten as an economist. Instead, Schumpeter's intuitive mind and conceptual grasp yielded the great insights for which he is well known. Almost unwittingly, he pushed economic theory to its boundaries. Despite his reductionist sentiments, he placed great emphasis on 'the broad patterns of economic evolution, on "Grand Questions" such as the determinants of long-term changes in the structure of the economy' (Dosi, 1990a, p. 335).

Overall, despite the manifest limitations, internal problems and logical conflicts within Schumpeter's theoretical system, he does surely rank as an outstanding economic theorist. In spite of his doomed attempt to grow a fully dynamic theoretical system in a Walrasian soil, Schumpeter remains a worthy inspiration for theorists of dynamic economic systems, and is full of insight and potential for further development. Contrary to many admirers, however, Schumpeter provides neither a systematic theory nor an ideal epitome for a new evolutionary economics, if that is to be a precise and meaningful term.

11

The Evolution of
Friedrich Hayek

The evolutionary thinking of Friedrich Hayek is covered here in two chapters. This present chapter deals with some fundamental evolutionary concepts and issues, namely Hayek's attitude to Darwin, Social Darwinism and sociobiology, his view of primordial instincts, and the question of his chosen analogy to the gene and its relation to his methodological individualism and his focus on individual choice. The subsequent chapter focuses on Hayek's theory of group selection, his notion of 'spontaneous order', his conception of the market and his policy conclusions.

Hayek places himself in the Austrian tradition of economists, emanating from the work of Carl Menger in the nineteenth century. He claims to follow Menger in embracing an 'evolutionary' approach to economics, although it is much more explicit in the case of the more recent author, and with specific allusions to biology. However, this approach is prominent in Hayek's later writings only, particularly those dating from the 1960s.

A number of questions hang over Hayek's characterization of the nature and processes of evolution. For instance, he repeatedly and proudly displays his own intellectual genealogy through Carl Menger, back to Adam Smith, David Hume and Bernard Mandeville. However, he does not seem to realize that their work is not equivalent to Darwinian evolution or natural selection in a fully specified sense. This search for genealogical roots in the works of Mandeville and the Scottish School thus leads to an attempt to diminish the significance of the Darwinian revolution and even the novelty of Darwin's own contribution to evolutionary theory.

This problem manifests itself at the theoretical level both in terms of conceptual vagueness and a tension between phylogenetic and ontogenetic conceptions of change. Aware of the modern prestige awarded to Darwinism, Hayek admits some kind of selection process and phylogeny in his evolutionary theory. But in so far as his theory is still rooted in methodological individualism and the ideas of the

Scottish School, it shall be argued that it largely remains in the confines of ontogeny.[1]

Nevertheless, his conception of socioeconomic and cultural evolution is the centrepiece of his mature theory, and it relates to such topics as his theory of law, the structure of political institutions, the nature of markets, and the critique of socialism and 'constructivism'. In view of its centrality, the relatively late development of the evolutionary idea in Hayek's work is, therefore, somewhat surprising.

It will be suggested in this and the following chapter that Hayek's evolutionary theory, while containing important insights, is sketchy and sometimes ambiguous. And finally, it does not support the kind of political and policy conclusions that Hayek wishes to sustain. Nevertheless, it stands alongside the work of Thorstein Veblen and Herbert Spencer as one of the more developed and most important applications of the evolutionary analogy in the socioeconomic sphere.

Given the importance of the comparison undertaken here between Hayek's evolutionism and his methodological individualism, the following section addresses this latter idea. Methodological individualism may claim some priority because of its explicit longevity in Hayek's work. Subsequently we return to a discussion of Hayek's evolutionism, as presented more prominently in his mature writings.

Methodological Individualism

As noted in the preceding chapter, the term 'methodological individualism' was originally devised by Joseph Schumpeter (1908, ch. 6). It was adopted by thinkers of the Austrian School, including Hayek, and classically defended by Ludwig von Mises (1949). A clear and useful definition of methodological individualism is provided by Jon Elster (1982, p. 453): 'the doctrine that all social phenomena (their structure and their change) are in principle explicable only in terms of individuals – their properties, goals, and beliefs.' Note the unqualified key words 'all' and 'only', and the appropriate focus on explanation in this definition. It is consistent with the definition of von Mises.

Methodological individualists in a sense take the individual 'for granted'. The individual, along with his or her assumed behavioural characteristics, is taken as the elemental building block in the theory of the social or economic system. As Steven Lukes (1973, p. 73) puts it, 'individuals are pictured abstractly as given, with given interests, wants, purposes, needs, etc.' In short, according to the methodological individualist, individuals do not evolve. Clearly, assumptions of this type are typical of neoclassical economics, as well as the economics of Hayek.

The obvious question to be raised is the legitimacy of stopping short at the individual in the process of explanation. If individuals are affected by their circumstances, then why not in turn attempt to explain the causes acting on individual 'goals and beliefs'? Why should the process of scientific enquiry be arrested as soon as the individual is reached?

After all, if 'the scientific practice is to seek an explanation at a lower level than the explanandum,' as Elster (1983, p. 23) puts it, then why stop with the individual? Why not delve into the psyche, and further, observe the firing of the neurons and the electrochemistry of the brain?

Also, as Barry Hindess (1989, p. 91) suggests, just as there may be conflicts of objectives within organizations, thereby ruling out a unitary conception of their operation, there may be diverse and sometimes conflicting objectives within the minds of single individuals. A paradox of methodological individualism is that by its own reductionist canon it is not reductionist enough.

Hayek's own way out of these difficulties seems to be presented in quotations such as the following: if 'conscious action can be "explained",' he writes, 'this is a task for psychology but not for economics ... or any other social science' (1948, p. 67).

This amounts to a dogmatic statement that economists and other social scientists should not concern themselves with 'psychology' and explanations of purpose and preference. There are a number of points to be raised here, some relating to the question of psychology. The idea that such explanations, if pursued, have to be purely in psychological terms is called 'psychologism' and is rebutted by Karl Popper (1945), Lawrence Boland (1982) and others. Second, it is impossible to exclude psychology – especially social psychology – from the domain of social science. In fact, Hayek suggests a questionable bifurcation between the sciences of social and of natural phenomena: a dubiously hermetic division between the natural and the social world.

The most important objection to Hayek's statement is that it involves a dogmatic and over-restrictive conception of the domain of the social sciences. It amounts to saying that we should not try to explain individual preferences and purposes simply because such explanations are deemed to be outside social science. All alternative conceptions of the disciplinary domain are thus dismissed. Similar dogmatism is expressed in the oft-repeated statement by orthodox economists that tastes and preferences are not the *explananda* of economics. It involves equivalent intolerance of alternative pictures of the content and boundaries of this discipline.

A more sophisticated defence of the idea that analysis may stop at the level of the individual is advanced by George L. S. Shackle (1989, p. 51) and Ludwig Lachmann (1969, p. 63). These Austrian-inspired writers suggest that individuals make choices which are primary, spontaneous and essentially 'uncaused'. They posit the uncaused nature of imagination and expectation and the indeterminacy of the economic process.

In arguing that the forces moulding expectation and decision cannot be explained at all, the Lachmann–Shackle position is different from that of Hayek, who suggests that they could possibly be explained by psychology but that it would not be legitimate to do so, and also from that of neoclassical theorists, who give a limited 'explanation' of behaviour by reference to all-determining and exogenous preference functions.

The possibility of such uncaused causes may be admitted, but the defender of methodological individualism has to go further than this. It has to be proposed that *all* human purposes or preference functions are entirely uncaused and unmoulded. If, on the contrary, it is admitted that some human goals and desires can be caused or moulded by circumstances, then the attempt to explain *those* preferences or purposes cannot be excluded by the Lachmann–Shackle argument.

Furthermore, if such uncaused causes are admitted, why should their location be confined to the human mind? If such indeterminacy is possible, why shouldn't it be located in other living things, or even elsewhere in the universe? With the development of quantum theory, Pandora's box has indeed been opened. Hence the trouble with the Lachmann–Shackle defence of reductionism is that it cannot ultimately control the demon of indeterminacy that it has chosen to release.

The above assessment upholds that the exclusion of the analysis of changes in goals or preference functions from social theory is an important component of methodological individualism: it is proposed by followers of this creed that the individual should be taken as given.

In sum, the methodological individualists have provided us with no good reason why explanations of social phenomena should stop short with the individual. We cannot exclude the idea that at least some human intentions have causes which are worthy of investigation. It shall now be explained why the above conclusion is fatal for methodological individualism, at least as the term is defined above.

If there are determinate influences on individuals and their goals, then these are worthy of explanation. In turn, the explanation of those may be in terms of other purposeful individuals. But where should the analysis stop? The purposes of an individual could be partly explained by relevant institutions, culture and so on. These, in their turn, would be partly explained in terms of other individuals. But these individual purposes and actions could then be partly explained by cultural and institutional factors, and so on, indefinitely.

We are involved in an apparently infinite regress, similar to the puzzle 'which came first, the chicken or the egg?' Such an analysis never reaches an end-point. It is simply arbitrary to stop at one particular stage in the explanation and say 'it is all reducible to individuals' just as much as to say it is 'all social and institutional'. As Robert Nozick (1977, p. 359) remarks: 'In this apparent chicken and egg situation, why aren't we equally methodological institutionalists?' The key point is that in this infinite regress, neither individual nor social factors have legitimate explanatory primacy. The idea that all explanations have to be in terms of individuals is thus unfounded. Accordingly, methodological individualism is fatally flawed.

Methodological individualism implies a rigid and dogmatic compartmentalization of study. It may be legitimate in some limited types of analysis to take individuals as given and examine the consequences of the interactions of their activities. This particular type of analysis, be it called 'situational logic' or whatever, has a worthy place, alongside other approaches, in social science. But it does not legitimate methodological individualism because the latter involves the further statement that *all* social explanations should be of this or a similar type.

In theoretical terms, the rejection of methodological individualism opens up space for a non-atomistic and social conception of the individual. It may be argued that there are external influences moulding the purposes and actions of individuals, but that action is not entirely determined by them. The environment is influential but it does not completely determine either what the individual aims to do or what he or she may achieve. This approach, elaborated in later chapters, involves a rejection of the extremes of both determinism and individualistic indeterminacy.

Culture and Methodological Individualism

Notably, Hayek's emphasis on the concept of culture does not itself imply a departure from methodological individualism. Indeed, there is an alternative tradition within anthropology which proselytizes an individualistic conception of culture. Likewise, sociobiologists such as Charles Lumsden and Edward Wilson (1981) offer a theory of culture which is redolent of methodological individualism. They write: 'culture is in fact the product of vast numbers of choices by individual members of the society' (p. 206).[2]

In a critique of individualistic conceptions of culture, Anne Mayhew (1980, 1987a) explains that there is a difference between regarding it 'as a consequence of the way in which people act' and of seeing behaviour, in part at least, as a consequence of culture. If the individual is to be taken as given, as Hayek and other methodological individualists seem to insist, then culture can only be embraced in the former sense and not fully in the latter.

This line of argument is of even greater relevance with the move to an analysis of an evolutionary kind. With investigations into short-run processes, or partial equilibria, tastes and preference functions could be taken as given. But in an unfolding and evolutionary perspective, involving long-run changes and developments in a social context, this compartmentalization is arguably out of place.

Biotic evolution involves natural selection of genes, which may themselves be taken as virtually invariant. However, the composition of the gene pool changes and it is necessary to explain this change. Moving to the socioeconomic sphere, individuals are clearly not as invariant as genes: our attitudes and beliefs often change dramatically during the course of our lives. Yet even if particular individuals were wrongly regarded as invariant and akin to the genes, then the population of individuals would change through time. As selection takes place the overall set of individual preference functions will change. These, in turn, would have to be explained.

It is thus necessary to take all possible changes into account, and treat change itself, as Veblen argued, as 'cumulative' in scope. In contrast to both Austrian and neoclassical theory, Veblen (1919, p. 75) saw 'both the agent and his environment being at any point the outcome of the last process'.

Thus there is an inconsistency in Hayek's work between, on the one hand, the ideas emanating from his individualist roots, and, on the other, his growing commitment to an evolutionary perspective. In an evolutionary context, methodological individualism has to be either redefined or abandoned. There have been some shifts in Hayek's work over the years, and it may be that 'Hayek is by no means the champion of methodological individualism that he claims to be,' as Stephan Böhm (1989, p. 221) alleges. He is more a systems thinker: one moreover with strong traces of functionalism.

Hence the development of Hayek's thought has not been continuous, or free of major internal contradictions. In particular, the kind of evolutionary notions which Hayek tries to embrace imply a conflict with many of his original presuppositions. This point is reinforced by a consideration of other aspects of Hayek's thought.

Evolution and Purposeful Behaviour

A notable difficulty is created in his mature theory. On the one hand, there is the typical emphasis of the Austrian School on purposeful behaviour, guided by expectations of an uncertain future. On the other, there is the modern biological idea of evolution in which intention plays no explicit part, and his unremitting emphasis of the concept of 'tacit knowledge' derived from the work of Michael Polanyi (1957, 1967).

Consequently, if socioeconomic development is determined by some process of natural selection, then what role remains for the notions of intentionality, purposefulness or choice, which economists in Hayek's tradition have held so dear? As John Gray (1984, p. 53) remarks: 'The problem with the natural-selection approach is that in accounting for individual character traits, dispositions, and so on by reference to their survival values, it deprives individual choices and purposes of their place at the terminal level of social explanation.'

Clearly, if Hayek's notion of cultural evolution is to retain the notion of purposeful action, it must be distanced from an evolutionary process of a strictly Darwinian kind. However, Hayek does not seem to recognize the full gravity of this problem. It is not until his work of the late 1980s that he describes cultural evolution as being specifically Lamarckian rather than Darwinian.[3] Even then it is without mention of the opening thus created for a notion of truly purposeful behaviour, in contrast to the orthodox Darwinian scheme within which purpose is regarded merely as programmed or goal-seeking activity.

The Emergence of Hayek's Evolutionism

The delay in the emergence of the biological metaphor in Hayek's writings may stem in part from his earlier critique of 'scientism' in social theory (Hayek, 1952). There he denounces social theory for a 'slavish imitation of the method and language of science' (p. 15). Later, however, in the preface to his *Studies in Philosophy, Politics and Economics*, Hayek (1967, p. viii) notes a change in 'tone' in his attitude to 'scientism', attributed to the influence of Karl Popper. This is not, needless to say, a matter of mere 'tone', and as the door is progressively opened for the entry of the biological analogues, the row with the allegedly scientistic neighbours diminishes nearly to the point of insignificance. In so far as the polemic against scientism remains, it changes its form as well as its tone, but still poses an inconsistency with the evolutionism of his later works.

Although the idea had been raised earlier, suggestions of a more prominent 'evolutionary' approach in Hayek's work are found in a few passages of a collection of essays published in the 1960s (Hayek, 1967, pp. 31–4, 66–81, 103–4, 111, 119). The bulkiest of the above extracts refers to 'the evolution of systems of rules of conduct' but direct references to the biological analogy therein are slight. The 1960s also saw the original publication of his important essay on Bernard Mandeville, wherein there are few further references to evolutionary biology (Hayek, 1978, p. 265).

In the 1970s the main exposition of Hayek's evolutionary theory is found in his three-volumed *Law, Legislation and Liberty*. Once again, however, the references to the biological literature and biological conceptions of evolution are patchy (Hayek, 1982, vol. 1, pp. 9, 23–4, 152–3, and vol. 3, pp. 154–9, 199–202). In fact, by far the longest discussion of the concept of evolution is in the 'Epilogue' to that work and its footnotes.

Strangely, we have to wait until the late 1980s to receive the fullest explicit statement of Hayek's evolutionary conception, in a few pages of *The Fatal Conceit* (Hayek, 1988, pp. 9, 11–28). Given the significance of an idea of the 'evolution' of social institutions in Hayek's mature work, it is odd that it receives so little elaboration.

The Underestimation of Darwin

Despite this reticence, Hayek repeats in several places a rather curious account of the nature and origin of evolutionary theory. In these narratives there is a tendency to underestimate the prominence of some key figures, to the benefit of others. With a social theorist as prominent as Hayek, the errors and travesties are likely to be replicated by his followers, and must be corrected. Furthermore, as argued below, this recurring historical error is of some analytical significance in understanding the nature of Hayek's own theoretical system.

Hayek's omission of the role of Thomas Robert Malthus in the Darwinian revolution has already been noted in chapter 4. Even more seriously, however, there is a tendency to underestimate the role of Charles Darwin in the development of evolutionary theory and both the originality and significance of his scientific work. For Hayek (1967, p. 32), the 'basic conception' of the theory of evolution by natural selection is 'exceedingly simple'.[4] Clearly these appraisals are likely to some extent to reflect on the nature and content of Hayek's own evolutionary theory.

The trouble seems to have started quite early on, where Hayek (1967, pp. 103–4n) approvingly quotes a very outdated passage by the legal theorist – not biologist – Sir Frederick Pollock (1890, pp. 41–2) to the effect that: 'The doctrine of evolution is nothing else than the historical method applied to the facts of nature. . . . Savigny . . . [and] Burke . . . were Darwinians before Darwin.' Pollock's trivializing estimation of Darwin's importance stems from a period when the influence of the famous biologist was at a low ebb (Bowler, 1983, 1988), yet it seems to have affected Hayek adversely ever since.[5]

Hayek (1978, p. 265) further argues that writers like Johann von Herder, Wilhelm von Humboldt and Friedrich von Savigny 'made the idea of evolution a commonplace in the social sciences of the nineteenth century long before Darwin'. Repeating this theme elsewhere, Hayek writes:

> It was in the discussion of such social formations as language and morals, law and money, that in the eighteenth century the twin conceptions of evolution and the spontaneous formation of an order were at last clearly formulated, and provided the intellectual tools which Darwin and his contemporaries were able to apply to biological evolution. . . . A nineteenth-century social theorist who needed Darwin to teach him the idea of evolution was not worth his salt. (Hayek, 1982, vol. 1, p. 23)

Although in a later work Hayek (1988, p. 26) concedes that Darwin's theory 'is one of the great intellectual achievements of modern times,' he still continues to deprive the great biologist of much of his glory. He writes that 'Darwin's work was preceded by decades, indeed by a century, of research concerning the rise of highly spontaneous orders through a process of evolution' (p. 24).

Note the imprecise use of the word 'evolution' here. Hayek slurs over the fact that the typical story of the emergence of 'spontaneous orders', as found in the works of the Scottish School, is ontogenetic in character, and is not strictly analogous either to a Darwinian process of natural selection or even to evolution of a Lamarckian kind. Hayek (ibid., p. 23) also writes that Darwin's

> painstaking efforts to illustrate how the process of evolution operated in living organisms convinced the scientific community of what had long been a commonplace in the humanities – at least since Sir William Jones in 1787 recognised the striking resemblance of Latin and Greek to Sanskrit, and the descent of all 'Indo-Germanic' languages from the latter.

However, in so far as Herder, Jones and Savigny introduced an idea of evolution in their writings on the development of language and law, it was one merely of lineal descent. The Darwinian idea of natural selection is not therein to be found. In so far as 'the idea of evolution' was 'a commonplace in the social sciences in the nineteenth century' its main proselytizer was Herbert Spencer, who was not truly a Darwinian and whom, incidentally, Hayek fails to mention in this context.[6] Unfortunately, these are not unique cases of a casual attitude to sources and scholarship in Hayek's work.[7]

In regard to the alleged forerunners of Darwin's theory, Ernst Mayr (1985b, p. 769) argues that 'virtually all of these so-called prior cases of natural selection turn out to be a rather different phenomenon, which is only superficially similar to selection.'[8] Hayek's attempt to belittle the importance of the Darwinian revolution by claiming multiple precedence is thus without foundation in the modern history of biology. It betrays both a misreading of the sources and some misunderstanding on Hayek's part.

Let us illustrate the kind of problem thus created. Note that, on the one hand, Hayek (1982, vol. 1, p. 24) mentions some kind of process of selection and rejects the old definition of evolution as *evolvere*, that is as unfolding or unwinding. However, on the other hand, these statements sit uneasily with the slurred account of the development of evolutionary theory in Hayek's work. In fact, the most prominent idea of social evolution which was 'a commonplace in the social sciences of the nineteenth century long before Darwin' was not one of selection in the Darwinian sense but simply of *evolvere*. Furthermore, in tracing his own intellectual pedigree from Hume and Smith, Hayek fails to notice the rarity of the idea of natural selection in their works, merely hinted at by Hume and never explicit in the economic writings of Smith.

When Hayek (1967, p. 72) writes that 'the whole of economic theory ... may be interpreted as nothing else but an endeavour to reconstruct from regularities of the individual actions the character of the resulting order' he is letting the cat out of the bag. Biological ontogeny is precisely the endeavour to explain the development of organisms from the regularities of their genetic endowment, in contrast to phylogeny which considers the sifting and changing of the gene pool through natural selection or drift. Hayek's statement clearly suggests ontogeny rather than phylogeny.

Thus, in implicitly comparing his theory to the kind of economic ontogeny found in the writings of Walras or Smith, Hayek makes the addition of the idea of 'natural selection' a mere appendage. Darwin is then reduced in stature because he is not significant for the Hayekian theory. Without further clarification, the latter can easily be reduced to the post-Humean ontogeny of the emergence of the coherent social order. With the epigenesis of Karl Ernst von Baer, for example, ontogeny was well established before Darwin. It is thus no accident that Hayek simultaneously upgrades ontogenesis and downgrades Darwin's contribution.

The Rejection of Biologism and Social Darwinism

We now turn to a more positive aspect of Hayek's evolutionism. A strong and repeated aspect of Hayek's account of cultural evolution is his rejection of biological reductionism and Social Darwinism, and his related critique of sociobiology. Hayek convincingly argues that the Social Darwinists spoiled their case by wrongly 'concentrating on the selection of congenitally more fit individuals, the slowness of which makes it comparatively unimportant for cultural evolution, and at the same time neglecting the decisively important selective evolution of rules and practices' (1982, vol. 3, p. 154). Since cultural evolution 'differs from genetic evolution by relying on the transmission of acquired properties, it is very fast, and once it dominates, it swamps genetic evolution' (p. 156).

In short, Social Darwinism wrongly 'concentrated on the selection of individuals rather than that of institutions and practices, and on the selection of innate rather than on culturally transmitted capacities of the individuals' (Hayek, 1982, vol. 1, p. 23). A similar error, Hayek argues, is found in the modern 'sociobiology' of Edward Wilson (1975) and others: 'perhaps the chief error of contemporary "sociobiology" is to suppose that language, morals, law, and such like, are transmitted by the "genetic" processes that molecular biology is now illuminating, rather than being the products of selective evolution transmitted by imitative learning' (Hayek, 1988, p. 24).

Thus in this respect Hayek's conception of evolution is clearly different from that of, for example, Herbert Spencer and William Graham Sumner in the nineteenth century, as well as that of Edward Wilson in the twentieth. Hayek puts much more emphasis on the autonomy of culture, and of the evolution of institutions and rules themselves. In this respect, therefore, he continues in the direction that Veblen had taken, many decades before.

Hayek and the Atavistic Basis of Socialism

Despite the above, Hayek repeatedly refers to atavistic influences. These are prominent where Hayek tries to turn the tables on the socialists by arguing that the yearning for egalitarianism and collectivism is an *'atavism, based on primordial emotions'* (Hayek, 1982, vol. 3, p. 165). He thereby assumes that individuals have a primitive and innate disposition towards collectivism which had to be repressed if civilization was to develop: 'practically all advance had to be achieved by infringing or repressing some of the innate rules and replacing them by new ones which made the co-ordination of larger groups possible' (p. 161). Thus, for Hayek, and contrary to its claim to represent progress, socialism is driven on by savage instincts and its consummation would mark a return to the social organization of the primitive tribe.

For Hayek, the establishment of civilization is the repression of much of our human nature that is determined by our genetic inheritance. It involves the supervening of the 'primitive' instincts of collectivism by the learned rules of the emergent individualistic culture appropriate to the Great Society. The growth of civilization is thus seen as the slow subversion of much of our biological nature.

The problem with this argument is not that Hayek assumes that to some degree our behaviour may be affected by our genes. This matter remains controversial, but it is difficult to dismiss entirely the idea that our genes affect our behaviour to some significant degree. It can be accepted that cultural influences are much more important, but it is difficult to dismiss entirely the influence of the genes.[9]

On the contrary, more transparent and ultimately fatal difficulties are found in Hayek's crude dichotomy: between collectivism as largely associated with instinct, and individualism seen primarily as a derivative of sophisticated and civilized social rules. Take the question of instinct first. Surely instincts of self-interest, competition, rivalry and even aggression are part of our biological inheritance, along with other dispositions towards caring and cooperation? Hayek dogmatically assumes that we inherit one type of instinct but not the other.

Hayek's black-and-white compartmentalization, where cooperation is seen to derive from biological instinct and individualistic civilization is seen to emanate from social culture, also breaks down on the social and cultural side of the divide. He ignores the strong possibility that socialism, far from being a return to primitive instincts, is actually an ideological product and extension of the kinds of liberal egalitarianism associated with the bourgeois epoch since its inception. Socialism has strong connections with the ideas of the Levellers and the Chartists, and libertarian or liberal thinkers such as Thomas Paine, William Godwin, John Stuart Mill and Henry George. In this sense, socialism is liberalism run to its rationalistic and egalitarian extremes. As Joseph Schumpeter wrote:

> capitalism creates a critical frame of mind which, after having destroyed the moral authority of many other institutions, in the end turns against its own; the bourgeois finds to his amazement that the rationalist attitude does not stop at the credentials of kings and popes but goes on to attack private property and the whole scheme of bourgeois values. (1976, p. 143)

Contrary to Hayek, socialist ideas emanate much less, if at all, from our genes and our primitive instincts. They are very much more an outcome of the ideological ferment of liberal capitalist society. Furthermore, through the development of large-scale industry in an urban setting, capitalism creates the working-class communities from which socialists have traditionally derived much of their political support. Notably, such ideas have often found the most fertile soils in an urban and industrial environment, not in some primitive and rural past.

The Selection of Rules

We now turn to Hayek's account of the mechanism of socioeconomic evolution. It is important to stress that in his work the account is more lucid than in the work of many preceding 'evolutionary' economists. Nevertheless, unlike Veblen for instance, Hayek's evolutionism is developed after the Darwinian synthesis and its popularization. There is thus a good reason to scrutinize his account more closely, even if some of the criticisms may apply to Veblen, and others, as well.

It will be argued that Hayek fails to clarify many crucial aspects of the processes involved. For instance, Hayek repeatedly associates evolution with the existence of some kind of selection mechanism, although its specification, along with that of the unit(s) of selection and the criteria of fitness, are somewhat vague.[10]

The possible ambiguity in the term 'selection' has been noted above, particularly in the chapter on Carl Menger. With Menger's theory of the 'evolution' of money, the medium of exchange is 'selected', but through cumulative reinforcement, and not necessarily through the sifting and winnowing of competing alternatives. Neither does it necessarily involve the 'natural selection' of the individual agents who are regarded as the 'genetic' elements driving the system. The process here is the 'selection' of a path of ontogenetic development, not the full 'natural selection' observed in phylogeny.

Hayek does not resolve this ambiguity. When he writes of the 'selective evolution of rules and practices' it is not clear whether rules are being selected in an ontogenetic or a phylogenetic sense. If it is ontogenetic selection then Hayek's conception of evolution is limited. In contrast, if it is phylogenetic selection then, as argued below, there is a contradiction between Hayek's methodological individualism and the idea of the selection of rules.

Furthermore, as Norman Barry (1979, p. 82) has pointed out, Hayek is unclear as to the criteria on which evolutionary selection takes place. Jim Tomlinson (1990, p. 47) has elaborated the same point, noting that

> Hayek . . . for example, suggests that religions which encourage strong families (undefined) provide favourable evolutionary conditions, but never spells out this point in any detail. This is a large hole in the argument, because he suggests that certain characteristics are crucial to evolutionary progress, but does little to identify what these characteristics are.

Hayek states that selection is not of individuals themselves but of 'institutions and practices' (1982, vol. 1, p. 23) and 'rules' related to individuals. However, as in the case of Hume discussed in chapter 4, the identification of what is being selected does not itself involve the specification of a selection mechanism. While Hayek makes it clear that the objects of selection are institutions or rules, this stance creates problems for Hayek's continuing adherence to methodological individualism, as explained further below.

Are Rules or Individuals Analogous to Genes?

Biological genes have a number of significant features. They are 'replicators', in that they pass on their information with some degree of fidelity. This information itself consists of coded instructions programming or directing behaviour or growth. Hence the gene could be described as an 'instructor' as well as a replicator.

If rules are seen as analogous objects of selection then they are attributed with both the functions of replicator and of instructor. When Hayek (1982, vol. 3, p. 199) writes of the 'genetic primacy of rules of conduct' he seems to be suggesting that the rule is analogous to the gene. This is prima facie a reasonable proposal because the rule does have the dual functions of replicator and of instructor.

However, Hayek's own standpoint, although vague and rarely elaborated, is more complicated. The first problem arises from the definition of the concept of 'rule'. Hayek (1967, pp. 66–7) writes: 'it should be clearly understood that the term "rule" is used for a statement by which a regularity of the conduct of individuals can be described, irrespective of whether such a rule is "known" to the individuals in any other sense than they normally act in accordance with it.'[11] This is an important clarification, as the word 'rule' is often associated by other authors with the idea of an explicit instruction or prescribed pattern of behaviour. In contrast, Hayek seems to have in mind the notion of a rule as a behavioural disposition or habit.

Despite his longstanding opposition to this philosophy, it should be noted that Hayek's definition of a rule is behaviourist, because of its exclusion of intent or design. To define a rule merely as a phenomenal 'regularity of conduct' is behaviourism pure and simple, and creates many problems for Hayek's theory, as we shall see.

What sustains the rule and gives it some durability through time? Once again, Hayek does not give us a sufficiently clear answer, but in discussing the process of cultural transmission he puts emphasis on the role of imitation.[12] The possibility of rule replication through imitation plausibly accounts for the much faster rate of cultural evolution, compared with the sluggish biotic processes of genetic change and selection. Genetic evolution, Hayek (1988, p. 16) rightly argues, is 'far too slow' to account for the rapid development of civilization. Instead, new practices were spread by imitation and acquired habit. 'This gradual replacement of innate responses by learnt rules increasingly distinguished man from other animals.'[13]

However, if the rule is simply an existing regularity of conduct then it is not entirely clear how other agents imitate existing rules. We could assume that humans act as if programmed to blindly follow others: but this would rob them of choice and the purposive ability to break rules, which Hayek is rightly keen to retain. Furthermore, do we follow rules simply as rules, or because they are embodiments of the wills of others? The mechanisms of rule replication are not clarified or explained. The mere suggestion of imitation is not enough.

Further, if the rule is simply an existing regularity of conduct, and need not take a prescriptive or codified form, as Hayek insists, then it is not entirely clear how it acts as an instructor for the human actor. What are the mechanisms involved in the genesis of action: the transformation of a rule into an act? Hayek (1967, p. 69) writes vaguely of the 'external stimulus' and the 'internal drive', without giving us much more to go on. Here there is another unfilled gap in his theory and it is necessary to interpolate and to conjecture so as to attempt to understand his theoretical system as a whole.

Are rules 'instructors' in themselves, or only because they reflect the decisions and actions of individuals? Perhaps a methodological individualist should deny the capacity of rules to 'instruct' behaviour by themselves, and see them as the intended or unintended outcomes of individual and purposeful behaviour. Yet this is to remove the 'instructor' function of the rule and to undermine its analogy with the gene. The 'instructor' thereby becomes the individual rather than the rule.

Individual genes replicate biologically. Individual actions and thoughts are sustained by habit. Rules replicate by conformism, obedience and imitation. However, as Hayek himself would agree, human choices are potentially novel. We may choose between existing rules, and there is always the possibility of novelty and creativity which is not mirrored in existing rules. Thus the replicative fidelity of rules can be undermined by real choices, even if choices are themselves replicated through their establishment as rules. While rules are clearly objects of replication in socioeconomic evolution, humans are not 'instructed' by rules alone; they also make choices. If choice is made supreme in the human sphere, then the analogy between the chosen rule and the gene becomes imperfect.[14]

Hence the question whether rules can be endowed with the qualities of an 'instructor' depends on the general methodological and ontological position that is taken. For this and other reasons Hayek's own explicit adherence to choice, purposeful behaviour and methodological individualism would seem to be inconsistent with his own supreme emphasis on the object of selection being rules.

In sum, in the social context, neither rules nor individuals provide exact parallels to the biological gene. Both individuals and rules, and perhaps additional entities as suggested below, are units of selection in socioeconomic evolution. Individuals, individual acts, and rules both replicate and are 'selected' in different ways, making the exact analogy with conventional biology problematic.

Despite having written on cultural evolution for over 20 years, Hayek not only fails to present an adequate solution to the above problems but also fails to articulate them clearly. Without a satisfactory solution Hayek's evolutionary theory remains incomplete. As we have noted, part of the problem is the juxtaposition in Hayek's writings of methodological individualism with evolutionary ideas. For instance, the retention of methodological individualism would seem to require a solution with all its weight on individual purposefulness and choice, to the neglect of conditioning and structure.[15] In which case the notion of the rule takes second place, and much of Hayek's emphasis on rule following would have to be removed.

Should a Reductionist Choose the Individual or the Gene?

As discussed in more detail in the next chapter, Viktor Vanberg (1986) has attacked Hayek's version of cultural evolution precisely because it is inconsistent with methodological individualism. Appealing for support for his view, Vanberg cites the works of biologists such as John Maynard Smith (1976, 1980), Robert L. Trivers (1985) and Edward O. Wilson (1975). There is also the seminal work of George C. Williams (1966) and the popular books of Richard Dawkins (1976, 1982, 1986, 1989). The theoretical position of Dawkins, G. C. Williams and others is widely described as 'genetic reductionist' because it involves an attempt to break down the explanation of biological phenomena to the basic unit of the gene.

It should be emphasized that the 'genetic reductionist' mode of explanation that is developed by Dawkins, Maynard Smith, G. C. Williams and others, relies on the important fact that the gene is not only a 'replicator' and an 'instructor', but that its features are much more stable and potentially longlasting than those of the individual, the group or the population. It is the stability of the gene and of the information within it, as well as its particular role in the evolutionary process, that is an important element in their case for regarding the gene as the unit of selection. If we are to regard individuals or rules as analogous to genes then we have to authenticate a sufficient degree of stability in these terms as well.

In social science, however, reductionist explanations typically focus on the individual, as in the case of methodological individualism (Lukes, 1973; Hodgson, 1988, ch. 3). Given that individuals are much more malleable than genes, this makes an appeal to 'genetic reductionist' biology in support of methodological individualism somewhat dubious.

There is a further problem in Vanberg's attempt to rescue Hayek by making him a consistent methodological individualist. If the impetus for a methodological individualist account is a reductionist attempt to explain the whole in terms of its parts then the true reductionist should embrace the gene rather than the individual as the basic unit of explanation.

Accordingly, as noted in the next chapter, David Sloan Wilson and Elliott Sober (1989) go so far as to argue that to settle on the individual as the unit of selection involves an inconsistency. The same arguments concerning explanatory reduction from groups to individuals apply equally to explanatory reduction from individual to gene. If we can reduce explanations to individual terms why not further reduce them to the terms of genes? This argument would seem especially apposite for one who appeals to the biological works of Maynard Smith, Trivers and E. O. Wilson. Or can these two alternatives – individuals and genes – be somehow reconciled?

One possible means of reconciliation, it would seem, would be to adopt Dawkins's (1982) distinction between 'replicators' and 'vehicles' in the natural selection process. Dawkins sees the genes as replicators, and the individuals or groups are 'vehicles' in which the genes are always carried. Natural selection works directly on the phenotypical 'vehicles'; some are selected and others are not. Only indirectly does this affect the genotypes, through an extended period of time in which different genes are selected.

Hayek (1967, pp. 67–8) says that the selection of rules will operate on the bases of the greater or lesser efficiency of the resulting order or system to which they relate. He could be loosely interpreted as saying that 'the selection of rules will operate on the basis of the fitness of the resulting individuals and groups.' In this particular formulation the rules are clearly analogous to the genes, and the individuals or groups are analogous to organism (or possibly group) phenotypes. The rules are thus the replicators, and individuals (or groups) are the vehicles.

At first sight, this reformation of Hayek's theory would seem to neutralize some of the features of Vanberg's (1986) critique, and within the terms of a genetic reductionist biology. However, there is a serious problem in this reformulation. In biological evolution, the genes of a given organism do not change; they endure as long as that organism remains alive, and may even be passed on to its offspring. This is clearly not the case with the rule in socioeconomic evolution; both individuals and groups can change rules. In consequence, these 'vehicles' can alter the replicating material they are carrying.

This is not normally the case in the biotic sphere. Here it is not necessary to explain further why a given vehicle sustains its genetic material, because at least in modern evolutionary theory it is imprinted in the DNA and cannot easily be altered. However, in contrast, in cultural evolution the maintenance of given rules by a given individual or group 'vehicle' is not automatic.

This important difference between biological and cultural evolution provides a source of serious error. While in biology it can be assumed that the genes have considerable stability and may maintain themselves with fidelity through time, we cannot assume the same in the cultural evolution. This has an important implication for the patterns of explanation involved. In biology we can sometimes assume that the known contribution of a gene to the overall fitness of an organism helps to explain its very existence. This is not the case in cultural evolution, because if a trait or rule is selected because of its contribution to the fitness of an individual or group then we have to further explain why that trait or rule sustains itself beyond the instant of its selection.

Consequently, Vanberg (1986, p. 83) is right to suggest that Hayek's argument has a functionalist quality; it assumes that the contribution of a rule to the maintenance of a system is sufficient to explain the existence of that rule. Absent in Hayek's argument is the specification of a process by which a rule that is advantageous to the system is sustained in operation within that system.

Hayek is rightly criticized for assuming that the contribution of a rule to the maintenance of a system is sufficient to explain the existence of that rule. But note that this argument applies to individuals as well as to groups. An individual could be regarded as a kind of system, as well as a group. Do we assume that the contribution of a rule to the welfare of an individual is sufficient to explain the adoption of that rule? Absent in such an argument is the specification of a process by which a rule that benefits a number of individuals is sustained in operation by those individuals.

If such anti-functionalism is combined with the kind of reductionist approach that Vanberg seems to prefer, then we encounter once more the problem of finding a sufficiently stable and enduring unit. Both individuals and rules have a transient quality, so the reductionist is impelled, once more, to turn to the gene. Hence, Vanberg's strong critique of functionalism, combined with an incautiously reductionist thrust, erodes his own chosen reliance on the individual as the basic explanatory unit.[16]

The Fatal Conflict

It has been shown that it is not enough to follow Hayek and simply assume that a rule is a manifest behavioural regularity in individuals, without examining the procedures and mechanisms involved in its adoption by each individual. Clearly, such an explanation would have to delve into psychology, habit formation and the nature of individual choice, among other factors. The endurance of rules should not be taken for granted; it has to be explained by detailed examination of both the cultural and psychological processes involved.

However, in line with his methodological individualism, Hayek (1948, p. 67; 1952, p. 39) suggests that in social science the given individual should be taken as the irreducible unit of explanation, excluding psychology in explanations of social phenomena. Yet these rigid statements specifically exclude an examination into some of the processes involved in the sustenance and replication of rules. Once again, the methodological individualist perspective that Hayek adopts from Austrian heritage would seem to block the development of his evolutionary thinking.

It is in assuming that the benefits of a rule are sufficient to explain its continuing adoption by an individual that Hayek is posing too direct a connection between individuals and rules. Either the explanation rests on the rule rather than the individual, or it has to explain the adoption of rules by individuals. In the former case, rules not individuals become the ultimate elements of explanation. The latter explanation involves psychology and other matters. In both cases there is a clash with methodological individualism – at least the kind that Hayek has advocated in the past.

In the following chapter this 'fatal conflict' in Hayek's mature thought is shown to reach even greater dimensions, when his juxtaposition of methodological individualism with group selection is examined.

12
Friedrich Hayek and Spontaneous Order

This chapter continues the examination of the evolutionary thought of Friedrich Hayek. Here we focus on his central concept of 'spontaneous order'. This is associated with the idea of group selection which Hayek has taken from biology. Despite prominent criticism of group selection, here a defence is presented of this notion in regard to both biotic and socioeconomic evolution. However, this defence leads to rejection rather than vindication of Hayek's policy stance. Further criticisms of Hayek's policy outlook are raised towards the end of this chapter.

Group Selection and the Concept of an Order

Hayek makes an important distinction between an *order* of actions and the set of *rules* of action through which it emerges: 'A particular order of actions can be observed and described without knowledge of the rules of conduct of the individuals which bring it about: and it is at least conceivable that the same overall order of actions may be produced by different sets of rules of individual conduct' (1967, p. 68). Although individual actions are governed by rules, orders are the unintended outcome of interactions, not the product of a single will.[1]

Hayek (1988, p. 20) states that rules are selected 'on the basis of their human survival-value'. In attempting to clarify what this might mean, Hayek (1967, p. 70; 1982, vol. 1, p. 164; 1982, vol. 3, p. 202) embraces the notion of 'group selection' as advanced by Vero C. Wynne-Edwards (1962) in biology. He argues that habits and rules are indirectly selected, through their association with a particular type of group: 'Such new rules would spread not because men understood that they were more effective, or could calculate that they would lead to expansion, but simply because they enabled those groups practising them to procreate more successfully and to include outsiders' (Hayek, 1988, p. 16). While the '*transmission* of rules of conduct takes place *from individual to individual*, the natural *selection* of rules will operate on the basis of the greater or less efficiency of the resulting *order of the group*'

(Hayek, 1967, p. 67). More particularly: 'The evolutionary selection of different rules of individual conduct operates through the viability of the order it will produce' (p. 68). Thus 'institutions and practices' which had first 'been adopted for other reasons, or even purely accidentally, were preserved because they enable the group in which they had arisen to prevail over others' (Hayek, 1982, vol. 1, p. 9).

As noted in the preceding chapter, such passages have a distinct functionalist quality. Hayek's argument assumes that the contribution of a rule to the maintenance of the group is sufficient to explain the existence of that rule. He fails to specify a process by which a rule that is advantageous to a group is sustained in operation, and not, for instance, replaced by other rules.

For similar reasons, the group selection idea has been the subject of a number of critiques from biology (Maynard Smith, 1976, 1980; Trivers, 1985; G. C. Williams, 1966) including a bestselling work by Richard Dawkins (1976). These works explain the survival of specific group behaviours in terms of mechanisms involving the natural selection of the related genes, not in terms of the selection of the group as a whole.[2]

A prominent argument against group and cultural selection, allied to the critique of functionalism noted above, is that there is no clear mechanism to ensure that an advantageous pattern of behaviour for the group will be sustained in operation within that system, or replicated by the actions of the individuals concerned. In particular, such a mechanism must ensure that 'free riders' do not become dominant in the groups that exhibit socially useful altruistic behaviours. Free riders would have the benefits of being members of a group whose other members perform socially useful and self-sacrificial acts, but would bear no personal costs or risks in terms of self-sacrificial behaviour themselves. Consequently, in the absence of any compensating mechanism, it is likely that free riders within the group will expand in numbers, crowd out the others, and alter the typical behaviour of the group as a whole.[3]

Thus, despite the possible benefits to the group of self-sacrificial behaviour, Hayek indicates no mechanism that will ensure that groups with these characteristics will prosper above others. What thus seems crucial is the selection of the constituent individuals and not the groups as a whole. Accepting this rationale, Viktor Vanberg further argues that Hayek's idea of group selection and his theory of socioeconomic evolution is inconsistent with methodological individualism. He thus concludes that the 'notion of cultural group selection is theoretically vague, inconsistent with the basic thrust of Hayek's individualistic approach, and faulty judged on its own grounds' (Vanberg, 1986, p. 97).

However, Vanberg is wrong to dismiss group selection so easily. It is shown in the appendix to this chapter that a number of biologists now argue with good reason that there are levels of selection other than the gene, including group selection. Furthermore, apart from biology, there are additional reasons to assume that group selection may operate in cultural evolution. Some of these reasons will be discussed below.

As already noted, the idea of 'group selection' does seem to conflict with a thoroughgoing methodological individualism, and there is a major internal inconsistency in Hayek's work. Further, as Vanberg argues, Hayek's support for group selection is inconsistent with genetic reductionism of the Dawkins–Trivers–Williams type. There seem at first to be two ways out of the difficulty: either to abandon group selection or to at least modify the individualistic thrust. Vanberg suggests the former, claiming an accord with both methodological individualism and attempts in biology to explain group phenomena in genetic terms.

The Possibility of Group Selection

Biologists who argue the case for the possibility of group selection do not suggest that group selection will always operate; it depends on the processes and structures involved. Essentially, group selection is seen to act if all organisms in the same group are 'bound together by a common fate' (Sober, 1981, p. 107). A population of (diverse) units is so interlinked, with spillover effects and externalities, that it is selected upon as an entity.[4]

But what if the behaviour of this interlinked group could somehow be explained in terms of the genes or individuals involved? Philosophers of biology such as Elliott Sober (1981) point out that a reductionist explanation in terms of genes – if one were possible – leaves open the question of what causes the gene frequencies themselves to alter. Although all information about ostensible group selection may be reduced to and represented by selection coefficients of organisms or genes, such a formal reduction to the genic or individual level leaves the question unanswered as to what causes the frequency of genes in the gene pool to change. Likewise, methodological individualist explanations leave open the questions of the origin or moulding or composition of a population of individuals with their preferences and purposes.

In turn, the response to this argument from the genetic reductionist may be that the gene is the single unit of replication. However, while biological objects pass on their characteristics via their genes, this leaves open the question as to what causes their differential transmission. Just as individuals may be regarded as groups of genes that have become functionally organized by natural selection to perpetuate themselves, groups can be seen as groups of individuals similarly functionally organized.

Given the possibility of group selection in biology, it can be conjectured that the same phenomenon occurs in the socioeconomic sphere.

Considerations of institutions, rules, norms and culture are apposite. Assume that a particular characteristic affects all members of a group to a similar degree, such as the enforcement of different modes of diet, dress or behaviour. Assume further that this characteristic affects the future growth and prosperity of the group. Then there may be grounds for considering that group selection is at work. Thus, for example, the Shakers as a religious sect have approached demise because of their internal law of celibacy. In earlier times, as Max Weber argues in *The Protestant Ethic and the Spirit of Capitalism*, Protestant communities or nations prospered relative to Catholic ones, partly because of their relatively individualistic culture and their disposition to accumulate worldly wealth (Weber, 1978).

Note that these examples are not straightforward cases of individual selection; it is not simply individuals with given behavioural propensities that are being selected. Although there was selection in favour of individuals who did not join Shaker sects, the preferences and behaviours of individuals were themselves changed, by indoctrination or cultural pressure, by becoming part of that group. Accordingly, groups and group cultures were being selected, or selected against, as well as individuals.

Indeed, it could be argued that group selection is more likely with cultural inheritance in human society than with genetic transmission in the biotic sphere. Hence although the parallel argument in biology is informative, the idea of cultural group selection does not depend upon it. Cultural transmission is more collective and conformist than genetic transmission. As Robert Boyd and Peter Richerson (1985, pp. 204–40) have shown, conformism provides a compensating mechanism to overcome the free-rider problem. Consequently, the potential free rider is under strong pressure not to free-ride but to conform to the group. The different nature of the transmission process establishes a strong case for cultural group selection.

Organizational Knowledge and Group Selection

There is another important reason for group selection which seems to be barred by Hayek's individualistic outlook. Following Michael Polanyi (1957, 1967) he stresses the importance of tacit knowledge. Like Polanyi, he relates this exclusively to individuals. However, experience suggests that it may in some sense reside in groups as well. An example is suggested by Sidney Winter (1982) who argues that the capabilities of an organization such as a firm are not generally reducible to the capabilities of individual members. He points out that:

> The coordination displayed in the performance of organizational routines is, like that displayed in the exercise of individual skills, the fruit of practice. What requires emphasis is that . . . the learning experience is a

> shared experience of organization members . . . Thus, even if the con-
> tents of the organizational memory are stored only in the form of memory
> traces in the memories of individual members, it is still an organiza-
> tional knowledge in the sense that the fragment stored by each individual
> member is not fully meaningful or effective except in the context pro-
> vided by the fragments stored by other members. (Winter, 1982, p. 76)

Clearly, there is an important question here concerning the possibility of collective knowledge.[5] Hayek is not the only theorist to deny
this and take an individualist position. For instance, Boyd and Richerson
develop a theory of cultural evolution in which they take the view of
culture as 'information capable of affecting individuals' (1985, p. 33).[6]
They (p. 37) approvingly quote Ward Goodenough (1981, p. 54) who
writes that: 'People learn as individuals. Therefore, if culture is learned,
its ultimate locus must be in individuals rather than in groups.' In
taking an individualistic view of knowledge, Hayek is thus a member
of an eminent collective.

In contrast, there is the 'collectivist' position of anthropologists such
as Marvin Harris (1971, p. 136), a stance more in accord with that of
Winter: 'Cultures are patterns of behavior, thought and feeling that
are acquired or influenced through learning and that are characteristic
of groups of people rather than of individuals.' Arguably, culture is
not simply 'information affecting individuals'; it consists not merely
of beliefs and assumptions, but also behaviour patterns, habits, language and signs, even rituals and patterns of behaviour (Keesing, 1974).
Furthermore, the kind of 'information' that is used and transmitted
in a culture is embedded in social structures and organizations, in the
sense that its existence and transmission depends on them. Even the
kind of information held by a single individual is typically context
dependent; information and structure are mutually intertwined.[7] It is
thus difficult to locate culture in individual persons. Culture and institutions transcend the individuals to whom they relate. By seeing
culture as a structured and interactive belief–action system its collective quality can be appreciated.

Winter's own argument suggests that although tacit or other knowledge must reside in the nerve or brain cells of a set of human beings,
its enactment depends crucially on the existence of a structured context in which individuals interact with each other. Otherwise, no such
knowledge can become operational. Furthermore, because organizational knowledge is tacit knowledge, by definition it cannot be expressed in a codified form. The knowledge becomes manifest only
through the interactive practice of the members of the group. It is both
learned and transmitted in a group context only.

There are many cases where the organizational knowledge is maintained within a structure, perhaps even for long periods of time, despite the turnover of its individual members. Just as our personal
memory of past events is retained, despite the loss and renewal of our

brain cells, organizational knowledge may survive the gradual but complete replacement of the individuals comprising the organization.

Clearly both individual and organizational outcomes depend on the nature of any such organizational knowledge. Here is a clear case of the fates of a number of individuals being bound together in a single group. Such organizational learning is thus feasibly associated with group selection.

Organizational knowledge can relate to a subset of the workers within a firm. If the knowledge relates to all the workers in a firm, or crucial aspects of its management, then the organization in which that particular organizational knowledge resides is the firm as a whole.

Selection may thus operate on a subset of the firm's routines, as in the selection process modelled by Richard Nelson and Sidney Winter (1982). If in contrast some aspects of 'organizational learning' are inextricably related to the firm as a whole, then this implies the selection of firms and not simply the capabilities or routines that may reside within them.

We have noted that for Hayek it is the individual rather than the organization which is the carrier of the rule. But if there is such a thing as organizational knowledge, as discussed above, it would be a mistake to attempt to account for this wholly in terms of the interaction of individuals. As Hayek (1967, p. 71) himself puts it: 'the existence of the whole cannot be accounted for wholly by the interaction of the parts but only in their interaction with an outside world both of the individual parts and the whole.' In the present context this would suggest that the existence of collective knowledge can be accounted for only by the interaction of individuals and by their interactions with the environment and the group. But this interpretation seems to conflict with Hayek's proposition that rules are carried by individuals alone. Once again, there seems to be a contradiction in Hayek's thought.

Organizational knowledge cannot be sustained at an individual level. Its group character means that it is quite different from individual altruistic propensities which are beneficial to the group but which can be progressively undermined by self-seeking 'free riders'. This will not necessarily occur in the case of organizational knowledge precisely because it is an attribute of groups rather than of individuals. Individuals have an incentive to conform to the group and gain access to its knowledge. Thereby a number of units are again 'bound together by a common fate'.

Markets and Still Higher Levels of Selection

As noted in the appendix to this chapter, the possibility of multiple and higher levels of selection is now accepted by a number of modern biological theorists, including the possibility of selection of species and even ecosystems. There is no apparent reason why multiple levels of selection should not also exist within the socioeconomic world as well.

Hayek sees selection as operating on a plurality of different groups or agencies, but seemingly always within a given (market) structure. Thus he ignores the possibility that selection may also be working at the level of structure and substructure, creating a diversity not simply of groups and agencies but also of types of economic system or subsystem (Hodgson, 1984), as well as a variety of market forms.

Hayek's very conception of the market is part of the difficulty here. In fact, Hayek is remarkably vague on how his image of the market fits into his picture of group selection and the spontaneous order. The fundamental dilemma here is this: does the market correspond to a particular type of *order*, or does it correspond to the general *context* in which the evolutionary selection of (all) orders takes place?[8] This unresolved dilemma is of vital importance, in both theoretical and policy terms.

In one passage Hayek (1988, pp. 38–47) puts the former interpretation. He sketches a history of the emergence of the market, suggesting that it is not itself the context of evolution but an evolved order: a specific outcome of evolution itself. However, this interpretation leaves open the nature of the context in which the selection of the market takes place. To assume that the market is itself selected in a market environment is either incoherent, or suggests the important but unacknowledged possibility of a nested set of market structures in which selection occurs: a market for markets.

Furthermore, such a formulation does not imply that the particular evolved market is necessarily optimal or ideal. It is a general but common mistake to regard evolution in such terms.

In contrast, in an earlier work, Hayek (1982, vol. 3, p. 162) supports the interpretation of the market as the general context of selection. The problem with this, however, is that Hayek does not explain how the specific rules and property rights associated with the market themselves emerge. The crucial question is left open as to how this longstanding general context of selection itself originally evolved.

Criticizing Hayek on this point, Vanberg (1986, p. 75) points out that the market 'is always a system of social interaction characterized by a specific *institutional framework*, that is, by a *set of rules* defining certain restrictions on the behavior of market participants'. Whether these rules are formal or informal the result is that there is no such thing as the 'true, unhampered market', operating in an institutional vacuum. 'This raises the issue of what rules can be considered "appropriate" in the sense of allowing for a beneficial working of the market mechanism' (ibid., p. 97).[9]

Notably, the market itself is not a natural datum or ether, but is itself a *social institution*, governed by sets of rules defining restrictions on some, and legitimating other, behaviours. Furthermore, the market is necessarily embedded in other social institutions such as the state, and is promoted or even in some cases created by conscious design.[10] Given that markets are themselves institutions, then they must all constitute objects of evolutionary selection, alongside other institutions of various types.

Given that the idea of supra-individual levels of selection is justified – an idea accepted by Hayek but not by Vanberg – then Hayek should be criticized, not for embracing group selection and eschewing a consistent individualism, but for failing to incorporate additional processes of selection above the group level.

This point, however, has embarrassing consequences for Hayek's theory. Clearly, such supra-individual selection must involve the selection of different types of institution, including varieties of both market and non-market forms. To work at such higher levels, evolutionary selection must involve different types of ownership structure and resource allocation mechanisms, all coexisting in a mixed economy.

It is thus important to emphasize that evolutionary theory does not justify the purified and ubiquitous market system that Hayek endorses. If the market is the *context* of selection then the origin of this framework is itself unexplained. If the market is an *object* of selection then for its selection to be real it must exist alongside other non-market forms. The rehabilitation of group selection, based on modern work in biology, thus rebounds on Hayek himself. His work presents multiple dilemmas from which there is no apparent escape.

Spontaneous Order and Evolution

Hayek writes repeatedly of the coupling of the 'twin ideas of evolution and spontaneous order',[11] implying that they are two facets of a single conception. But, as Ellen Paul (1988, p. 261) argues: 'The relationship between Hayek's concept of spontaneous order and his evolutionism is unclear.'[12]

Nevertheless, to bolster his central idea, he linked the concept of spontaneous order together with 'autopoiesis, cybernetics, homeostasis, spontaneous order, self-organisation, synergetics, systems theory' (Hayek, 1988, p. 9) as supposedly allied and similar ideas, and cited works by Ilya Prigogine and others (Hayek, 1982, vol. 3, p. 200) in their support. However, this list of topics is not itself conceptually or theoretically homogeneous. It further betrays a serious shortcoming of Hayek's work: a lack of clarity about the crucial concept of spontaneous order.

It should be noted at the outset, however, that the ideas listed are developments of cybernetics and systems theory, and the latter very much owes its development to biological theorists such as Ludwig von Bertalanffy and Paul Weiss.[13] Nevertheless, a key point of the development of these 'sciences of complexity' is their synthesis in the 1960s with non-equilibrium dynamics. This led to the distinctive ideas of autopoiesis and self-organization.[14] A crucial feature of autopoietic or self-organizing systems is the emergence of order from apparent chaos in a far-from-equilibrium state. In contrast, simpler systems are typically presented as being in equilibrium, or close to it.

The most charitable interpretation would be to associate Hayek's idea of a spontaneous order with the more sophisticated ideas of autopoiesis or self-organization. It is not clear, however, if he would want to take all the related baggage on board. For instance, a central idea in the literature on complex and evolving systems is that the occurrence of smooth economic growth over a long period is no guarantee that such a felicitous trajectory will continue. There is always the possibility of abrupt morphogenetic change. Interestingly, such structural disruptions do not need to come from exogenous sources. Working latently during the periods of peaceful development, built-in mechanisms can prepare for eventual catastrophic change.

Accordingly, Ervin Laszlo (1987, p. 46) argues, 'as no autopoietic reaction cycle is entirely immune to disruption, constant changes in the environment sooner or later produce conditions under which certain cycles can no longer operate. The systems encounter a point known in dynamic systems theory as bifurcation.' Unlike the intervening periods of relative macrostability, at the point of bifurcation the system is highly sensitive to minute changes. Small variations can affect the entire course and trajectory of development (Prigogine and Stengers, 1984). In sum, the notion of spontaneous order, if conceived in these terms, should embrace the twin idea of spontaneous disorder as well.

However, in particular contrast to the evolutionary thought of Veblen, there is no discussion of the possible breakdown of a spontaneous order in Hayek's work. The entire emphasis is on the emergence and stabilization of the order, as an unintended consequence of individual actors. He invests the idea of spontaneous order with a hallowed and inviolable mystery: suggesting that in general it should not be tampered with. Yet if the possibility of spontaneous *dis*order was accepted, then perhaps some grounds for interventionist policies could be readily sustained.

The idea of a self-organizing, 'dissipative structure' developed by Prigogine and his collaborators involves the emergence of order through the interaction of continuous fluctuations at the elemental level. Although such fluctuations introduce a limited type of variety into the system, they are kept within limits. Accordingly, Prigogine's work has been criticized by Peter Corning (1983, p. 75) for putting too much emphasis on the emergence of order: 'If there has been order through fluctuations, there has also been disorder through fluctuations.' Notably, Corning (pp. 70–6) also dwells at length on the similarities between the work of Ilya Prigogine and Herbert Spencer. Hayek seems to be willingly in the same boat.[15]

In sum, Hayek takes on board a one-sided view of evolution which stresses the emergence of order rather than the possibility of disorder. He even gives relatively little attention to the clash of rival orders in turmoil and war, reassuring us continuously that spontaneous order can and will emerge. With evolution, however, there is no guarantee that it will always be directed towards an ordered state: chaos and collapse are always possible.

Phylogeny Approaching Ontogeny Once More

Nevertheless, Hayek seems to want to relate the idea of a spontaneous order to a phylogenetic concept of evolution in which selection is taking place. In this case an important question emerges: Are there major sources of renewed variety and diversity in the system, and if so, from where? We can see novelty as emerging from the creativity of the inventor or the entrepreneur, and potential variety in microscopic fluctuations, or in the chaotic forces of non-linear development. These are plausible sources of variety, but none is made explicit in Hayek's presentation.

In one passage Hayek (1967, p. 32) writes of 'a mechanism of reduplication with transmissible variations'. Vanberg (1986, p. 81) sees this as a process of variation in which 'continuously new' transmittable variants are 'generated'. This is something, but not much, to go on. Notably, this remark of Hayek's is in the very same paragraph where he refers to the theory of evolution by natural selection as being 'exceedingly simple'. However, as we have seen, even quite complex accounts of evolutionary process may largely ignore the question of the ongoing source of variety. Although Hayek finds the idea of evolution to be simple, he has left a gaping hole in his account of it. Precisely how is variety generated and renewed? Here, clearly, Hayek's omission of Malthus is telling.[16] It is only in a few places elsewhere (e.g. Hayek, 1982, vol. 3, pp. 161, 167) where Hayek cautiously talks both of rule-breaking and the evolution of new rules.

In fact, Hayek's conception of evolution converges to that of Spencer at this crucial point. With the emphasis on the emergence of a stable order, and the corresponding neglect of the possibility of spontaneous disorder, Hayek's theory strongly resembles that of his nineteenth-century predecessor. Both theories are strictly phylogenetic in character, but with an outcome that converges to a near-stable state.

As in the case of Spencer, the spontaneous order could involve growth and change, just as the ontogenetic development of an organism with fixed genes involves growth. Ontogeny does not imply an equilibrium in a mechanical sense, but it does involve a degree of stability and continuity of form. It is thus indeed an equilibrium of a different kind. As Marina Colonna (1990, p. 64) notes, there is an assumption in Hayek's economic writings that 'whatever the disturbing factors may be, in a free market economy the inherent tendency towards equilibrium finally will prevail, or at least it is always at work.'

As we have noted, the movement towards such a well-formed outcome narrows the gap between phylogeny and ontogeny. With no further source of renewal or variety, the former converges on the latter. In this case, Hayek's theory of socioeconomic evolution again resembles Spencer's; it is asymptotic to ontogeny as the kind of variety that is introduced into the system becomes confined, or even progressively dries up. We find again, in Hayek's theory, another case where 'phylogeny approaches ontogeny' in a reversed Haeckel's law. Although strictly phylogenetic, Hayek's idea of evolution reduces essentially to an ontogenetic metaphor.

In view of this similarity with Spencer, it is uncanny that Hayek (1982, vol. 3, p. 158) approvingly quotes the following statement of Gregoire Nicolis and Ilya Prigogine: 'Wherever we look, we discover evolutionary processes leading to diversification and increasing complexity.' This strongly Spencerian idea of evolution creating increasing variety is also suggested elsewhere in his work (Hayek, 1988, pp. 26, 126–7), but without acknowledgement of its source in Spencer himself.

Hayek clearly differs from Spencer in regarding individual rules, rather than individuals or genes, as the units of selection. Also, unlike Spencer, he rejects the idea of explicit laws of evolution (Hayek, 1982, vol. 1, pp. 23–4; 1982, vol. 3, p. 198). However, in suggesting that evolution involves greater and greater complexity, Hayek has precisely and inadvertently reproduced the alleged 'law' of the 'transition from something homogeneous and general to something heterogeneous and special' originally found in the work of Karl Ernst von Baer and embraced and popularized by Spencer.

Consequently, 'spontaneous order' and 'evolution' are not necessarily 'twin ideas' at all. If evolution is phylogeny, then it conflicts with the more plausible ontogenetic interpretation of the emergence of a relatively durable and stable order. Phylogeny involves disorder as well as order, and chaos as well as equilibrium. It has been argued here that the greater interpretative weight should be put on the idea that Hayek has a concept of evolution in which there is an ongoing selection process, but in which the process of development, as in Spencer's theory, is asymptotic to ontogeny. The 'twin ideas' are not of spontaneous order and evolution in general, but of spontaneous order and ontogeny.

Hayek and the Perfectibility of Society

The above comparison of Hayek and Spencer suggests a further examination of their work for possible similarities. In a preceding chapter it has been shown that Spencer (1855, p. 492) proposed that 'life attains more and more perfect forms' and that evolution in general meant increasing progress and efficiency.

At first sight Hayek would seem to take a different view. For instance, he insists that there are no grounds to presume that any particular outcome of the evolutionary process is morally superior or necessarily just. As Hayek (1988, p. 27) puts it: 'I do not claim that the results of group selection of traditions are necessarily "good" – any more than I claim that other things that have long survived in the course of evolution, such as cockroaches, have moral value.'

Unlike Spencer, and with the benefit of the hindsight of the totalitarian horrors of the twentieth century, Hayek does not hold the view that evolution is automatically leading in the direction desired by the classic liberal. He acknowledges and bemoans the fact that history evinces far more examples of illiberal than liberal societies. Accordingly, he does not believe that society, left alone, will evolve towards perfection.

With these qualifications, however, there is still a similarity with Spencer on this point. Both Spencer and Hayek call for eternal vigilance in the name of liberty, and have similar visions of the better future that is its reward. Both propose a 'Great Society' emanating from the strong traditions of classic liberalism, manifest in a set of political and social institutions involving supposedly minimal government and maximum individual liberty, and resting squarely on a constitution protecting well-defined property rights and extensive free markets.

So while Hayek on the one hand rejects the suggestion that evolution automatically leads to progress, he has a clear criterion by which advance may be judged: to the extent that rules consistent with the Great Society emerge and function, and overcome the assumed atavistic and collectivist instincts of humankind, then progress is deemed to be made.

Although Hayek has less faith than Spencer in the felicitous outcome of the evolutionary process, he has a clear preference for a particular kind of socioeconomic system and he believes that such a system is attainable. Most of his written output is directly related to the investigation of the principles governing the operation of the Great Society. This utopian strain in his thinking is somewhat underestimated by some other commentators. Notably, Hayek himself (1933, p. 123) wrote: 'it is probably no exaggeration to say that economics developed mainly as the outcome of the investigation and refutation of successive Utopian proposals.' Just as there are utopians proposing planned and collectivist solutions, there are those, like Hayek, suggesting an alternative utopia based on private property and markets.[17]

Here the double similarity with Spencer is obvious; both writers are utopians and both propose utopias of a very similar variety. Both writers reject socialism, partly because of its apparent denial of diversity. However, while Hayek (1988, p. 80) quotes Wilhelm von Humbolt's celebration of 'human development in its richest diversity', for him, as for Spencer, diversity is to be limited. Both visions are based on the single and ubiquitous economic arrangements of markets and private ownership. They embrace a competitive plurality of economic agents but not a pluralistic diversity involving quite different structural forms. While the pluralism of individuals and entrepreneurs is endorsed, true structural pluralism is shunned.

Although in detail they have different conceptions of the evolutionary process, implicit in the ideas of both Spencer and Hayek is the common assumption of the eventual perfectibility of society. Strikingly, therefore, both thinkers are vulnerable to the Malthusian critique of the notion of such perfectibility. For Malthus, diversity itself was essential to progress, and for this reason alone the system could never take a perfect or purified form. To remain consistent with this view, the idea of a Great Society based on a single type of structure or economic arrangement has to be rejected. Arguably, any perfect society based on such a homogeneity of structure, even with an incorporated diversity of agents and cultures, is at risk. Stagnation and lack of moral impulse may be its fate. Or there could be crises due to insufficient internal structural variety, such variety being necessary so that novel responses may be generated to unanticipated change.[18]

This Malthusian line of argument finds in Hayek's kind of liberalism an Achilles' heel. Note the relevance here of the discussion of American liberalism by Louis Hartz (1955), as taken up by Albert Hirschman (1982). Both Hartz and Hirschman see a problem of potential or actual stagnation, of both a moral and an economic kind, in the kind of developed capitalist individualism that is most advanced in the United States of America: 'Having been "born equal," without any sustained struggle against . . . the feudal past, America is deprived of what Europe has in abundance: social and ideological diversity. *But such diversity is one of the prime constituents of genuine liberty*' (Hirschman, 1982, p. 1479). Thus, in contrast to the fake diversity that is proclaimed by devotees of the individualistic golden age, liberalism taken to extremes becomes its opposite: a monolithic order, embracing a species uniformity of both ideology and structure, the tyranny of the like-thinking majority and a 'colossal liberal absolutism' (Hartz, 1955, p. 285).[19]

The flaw in the kind of classic liberal utopia proposed by Hayek and Spencer is both to conceive of a perfectible type of system based on a ubiquitous kind of economic arrangement and to limit the indigenous diversity to that of agency rather than structure. The Malthusian argument provides an antidote to this conception, even if Malthus himself did not pursue it to the full. It is thus perhaps no accident that in Hayek's accounts of the influences on Darwin the name of Malthus is omitted.

The Policy Contradiction

A central problem with his policy stance is that Hayek has placed himself in a contradictory position. Essentially, he appeals to reason to limit the scope of rationalist thought. Hayek devises, as Michael Oakeshott (1962, p. 21) wittily remarks, 'a plan to resist all planning'. Yet he clearly admits that government 'is of necessity the product of intellectual design' (Hayek, 1982, vol. 3, p. 152). Jim Tomlinson (1990, p. 56) further elucidates this dilemma:

> there remains a problem in conceiving of how arguments about forms of social organization . . . can be conducted which are not substantially 'rationalistic' in character . . . Political arguments have to be framed in terms of rational principles, even if we know at the same time that human action can never be reduced to rationality in motion. But only the most unthinking conservative can resolve this dilemma by appeal to what *is*, rather than through any rational justification for forms of social organisation.

Hayek's evolutionism is often depicted as a kind of Burkean appeal to the sanctity of tradition, and a subtle investment of that which *is* with a moral *ought*. If this was the case then he would be a supreme advocate of laissez-faire. But he is not. The twentieth century has extinguished such conservative optimism, along with belief in the sure march of progress. As Chandran Kukathas (1989, pp. 211–12) notes: 'For all his criticisms of constructivist rationalism, his philosophical concern is not simply *description* but also *evaluation* and *prescription*.' Hayek thus appeals to reason and calls on the supporters of individual liberty to act against the collectivist threat.

However, this interventionist outcome creates still further problems for his system of thought. Hayek (1982, vol. 1, p. 32) writes: 'Liberalism . . . restricts deliberate control of the overall order of society to the enforcement of such general rules as are necessary for the formation of a spontaneous order, the details of which we cannot foresee.' But this is not *any* spontaneous order that Hayek has in mind. It concerns just *one* type: the Great Society. What happens if the foundations of the Great Society are yet unbuilt or under threat? Rather than a faith in evolution towards perfection, Hayek believes that socioeconomic intervention must be pushed down a particular track precisely by the creation of institutions and 'general rules' which are necessary for the formation and sustenance of the liberal utopia.

The interventionist temptation in Hayek's thought is masked by the fact that capitalist market systems are actually dominant in the modern world. In such real-world circumstances the advocate of free markets can then declare: when in doubt, do nothing. Accordingly, by placing the 'burden of proof on those wishing to reform' (Hayek, 1988, p. 20), most proposals for state intervention can easily be opposed.

After all, no advocate of reform can prove that the proposal will work precisely as intended, or predict with certainty the alternative outcome. The Hayekian argument is thus rigged. As long as the uncertainty of our predicament in a capitalist world is mutually accepted, the free marketeer can easily seem to win the argument.

But what if the tables are turned? What if we are faced with the dilemmas of reform in a country which is not dominated by market relations and private property? Such problems are illustrated no more graphically than by speculation on the Hayekian attitude to the post-1989 reforms of the former Eastern bloc economies. Gérard Roland (1990) points out that in the context of the introduction of private property rights in the East, Hayek is caught between two irreconcilable arguments: his support for markets, on the one hand, and his opposition to deliberate structural change or 'constructivism', on the other.[20] If he takes one horn of this dilemma he should oppose reform in the Soviet Union, as this is essentially interventionist and 'constructivist' in nature. But it would seem that the construction of the Great Society here takes priority. The 'burden of proof' is thus no longer placed on those advocating reform. In the context of Soviet-type societies that onus is seemingly now placed on the conservative elements who resist the growth of markets and private property. Clearly, and especially with Hayek's disposition of the 'burden of proof', there is a danger that a double standard may be operating here.

For Hayek, the heavy hand of political intervention must tear up and destroy the weeds of socialism and constructivism before the Garden of Eden can bring forth its bloom and its fruit. Even before the Hayekian dilemmas concerning perestroika were posed, the contradiction was clear. As Murray Forsyth (1988, p. 250) puts it:

> Quite unconscious of irony or paradox, he pushes onwards and proceeds to 'construct' models of government which will ensure that the right people with the right insight will make the right kinds of rules for the Great Society to proceed uninterrupted on its way, models that would do credit to the most rational of all eighteenth century rationalists. The spontaneous order has now suddenly lost its spontaneity.

Given the ravages of the twentieth century, the consequent loss of a Spencerian faith in the inevitability of progress means for Hayek the necessity of political intervention to check and reverse the socialist advance. Hence his critique of 'constructivism' loses its edge. While Hayek's warnings about the dangers of proposals to plan an entire society in some rational way remain pertinent, he himself slips back into the 'constructivist' project to build a liberal order whose broad features are themselves decreed by reason.

Hayek and others have inspired policies to extend 'free markets' and 'roll back the state'. It is no accident that governments committed to these ideas have often taken an authoritarian tone, such as in Britain in the 1980s under the premiership of Margaret Thatcher. As Karl Polanyi (1944) argued long ago, the extension of markets did not mean the diminution of the powers of the state, but instead led to increasing intrusion and regulation by central government. Accordingly, even in Victorian Britain, the introduction of free markets, far from doing away with the need for control, regulation and intervention, enormously increased their range. This was true *a fortiori* in France and Germany, where markets were often imposed from above and generally more closely regulated.

Polanyi argued that the creation and maintenance of private property rights and functioning market institutions require the sustained intervention of the state to eject economic forms and institutions which are antagonistic to the private market system. Paradoxically, therefore, 'free market' policies can lead to a substantial centralization of economic and political power. Hayekian policies in practice actually threaten both economic and political pluralism and grant extended powers to the central state. His extreme individualism becomes what could be described as a kind of totalitarian liberalism.

It should also be emphasized that the unqualified goal of the 'free' market ignores the fact that trade and markets rely on other antiquated and often rigid institutions and other traditional features of social culture. Joseph Schumpeter has argued persuasively that such older institutions provide an essential 'symbiosis' with capitalism, and are thus 'an essential element of the capitalist schema' (1976, p. 139). While capitalism tends to undermine these supports, 'no social system can work which is based exclusively upon a network of free contracts between (legally) equal contracting parties' (p. 423).

Hayek's molecular view of the modern economy in terms of entrepreneurial individuals periodically engaged in market contracts may conform with prevailing ideology but is far from the actual truth. As Herbert Simon (1991) has argued with great eloquence, the texture of modern capitalism is dominated much more by non-market organizations and their internal relations than markets and their contractual haggling.

Admittedly, the market continues to play an indispensable role in the modern era, but it is deceptive to suggest that it is the primary arena of social interaction for most agents. In contemporary economies much more daily activity is internal to organizations and outside the market. True, the growth of capitalism is characterized by the development and extension of markets on a global scale. Yet, in comparison to all earlier economic systems, the growth in organizational diversity, complexity and scale is also a vital feature of the capitalist order. Along with many other modern economists, Hayek obscures this fact with his individualistic and contractarian bias.

Conclusion

There is much of great value in Hayek's writing which should not be ignored. In particular, there is Hayek's (1935, 1948) argument that *complete* central planning is not feasible. This is both correct in its main conclusion and appropriate in its focus on the problems of gathering and processing sufficient or meaningful knowledge about the economy. Furthermore, it has been explicitly or implicitly confirmed by writers and politicians less sympathetic to the unrestricted economics of the free market.[21]

While Hayek may go too far in his warnings of possible excesses of over-rationalistic or 'constructivist' ideas to reform society or transform the economy, his arguments concerning the inevitable decentralization and parcellization of knowledge must still act as powerful counters to those who believe that it is possible to reconstruct the system according to some comprehensive, rational blueprint or plan.

On the negative side, Hayek's evolutionary argument has a number of problems and flaws. While it counters any attachment to one hundred per cent central planning, it does not support the policy of universal free markets either. Hayek's evolutionary argument has some resemblance to that of Spencer and Social Darwinists such as William Graham Sumner because it still falls back on some strange, detached and universal selective force emanating from the 'free' market. In crucial respects the mechanisms of evolution are unclear. In some areas Hayek's theoretical structure has internal contradictions which are difficult to rectify without major change.

In sum, Hayek's corpus of writings in social science is an immense achievement. Yet his attachment to an evolutionary analysis of socioeconomic evolution creates problems for his enduring attachments both to methodological individualism and to classic liberal ideology.

Appendix: Group Selection in Modern Biology

Despite the efforts of Richard Dawkins, Robert L. Trivers, George C. Williams and others, within biology the issue of group selection remains highly controversial and a number of authors have taken issue with the genetic reductionists on this point. These include prominent biologists such as Niles Eldredge, Stephen Jay Gould, Richard Lewontin and Ernst Mayr, who have all criticized such single-level explanations. For example, following his joint work with Stephen Jay Gould, Niles Eldredge (1985a) proposes that selection mechanisms are hierarchical, involving culls at higher levels that favour whole species rather than simply genes or organisms. In other words, selection operates simultaneously on different types of unit, depending on the time-scale and the type of selection process.

The idea of higher levels of selection is much resisted, particulary by biologists wedded to genetic reductionism. In contrast, group-selection ideas exemplify non-reductionist and hierarchical views of selection in biology, connecting with the similar work of earlier biological theorists such as Ludwig von Bertalanffy (1952, 1971) and Paul Weiss (Weiss et al., 1971). Other biologists and philosophers of biology who have recently formulated a defence of group or other levels of selection include Robert Brandon, Michael Wade, William Wimsatt and David Sloan Wilson.

The recent controversy over units of selection cannot be surveyed in detail here, but it is possible to draw out a few of the central themes and to touch on some of the major contributions. Notably, among biologists the notion of group selection is not so reprehensible as Viktor Vanberg (1986) suggests, and it retains some considerable support from a number of theorists and philosophers after a detailed and protracted controversy.

The Nature of Biotic Group Selection

Establishing the dependence of individuals on the group is itself not enough to establish the notion of group selection. Notably, although the properties of individuals may be influenced by the nature of the groups to which they belong, the individual selectionists argue that the relevant group properties are themselves the product of individuals and their interactions. After considering these points, Sober (1981, 1984a) reaches the conclusion that dependence on the group context is necessary but not sufficient to define group selection. His definition is as follows:

> Group selection acts on a set of groups if, and only if, there is a force impinging on those groups which makes it the case that for each group, there is some property of the group which determines one component of the fitness of every member of the group. (Sober, 1981, p. 107)

In other words, when group selection occurs, all the organisms in the same group are 'bound together by a common fate'. Although members of the group may not have identical fitness values, group selection works via a uniform effect.[22]

It may be that all such information about ostensible group selection may be reduced to and represented by selection coefficients of organisms or genes. But, contrary to Dawkins (1976, 1982), such a formal reduction does not imply that the concept of group selection is invalid or that it is individual or genic selection which is occurring. 'In particular, the computational adequacy of genetic models leaves open the question whether they also correctly identify the causes of evolution' (Sober and Lewontin, 1982, p. 158). That is, formal reduction to the genic or individual level leaves the question unanswered as to what propels changes in the frequency of genes or individuals.

Genetic reductionists respond that the gene is the single unit of replication. However, group selectionists 'do not deny that the gene is the mechanism by which biological objects pass on their characteristics ... this shared assumption about the unit of replication simply cuts no ice. That genes are passed along leaves open the question as to what causes their differential transmission' (Sober, 1981, p. 113).

In the view of Sober and his collaborators, group or other higher levels of selection are possible, and their existence is determined by examination of the processes and structures involved. Just as individuals may be regarded as groups of genes that have become functionally organized by natural selection to perpetuate themselves, groups can be seen as groups of individuals similarly functionally organized (Wilson and Sober, 1989, p. 41).

On this basis, Wilson and Sober go so far as to argue that to settle on the individual as the unit of selection involves an inconsistency. This is because individuals may be regarded as groups of alleles. Simple reduction to the individual level is unacceptable because the same arguments concerning reduction from groups to individuals apply equally to reduction from individual to gene. To avoid this 'double standard' one must either accept multiple levels of selection, or reduce everything to the lowest possible level in the manner of Dawkins (1976, 1982) and Williams (1966, 1986).

Notably, much of the controversy over units of selection results from semantic and conceptual confusion:

> Within levels-of-selection theory an entity must be a unit of selection to become functionally organized. Within selfish-gene theory an entity can be functionally organized without being a unit of selection.... If we remain within the framework of selfish gene theory, and ask the question 'What causes an entity to become an organism?', we find that selfish gene theory must give back exactly what it took away – a nested hierarchy of units which it calls 'vehicles of selection' rather than 'units of selection'. Thus, individuals are organisms because they are vehicles of selection, and if individuals can be vehicles then groups or communities can be as well. (Wilson and Sober, 1989, p. 351)

Dawkins (1982, p. 114) appears to recognize this, but then makes the claim that individuals rather than groups normally serve as vehicles of selection. Wilson and Sober reject this empirical claim, and with it Dawkins's suggestion that, to be units of selection, groups (or individuals) must be as resilient and immutable as the information in a gene. 'Even selfish gene theory must conclude that functional organization is distributed among a hierarchy of units' (Wilson and Sober, 1989, p. 351).

The Complexity of Evolutionary Models

Some of the major detailed arguments against group selection emanate from the mathematical work of John Maynard Smith (1964, 1976), Williams (1966) and their followers. However, mathematical expressions of evolutionary dynamics are highly complex and notoriously intractable. A problem with nine possible genotypes and independently specifiable fitness parameters is already more complicated than the three-body problem of classical mechanics. Like the three-body problem, it has been solved for a variety of special cases but has not been solved in general.

Williams (1966) attempts to deal with such problems by modelling the operation of selection coefficients acting independently at a number of loci, first by taking one locus at a time and then extending to a global solution by 'iterating over all loci'. However, as Wimsatt shows, this method is valid only in a restricted number of special cases:

> if variance in fitness at a given level is totally additive, the entities of that level are composed of units of selection, and there are no higher-level units of selection. If the additive variance in fitness at that level is totally analysable as additive variance in fitness at lower levels, then the entities at that level are composed of units of selection at those lower levels, rather than being units of selection themselves. . . . In their causal effects, they are then 'nothing more than' collections of the lower-level entities, and any independent causal efficacy is illusory. This is a necessary and sufficient condition for the truth of Williams's genetic reductionism. But, in general, we would expect this partitioning of variance in fitness into additive and nonadditive components at different levels to show a number of levels – genes, gene complexes, chromosomes, individuals, even groups – at which additive variance at that level appears only as nonadditive variance at lower levels. There are units of selection at each level at which this occurs, and if it does, genetic reductionism and determinism are false. (Wimsatt, 1980, p. 256)

As Wimsatt points out, Williams wrongly presumes that gene frequency alone is an adequate basis for a deterministic theory of evolutionary change, and ignores the fact that the fitness of a gene can depend on its context or environment, which among other things can generate significant feedback loops with non-linear effects.

This is reminiscent of a number of other arguments. Typically, Mayr (1963, p. 296) asserts: 'No gene has a fixed selective value; the same gene may confer high fitness on one genetic background and be virtually lethal on another.' As Elliott Sober has conjectured: 'If a gene raises the probability of a given phenotype in one context and lowers it in another, there is no such thing as the causal role that the gene has in general' (Sober, 1984a, p. 313). With such considerations in mind, Wimsatt (1980, p. 240) asserts: 'Illegitimate assumptions of context-independence are a frequent error in reductionist analyses.'

Oversimplifications in the Basic Selection Model

Although a number of models have been developed, their common characteristics justify their joint description as the 'basic selection model' (D. S. Wilson, 1980). While these models show that group selection is possible, the general conclusion of the modellers is that it is unlikely. The basic selection model suggests that the differential selection of groups cannot override the effects of individual selection within groups except for a highly restricted set of parameter values. On these grounds, group selection is considered to be relatively insignificant by Maynard Smith (1976), George Williams (1966) and others.[23]

The free-rider problem outlined by Vanberg (1986) and summarized above emanates from models of the type developed by Maynard Smith. Although the argument may be convincing at first sight, the mechanisms through which free-rider or other migrants emerge, and through which the migrations occur, must also be considered.

Notably, in order to build such mathematical models of selection several necessary simplifications must be made. A number of non-linearities and environmental interdependencies have to be excluded if a mathematical solution is to be obtained. As Wimsatt (1980, p. 241) points out, there is 'the practical impossibility of generating an exhaustive, quasi-algorithmic, or exact analysis of the behavior of the system and its environment'. As a result the reductionist must start simplifying. Given the interest in studying relations internal to the system, priority will be given to the simplification of the picture of the environment rather than of the system itself. The bias will be against simplifications internal to the system because of the danger of simplifying out of existence the very phenomena being addressed. This means that certain environmental changes and system–environment interactions will be excluded.

Wade's Theoretical and Empirical Critique

Addressing the simplifications in the basic selection model, Wade (1976, 1977, 1978) has provided a theoretical and experimental critique of the type of argument against group selection provided by Maynard Smith and Williams. First, Wade enumerates some of the underlying assumptions of the basic selection model so as to examine them in detail:

1   It is assumed that probability of survival of a population can be significantly dependent on the frequency of a single allele.
2   In the models all populations contribute migrants to a common pool, normally in a number independent of the population size, from which colonists are drawn at random to fill vacant habitats.
3   Variance between populations is assumed to be created primarily by genetic drift between populations, rather than by differential sampling from the migrant pool.
4   Group and individual selection are assumed to be operating in opposite directions with respect to the allele in question.

Wade (1978) then discusses these assumptions in turn, showing their weaknesses in each case:

Assumption 1   This is confounded in part by strong effects of the biotic environment on fitness by means of interactions between genotypes and other effects. As noted above, the environment is not simply given; it is affected by the process of evolution itself. Individual selection pressures vary in sign or magnitude among local populations, owing to frequency dependence, or other factors. Consequently, when the same allele is situated in different genetic backgrounds or different local habitats, this can result in variations in both the direction and the intensity of individual selection.

Further, depending on the initial genotypic composition of the population, individual selection could result in the attainment of any number of different gene frequencies corresponding to local 'adaptive peaks' on a non-linear fitness surface. The possibility of a 'multiplicity of adaptive peaks' was noted by Sewall Wright (1931, 1956, 1959) long ago. In this case an attained gene frequency may be a local rather than a global optimum, and a shift from the local peak to the global optimum may be ruled out. However, Wright's concept of a multiplicity of adaptive peaks is ruled out by the assumptions in the basic selection model.

Wade (1976) carried out a number of breeding and selection experiments on the flour beetle *Tribolium castaneum*. By comparing the repeated selection of groups with that of individuals, for either increased or decreased population size, Wade showed that significant differences emerged in several of the primary characteristics known to affect population size, such as fecundity, body size and developmental time. These experiments confirm theoretical arguments for the viability of group selection.

Importantly, Wade's experiments on flour beetles are cases of group selection by Sober's definition. By selecting groups for a given population size, every individual in a group is thus treated equally. Individuals in a group are bound together, their fitness values determined equally by their common membership of a group of a certain size (Sober, 1981, pp. 106–7). Incidentally, while group selection is occurring, *individual* selection is also going on simultaneously within the group. Finally, Wade's experiments show that group selection may exist without the phenomenon of altruism, which was central to Wynne-Edwards's earlier and unsuccessful formulation.

Assumption 2   Although the migrant pool idea facilitates the mathematical modelling of evolution in groups, Wade argues that in reality dispersion is unlikely to be uniform in this manner. With possible exceptions, such as wind-dispersed seeds, geographical barriers to migration as well as behaviourally restricted movement patterns will interact with and give rise to a non-uniform population structure.

According to this assumption, all populations are deemed to contribute equal numbers of migrants to the migrant pool, making the gene frequency in the pool the average frequency of all the contributing populations. It follows directly that there is no possibility of group selection by means of the differential proliferation of populations. In contrast, Wade points out, if more propagules are taken from large populations than from small populations, then significant differences in the pattern of group population size can emerge. Once again, this has been confirmed experimentally by Wade (1976, 1977).

Assumption 3   With the (mathematically convenient) idea of a migrant pool, with its own gene frequencies distributed around the overall mean, a portion of the genetic variance between populations is lost because of migration at each generation. Reducing the variation between populations means undermining the process of group selection. Experiments by Wade (1976, 1977) confirm that if an unmixed propagule pool is used, with differential contributions by different populations, then group selection can work.

Assumption 4   Wynne-Edwards (1962) has suggested that individual selection within populations generally tends to increase population size and this tendency is opposed by the extinction of large populations because of an overexploitation of resources. However, group selection could favour higher productivity. The possibility that group and individual selection work in the same direction has rarely been considered. Williams's (1966) principle of parsimony states that if the evolution of a trait can be explained by individual selection then there is no need to invoke group selection. This would seem to restrict the discussion of group selection to cases where individual and group selection work in opposite directions.

However, Wade showed experimentally that even when individual and group selection work in the same direction, they can lead to different results. Observing in one of his experiments that individual selection had reduced population size, Wade replicated the experiment but with group selection for decreased population size. The result was the development of more heterogeneity among the different populations, suggesting that group selection and individual selection, in the case where they worked in the same direction (i.e. towards reduced population size) were not identical.

Wade's work thus demonstrates that the mathematical selection models in the literature are based on oversimplifying and restrictive assumptions which reduce the apparent likelihood of group selection. He argues that when these assumptions are relaxed, group selection is much more plausible.

Wilson's Critique of the Basic Selection Model

The work of D. S. Wilson (1980, 1983) is in a similar vein, taking issue with at least one particular assumption of the basic selection model. He points out that all such models assume a spatial homogeneity in the genetic composition of populations. Although this assumption is mathematically convenient, it is neither necessary nor realistic.

In the basic selection model an individual will be selected even if its own fitness is decreased, if it decreases the fitness of others still more. This has been called 'spite' in the biological literature. Conversely, if an individual increases its own fitness, it will be selected against if it increases the fitness of others still more. Thus, as D. S. Wilson observes:

> this basic selection model predicts that selection is insensitive to the fitness of the population as a whole. *Natural selection is sensitive only to the fitness of a genotype relative to other genotypes within that population.* This feature is such a fundamental part of basic selection models in general that the majority actually define fitnesses relative to the most fit type in the population, thereby eliminating a consideration of population productivity from the start. (D. S. Wilson, 1980, p. 16, emphasis in the original)

In contrast to the basic selection model, D. S. Wilson argues (1977, 1980) that the population is subdivided into what he calls trait groups. These refer to spheres of influence where a given trait affects other individuals equally, such as a nest shared by birds. In the trait group, every individual feels the effects of every other individual, and within its bounds the individual-selection model with its assumption of spatial homogeneity in genetic composition is viable and realistic.

Given that the fitness of an organism is dependent on both the genotype and the characteristics of the trait group, two types of population unit are involved: one that is homogeneous with respect to ecological interactions (the trait group), and another that is homogeneous with respect to genetic mixing (the deme). The selection process is working on both types of population. The distinction between the trait group and the deme is ignored by any mathematical model, such as the basic selection model, that assigns a single frequency to its genotypes.

The possibility that the fitness of an organism may in part depend on the characteristics of its own trait group (the make-up of which is partly dependent on that organism itself) is an important one. D. S. Wilson (1980, 1983) considers examples of differential trait groups where fitness is frequency dependent. Instances can thus be constructed where altruistic behaviour can be selected in one trait group with a high frequency, even if it is less fit at the mean frequency level for the population as a whole. Once again, the assumptions on which the basic selection model is founded are shown to be overrestrictive and oversimplified.

Multiple and Higher Levels of Natural Selection

The possibilities are not exhausted by group and genic selection. Many of the arguments summarized above concerning group selection apply directly or with amendment to the prospect of other, higher levels of selection as well. In biology the idea of higher levels of selection has reemerged. Selection between species is considered in Leigh van Valen (1975), Gould (1980b) and Steven M. Stanley (1975), and between ecosystems in M. S. Dunbar (1960).

The general idea of multiple levels of selection is also being supported. Foreshadowing the important work of Niles Eldredge (1985a), Anthony Arnold and Kurt Fristrup (1982, p. 113) write: 'It is self-evident that evolutionary theory has acknowledged the utility of hierarchical structure in *describing* biological phenomena. However, this body of evolutionary theory does not incorporate hierarchical structure in its conventional modes of *explanation*.' Multiple levels of selection are also proposed by Brandon (1982) and Lewontin (1970).

In sum, biology does not give unanimous support to the individualistic or generally reductionist ideas which have been prominent in economics. Indeed, some of the pitfalls of oversimplified models are exemplified, particularly those of a linear type. Given the frequency of oversimplified modelling in economics, economists have much to learn from this controversy.

In one sense, however, it can be left on one side. As noted above, even if the cases of group selection in the biotic sphere are marginal, there are much stronger reasons to assume that group and higher levels of selection are operative when rules and routines surpass the genes as the stuff of inheritance. Cultural processes of 'emulation' (Veblen) or of 'conformism' (Boyd and Richerson) may be sufficiently strong to engulf any individualistic 'free rider' effects. Once we no longer take the individual as given, then emulation or conformism can ensure that the group as a whole is a unit of selection. Furthermore, group attributes such as organizational knowledge may also make group selection viable.

PART IV
Towards an
Evolutionary
Economics

The disadvantage of exclusive attention to a group of abstractions, however well-founded, is that, by the nature of the case, you have abstracted from the remainder of things. In so far as the excluded things are important in your experience, your modes of thought are not fitted to deal with them. You cannot think without abstractions; accordingly, it is of the utmost importance to be vigilant in critically revising your *modes* of abstraction. It is here that philosophy finds its healthy niche as essential to the healthy progress of society. It is the critique of abstractions. A civilization which cannot burst through its current abstractions is doomed to sterility after a very limited period of progress.

Alfred North Whitehead, *Science and the Modern World*

A good economist . . . is someone who has a difficulty for every solution.

Brian Loasby, *Equilibrium and Evolution*

13
Optimization and Evolution

It is widely, but wrongly, assumed that evolutionary processes lead generally in the direction of optimality and efficiency. The 'adaptationist' idea that natural selection is some kind of optimizing agent dates from the episode of Social Darwinism in the last century and has dominated biology until fairly recently. In biology it has been criticized extensively by Stephen Jay Gould and Richard Lewontin among others.[1]

Voltaire had Dr Pangloss insist in his novel *Candide*: 'Tis demonstrated . . . that things cannot be otherwise; for, since everything is made for an end, everything is necessarily for the best end.' Panglossian thinking stems in part from the 'naturalistic fallacy': the unwarranted assumption that what exists 'naturally' is good. It is also associated with the presumption that 'natural' and competitive social processes lead to optimal results: that nature is an optimizer. Although connected, these two propositions are different. The former is more directly a matter of a value judgement, and in the present chapter we are more concerned with the latter proposition.

In a loose sense, processes of natural selection can lead to improvement, because adaptation to the environment does occur. But it is a mistake to go further than this and assume that natural selection is a strong optimizing force. On the contrary, natural selection is always an imperfect instrument, and it can sometimes lead to clearly suboptimal, even disastrous, outcomes. The adaptationist fallacy is the assumption that all adaptations are necessarily functional and (near) optimal. It has reappeared in modern economics in two principal and related forms.

The first is the attempt to justify the hypothesis of maximizing or rational behaviour by appeals to the notion of 'natural selection', by Milton Friedman and Friedrich Hayek. Hayek and Friedman thus assume that the kinds of behaviours that are selected in a competitive evolutionary process are necessarily superior and relatively efficient.

The second is the proposition that capitalist competition acts like an evolutionary process, favouring the 'fitter' and more efficient institutional forms and modes of industrial organization. This notion is found in the works of Michael Jensen, William Meckling, Douglass North, Oliver Williamson and others. Jensen, Meckling and Williamson take a further step, and presume that the typical, hierarchical, capitalist firm is more efficient, principally because it is predominant in the modern competitive world.

However, when economists such as these have dabbled in biology to find some sustenance for their ideas, often the conclusions of that natural science are presumed rather than closely examined. Many economists seem unaware of developments in modern biology and general evolutionary theory that undermine the idea that evolution is necessarily a progressive and optimizing force. A point emphasized in this chapter is that Panglossian conceptions of evolution have little foundation in modern evolutionary theory, and therefore should be severely qualified or discarded.

The question arises as to whether the matters thus uncovered within biological theory are of relevance for economic evolution. It will be suggested that the parallels are sufficiently close to take heed of these arguments from biological science. Although the biological analogue should always be handled with care, it does seem to be of relevance in addressing some evolutionary ideas which are utilized in economics.

Accordingly, in an economic context, evolutionary processes do not necessarily lead to – by any reasonable definition – optimal outcomes. The possibility and indeed desirability of some limited form of state intervention in economic life – be it an industrial policy, some form of indicative planning, or whatever – is thus highlighted by modern evolutionary theory.

Economic Evolution as a Promoter of Rational Maximization

In 1950 Armen Alchian published his famous argument that maximizing behaviour by economic agents does not have to be justified in terms of their explicit or implicit objectives, but by the 'evolutionary' contention that maximizing and thus 'fit' firms and individuals are the ones more likely to survive and prosper. Selective success, Alchian (1950, 1953) argues, depends on behaviour and results, not motivations. If firms never actually attempted to maximize profits, 'evolutionary' processes of selection would ensure the survival of the more profitable enterprises. He further argues that the type of firm, or firm behaviour, that is conducive to survival and prosperity will tend to spread, through the failure of less efficient firms and by the general imitation of the more successful. Thus Alchian sees the idea of evolutionary selection less as a bulwark and more as an alternative to the assumption that individual firms are actually maximizing profits.

Stephen Enke (1951) shifts the emphasis somewhat, first by arguing that with sufficient intensity of competition all firms except the optimizers would fail the survival test. Consequently, 'in the long run', conditions of intense competition mean that only the optimizers will remain viable. Friedman (1953) went one step further and argued that this 'evolutionary' argument constituted a justification of the maximization hypothesis: it is meant to show that evolutionary selection leads to optimizing behaviour by agents and firms. Thus Friedman sees 'natural selection' as grounds for assuming that agents act 'as if' they maximize, whether or not firms and individuals actually do so.

However, like others, Friedman is vague about the mechanisms of selection and the nature of the evolutionary process. Alchian suggests that other firms will 'imitate' the profit maximizers. Not only does this contradict Friedman's view that intentional behaviour has to be disregarded in the theoretical explanation, but also it leaves open the non-trivial question as to how other firms know what characteristics to look for and to imitate.

A related argument is found in Friedrich Hayek's (1982, vol. 3) work. He argues that 'competition will make it necessary for people to act rationally to maintain themselves ... a few relatively more rational individuals will make it necessary for the rest to emulate them in order to prevail. In a society in which rational behaviour confers an advantage on the individual, rational methods will progressively be developed and spread by imitation' (p. 75). Although imitation is again highlighted, this insufficiently precise statement is unacceptable for several reasons which are raised below.

Appropriately, in response to Alchian (1950, 1953), Edith Penrose (1952, 1953) argues that the analogy with natural selection in biology is weak because there is no economic equivalent to heritable traits. As Sidney Winter (1964) insists, such an equivalent and relatively durable element has to be found if the evolutionary analogy is to be employed.

Economic Evolution as a Promoter of Efficiency

Appeals by economists to simplistic 'evolutionary' arguments to infer efficiency from competition are common. For instance, North (1981, p. 7) writes: 'competition in the face of ubiquitous scarcity dictates that the more efficient institutions ... will survive and the inefficient ones perish.' Likewise, Williamson (1975, 1985) argues repeatedly that evolutionary competition leads to greater efficiency. He asserts that because hierarchical firms exist, then they must be both more efficient and most suited to survival. He thus argues that evolution leads to the selection of relatively superior or near-optimal organizational forms.

Williamson repeatedly refers to 'evidence' in support of his contention that efficiency considerations will tend to win out. However, this particular evidence simply consists of the observation that hierarchical firms – rather than non-hierarchical worker cooperatives etc. – are clearly more numerous in the real world.

Support for the proposition that participatory and cooperative firms enjoy greater productivity and longevity comes from a large amount of additional case study and econometric evidence.[2] Like most empirical evidence relating to complex issues, it is problematic and controversial, but the weight of testimony in favour of a positive correlation between participation and productivity does not justify its neglect in the work of Williamson and other like-thinkers. This empirical evidence is largely disregarded by them because it seems to be inconsistent with the undisputed observation that in the real world hierarchical firms are far more plentiful.[3] However, as shown below, the two sets of empirical evidence are not inconsistent.

Williamson (1988) tries to evade the charges of Panglossian excess by his insistence that selection is weak or imperfect. While he disclaims adherence to the stronger proposition 'that all is for the best in this best of possible worlds', he still holds to the view that competition performs some kind of sort and shifts resources in favour of the more efficient forms of organization.

Also alluding to Darwinian 'natural selection', Jensen and Meckling (1979, p. 473) make the very same point as Williamson when they discuss worker participation: 'The fact that this system seldom arises out of voluntary arrangements among individuals strongly suggests that codetermination or industrial democracy is less efficient than the alternatives which grow up and survive in a competitive environment.' However, as indicated below, arguments from theoretical biology and elsewhere no longer sustain such unqualified propositions.

The evolutionary 'selection of rational maximizers' and 'selection of efficient institutions' arguments have much in common, and we can address both, in the form of a list of 'Problems for Dr Pangloss'.

Problems for Dr Pangloss: (1) Selection and Survival

Panglossian modes of thought often involve the assumption that evolution always means increasing progress and efficiency, a beneficent journey from the lower to the higher form of organization or life, and from the inferior to the superior. This view is now widely disputed in biology (Dupré, 1987; Nitecki, 1988) and has already been countered in chapter 6 above in the context of a discussion of Herbert Spencer's thought.

As already noted, and as Theodosius Dobzhansky et al. (1977, p. 98) point out, natural selection does not lead to the superlative fittest, only the tolerably fit. But even in a weaker sense, evolution is not necessarily a grand or natural road leading generally towards perfection.

Change can be idiosyncratic, error can be reproduced and imitated, and a path to improvement can be missed.

Furthermore, an evolutionary process involving selection cannot be an optimizing one, at least in the strict sense, because for evolution to work there must always be a variety of forms from which to select. Without such variety there would be no evolution. Furthermore, the obverse of selection is rejection, and the evolutionary process must thus involve ceaseless and systematic error-making as well. As Gould (1987, p. 14) puts it: 'imperfections are the primary proofs that evolution has occurred, since optimal designs erase all signposts of history.'

Also, as already noted in chapter 6, 'survival of the fittest' is an ill-conceived slogan. Indeed, the process of 'natural selection' in modern biology does not even necessarily lead to survival, and the mere fact of survival, even to a numerous and sustained extent, need not always imply efficiency at all.

Panglossian writers like Friedman and Williamson take it for granted that survival means efficiency. However, Edna Ullmann-Margalit (1978) shows that this is invalid. Strictly, in order to explain the existence of a structure it is neither necessary nor sufficient to show that it is efficient. Inefficient structures do happen to exist and survive, and many possible efficient structures will never actually be selected. As Simon (1976, p. 247) insists: 'the assumption so often made in administrative studies, that an arrangement is effective because it exists, is a circular argument of the worst sort.' Gregory Dow (1987, p. 32) similarly observes, 'it is all too easy to abuse economic selection arguments by simply declaring that surviving forms of organization are efficient ipso facto.'

Alchian, Friedman, Hayek, Williamson and others argue that evolution performs some kind of sort in favour of the more competitive or efficient agents or firms. However, such apologetic abuses of the evolutionary metaphor typically fail to specify any plausible and detailed causal process to sustain this conclusion. Thus, in response to Friedman, it has been pointed out by Penrose (1952) and Winter (1964, 1971, 1975) that his argument lacks an explanation of a clear evolutionary mechanism, particularly in regard to the transmission of heritable determinants of fitness. Similar remarks apply to the other aforementioned authors.

Responding to this gap in orthodox theory, Richard Nelson and Sidney Winter (1974, 1977, 1982) argue that such heritable fitness must be explained by relatively durable routines within the firm. This also prompts an examination of the processes of internal cultural transmission within the firm. Robert Boyd and Peter Richerson (1980) suggest that if managers have conformist tendencies, then the conditions of emergence and competitive selection of efficiency regimes within firms are restrictive. For further reasons discussed below, there are other good reasons to assume that such routinized behaviour within institutions will not generally be on an optimal track.

Problems for Dr Pangloss:
(2) Fecundity and New Entrants

Undermining the idea of natural selection as a universally optimizing agent, Gould and Lewontin (1979) point out that selection and adaptation could be decoupled, as in the case of a mutation which doubles the fecundity of individuals. As natural selection always favours greater fecundity, a gene promoting it would sweep through a population rapidly, but it need not imply greater survival value. Indeed, if a predator on immature stages is led to switch to the species in question, now that young organisms are more plentiful, the overall population size may actually decrease as a consequence. This argument suggests that selection does not simply depend on considerations of fitness of given units but also on the capacity of the type of unit to procreate.

The economic relevance of this can be illustrated in the following case. Williamson (1975, 1985) has proposed that the greater density of hierarchical and non-cooperative firms in the real world must relate to their superior efficiency. However, referring to Mancur Olson's (1965) analysis of the difficulties of forming collective organizations where individual benefits do not seem to justify the trouble and expense of organizing, Nathan Rosenberg and Luther Birdzell (1986, p. 316) point out that, by comparison with cooperative enterprises, 'the promoter of an investor-owned enterprise can, by retaining part or all of the ownership interest, profit handsomely if the enterprise succeeds. So one might expect more investor-owned enterprises, small or large, to survive simply because far more of them are likely to be born.'

Consequently, even in a rational-choice framework, such as that employed by Olson, there is good reason to doubt that the existence of a greater number of non-cooperative rather than cooperative firms would imply that the former is more efficient than the latter. The greater density of a given organizational form does not necessarily imply greater efficiency. It may be that cooperative firms are less numerous, not because they are less efficient, but simply because they are less likely to emerge than firms created on the basis of individual ownership, involving one person, a partnership or a small group. If circumstances favour the birth of greater numbers of hierarchical firms they may grow in size or number to swamp the non-hierarchical businesses, whatever the relative efficiencies. The evaluation of the performance and optimal scale of cooperatives is complex, and no simple verdict is being suggested here. It is simply argued that neither existence nor non-existence, neither survival nor extinction, may be taken to imply either greater or lesser efficiency.

Considerations of fecundity in biology do not simply involve the conditions governing the birth of firms. They also lead us to focus directly on the characteristics of new entrants into an industry. Evolution will also favour the forms more likely to emerge in a given sector in given circumstances, rather than simply the more efficient. In relation to a particular subsystem, such as a national or regional economy, evolution will also favour the more mobile 'immigrant' firms and the subsidiaries thus created. Thus multinational corporations may predominate, not because they are more efficient, but simply because their assets and expertise are able to penetrate national and regional boundaries to become reproducible therein.

If the industry is subjected to a rapid flow of new entrants of hierarchical form, then they may swamp the less hierarchical firms even if other selection processes are working in favour in the latter. The selection of hierarchical or non-hierarchical firms may depend not simply on the existing population, but on the capacity of new entrants to acquire or imitate their characteristics. In general, therefore, the rate of immigration, the characteristics of the entrants and the relationship of these characteristics to the selected population will affect the chances of particular types of organizational forms being selected. This conclusion is important because it shows that the particular kind of mechanism governing the creation of new entrants is as significant as the selection process *per se*.

To recapitulate the general point here, most 'evolutionary' arguments for the alleged superiority of hierarchical firms concentrate simply on the question of the extinction of the allegedly unfit. However, as Gould (1982b, p. 101) writes: 'Natural selection operates either by differential death or differential birth.' Each is important, and the matters promoting or hindering the creation of new firms cannot be ignored in an evolutionary process. As the biologist Ernst Mayr (1985b, p. 768) puts it, 'selection in leaving progeny' is just as important as mortality selection. As we have seen, this biological issue of fecundity is directly relevant for the economic sphere, in terms of the birth and immigration of firms.

Problems for Dr Pangloss: (3) Path Dependency

We turn to the very important issue of path dependency. This phenomenon is introduced in this section, but the succeeding sections also include pertinent examples. Although the general problem was recognized long ago,[4] many economic theorists have now accepted that the future development of an economic system is affected by the path it has traced out in the past. This contrasts with the preceding view that, within limits, from whatever starting point, the system will eventually gravitate to the same equilibrium, and thus real time and history could be safely ignored.

Path-dependent processes are now widely discussed in biology. Gould, in particular, has long argued that evolution often depends on initial 'accidents' that somehow dispose it to take a suboptimal and often eccentric path.[5]

Modern mathematics, especially the study of non-linear dynamic models, has also helped to put path dependency back on the agenda. There are at least two mathematical arguments which convey the basic idea. First, whenever a dynamic system has more than one stable critical point, the particular equilibrium towards which the system gravitates will depend upon the path taken out of equilibrium, the initial conditions and the external shocks. Second, in chaotic models the dynamic path is extremely sensitive to initial conditions in such a way that the outcome can change dramatically with a small change in the latter. Further, as each present instant embodies a set of 'initial conditions' for the future development of the system, the 'initial conditions' change at every moment of time.

In the context of economic history, path dependency suggests that the development of the factory system and the modern capitalist firm is not simply a question of the evolutionary selection of the most efficient organizational configurations. For example, some historical researchers have suggested that the developing factory system was influenced at its origin by the military structures of the time: in Britain during the Napoleonic wars and in the United States around the time of the Civil War. The circumstances of war prompted militaristic forms of industrial organization, and the hierarchical regimentation of the soldiery has its parallel in the similar organization of the workforce.[6]

In another discussion of the formative years of the industrial revolution, Michael Everett and Alanson Minkler (1991) show in more detail that labour-managed firms were originally at a substantial disadvantage compared with their capitalist counterparts. They argue that in Britain the situation of unlimited liability before the Companies Act of 1856 imposed additional risks and costs on labour-managed firms. Furthermore, early financial instruments were ill-suited to the establishment and continuation of worker cooperatives. The subsequent coevolution of firms and supporting institutions involved a path-dependent process where labour-managed firms were at a continual disadvantage, even after many of the earlier impediments were removed.

Charles Sabel and Jonathan Zeitlin (1985) argue on the basis of historical evidence that in Europe there was an alternative path to industrialization based on small-scale firms and flexible specialization. Also looking at the evolution of the factory system, Maxine Berg (1991) compares explanations based on the supposed dictates of technology with the idea of such an alternative road. She concludes that industrialization could have taken many possible pathways and occurred in different sequences. Ugo Pagano (1991, p. 327) considers the two-way and cumulative interaction of technology with property rights, pointing out that: 'In this context, simple efficiency stories may well lose their meaning. Each outcome is likely to be path dependent and inefficient interactions between property rights and technology are likely to characterise the history of economic systems.'

In the context of modern industrial structures, Richard Langlois (1988) argues explicitly that path dependency may be relevant in the evolution of organizational form. Likewise, and contrary to his earlier view, Douglass North (1990) now accepts that path-dependent processes also apply to institutions, and therefore the surviving arrangements are not necessarily the most efficient. The kind of economic history which ignored path dependency and inefficient equilibria, and assumed that historical change involved a sequence of discrete steps to ever more efficient institutional arrangements, is now widely criticized (Binger and Hoffman, 1989).

Williamson's identification of existence with efficiency would deem the military-industrial parallel to be irrelevant: whatever the original circumstances the more efficient forms would prosper and survive. Also, the alternative industrial roads of flexible specialization or labour management would be deemed to have been avoided because of their inefficiencies. On the contrary, the possibility of path dependency suggests that alternative, less hierarchical or less regimented forms of organization could have been just as viable. Only painstaking historical research, rather than bold evolutionary generalizations based on dubious 'biological laws', can adjudicate on this and related questions.

Problems for Dr Pangloss:
(4) Lock-in and Chreodic Development

Path dependency can be associated with particular kinds of inflexibility in economic processes. It has been observed that evolving systems, whether biotic or economic, can get locked into given paths of development, excluding a host of other, perhaps more 'efficient' or desirable possibilities.[7] A relevant economic example, discussed by Michael Best (1982), is the development of the system of transport based on the motor car, which once it had occurred tended to preclude the gradual development of other alternatives. In such cases, marginal adjustments towards perhaps more optimal outcomes are often ruled out.

This is redolent of the idea developed by the biologist Conrad Waddington (1957, 1972) of a 'chreod' (from the Greek *chre*, meaning it is fated or necessary, and *hodos*, a path). A chreod is a relatively stable trajectory of development for a species, caused in part by the evolution of hierarchical control sequences in the genotype. This kind of evolution is not homeostatic: it does not stabilize at one point or on one set of characters. Instead – to use another word coined by Waddington – it is 'homeorhetic' (from the Greek *rheo*, to flow), in that it stabilizes on one course of development through time. Evolutionary selection thus produces constant incremental change. Furthermore, the path of change is relatively stable: 'Environmental influences may operate in such a way as to tend to push the system off the trajectory, but the canalization of the chreod, or, otherwise expressed, its tendency towards homeorhesis, will tend to bring the system back on to the normal path again' (Waddington, 1969, p. 366).

As Devendra Sahal (1981, 1985) and Norman Clark and Calestous Juma (1987) argue, there are technological trajectories each of which develops a hierarchical control sequence very similar to the chreod. Once a technological 'paradigm' is adopted, this predetermines a general direction or path of development. 'For example, early alternatives in car design included electric, gasoline and steam' (Clark and Juma, 1987, p. 171). Once the choice was made the course of development was set, but with further choices as to more particular details further down the line.

This idea of a 'branched' pattern of directed technological development, with each branch confined to a chreod, means that what exists is not necessarily the most efficient, and the world could easily be otherwise. As Joel Mokyr (1990a, p. 285) writes: 'Had things been different, we could all be driving steam-driven cars, running our factories on water-power, [and] crossing the Atlantic on Zeppelins.'

In some respects the idea of chreodic development is similar to the biological idea of 'hyperselection'. This can occur if the growth rates of strategies or species are coupled in a non-linear and dynamic way (Silverberg, 1988, p. 549). The result is that very different evolutionary outcomes can emerge from small variancies in initial conditions, as in the more general case of the 'butterfly effect' in dynamic, non-linear systems. An example is the almost exclusive preponderance of 'left-handed' organic molecules – although *a priori*, right-handedness is equally viable – which has evolved from an 'accident' long ago in evolutionary time. Another case is the uniqueness of the genetic code.

Hyperselection emerges from strong positive feedback effects that 'freeze' a given attribute or structure, making further amendment difficult, even if the initial configuration is imperfect. Technological analogues are plentiful, from the emergence of the immutable but suboptimal 'QWERTY' typewriter keyboard, discussed by Brian Arthur (1983, 1989), Paul David (1985) and Stephen Jay Gould (1987), to the spread of standard gauge railways (Kindleberger, 1983), and the victory of the inferior VHS video system over Betamax (Arthur, 1988). The externalities involved with the introduction of standards – such as those pertaining to computers or railways – are discussed by Michael Katz and Carl Shapiro (1985, 1986).

The concept of chreodic development seems more general in scope than these examples of hyperselection. The latter idea is generally applicable to the detailed structures of individual components or units where little or no variation can take place once hyperselection occurs. In contrast, the idea of a chreod is most often applied to dominant characteristics and overall structures, where small perturbations can take place but the system is often pulled back on to a chreodic channel.

In the case of both chreodic development and hyperselection the outcomes have a path dependent and arbitrary quality, depending much on initial conditions. In the economic context the possibility is thus raised of some form of state intervention to set out or change the contours of chreodic development, or to initiate a more desirable hyperselective scenario.

Problems for Dr Pangloss:
(5) Context and Frequency Dependence

It should be emphasized that in biology there is no fixed or eternal genotypical formula for success. Evolution does not generate eternal attributes, or characteristics in accord with some absolute standard of 'fitness'. As Mayr (1963, p. 296) argues: 'No gene has a fixed selective value; the same gene may confer high fitness on one genetic background and be virtually lethal on another.' Likewise, as Waddington (1969, p. 364) observes: 'The same genotype can therefore produce a number of phenotypes according to what the environment of the developing system has been.' Equivalent or analogous propositions are valid in the economic sphere as well. What is 'fit' is always relative to an environmental situation.

Thus even if the 'selected' characteristics of firms were the 'fittest' then they would be so in regard to a particular, economic, political and cultural environment only; they would not be the 'fittest' for all circumstances and times. Consider the following illustrative example of a type of context dependence where the chief effect on fitness is of the frequency of the population, called 'frequency dependence' (Lewontin, 1974).

In economics, the case of perfect competition doconplays frequency dependence, because each new entrant to the market by definition has no significant effect on prices. More realistically, however, firms or economic agents have market power, as in the case of oligopoly. Mark Schaffer (1989) considers a situation where firms have the choice of either maximizing profits or behaving 'spitefully' by using their market power. In the latter case the firm is not profit maximizing but is hurting the profit maximizing firms more than it hurts itself. With these assumptions it can be shown that profit maximization is not an evolutionary stable strategy, and can be driven out by the spiteful firms. Consequently the argument of Friedman (1953) and others that 'natural selection' necessarily favours the profit maximizers turns out to be wrong.

Consider another example of frequency dependence. Assume two types of firm, type A and type B. The population as a whole is a mix of type A and type B firms, with the associated culture and interfirm relations. Given that a new entrant can be of either type, their profits can be given by one of the following formulae:

Profit of type A entrant firm = 50 + (% of type B firms)

Profit of type B entrant firm = (% of type B firms)

Such illustrative profit values can be justified in terms of the different types of organizational form and interfirm relations. For instance, type B firms can be associated with more open and participatory structures and more cooperative interfirm behaviour, including perhaps the informal exchange of technical know-how (Hippel, 1987, 1988). Accordingly, there could be positive externalities associated with firms of such a type.[8]

Assume, first, that the initial (large) population is composed entirely of type A firms. In this case the profit for each type A new entrant will be 50, and of each type B new entrant will be 0. Clearly, type B firms are unlikely to become established if type A firms are dominant. However, if the initial population is composed entirely of type B firms then the profit for each type A new entrant will be 150, and of each type B new entrant will be 100. Consequently, in this case, type A firms can successfully invade the type B population. In sum, type A firms are likely to become or remain dominant, whatever the starting position. This will happen even if average profits are greater in an industry composed entirely of type B firms than one composed entirely of type A. Assume that the above equations apply to all firms, and not simply new entrants. Then the average profits of a type A population will be 50 and of a type B population will be 100. Yet type B firms are always at a relative disadvantage.

Furthermore, if the industry was dominated by type B firms then the situation may not last because new entrants of type A would be at a great advantage in those circumstances. Unless corrective action were taken – such as some arrangement for formal or informal regulation of the industry by the state or by an industrial association – the greater overall benefits related to type B dominance would be eventually undermined and destroyed by incoming type A firms.

This hypothetical example illustrates a number of general points. First, given that payoffs are dependent on the nature of the industry as a whole, then the selected characteristics likewise depend on the overall environment. Indeed, research on cooperatives suggests that their success is highly dependent on the type of financial and cultural regime that prevails in the regional or national economy (Horvat, 1975; Milenkovitch, 1971; Thomas and Logan, 1982).

Second, 'natural selection' does not necessarily favour the more efficient units, or always the optimal or near-optimal outcomes. The low density of cooperative or participatory firms in the real world should not be taken to mean that either individual firms of this type, or an industry dominated by them, is necessarily less efficient.

Third, and consequently, such circumstances may constitute a pretext for some kind of intervention in the economy, because there is no guarantee that efficient firms will actually be selected in a competitive, evolutionary process.

Problems for Dr Pangloss: (6) Multiple or Shifting Adaptive Peaks

Biologists use the analytical device of the fitness surface to trace out the description of the fitness of a population in regard to characteristic space. The possibility of a 'multiplicity of adaptive peaks on a fitness surface' was noted by Sewall Wright (1931, 1956, 1959). In these circumstances the selection process may lead to the congregation of units around a local, rather than the global, maximum, and a journey to the global maximum may be ruled out by the distance involved and the depth of the valleys in between. Clearly this possibility could apply to economic as well as biological evolution, with firms congregated around a local profit or efficiency maximum. With a multiplicity of adaptive peaks the route followed and thus the peak obtained is again path dependent: a result of history.

Most importantly, the environment in which selection proceeds includes not simply the climate, soil, etc., but also other species and even sometimes the 'social relations' or 'culture' of the subject species itself. Consequently, as pointed out by Waddington (1975, p. 170), behaviour is not simply a result of environmental change but also in part its cause.[9]

This compounds the problems for Dr Pangloss, because as a result the fitness surface may not be static. Consider a favourable adaptation that may take place in relation to a given environmental situation. Further adaptations take place along similar lines. However, while the first few adaptations may be favourable for the units concerned, the accumulation of such adaptations may alter the environment itself, and the result may be that the same adaptation no longer yields beneficial results for any individual unit.

For example, a firm may find a market niche involving the manufacture of a new type or variety of product. Initially, the firm may make large profits from the venture. Indeed, it may initially be at a global maximum on the fitness or profits surface. However, if a large number of other firms perceive and grasp the same opportunity, the market may become flooded and the product may no longer be profitable. Of course, we must assume a downward-sloping demand curve and some kind of profit-seeking firm, but not necessarily strict profit maximizing behaviour or other textbook fictions, for this to happen. Crucially, the 'environment', that is the state of market demand, itself may alter as other firms seek out buyers. What was profitable for one or a few may not be profitable for many. Being placed in this deteriorating situation, it may be difficult for the firms congregating in the niche to move elsewhere, because of the specificity of their assets or skills.

The changing topography of the fitness surface resulting from such frequency dependency effects may further inhibit the selection of optimizers. A group of hill climbers having climbed a sometime global maximum might find themselves overshadowed by a new and unobtainable global peak, or even plunged into a new depression. A group of sluggish non-optimizers might find themselves lunged upwards by earth movements in their favour. The possibility of a fitness surface with such a changing topography is considered in biological theory, by Waddington (1972) among others. It is sometimes referred to as the 'dancing landscapes' problem (Kauffman, 1988). With a shifting fitness surface we often have no reason for asserting that one 'optimal' solution will prove to be lastingly better than another.

This important possibility, deriving from a cybernetic or 'feedback' relationship between a unit and its environment, is as significant in economic evolution as it is in the biological sphere. We have already discussed the 'frequency dependency' effect where selection coefficients are dependent on population frequency, and clearly these cases have a direct application to economics. The neglect of such eventualities could involve another case of the 'fallacy of composition': the erroneous presumption that the selection of fitter individuals always leads to the selection of fitter populations. The repetition of this type of error in our science can likewise have damaging consequences for economic theory and policy.[10]

Problems for Dr Pangloss:
(7) Critical Mass and Intransitivity

We may note here Robert Axelrod's (1984) famous experiments on 'the evolution of cooperation' in an iterated Prisoner's Dilemma. Via a celebrated computer tournament he showed that a simple 'tit for tat' strategy where cooperation is met with cooperation, and hostile 'defection' is met with defection, can rival a formidable sample of rival and often more complex strategies.

Axelrod further shows that in some cases the prosperity of the 'cooperators' may depend on them reaching a critical mass in the population as a whole. Further, the viability of certain populations may depend on the initial population structure (Axelrod and Dion, 1988). In general, this means that what is efficient in one context may not be efficient in another. More particularly, the 'failure' of a type of unit may result not from any inherent deficiency but from the fact that it has not reached a critical mass in the general population. Clearly this is another case of frequency dependence.

Further relevant repercussions of this prisoner's dilemma model are suggested by Philip Kitcher (1987, p. 92) and reportedly also by Jack Hirshleifer. It is pointed out that a population dominated by units playing the tit-for-tat strategy could plausibly be invaded by an influx of others who will always cooperate. If this occurs then the consequent population of cooperators would clearly be vulnerable to an invasion by a species of unit which consistently defects. The tit-for-tat strategy would thus be completely overturned, and the population would 'regress' to the strategy of defection and non-cooperation.

However, such a population could then be invaded by units playing tit for tat, as long as the problem of critical mass is overcome by, for example, a sufficiently high rate of immigration. Clearly there is a case of intransitivity here. A population of tit for tats is vulnerable to invasion by cooperators; but a population of cooperators is vulnerable to invasion by defectors; and finally a population of defectors is vulnerable to invasion by tit for tats. Replace each occurrence of the phrase 'is vulnerable to invasion by' in the preceding sentence with 'is less efficient than' or with 'is less fit than' then we can see the problem that is raised by such intransitivity. Not only is the general notion of the 'survival of the fittest' questioned, but more particularly any ordinal notion of efficiency becomes groundless. The very idea that 'natural selection' sorts out units in accord with some absolute or relative notion of efficiency is highly dubious in such circumstances.

The idea of critical mass has been examined in other contexts in economics, for example in regard to the establishment of technological regimes (David, 1987), to the emergence of particular consumer behaviours in situations of interdependence (Granovetter and Soong, 1986), to the stabilization of conservative regimes (Kuran, 1987), to speculation about other individuals' behaviour (Schelling, 1978), to solutions to the prisoner's dilemma by collective learning (Witt, 1986a), and to the emergence of social institutions (Witt, 1989).

The prisoner's dilemma also corresponds to cases in the sociobiological literature describing the evolution of tendencies to either 'selfish' or 'altruistic' behaviour. While universal altruism may be most beneficial for all members of the species, the possible existence of such a prisoner's dilemma can lead to the breakdown of the arrangement of universal altruism with its advantages for all. Thus there is not necessarily any universal mechanism by which natural selection tends to favour the survival of the group. Given that the mechanism of natural selection in modern biology does not even necessarily lead to survival, the mere fact of survival, even to a numerous and sustained extent, need not always imply absolute fitness or efficiency at all.

In some cases there can be a problem of symbiosis rather than critical mass, where the efficient behaviour of the rational depends on a sufficient number of less rational agents. Consider the fisheries model of Peter Allen and J. M. McGlade (1987a) in which individual fishing boats are divided into maximizing 'Cartesians' who move to places which are most likely to yield fish on the basis of information available, and 'Stochasts' who take risks and search randomly. Given that a fleet composed entirely of Cartesians would overfish specific locations and be unlikely to find new ones without the help of some wandering Stochasts, Allen and McGlade conclude that a mixture of Cartesians and Stochasts is overall more productive than a pure population of maximizers.

John Conlisk (1980) shows that under plausible conditions evolutionary selection will not necessarily produce a homogeneous population of optimizers. After assuming that optimizing behaviour is relatively costly, he finds that a mixed population of rational optimizers and slavish imitators can evolve to an equilibrium still involving a mixture of both types. As a result the evolutionary outcome is a mixture, rather than a pure race of optimizers.

Concluding Observations

It has not been established here that state intervention or economic planning are necessarily superior to laissez-faire. It has been demonstrated, however, that the nineteenth-century idea of unhampered evolution necessarily reaching optimal outcomes is misconceived. Both in the biological and the economic context, evolution is not a grand optimizer, or a perfectionist. Evolution is awesome and inspiring, but also messy, stupid and tragic.

Consequently, while the positive case for state intervention has not been made in this chapter, one of the principal arguments in opposition to such 'interference' has been removed. The outcome is that we cannot appeal to natural selection to support either general reliance on markets or general support for state intervention: the case for one or the other policy has to be made in regard to specific circumstances.

Although the policy conclusion is neither generally pro-state nor generally pro-market, its significance should not be underestimated.

The legacy of Spencer and others is found in innumerable common-place remarks concerning the alleged benefits of 'free' market forces and competition. But evolution has its revenge; the very notion of 'the survival of the fittest' will not itself endure the test of time.

14
Evolution, Indeterminacy and Intention

The modern, neo-Darwinian, 'synthesis' in biology explains evolution in terms of random variation and natural selection. The notion of causality is neither straightforwardly mechanical nor strictly deterministic, because of the role of random mutation. It is, to use Jacques Monod's (1971) phrase, a combination of 'chance and necessity'. However, what is notable is the absence, at least within neo-Darwinian orthodoxy, of any explanation in terms of intentional behaviour. The element of chance is confined to mutation, not to purpose or action. Given its environment, once an organism is born its behaviour is regarded as being determined simply by its genes. It may be deemed that an organism is goal-seeking, but it is argued below that this is not purposeful behaviour in the fullest sense. Hence the Darwinian theory of evolution gives a largely causal explanation of animal behaviour and evolution, undermining the preceding domination of teleology in biology.

In the present context, the problem with this has already been stated earlier in the present work: if economic development is determined by some process of natural selection, with something analogous to genetic replication and to random variation or mutation, then what role remains for the notions of intentionality, purposefulness or choice, which economists from many schools of thought have held so dear?[1]

Thus the preservation of a genuine notion of purposeful behaviour is a problem for those who wish to apply to society the metaphor of evolution in biology. As Gerald Silverberg (1988, p. 539) observes: 'Almost without exception, workers in the field of social evolution acknowledge that human societies are characterised by an emergent property almost totally absent from the biological domain – the presence of conscious goal-seeking behaviour partly guided by mental models of the world which attempt to anticipate the future course of the individual's environment.'

Both the biological and the physical sciences have generally rejected the concept of intentionality as an explanation of events. Despite being the science of life, biology follows physics in identifying merely cause and effect. Intention or purpose are not recognized, except as the determinate consequences of another cause. There is no teleology. Alfred North Whitehead (1938, p. 211) addresses this mainstream scientific view: 'Science can find no aim in nature: Science can find no creativity in nature; it finds mere rules of succession. . . . The disastrous separation of body and mind which has been fixed on European thought by Descartes is responsible for this blindness of Science.'

Remarkably, despite this enduring blindness, the idea that purpose is meaningful in evolution has haunted biology ever since its inception as a science. Aristotle believed that everything had its own predestination, and a teleological view of nature was widespread in the two centuries before Darwin. Although revivals of Lamarckism have often concentrated more on the mechanisms of acquired character inheritance, the ascription of purpose to organisms is a feature of Jean Baptiste de Lamarck's work (see *Zoological Philosophy* of 1809 – Lamarck, 1963; Burkhardt, 1977). Accordingly, the Lamarckian biologist Paul Kammerer (1924) wrote: 'It is not merciless selection that shapes and perfects the machinery of life; it is not the desperate struggle for survival alone which governs the world, but rather out of its own strength everything that has been created strives upwards towards light and the joy of life.'[2]

Likewise, in a number of novels and essays Samuel Butler periodically lambasted Darwinism for its apparent denial of consciousness and free will, and this was echoed by George Bernard Shaw in his famous Preface to *Back to Methusalah*, along with the iteration of other Lamarckian notions. Other dissenters from strict Darwinism, including Pierre Teilhard de Chardin (1959), Jean Piaget (1979) and Arthur Koestler (1967, 1971, 1978, 1980) have concerned themselves with similar themes.

There is a related area of tension in mainstream biology because of the role of random variation in the evolutionary process. The tension is between the commonplace belief that causal explanation should be supreme in the physical sciences and the need to admit 'random' variation in an evolutionary theory. Such an idea sits uneasily with the prevailing emphasis on determinate causality. As Ernst Mayr (1985b, p. 770) points out: 'Curiously, in the controversies over natural selection, the process has been described sometimes as "pure chance" . . . or as a strictly deterministic optimization process.'

In fact, biology may point to a different kind of causal explanation, surpassing the dichotomy of randomness and determination. As Sewall Wright (1967, p. 117) suggests: 'The Darwinian process of continued interplay of a random and a selective process is not intermediate between pure chance and pure determination, but in its consequences qualitatively utterly different from either.'

In this recurrent challenge from biology to the incursions of mechanistic causality, the Aristotelian ghost of teleology waits in the wings, as if waiting to recover some of its lost estates. As John Campbell (1985, p. 163) points out, using a different metaphor: 'nearly every scientist who has written on the general nature of evolution has felt compelled to show how deftly he can skate towards the abyss of tele-ology without falling in.' Campbell's own response to this issue is presented near the end of this chapter.

Although evolutionary thinking may eventually lead to a tran-scendence of the dichotomy between determinism and chance, as yet mainstream biology does not satisfactorily address the question of purposefulness and intentionality. Its notion of purpose is limited to programmed, goal-seeking behaviour. It is the aim of this chapter to explore the deeper issue of intentional behaviour in an evolutionary context. In the following section the notions of choice and purpose in economics are briefly surveyed. It will be argued that while econ-omists have traditionally emphasized purposefulness and choice, these concepts are not well founded in orthodox economic theory, neither is their space in existing ideas for an evolutionary approach well defined.

This chapter goes on to suggest a preliminary theoretical framework for dealing with the problems that have been raised. This features several overlapping and multilevelled hierarchies, where there are different degrees of purposefulness and a spectrum of notions of causality, with an important place for both habits and institutional routines. While the stress on habit and routine provides a basis for both sustaining the evolutionary analogy in economics, and for build-ing economic models with some tentative capacity to estimate the future, it is nevertheless argued that there must also be a space for some degree of purposefulness and choice, and this must be founded on some notion of objective indeterminacy.

Thus the main thrust of the chapter is to propose a means of com-bining ideas of purpose and determination, causality and evolution, which previously many have regarded as difficult to reconcile.

The Rhetorical Background in Economic Theory

The idea of individuals with preferences is so central to the discourse of orthodox economics that the subject itself has sometimes been defined as 'the science of choice'. The elevation of this concept to this position of supremacy occurred with the 'marginal revolution' in the 1870s. Subsequently, the notion has often been taken for granted. Clearly, to be meaningful, the idea of choice must involve intentional or purposeful behaviour by the actor, and not merely a programmed response.

The concept of intentional behaviour is found in a wide variety of economic writings. For instance, when discussing the production process, Karl Marx wrote that 'what distinguishes the worst architect from the best of bees is that the architect builds the cell in his mind before he constructs it in wax' (1976, p. 284). Not only is work a 'purposeful activity' for Marx, in the sphere of exchange the juridical contract is seen as 'a relation between two wills' (p. 178).

Léon Walras, the most formalistic of the founders of neoclassical theory, saw economic agents as 'endowed with reason and freedom'. Indeed, for Walras and many other writers, it is the 'exercise of the human will' which distinguishes the social from the natural world (Walras, 1954, pp. 55, 61).

The American institutionalists also had an explicit notion of purposeful, individual human action. John Commons (1950, p. 36), in particular, argues that the 'science of the human will' acting in both 'individuals and all collective organizations' is the 'twentieth century foundation' of economic science.

The idea of action as purposeful behaviour is emphasized by the Austrian School. Thus in his *Human Action* Ludwig von Mises (1949) forcefully asserts that the analysis of economic and social phenomena requires the premise that human action is purposeful and goal directed.

However, the notion of purposeful behaviour is not deeply rooted in orthodox theory. This is demonstrated when attempts are made to incorporate Darwinian ideas. In particular Armen Alchian (1950) argued that maximizing behaviour by economic agents does not have to be justified in terms of their explicit objectives but by the 'evolutionary' contention that maximizing, and thus 'fit', firms and individuals are the ones more likely to survive and prosper. Such an argument clearly downgrades the theoretical status of the concept of purposeful behaviour, making it irrelevant to the explanation of the competitive process. It is somewhat paradoxical that a similar argument has been taken up by Milton Friedman (1953) in his famous methodological essay, given his political emphasis on the desirability of 'choice'.

Determinism and Choice

We may define determinism broadly here, as the view that outcomes are governed by causal laws. Free will is taken to imply that under given conditions an agent can act in a variety of possible ways. The latter implies that the chosen outcome is not completely determined or caused. This definition of free will is different from that of the 'compatibilists' (Ayer, 1954) who argue that freedom and determinism can be reconciled. Both supporters and opponents of compatibilism can be found among modern philosophers.

Although neoclassical theory is today associated with a liberal and individualistic ideology, at the theoretical and conceptual level it is implicitly deterministic. Against the compatibilists, it can be argued that it denies free will by making the individual a prisoner, not simply of the social environment, but of his or her immanent and often invariable preference functions and beliefs. In neoclassical theory, a unique choice is determined by given, individual preference functions; the individual is seen as maximizing utility with given preferences and objective constraints. On the basis of such a deterministic model it is difficult to find any space for real choice (Mini, 1974, p. 42; De Uriarte, 1990). As Brian Loasby (1991, p. 1) remarks: 'the rational choices that economists attribute to economic agents exhibit no signs of purposeful reasoning; they are programmed responses to the circumstances in which those agents are placed.'

The full consequences of this deterministic view are rarely made explicit. An exception is Vilfredo Pareto (1971, p. 120), when he wrote: 'The individual can disappear, provided he leaves us this photograph of his tastes.' With such a taste-satisfying machine, questions of real will or purpose fade away. As George Shackle (1972, p. 122) puts it: 'if the world is determinist, then it seems idle to speak of choice.'

Furthermore, to be meaningful, choice must take place in conditions of uncertainty. Loasby (1976, p. 5) has argued this concisely: 'If knowledge is perfect and the logic of choice complete and compelling then choice disappears; nothing is left but stimulus and response. If choice is real, the future cannot be certain; if the future is certain, there can be no choice.'

Even with the relaxation of the assumption of perfect knowledge in recent neoclassical models, choice is not necessarily reinstated. A Bayesian (or other similar) model with a random element does not necessarily admit true sovereignty or spontaneity for the individual concerned. Action enslaved by the throw of the dice may not be quite as rigidly determined, but it is no more purposeful or free.

Purposefulness and Goal Directedness

In a sense, the problem is one of distinguishing between a purposeful human agent and a goal-directed machine. Notably, two systems theorists, Russell Ackoff and Fred Emery (1972), have elaborated a relevant distinction between purposeful and goal-directed behaviour. The difference lies in the set of possible responses to the structural environment faced by the individual. Simpler goal-seeking devices (such as a thermostat) respond in a single and predetermined manner to changes in their environment.

The most sophisticated type of goal-seeking behaviour is that of a computer or machine that can 'learn' from its mistakes in pursuing goals, and thus can respond in different ways to the same repeated problem. However, in both these cases, the goals are still themselves determined or fixed.

The human, purposeful agent is essentially different in that he or she can change goals, and furthermore this may happen without any stimulus from outside. There is, so to speak, an 'uncaused cause'. The capacity to change both behaviour and goals without external stimulus means that humans have a will, and that some of our choices are real ones. As Nicholas Georgescu-Roegen (1971, p. 179) puts it: 'If man can *will* his motives freely, then man is free in spite of the fact that all actions follow with necessity from motives.' Real choice must stem from the ability to do otherwise, and must be contrary to the rule of either passions or fixed preference functions.[3]

Typically, much of orthodox economic theory does not include purposeful behaviour in this sense, and its models are of goal-seeking behaviour of the simplest type. Behaviour is regarded as a determinate result of external inputs to given preference functions. In recent years there have been more sophisticated developments, such as with models where a kind of learning is involved. But, for the reasons given above, the agent is still not endowed with real choice.

Free Will and the Uncaused Cause

Such changes in goals mean that all human action must contain an element of indeterminacy in the sense of an uncaused cause. Hence Shackle (1989, p. 51) asserts that 'economics is about choice as a *first cause*, that is the coming into being of decisive thoughts not in all respects to be explained by antecedents.' Shackle's anti-determinism is based on a conception of the essential indeterminacy of human decision-making: of individual decision and action as a first or uncaused cause.

Shackle expresses with eloquence an idea that is found in the Austrian tradition of economic thought. Similarly, much earlier, Frank Knight (1933, p. 221) argued: 'If there is real indeterminateness . . . there is in a sense an opening of the door to a conception of freedom in conduct.' Ludwig Lachmann (1969, p. 93) comes from the same intellectual tradition, arguing that individual plans cannot be a response 'to anything pre-existent' and thus they are wholly spontaneous and undetermined.

The idea that free will must be rooted in an uncaused cause has been taken up more recently by the non-compatibilist philosopher John Thorp (1980). He argues that the defence of free will has precisely to be located in the neurophysiological indeterminacy of the nervous system, and, following a suggestion of John Eccles, that such indeterminacy is both real and indeterminate in the deeper sense that it is not governed by a probability function.[4]

If the idea of freedom of the will can be established in this manner, then the notion of intentional or purposeful behaviour is given greater meaning and substance. Furthermore, there is a clearer basis for a distinction between the explanations of events in terms of human intentions and explanations in terms of causality: that is intentional explanations are distinguished from causal explanations (Elster, 1983).

The question of the possibility of purposes and actions which are not determined by the external environment may appear to hinge on the issue of the existence of (non-probabilistic) indeterminacy in the real world. This matter cannot, of course, be resolved here. There is no way in which either the existence of a causal relation, or the lack of one, can be definitively established. Yet modern physics now embraces some notion of indeterminacy. As Karl Popper points out: after the deterministic drift of nineteenth-century science, now the ' "natural" view of the universe seems to be indeterministic' (Popper and Eccles, 1977, p. 32).

We find important arguments in favour of chance and against mechanical necessity in the philosophical writings of Charles Sanders Peirce. He was one of the first modern philosophers to broach the notion that we have to assume objective indeterminacy in order to understand the manifest diversity of the universe. He conjectured that underneath apparent order and regularity, the world was governed by chance and disorder, thus 'admitting pure spontaneity or life as a character of the universe'. Crucially, 'variety can spring only from spontaneity' (Peirce, 1935, p. 41).

Significantly, Peirce was a major influence on Thorstein Veblen, but his ideas on indeterminacy remained underdeveloped within American institutionalism and elsewhere.[5] It was after the development of quantum theory that a small number of post-quantum theory economists, such as Knight, discussed and endorsed the idea of the objective indeterminacy of the world.[6]

However, this appeal to quantum physics creates difficulties for those who wish to compartmentalize explanations into intentional terms, on the one hand, and causal terms, on the other. For quantum theory points to ubiquitous indeterminacy, not simply in the recesses of the human brain but within each and every atom of matter. Of course, the indeterminacy of the quanta is probabilistic, in contrast to the non-probabilistic notion of indeterminacy discussed above. Nevertheless, quantum theory involves something quite different from the deterministic idea of cause and effect.

Popper's (1982b) own arguments for the indeterminacy of the universe also go much further than the mysteries of the human mind. He makes a useful distinction between 'scientific' and 'metaphysical' determinism. 'Scientific' determinism involves the view that, in principle, any event can be rationally predicted with a sufficient degree of accuracy. This is rejected on the grounds that we can never know the complete description of cause and effect, even if the universe is fully deterministic. Even more interestingly, 'metaphysical' determinism is rejected on the grounds that it involves an untenable description of the space–time continuum in terms of a four-dimensional 'Parmenidean' block. In this block, the past, present and future are all contained; the past is symmetrical with the future along a single dimension – there is no arrow of time. Consequently, Popper inclines towards an ontology involving indeterminism, even if the 'metaphysical' character of this proposition means that it cannot be falsified.

It appears that in discovering indeterminacy we may well have opened a Pandora's Box. It may not be possible to confine discussion of such a phenomenon to the human brain. On the one hand, quantum theory points to a wider indeterminacy of the universe. On the other, the idea that free will emanates from the indeterminacy of the firing of the neurons suggests that all animals with a nervous system are endowed with some kind of free will, not humans alone. This runs counter to the idea, which pervades much of economic theory, that humans alone are endowed with will and choice. However, Robert Rosen (1987, pp. 13–14) sees anticipatory mechanisms at many levels in biological systems. The more radical idea that animals may have a free will is accepted by Thorp (1980, pp. 140–1), and Popper argues, contrary to strict Darwinism, that animal preferences and consciousness could be decisive in evolution (Popper and Eccles, 1977, pp. 12–13). For Whitehead (1938, p. 207) too, the notion of creation, involving purposeful organisms, 'is essential to the understanding of nature'.

Chaos Theory and Indeterminacy

We can never demonstrate the existence of indeterminacy because there is always the possibility of a hidden and unknown causal mechanism at work. However, what we do know from the mathematical theory of chaos (Gleick, 1988; Stewart, 1989) is that even if the world is deterministic it would almost certainly behave in an apparently random, even non-probabilistic, and unpredictable way. The possibility of 'deterministic chaos' is thus established.

Nevertheless, this does not give outright victory to determinism in its old battle against indeterminacy. On the contrary, chaos theory suggests that the rules of engagement have changed. Even if the world is deterministic, the theory suggests that we would have to treat it as if it were indeterministic and unpredictable. Even if novelty is caused, it may appear as entirely spontaneous and free. Thus the very distinction between determinacy and indeterminacy is undermined. We can never know for sure if any event is caused or uncaused, but chaos theory suggests that we have to treat complex systems as if they were indeterministic. Rather than the victory of determinism, and as Philip Mirowski (1990a, p. 305) writes: 'The chaos literature instead reveals the curious symbiosis of randomness and determinism, the blurring of the boundaries between order and chaos.' Chaos theory simultaneously breaks the reductionist bonds and suggests the possibility of emergence, even in a system which is deemed to adhere to deterministic rules.

The chaos theorists have shown that tiny changes in crucial parameters can lead to dramatic consequences, known as the 'Butterfly Effect – the notion that a butterfly stirring the air today in Peking can transform storm systems next month in New York' (Gleick, 1988, p. 8). There are parallels here with James Maxwell's (1882, p. 443) account of indeterminacy, 'the little spark which kindles the great forest', and more recently with the account of 'bifurcation points' in the work of Ilya Prigogine and Isabelle Stengers (1984). After behaving deterministically, a system may reach a bifurcation point where it is inherently impossible to determine which direction change may take; a small and imperceptible disturbance could lead the system into one direction rather than another.

Chaos theory suggests that apparent novelty may arise from a deterministic system. Accordingly, James Crutchfield et al. (1986, p. 49) make explicit some connections between chaos, evolution and the emergence of novelty:

> Chaos is often seen in terms of the limitations it implies, such as lack of predictability. Nature may, however, employ chaos constructively. Through amplification of small fluctuations it can provide natural systems with access to novelty.... Biological evolution demands genetic variability; chaos provides a means of structuring random changes, thereby providing the possibility of putting variability under evolutionary control.

Chaos theory thus provides an interesting challenge; suggesting even that the distinction between determinacy and indeterminacy is blurred. From an apparently deterministic starting point, we are led to novelty, quasi-randomness and evolution. Although the philosophical implications of chaos theory have not yet been spelt out in detail, the dualistic separation between determinacy and indeterminacy is questioned. The seemingly 'uncaused cause' may have chaotic origins. The point, however, is that we can never know.

In sum, chaos theory brings mechanical determinacy to its limits, and undermines the whole edifice of predictive and reductionist science. The seeds sown on the traditional ground of mechanistic causality thus grow into the very monstrosities – chaos, indeterminacy, free will, organicism, holism – which many modern scientists would claim to have felled long ago.

The Limits to Indeterminacy

So far, we have raised many more questions than answers. Clearly, most of the fundamental philosophical issues cannot be resolved here. Nevertheless, there are strong grounds discussed above to reject two extreme kinds of position. The first involves some variant of determinism, in which it is assumed that science proceeds exclusively through analysis of cause and effect. On both ontological and methodological grounds this may be rejected. Chaos theory, furthermore, has put paid to the idea of predictability, even if we live in a fully determined world.

The second extreme position, traditionally associated with the Austrian School and with those under their influence, is that human action is based exclusively on decision and choice which are themselves wholly uncaused. The emphasis is on expectation and imagination: on action in an uncertain world. In such a view, the external world of institutions and natural resources impinges on the actor principally as a constraint, not as factors affecting choice itself. The sphere of choice in the human mind is sacred, undetermined and free: unsullied by the relations of cause and effect to be found in the external world.

Such a view, however, neglects the forces that themselves may mould – but not necessarily or completely predetermine – some individual purposes and goals. In the view of the Austrian School the individual is taken as a given. He or she descends on the social world, already formed and without a natural history. The consequences for Austrian theory are that it is incapable of building a model of the economy where the formation or moulding of some individual purposes and goals is taken into account, to complement the complex portrayal of social institutions as the unintended consequences of interacting individuals. Half the picture is missing.

Thus, while creating a space for real choice, Shackle and the Austrian theorists seem to deny the legitimacy of enquiry into the framing or moulding of purposes or preference functions. For instance, the role of institutions and culture in shaping human cognitions and actions is ignored. I have argued at length elsewhere that intentional explanations may rely on cultural and institutional props (Hodgson, 1988). Arguably, therefore, Shackle and the Austrian theorists go too far, proposing that it is beyond the scope of economic theory to enquire as to how *any* purposes and actions may be framed or moulded by circumstances. It seems untenable to deny any possible external influence on the thought processes and purposes of the individual, other than mere constraints.

Indeed, it is possible to retain some notion of non-probabilistic indeterminacy on which there are real constraints and thereby limited possibilities. For instance, Thorp (1980, p. 68) considers the idea of 'partial indeterminacy'. In this instance 'it is not the case that at a certain moment literally anything may happen next – rather that several different things could happen and one of them will.' In other words, 'partial indeterminacy' involves not simply exogenous constraints on the set of possible outcomes but also endogenous constraints which are associated with the indeterminate process itself.

Accordingly we may consider that although novelty and creativity are possible, each human mind has limited powers of imagination and expectation. Furthermore, these limits will be a result of experiences and habits of thought which are bounded and framed by the culture of which the individual is a part. Hence, although there is still real indeterminacy, we may be internally constrained in our imagination and choice.

To illustrate: A slave may be able to imagine and desire the state of freedom, but accommodation to enslavement rather than a striving for liberty is the more likely state of mind. A feudal peasant may frequently engage in buying and selling, but will not necessarily have the kind of deliberative and calculative mentality associated with the pursuit of money-making in the capitalist era. A traditional housewife may be able to imagine a career of professional employment, but she will face internal constraints on her own expectations formed by her own subculture as well as the externally imposed limits to choice. An industrial worker will come from a kind of collectivist culture in which individualism and the drive to entrepreneurship are often over-shadowed. A resident of Eastern Europe emerging in the 1990s from more than half a century of totalitarianism will not necessarily be endowed with the habits of thought associated with the acceptance of personal responsibility, and may be inclined to leave initiatives to others.

In all of these cases there is non-probabilistic indeterminacy and space for choice. Nevertheless, the indeterminacy is partial. Consequently the set of possibilities is limited and accordingly there is even some scope for prediction. Such a standpoint avoids the extremes of either determinism or complete indeterminacy.

There are external influences moulding the purposes and actions of individuals, but action is not entirely determined by them. The environment is influential but it does not completely determine either what the individual aims to do or what he or she may achieve. The individual is ridden by habits of thought but not bereft of choice. There are actions which may be uncaused, but at the same time there are patterns of thought or behaviour that may relate to the cultural or institutional environment within which the person acts. Action, in short, is partially determined, and partially indeterminate: partly predictable but partly unforeseeable. The economic future is still uncertain, in the most radical sense; at the same time, however, economic reality displays a degree of pattern and order.

In sum, it is desirable to assert the importance of indeterminacy and spontaneity in human action but also to recognize its limits at the same time. In some ranges or dimensions, action may be indeterminate, but in others it is not. To assert indeterminacy is not to deny its limits: that action is also bounded and moulded by the influences of culture, institutions and the past.[7]

Levels of Consciousness

The acceptance that imagination and choice may be culture-bound leads us to consider the nature and limits of conscious, purposeful behaviour. The limits on imagination and choice do not simply concern their boundaries: culture moulds their very nature and substance. Reason and imagination depend on concepts and are bounded by cognitive frames, and these in turn are affected by our social culture.

However, the purpose of this argument is not to reduce the explanation of human action to culture alone, in the manner of some schools of thought in anthropology. In contrast, the intention here is to reconceptualize the conscious and purposeful aspects of human behaviour so that they are situated in both a cultural and a natural context.

In contrast, in economics and elsewhere, a Cartesian and dualistic view is frequently taken; the realm of thoughts and intentions is simply divided from the physical and natural world, and consciousness itself is regarded as undifferentiated. As Whitehead (1938, pp. 204–5) argues, for Descartes

> there are material substances with spatial relations, and mental substances. The mental substances are external to the material substances. Neither type requires the other type for the completion of its essence. Their unexplained interrelations are unnecessary for their respective existences. In truth, this formulation of the problem in terms of minds and matter is unfortunate. It omits the lower forms of life, such as vegetation and the lower animal types. These forms touch upon human mentality at their highest and upon inorganic nature at their lowest. The effect of this sharp division between nature and life has poisoned all subsequent philosophy ... there is no proper fusion of the two in most modern schools of thought. For some, nature is mere appearance and mind is the sole reality. For others, physical nature is the sole reality and nature is the epiphenomenon.

Equally in opposition to Cartesian dualism, Veblen (1914, p. 30n) urged that 'a substantial dichotomy between physiological and psychological activity be abandoned'. Yet such a view is the exception rather than the rule. Much of social science has cut human mentality and action adrift from its natural foundation.[8]

As one who is typical of the subjectivists who downgrade the connections between nature and human action, von Mises (1949, p. 8) writes: 'Reason and experience show us two separate realms, the external world of the physical, chemical and psychological phenomena and the internal world of thought, feeling, valuation and purposeful action.' With such a 'dualistic philosophy' (von Mises, 1957, p. 1), the individual, now virtually a ghost in the machine, is seen to animate the bodily mechanism.[9]

Notably, the dualistic philosophy, with its unbridgeable divide between the mental and physical, cannot easily accommodate the concept of habit, in the fullest and most meaningful sense, or recognize its significance in a complex world. For the dualistic philosophy, action is purposeful, and without purpose there is no action. There are no gradations or blurred edges. Habit, which has been defined as 'a more or less self-actuating disposition or tendency to engage in a previously adopted or acquired form of action' (Camic, 1986, p. 1044) is either dismissed, devalued or ignored.

In general, neoclassical theorists assume that individual objectives emanate from a single-valued utility function. While doubt has already been cast on the ability of such mechanistic functions to represent purposeful behaviour, it is clear that all actions are, so to speak, on the same level. If habits exist they are deemed to result from utility maximization just like anything else.[10]

Likewise, when confronted with the possibility of such a grey area between the two, Austrian theorists generally react by placing all actions in the same category, that of conscious and creative choice. This even applies in cases where an individual refrains from action. Accordingly, von Mises (1949, p. 13) asserts that 'to do nothing and to be idle are also action, they too determine the course of events. ... Action is not only doing but no less omitting what possibly could be done.'

However, if the abstention from action is to be regarded as purposeful in the manner suggested, then it would imply that we continuously scrutinize not only ourselves but also our entire environment for opportunities to act: a continuous and omniscient monitoring process governing all potential deeds.

Ironically, the reason why such a monitoring process is not feasible derives from the very sort of consideration that the Austrians have quite rightly brought to the fore in a different context: the impossibility of dealing with and processing the vast quantity of information that is involved in the planning of a modern economy (Hayek, 1935, 1948). But a similar point applies to the human mind as well. Both our physiology and our environment are so complex that the human mind cannot commit all the sensory data it receives to the same level of conscious deliberation.

Consistent with this argument, it is appropriate to regard decision-making as operable on different levels, and subject to different degrees of deliberation. As Koestler (1967, p. 238) argues, consciousness 'is not an all-or-nothing affair but a *matter of degrees*. There is a continuous scale of gradations which extends from the unconscious ... up to bright, wide-awake states of arousal'.

To reassert the importance of the notion of purposeful action it is necessary to establish habitual, unreflexive behaviour, as its real and conceptual opposition. For without such an irreducible hierarchy of levels of consciousness and intent (as proposed by Koestler, 1964, 1967, 1978, 1980) there is the danger that one level or type of consciousness and purposefulness will dissolve conceptually into another.

Matters of Habit

An excellent illustration of the perils of a dualistic view is found in the story of the relegation of the concept of habit in sociology, as related by Charles Camic (1986). After occupying pride of place in the writings of Émile Durkheim and Max Weber, and in sociology generally around the beginning of the twentieth century, the concept of habit was purposefully excised from the discipline. Arguably, a similar process has occurred within economics as well (Waller, 1988).

Camic argues that this excision was a defensive response to the conceptual homogenization of action by the behaviourist psychologists after the First World War. In contrast to the Social Darwinists, the behaviourists put supreme emphasis on environmental conditioning, to the point of denying any space for human agency.

Under the influence of behaviourists such as John B. Watson and Burrhus F. Skinner, there has been a reluctance, even outside psychology, to use 'intangible' concepts such as consciousness and intent: 'Merely to mention these pariah words in scientific discourse is to risk immediate loss of attention and audience' (Matson, 1964, p. 174). Skinner's behaviourism represents the opposite end of the same false Cartesian dichotomy to that which is occupied by the Austrians. The behaviourists import mechanistic scientism into the study of human action: for them all is mechanical cause and effect. In contrast, others such as the Austrian School eschew the natural and physical aspects of humanity, placing supreme stress on intention and thought instead.

However, the relegation of the concept of habit in the social sciences was also bound up with the persisting influence of Social Darwinism, up to the Second World War. By the interwar period there was a strong reaction against all tendencies to relate socioeconomic to biological phenomena, whatever their perceived ideological connotations (Degler, 1990; Weingart, 1990). Concepts like 'habit' and 'instinct' were the casualties, because they were regarded as being part of the Social Darwinian emphasis on heredity and genes.

Reacting against the behaviourist denial of consciousness, reflexivity and rational deliberation, social scientists became concerned to reclaim a space for agency and choice. Concerned to rebut any suggestion that action, even at the habitual level, was driven by the genes, the concept of habit was either removed entirely or subsumed within the higher levels of consciousness and deliberation. Thus, with a concern to maintain what it saw as its scientific credentials, social science cut loose from the biological and psychological world and abandoned any attempt to relate the two.

While both sociology and economics both took this anti-naturalistic turn in the 1920s and 1930s, they then immediately parted company, establishing different kinds of dualisms. For many sociologists, a freestanding concept of culture became the medium and motivation of action. Culture itself was demarcated from its natural and biological foundations. Mystically self-reinforcing and floating free, culture in some cases became a *deus ex machina*.

In contrast, for the orthodox economist, particularly after Lionel Robbins's famous *Essay on the Nature and Significance of Economic Science* (1935), the presumptions of rationality became the fountainhead of theory. Not only was a separation made from the psychological and physiological foundations of human wants and needs, there was an explicit denial of realism, culminating in Milton Friedman's (1953) famous defence of the assumptions of rational maximization. The pure utilitarian calculus was justified in terms of an instrumentalist methodology, and the separation from the real world – biological and social – was complete.

While these developments in sociology and economics are clearly different, both ignore the biological foundation of human society. Action is homogenized at a single level: that of human action or choice. Both embody a Cartesian view of mind, separated from the remaining world by an impenetrable conceptual barrier. Having established this divide, the intermediate levels of consciousness and deliberation, namely habits, are either denied or incorporated at the conscious level.

In effect, economists actually confounded the substance of purposefulness and choice, by denying the obverse with which it could be contrasted. Sociologists actually diminished the concept of culture by making all action culture-bound. Similarly, behaviourist psychology, by excising consciousness, neglects the essence of habit as well; all is mere behaviour, or all is undifferentiated action. Thus, by collapsing all levels of action into one, social science effectively undermined its own conceptual foundations. It is only by situating such key concepts in a conceptual system in which their obverse may be addressed that such key concepts can be given full substance and meaning.[11]

The reinstatement of the concept of habit is important in a number of respects, already noted in chapter 9 above. By establishing a non-deliberative category of behaviour it is possible, first, to find the basis for some degree of stability and continuity in social life; second, it enhances the idea of choosing or deliberative behaviour with which it contrasts; and third, it provides a basis, through the provision of an equivalent to the gene, for a genuinely evolutionary theory in economic and social science.

Habit has a place in the hierarchy of thought and action, and infuses a number of its levels. Even the most deliberative kinds of thought and reason are themselves governed by habits of thought, involving particular kinds of concept and method of calculation. Although real choice may be exercised, the very concepts and methods of calculation may not themselves be deliberated upon.

Instead of the Humean idea of atomic units of experience, habits provide continuity in thought and action. Against Hume's atomization of experience, John Dewey (1938, pp. 245–6) saw habits as part of an organic and temporal web: 'Some sort of sequential connection is ... as inherent a quality of experience as are the distinctive pulses of experience that are bound together. Cultural conditions tend to multiply ties and to introduce new modes of tying experiences together.'

Although many rules and habits that infuse experience and behaviour may be fixed, it is argued by Koestler (1980, pp. 455–9) that there is always room for different and variable strategies. In fact, Koestler (1980, p. 455) sees the distinction between fixed codes and variable strategies as 'fundamental to all purposeful behaviour'.[12] It may appear paradoxical, but the very idea of purposeful action depends on the fixity of a number of concepts, rules and conceptual frames.

Habit is not mere automatic behaviour; that mistake reproduces the Cartesian dualism of thought and machine. Even the most ingrained habits are the objects of recurring mental activity and evaluation.[13] This is partly because all habits are triggered and interlocked with other habits. However, this does not imply that habits are frequently deliberated on at higher levels of awareness. Instead, they are addressed at the level of 'practical consciousness' (Giddens, 1984), typically with the day-to-day mentality of routine and work. As pragmatist philosophers such as Peirce recognized long ago, the concept of habit is a strong challenge to the Cartesian dualisms of matter and mind, of automatism and thought.

Consequently, habits have both intentional and causal facets. Furthermore, we do not have to regard the evolutionary selection process as operating simply on the raw material of programmed action. There should be a place in an evolutionary explanation for some freedom of the will, but not in quite the same sense as the fully deliberating and choosing agent found in the rhetoric of economic theory.[14]

Biology and Teleology

It was noted near the beginning of this chapter that biology has tended to ape physics by eschewing intentional explanations. However, a recent paper by John Campbell (1985) develops an important challenge to this view. It is briefly summarized here to suggest a direction in which the philosophy of biology may move on the question of teleology and causality. Furthermore, Campbell develops a typology of relations between causality and organization which is of great significance for all social and physical sciences.

Campbell's starting point is to draw a distinction between selection for 'evolutionary functions' and selection for 'adaptive functions'. Traditional Darwinism involves selection for adaptive functions, relating to the fitness or fecundity of the individual:

The individual organisms best able to carry out adaptive functions automatically have selective advantages in propagating their particular genes. Selection for evolutionary functions is not that direct. Structures that help the species to evolve do not increase the competitive fitness or fecundity of the individual. (Campbell, 1985, p. 139)

The 'Red Queen' hypothesis or paradox of Leigh van Valen illustrates this (Van Valen, 1973; Stenseth and Maynard Smith, 1984). Van Valen considers a situation where, like the Red Queen in Lewis Carroll's *Through the Looking Glass*, organisms must run fast to stand still. Different species coexist and form part of each other's environment. As each species evolves, this itself constitutes an alteration of the environment of the other species, giving rise to further evolutionary change and cumulative feedback effects on the other species. Campbell (1985, p. 139) points out that in this situation:

In the long run competition is not just for fitness with the environment but it is for the ability to out-evolve other species. Those forms most facile at evolving will predominate. Ultimately, evolutionary success for each competitor comes from acquiring tricks, skills, and strategies to evolve faster and more effectively than the competition.

It is the evolution of these 'tricks, skills, and strategies' to deal with a repertoire of possible changes, as well as the evolution of adaptations to a specific change, which concerns Campbell. A phenotypic trait that develops through direct natural selection helps to adapt the species to its environment. The trait may then be modified so that it also performs a more general evolutionary function, enabling the organism to adapt more easily to future change.

This idea is redolent of similar second-order selection effects, such as the famous 'Baldwin effect' and Conrad Waddington's (1953) idea of 'genetic assimilation'. Waddington (1969, p. 373) argues that:

Natural selection has built into all the more highly evolved organisms some capacity for reacting to stress in ways which tend to make the organism more effective in dealing with it. Such responses can be considered as a very generalized form of learning. It is clear enough that responding to a stress in this way would be useful to the organism and would therefore be favoured in natural selection. (Waddington, 1969, p. 373)

In other words, natural selection may lead not simply to the development of species which are more adapted to their environment, but also to different capacities to respond by further adaptation to changes in the environment.[15]

Given such processes of genotypic selection, one possibility is that the general direction or drift of genotypic evolution may keep in step with the environmental changes. This Campbell (1985, pp. 142–3) calls an evolutionary director, which may 'direct or channel the pathway of evolution without actually powering the change'. This is precisely the

Causality and organization

Type of organizations	Emergent causal property	Format for causal analysis
None (elementary) particles only)	Acausal	Quantum mechanics
Mechanical objects	Deterministic cause and effect	Newtonian mechanics
Negentropy	Unidirectional cause and effect	Thermodynamics
Information		Cybernetics
Information about self	Recursive causes are their effects	Self-reference
Information about future self	Future causality	Future self-reference

Source: J. H. Campbell, 'An Organizational Interpretation of Evolution', in *Evolution at the Crossroads: The New Biology and the New Philosophy of Science*, ed. D. J. Depew and B. H. Weber (Cambridge, Mass.: MIT, 1985), p. 155.

conclusion drawn by Waddington (1957) with his idea of chreodic development (discussed briefly in chapter 13 above).

Campbell goes on to consider *sensory evolution* as a possible case where 'an organism detects relevant information about its environs and influences the way it evolves accordingly' (1985, pp. 146–7). Directors for sensory evolution have been found, even in bacteria. *Projective evolution* is the next case, involving 'access to multiple sources of information about self and the environment' (p. 149). Anticipatory mechanisms have been identified at many levels in biological systems (Rosen, 1987, pp. 13–14). The nervous systems of the higher animals enable projective evolution. The domestication of animals and artificial selection are examples.

Clearly, Campbell is attempting to expand the repertoire of causal explanation in biology. He writes:

> The study of evolution is expanding inexorably to include structure-function interpretation. Accordingly it becomes increasingly evident that organisms evolve special structures to promote their capacities to evolve, and that these structures enormously expand the scope of the evolutionary process. Nevertheless, function is fundamentally a teleological concept, especially when applied to the evolutionary process. (1985, pp. 152–3)

With this reinstatement of the concept of teleology, Campbell goes on to argue that:

> Contrary to its superficial appearance, causal behaviour is not an inherent property of matter as such. Instead, causality emerges only from organization of matter. Poorly organized material admits only rudimentary forms of causality. As matter becomes progressively more organized it sequentially acquires new capacities for causal interactions. (pp. 154–5)

This controversial argument is reminiscent of the proposition of Charles Sanders Peirce (1935, p. 84) that there are no immutable laws of nature. He argued that physical laws themselves evolve over time and are context dependent. Reproduced above is Campbell's own table of the relationship between different kinds of organization and different types of causality.

Campbell's argument is provocative and debatable, but it does provide a framework within which there are places for both causality and finalism. This has simultaneous potential applications to both the biological and the social sciences. Different relationships between the organization of matter and types of causality are arrayed in a hierarchy, and are compatible with the earlier arguments in this chapter.

Conclusion

As discussed in the next chapter, a hierarchical view of the organization of nature has been developed by biologists such as Ludwig von Bertalanffy (1971), Niles Eldredge (1985a), James Miller (1978) and Paul Weiss (1973). This continues the long relationship between systems theory and biology, influenced in part by philosophers such as Whitehead (1926, 1938). Clearly, this hierarchical idea may be extended to the social and psychological domains, and this concern is reflected in the work of Koestler (1967, 1978, 1980). He proposes an organicist and hierarchical view of the universe, and attempts to transcend the Cartesian dualisms of mind and matter, intention and causality.[16]

Remarkably, in such a hierarchical ontology there is once again a place for intentional, as well as habitual, behaviour. Indeed, in a prolonged polemic with Darwinian biology, Koestler likewise argues that intention and purpose should not be excluded from the evolutionary process. Although Koestler's ideas have not proved to be very influential, it is notable that the questions he raised will not go away. Many biologists may still treat life in mechanical or physicalist terms, but countervailing quasi-vitalistic or teleological ideas periodically resurface. Thus Jonathan Jacobs (1986) has made a plea for the adoption of teleological notions in biology, and he shows that they imply a nonreductionist theoretical approach.

It is also important to note that such a view provides a place for novelty and creativity, and this is clearly of great significance in an evolutionary framework. However, some writers, notably Ulrich Witt

(1991a, forthcoming), have taken the cue from the Austrian School and suggested that the indeterminacy of individual imagination and choice is the primary source of novelty in economic evolution. A slightly different view has been suggested here, in which there are both limits to individual indeterminacy and even sources of spontaneity and novelty elsewhere.

Clearly, all technical and institutional innovation involves individuals, but we must be concerned with the culturally determined limits to imagination as well as imagination itself. Innovation and novelty are much more likely when these limits are being altered or broken down, such as when different cultures collide, or in periods of major socioeconomic turbulence. An individualistic focus on the subjectivism of the human imagination pays insufficient heed to the limits of spontaneity and the ever-changing textures of institutions and culture. These both limit and mould the possibilities for innovation and novelty in an evolutionary process.[17]

15

The Problem of Reductionism in Biology and Economics

Inspired in particular by classical physics and its apparent analytical and practical successes, orthodox economists have long been labouring under a reductionist research programme. The complexities of economic systems have been addressed by attempting to build up a composite picture from atomistic, individual units, just as the particle forms the elemental unit in Newtonian mechanics. Accordingly, the attempt has been to explain the whole through its analytical reduction to its presumed microfoundations and component parts.

Yet after well over a century, and an enormous cumulative effort in the application of mathematical technique to this task, economics today is in more confusion and disorder than it was 30, 50 or even 100 years ago. Just as a consensus was seemingly achieved in the 1950s and 1960s, it dissipated in the 1970s into increasing disarray. Interestingly, this occurred simultaneously with a renewed effort to complete the reductionist programme, undermining the macroeconomic side of the consensus with the appeal for 'sound microfoundations'. Now, instead of consensus – in either macroeconomics or microeconomics – there is a plethora of rival approaches and schools.

Furthermore, 'hard core' notions such as rationality and equilibrium are being questioned, even by mainstream theorists. Textbook attempts to make neoclassical theory operational, with aggregated functions, the 'law of demand' and so on, have been found to lack generality and to depend on a seemingly increasing number of auxiliary presuppositions. The precise resolution of the crisis in this subject is not, of course, an easy matter. But nevertheless an examination of some of the fundamental ontological and methodological issues suggests a route of advance that may well repay further intellectual investment.

This chapter addresses some of the ontological and methodological issues involved in the atomistic world-view, and in the individualistic version of atomism found in orthodox economics. It includes a brief review of some developments in biology which lead away from atomistic and reductionist philosophies. Some tentative ideas concerning the future development of economics are proposed, influenced in particular by developments in biology, and involving a discussion of the appropriate levels of reduction in economic science.

It should be pointed out at the outset that the general idea of a reduction to parts is not being overturned here. Some degree of reduction to elemental units is inevitable. Even measurement is an act of reductionism. Science cannot proceed without some dissection and some analysis of parts.

However, although some reductionism is inevitable and desirable, complete reductionism is both impossible and a philosophically dogmatic diversion. What is important to stress is that the process of analysis cannot be extended to the most elementary sub-atomic particles presently known to science, or even to individuals in economics or genes in biology. Complete reductionism would be hopeless and interminable. As Karl Popper has declared: 'I do not think that there are any examples of a successful reduction' to elemental units in science (Popper and Eccles, 1977, p. 18). Reduction is necessary to some extent, but it can never be complete. What is contentious is not reductionism *per se*, but its chosen scope and extent, and the ultimate reliance placed on it in comparison with, or to the exclusion of, other general methodological procedures.

Atomism in Science

In an atomist ontology, entities possess qualities independently of their relations with other entities. In the world of atoms 'all qualitative diversity is reduced to differences in configuration and motion of the homogeneous and permanent elements' (Capek, 1961, p. 5). The origins of atomism in the West can be traced back to Greek civilization, and to Leucippus and Democritus in particular. Additionally embracing a deterministic outlook, they believed that everything is composed of atoms which are physically indivisible.

In contrast, Aristotle rejected atomism, and his ideas were prominent in medieval Europe. The move back to atomism, led by Galileo, Descartes, Newton and others, helped to establish the foundations of modern science. In particular, Newtonian physics was built on the analysis of particles and their motions in accord with the assumed fundamental laws. The analytical success of atomism related to the development of methods by which complex phenomena could be broken down and understood in terms of their fundamental components and the interactions between them, involving an impressive analytical reduction of wholes to parts. The new scientific method was thereby characterized by its fusion of an atomist ontology with a reductionist approach to analysis.

This post-medieval rebirth of atomism coincided – not accidentally – with the development of liberal and individualistic doctrines in political science, in the writings of Hobbes and Locke, for example. There is a familiar yet resilient argument that the growth of these ideas was related in some degree to the social and economic changes associated with the development of commodity trade. We do not have to embrace a vulgar Marxism to see the substance of this. The organicist world-view of the Middle Ages had to be displaced as a precondition for both the development of modern science and for the establishment of a conducive legal, political and institutional environment for exchange and markets. It is no accident that the development of classical physics occurred in the period and in countries where individual property, plus banking and accountancy systems based on common monetary measurement, were also becoming paramount. The historical coincidence of these developments is too striking to be ignored.

In the social sphere the human individual became the fundamental unit of analysis: the indivisible particle in motion. Of course, it is accepted that individuals, like particles, are affected by their circumstances in the manner of the forces and constraints that impinge upon them. But in such an atomist social ontology the essential aspects of human personality and motivation are conceived of as independent of the social relations with others. As a typical, and most simple, expression of this outlook, individual taste and preference functions are taken as given, at least for the purpose of analysis.

Many examples of atomism and reductionism can be found in both the natural and the social sciences to the present day. For instance, the physicist and Nobel Laureate Steven Weinberg (1974, p. 56) has written: 'One of man's enduring hopes has been to find a few simple laws that would explain why nature with all its seeming complexity and variety is the way it is. . . . At the present moment the closest we can come to a unified view of nature is a description in terms of elementary particles and their mutual interactions.'

Alternatively, there is a long history of biological reductionism in regard to social phenomena, from Herbert Spencer and the Social Darwinists to this day. As a recent example some theorists of social culture, such as Alexander Alland (1967) argue that it is a kind of biological adaptation. A similarly biological-reductionist response is given by Jerome Barkow (1978, p. 13): 'Human social institutions are and can only be patterned expressions of biologically based learning preferences, predispositions and motivations, characteristics which are there because they once maximised inclusive fitness.' These statements deny the autonomy of the cultural and institutional level of human society.

Atomism, Individualism and Reductionism in Economics

With a few notable exceptions, the ideas of atomism and its special expression as a form of individualism have dominated economics since

its emergence as a science.[1] Since Adam Smith, mainstream economists have taken for granted the analytical primacy either of the individual or of the household (the household itself being seen as the
estate of a single individual: its male head). Topics such as growth and
distribution have been frequently addressed, but it has been a general
belief that such aggregate or social phenomena should, where possible, be explained via an understanding of the behaviour of the individuals involved.

The rise of neoclassical economics after 1870 further consolidated
this reductionism by providing an analytical framework in which to
place the choosing individual, adjusting his or her endowments according to given individual functions of utility or preference and with
due heed to prices and constraints.

Thus the dilemmas of choice under constraint increasingly became
the dominant theme, reinforcing the idea of the maximizing and
utility-driven individual as the elemental component of the science.
This development has been further consolidated in recent years with
attempts to break down the analysis of previously undivided units,
such as the government or the family or the firm, into the individual
behavioural elements composing them.[2]

At the core of general equilibrium theory the individual atom still
remains. Like others, general equilibrium theorist Kenneth Arrow (1968,
p. 641) reflects the view that explanations of economic phenomena
should be reduced to the behaviour of individuals, seeing this as a
salutary 'rejection of the organism approach to social problems'. In a
mood of disenchantment with aggregative macroeconomic theory, there
has been a strong movement since the 1970s to place that arm of the
subject on secure microeconomic foundations derived from Walrasian
general equilibrium theory (Weintraub, 1979).

The atomistic and reductionist outlook is also endorsed by non-
neoclassical authors, such as the Austrian School led by Ludwig von
Mises and Friedrich Hayek. It is even ratified by the new type of
'rational choice' or 'analytical' Marxism which proudly employs
'standard tools of microeconomic analysis' (Roemer, 1988, p. 172),
including versions of general equilibrium and game theory.

Jon Elster, a leading member of the latter school, expresses well the
individualistic and reductionist presumptions which he shares with
orthodoxy: 'The basic building block in the social sciences, the elementary unit of explanation, is the individual action guided by some
intention. . . . Generally speaking, the scientific practice is to seek an
explanation at a lower level than the explanandum. . . . The *search for
micro-foundations*, to use a fashionable term from recent controversies
in economics, is in reality a pervasive and omnipresent feature of
science' (Elster, 1983, pp. 20–4).

Methodological individualism is an important expression of reductionism in social science. It amounts to the view that explanations of

social and economic phenomena should be made in individual terms. However, it has been argued in a preceding chapter that adequate reasons why explanation should be reduced simply to the level of the individual, and stop there, have not been provided.

Lars Udéhn (1987) has argued convincingly that not only is methodological individualism flawed, but that it is inoperable as a methodological approach because of the problems of analytical intractability involved. The reductionist explanation of all complex socioeconomic phenomena in terms of individuals is over-ambitious, and has never succeeded. Aggregation and simplification are always necessary. The general problem of analytical intractability is discussed further below.

The obverse position to methodological individualism could be described as 'methodological holism' and it would amount to the proposition that all social phenomena are explicable only in terms of social structures, social institutions, or social culture. In the case of methodological individualism, explanation reduces to the exclusive matter of the individual parts; in the case of methodological holism, explanation reduces to the exclusive matter of the social whole. Both of these are thereby reductionist positions. It will be suggested below, however, that both standpoints are unsatisfactory and that there are non-reductionist alternatives to both methodological individualism and methodological holism.

The Failure of the Microfoundations Project

Mainstream theory has been engaged in a longlasting attempt to place economics on secure and individualistic microfoundations. However, it was quickly realized that the potential diversity among individuals threatened the feasibility of this project. Many types of interaction between the individuals have to be ignored to make the analysis tractable. Indeed, it was not easy to develop a composite picture from a diversity of types of individual agent.

Even with the standard assumptions of rational behaviour, and its drastic psychological and epistemological limitations, severe difficulties are faced. As Arrow (1986, p. S388) has been led to declare: 'In the aggregate, the hypothesis of rational behaviour has in general no implications.' Consequently, it is widely assumed that all individuals have the same utility function. Among other things this denies the possibility of 'gains from trade arising from individual differences' (ibid., p. S390).

Fabrizio Coricelli and Giovanni Dosi (1988, p. 126) argue that 'the project of building dynamic models with economic content and descriptive power by relying solely on the basic principles of rationality and perfect competition through the market process has generally failed.' Attempts to base macroeconomics on neoclassical microfoundations involve faith in the 'invisible hand' and in the substantive capabilities of individuals to calculate endlessly and make supremely rational choices. Yet the results of this theoretical endeavour show no more than a very crippled hand, incapable of orderly systemic coordination even in relatively simple models:

> Moreover, note that these results are obtained despite an increasing attribution of rational competence and information processing power to individual agents. Certainly ... the attempt to 'explain' macroeconomics solely on the basis of some kind of 'hyper-rationality' of the agents ... and the (pre-analytical) fundamentals of the economy (i.e. given technology and tastes) has failed. (Coricelli and Dosi, 1988, p. 136)

Hence it is no exaggeration to say that the microfoundations enterprise has effectively collapsed, and for reasons well known to and understood by the leading theorists of the genre. The gravity of the present crisis for mainstream economics can be illustrated by considering a number of central theoretical topics.[3]

First, theoretical work in game theory and elsewhere has raised questions about the very meaning of 'hard core' notions such as rationality. Yanis Varoufakis (1990) surveys some of the recent results concerning the problems of rational decision-making in the circumstances where a limited number of other actors are believed to be capable of 'irrational' acts. Such 'irrationality' need not stem from stupidity; it is sufficient to consider the possibilities that rational actors may have incomplete information, limited computational capacities, slight misperceptions of reality, or doubts concerning the attributes of their adversaries. Agents do not have to be substantially irrational for irrationality to matter. Irrational behaviour may emerge simply where some people are uncertain that everybody else is rational.

Second, after the neglect of decades, mainstream theorists now, albeit in a limited fashion, admit discussion of problems of imperfect or asymmetric information and even 'bounded rationality'. While these are welcome developments they have created havoc with orthodox presuppositions. For instance, as Joseph Stiglitz (1987) has elaborated, where prices signal quality to the consumer, standard demand analysis and the so-called 'law of demand' get overturned.

Third, the intrusion of chaos theory into economics has put paid to the general idea that economics can proceed simply on the criterion of 'correct predictions'. With non-linear models, outcomes are oversensitive to initial conditions and thereby reliable predictions are impossible to make in regard to any extended time period. In particular, chaos theory has confounded the rational expectations theorists by showing that even where most agents know the basic structure of the economic model, in general they cannot derive reliable predictions of outcomes and thereby form any meaningful 'rational expectations' of the future (Grandmont, 1987). We shall discuss some further implications of chaos theory below.

Fourth, recent research into the problems of the uniqueness and stability of general equilibria has shown that they may be indeterminate and unstable unless very strong assumptions are made, such as the supposition that society as a whole behaves as if it were a single individual (Coricelli and Dosi, 1988). This demolishes the entire microfoundations project. Facing such profound problems, Alan Kirman (1989, p. 138) concludes: 'If we are to progress further we may well be forced to theorize in terms of groups who have collectively coherent behaviour.... The idea that we should start at the level of the isolated individual is one which we may well have to abandon.'

The theoretical implications of these uniqueness and stability results for general equilibrium theory are devastating and dramatic. A fundamental consequence is the breakdown of the types of analysis based on individualistic or atomistic ontologies. The indeterminacy and instability results produced by contemporary theory lead to the conclusion that an economy made up of atomistic agents has not structure enough to survive, as its equilibria may be evanescent states from which the system tends to depart (Ingrao and Israel, 1985, 1990; Kirman, 1989). Furthermore, as Donald Katzner (1991) has argued, it is not possible to aggregate from individual supply and demand functions to such aggregated functions at the level of the market if considerations of ignorance and historical time are taken into account.

Typically, the textbook macroeconomics that is spun out of neoclassical theory goes well beyond the rigours of general equilibrium theory, to make bold and general claims concerning the relationship between wages and unemployment, and inflation and the money supply. Only the more honest and careful neoclassical theorists have questioned such macroeconomic derivations from microeconomic assumptions. For instance, Arrow (1986, p. S386) states that he knows 'of no serious derivation of the demand for money from a rational optimization'. In an extensive examination of orthodox, textbook, macroeconomic theories, John Weeks (1989, p. 236) shows that they 'suffer from serious flaws of internal logic. Accepting these models and proceeding as if they were analytically sound is essentially an act of politically-motivated faith.'

There are many other problems in modern economics, from capital theory to monetary analysis, from the theory of the firm to the economics of welfare. For the moment we have confined ourselves to some special cases only. These conspire to undermine the very ontological and methodological foundations of orthodoxy.

The Ubiquitous Problem of Analytical Intractability

As in other sciences, there is a strong reductionist tradition in biology. In the nineteenth century, after the publication of Charles Darwin's

Origin of Species, there was a prominent tendency on behalf of his followers to assume that explanations of social phenomena were reducible to biological terms. One of the best-known equivalent cases in the twentieth century is the work of Richard Dawkins (1976), where he takes the view that the behaviours of organisms, groups and whole species can be largely explained in terms of their genes. Similarly, sociobiologists such as Edward Wilson (1975) attempt to explain the social behaviour of animals and humans in terms of the constituent genes, without sufficient recognition of the explanatory autonomy of social culture. Culture cannot be understood simply as an expression of the genes; it has little or nothing to do with genetic concepts such as 'inclusive fitness'. Of course, it is not being suggested here that biology has no relevance at all for the study of social phenomena. Instead, the contrary and extreme view that they can be understood wholly or largely in biological terms is being challenged.

Yet biological reductionism has unmanageable computational problems. Consider the prediction of evolution with multiple loci or alleles: 'even the simplest multi-locus case of two alleles at each of two loci is analytically intractable. This should not be surprising: the problem of dimensionality nine (there are nine possible genotypes, with independently specifiable fitness parameters) is already more complicated than the three-body problem of classical mechanics' (Wimsatt, 1980, p. 223). Like the three-body problem, this biological computation has been solved for a variety of special cases (Roughgarden, 1979, pp. 111–33) but has not been solved in general. Similar problems of intractability arise from the Schrödinger equations for subatomic particles.

To assess the dimensions of analytical difficulty, let us address the 'less complex' case of the three-body problem in mechanics. While this problem has been solved for two bodies, the differential equations that result from applying these laws to three bodies are so complicated that a general solution has not been found. Instead, partial solutions have been achieved by resorting to approximations or constraints of various kinds, such as the assumption that one body has negligible mass (H. D. Young, 1968, p. 258; Stewart, 1989, pp. 66–72). Hence mathematical solutions cannot be found to configurations of this very first level of complexity, involving just three bodies.

This does not mean, of course, that ontological reductionism is invalid; the system may still be regarded as being composed of three atomistic units. But it indicates the operational limits of reductionism; the hope that predictions can be made with such a simple three-body system is in vain. Furthermore, this gives little consolation to the biological or economic reductionist who aims to predict by breaking down all complex phenomena to the interactive behaviour of atomistic or individual parts.

Chaos theorists have shown that in non-linear systems, tiny changes in crucial parameters can lead to dramatic consequences (Gleick, 1988;

Stewart, 1989). The result is not simply to make prediction difficult or impossible; there are serious implications for the notion of reductive explanation in science. We cannot with absolute confidence associate a given outcome with a given set of initial conditions, because we can never be sure that the computations traced out from those initial conditions are precise enough, and that the initial conditions themselves have been defined with sufficient precision. Hence in chaos theory the very notion of explanation of a phenomenon by reference to a system and its initial conditions is challenged.

As leading mathematicians of chaos have themselves proclaimed, chaos theory 'brings a new challenge to the reductionist view that a system can be understood by breaking it down and studying each piece' (Crutchfield et al., 1986, p. 48). The impact of chaos theory for science as a whole is likely to be profound. Not only is the common obsession with precise prediction confounded; the whole atomistic tradition in science of attempting to reduce each phenomenon to its component parts is placed into question.

However, this does not mean that such non-linear equations relating to a lower level of analysis are worthless. Although they may be of limited computational or predictive use, they retain some explanatory power. Furthermore, as noted later below, chaotic systems do exhibit some kind of order about which deductions may be drawn.

The Limitations and Biases of the Counterstrategies

Strategies have been devised to attempt to deal with the general analytical problems associated with complex systems. For instance, Herbert Simon (1968) has examined 'the hypothesis of near decomposability' through which it is assumed that a complex system can be decomposed into a set of subsystems. For this to be feasible, all strong interactions must be contained within the boundaries of subsystems, and interactions between variables or entities in different subsystems must be appreciably weaker than those relating variables or entities in the same subsystem. If this is the case then a short-run approximation to the behaviour of the system can be made by ignoring the interactions between subsystems, and analysing each one as if it were isolated.

However, the general applicability of this principle is in doubt. Apart from the remaining problem of long-term interactions, biologists have shown that under feasible conditions there can be permanent and substantial linkage disequilibrium between subsystems (Maynard Smith, 1978a, ch. 5; Roughgarden, 1979). This suggests that systems can be treated as being nearly decomposable only in a limited number of special cases.

In a seminal work of genetic reductionism, George C. Williams (1966) claims that reductive problems can be solved one locus at a time and then extended to a global solution by 'iterating over all loci'. This is now recognized by critics as invalid. Williams wrongly presumes that gene frequency alone is an adequate basis for a deterministic theory of evolutionary change, and ignores context dependence. This refers to a situation where the fitness or behaviour of an organism may be significantly dependent on its environmental context, often leading to two-way interactions between a unit and its environment. As William Wimsatt (1980, p. 240) argues: 'Illegitimate assumptions of context-independence are a frequent error in reductionist analyses.'

In the course of his argument, Wimsatt highlights 'the practical impossibility of generating an exhaustive, quasi-algorithmic, or exact analysis of the behaviour of the system and its environment'. In response to this complexity

> the reductionist must start simplifying. In general, simplifying assumptions will have to be made everywhere, but given his interest in studying relations *internal* to the system, he will tend to order his list of economic priorities so as to simplify, first and more extremely, in his description, observation, control, and analysis of the environment than in the system he is studying. After all, simplifications internal to the system face the danger of simplifying out of existence the very phenomena and mechanisms he wishes to study. (Wimsatt, 1980, p. 241)

However, there are clear pitfalls in ignoring the complexities of the environment and some of its interactions with the system in question. Therefore the reductionist research strategy, Wimsatt rightly concludes, has an inbuilt bias towards the inclusion of certain types of relations and the exclusion of others. (This is exemplified in the group selection controversy outlined in chapter 12 above.)

The Revival of Organicism in Biology

The dispute between reductionists and non-reductionists in biology has flared up periodically. Partly because of the ongoing prestige enjoyed by the basic physical sciences, ever since Darwin published his *Origin of Species* biologists have been faced with the claim that biological phenomena could be reduced to and explained in terms of classical physics and chemistry. It has been upheld that every living organism must obey the same laws as those that apply to inert matter and that there are no other laws. In the past, some biologists adopted this physicalist viewpoint, and ventured to explain biological phenomena mechanistically and deterministically in terms of particles, movements and forces. Max Hartmann, Hermann Helmholtz, Jacques Loeb, Carl Ludwig, Julius Sachs and August Weismann took this physicalist view. Although it has since made limited headway, it persisted as late as the postwar period. Note the words of Nobel Laureate

Francis Crick (1966, p. 10): 'the ultimate aim of the modern movement in biology is in fact to explain *all* biology in terms of physics and chemistry.'[4]

For a long time the opposition to physicalism from within biology came from those who followed Aristotle and proposed that a living organism had some kind of constituent that clearly distinguished it from inert matter. This 'vital force' was deemed not to obey the laws of physics and chemistry. As Ernst Mayr (1985a, p. 45) puts it: 'For a vitalist, at least an extreme vitalist, there are two entirely separate worlds, that of the physical sciences and that of the world of life.' The philosopher Henri Bergson and leading biologists such as Hans Driesch and John B. S. Haldane inclined to vitalism. Mayr (p. 46) evaluates this group as follows: 'There is little doubt that some of the much-maligned vitalists had a far more profound understanding of the living organism than their mechanistic opponents.' Since the 1940s, however, vitalism has had no significant following.

With conceptual developments in postwar biology, physicalism also went into decline. Instead, the refined synthesis between Darwinism and Mendelian genetics focused the attention of many on the gene as the unit of analysis. However, a thoroughgoing reductionist should not be content with explanations based on the gene alone. This unit should in turn be reduced to its constituent elements. Accordingly, there is a controversy over the possibility of the reduction of Mendelian genetics to molecular biology.[5]

In addition, there is a related quarrel over the unit of evolutionary selection. On this central issue there is as yet no consensus among biologists, and views range from the idea of the gene as the exclusive unit of selection as in the work of Dawkins and others, through the possibility of group or species selection, up to the selection of ecosystems.[6]

Even with such a diversity of views, biology fosters an intuition about the wholeness of living systems. As Mayr (1985a, p. 44) retorts: 'every biologist would insist that to dissect complex biological systems into elementary particles would be by all odds the worst way to study nature.' Mayr's own argument goes further: 'Nowhere in the inanimate world can one find a system, even a complex system, that has the ordered internal cohesion and coadaptation of even the simplest of biological systems. And this requires an entirely different approach from that of the classical philosophy of science' (pp. 57–8).

An earlier postwar challenge to atomism and reductionism came from the set of biologists, including Ludwig von Bertalanffy (1971) and Paul Weiss (1973), who had become the pioneers of general systems theory. Although the reductionist tradition remains strong, there have been further moves against genetic reductionism in biology in recent years. These are found in the work of Niles Eldredge, Stephen Jay Gould, Richard Lewontin and Ernst Mayr, among others.[7]

It should not be assumed, however, that reductionism is on the point of extinction in biology. In a rather obvious attempt to preserve as many of its tenets as possible, Alexander Rosenberg (1985) has developed the concept of supervenience, and this has many adherents amongst philosophers of biology. Supervenience applies to the situation where the identity of two or more entities at the macro level does not assume identity at the constituent micro level, but identity at the micro level does guarantee identity at the macro level. In this case the macro level can be said to be supervenient. Rosenberg (1976) applied a related argument to economics, defending a qualified form of reductionism there.

Clearly, the concept of supervenience is a direct counter to the rival conception of emergent properties that was discussed in the preceding chapter. Supervenience retains ontological reductionism and the priority of the physical and micro level over other, higher levels. It is impossible to deal with this complex philosophical issue here, but it may be noted that the supervenience concept was developed before chaos theory was seen to pose a severe challenge to reductionism. In chaotic systems, almost exact identity at the micro level does not guarantee identity at the macro level, and supervenience is eluded. It remains to be seen whether supervenience as a concept will survive the consequences of chaos theory and related developments.

The entropy concept in thermodynamics involves a shift away from the kind of mechanistic thinking with which reductionism is associated. The entropy law enforces the concept of irreversibility, where macroscopic change has direction in time. The law presumes that the universe is moving from a relatively ordered and organized state to the chaotic outcome of maximum disorder or entropy. However, this process is not instantaneous, and it is constrained by the transient rigidities and barriers in ordered systems. Biotic evolution, furthermore, creates local islands of order, which seem to resist the march of entropy for a while.[8]

However, while the entropy law implies irreversible and universal decay, the time-scale involved is immense. Clearly it is important to examine the detailed processes involved. Here the concept of boundary constraint, applicable to each level of any ordered structure, is important. Accordingly, 'successively higher levels of the hierarchy are dependent, reductionistically, not so much on the *elements* at the lower levels, but on the nature and existence of the boundary constraints. If one removes the constraints at a given level, the systemic (or holistic) properties of all higher levels potentially collapse' (Kell and Welch, 1991, p. 15). For example, the severe lesion of a cell membrane can cause not only the decomposition of the cell, but, by the release of enzymes, the disorganization of a whole organism.

Hence the rigidities and boundary constraints provided by the whole structure play an essential role in maintaining its integrity and coherence. They provide boundaries in the real world between levels within complex systems. Just as we cannot fully understand the strange attractors and strands of order in the chaotic systems of modern mathematics by following and replicating each stage in the computation, we cannot understand complex, evolving systems by focusing simply on their parts. The system has to be understood both in terms of the movements of the parts and the systemically imposed constraints that bear upon them at each level.

The Principles of Hierarchy and Emergence

Hence one of the deepest problems with reductionism is the question of the transition between concepts on different analytical levels. While the reductionist believes that analytical progress towards explanations in terms of smaller and simpler components can eventually be complete, there are concerns about the conceptual transitions involved. A good illustration has been provided by the philosopher of science Paul Feyerabend (1965, p. 223) in regard to the relationship between the movements of molecules, at one level, and the concept of temperature, on another. He has argued that although the concept of temperature can be associated with statistical mechanics and the movements of molecules, the kinetic theory cannot 'give us such a concept' as temperature, which relates to an interactive level above and beyond the combined movements of molecules. It is an error to attempt to reduce completely the concepts of one science to those of another.

The view is proposed here that the key to an alternative approach is through an exploration of the organizing principles of complex, hierarchical, open systems. Some of the ideas involved have been discussed already in this book. Systems or subsystems at each level of the hierarchy have a dual character, acting both as wholes themselves and as parts of other wholes (J. G. Miller, 1978; Pattee, 1973).

Arthur Koestler (1967, ch. 3) has attempted to capture this dual quality of each system with the term 'holon'. Each holon displays 'both the autonomous properties of wholes and the dependent properties of parts' (p. 383). This is described as the 'Janus effect'. Every organism (holon) is possessed of two opposite polarities: 'an *integrative tendency* to function as part of the larger whole, and a *self-assertive tendency* to preserve its individual autonomy' (Koestler, 1980, p. 465).

A holon is subject to the influences not only above and below in its own hierarchy but also through the connections with other hierarchies or systems. Such hierarchies are interlaced with each other: in overlapping, net-forming, or 'reticulating' (Koestler, 1967, p. 387) patterns.

Also contrary to straightforward reductionism, Donald Campbell (1974, p. 182) has drawn attention to the way in which wholes, through what he calls downward causation, can affect the properties of components at lower levels. Thus in addition to the notion of the whole being greater than the sum of the parts, to some extent the whole determines the properties of the parts.

In a related vein, Mayr argues:

> Systems at each hierarchical level have two characteristics. They act as wholes (as if they were a homogeneous entity), and their characteristics cannot (not even in theory) be deduced from the most complete knowledge of the components, taken separately or in other partial combinations. In other words, when such systems are assembled from their components, new characteristics of the new whole emerge that could not have been predicted from a knowledge of the components. (1985a, p. 58)

This principle of emergence is a fundamental characteristic of complex, hierarchical systems. Reductionism is thwarted by the existence of such emergent properties at each level of the hierarchy. As Mayr contends: 'Recognition of the importance of emergence demonstrates, of course, the invalidity of extreme reductionism. By the time we have dissected an organism down to atoms and elementary particles we have lost everything that is characteristic of a living system' (ibid.).[9] Furthermore: 'Such emergence is quite universal, occurring also, of course, in inanimate systems, but nowhere else plays the important role that it does in living organisms.'

This hierarchic ontology also counters strict determinism, for the existence of emergent properties suggests that some phenomena are uncaused, at least in the traditional sense in terms of the dissectable combination of forces acting upon them. As Popper (1974, p. 281) has remarked: 'We live in a universe of emergent novelty'; a novelty which is as a rule 'not completely reducible to any of its preceding stages' (Popper, 1982b, p. 162). 'Our universe is partly causal, partly probabilistic, and partly open: it is emergent' (ibid., p. 130). Popper here reflects the earlier views of other notable philosophers. For instance, Charles Sanders Peirce (1923, p. 190) saw 'an element of indeterminacy, spontaneity, or absolute chance in nature'. Alfred North Whitehead (1926, 1929a, 1929b, 1938) also regarded the notions of emergence and creativity as essential to our understanding both of human society and of nature.

The arguments of Whitehead, Koestler and others involve attempts to break down the dualistic barriers not only between mind and matter, but also between the purposeful and the mechanical, between atomism and holism, and between finalism and deterministic causality. Clearly such a view involves a break not only with reductionist methods of analysis, but also with the opposing extremes of determinism and indeterminacy that were discussed in the preceding chapter.

It has already been noted that chaos theory provides nothing more than a hollow victory for determinism. Indeed, chaotic behaviour 'can provide natural systems with access to novelty' (Crutchfield et al., 1986, p. 49). Hence chaos theory may lead us to a composite ontology, in which both causal and indeterministic relations reside. Notably, a dynamic system that exhibits chaotic behaviour may in fact be performing complex oscillations around an attractor. Chaotic attractors are complex configurations within which the behaviour of seemingly random and unpredictable systems is constrained. As Ervin Laszlo (1987, pp. 41–2) puts it, chaos theory 'studies processes that appear chaotic on the surface but on detailed analysis prove to manifest subtle strands of order'.

Thus the chaos generated out of orderly, non-linear, mathematical functions may often lead to a kind of order at a higher level. Prigogine and Stengers (1984) and Kauffman (1991) start from chaotic interactions and show that self-organization and order can arise in complex systems. In both these cases the traits of the self-organizing system emerge from its basic structure, despite the chaos at the micro level.[10] Just as chaos can be spun from the 'order' of simple non-linear functions, order can emerge from chaos. Hence chaos and 'antichaos' are entwined.

In sum, chaos theory suggests the possibility of structure and order coexisting with chaos. This insight makes it possible to concentrate on the general structural characteristics of the system, while it is simultaneously impossible to make firm predictions from knowledge of the individual components; we may study the psychology of crowd behaviour without knowing every detail of every person in the crowd. While chaos confounds any attempt at complete reductionism, the structure makes analysis possible.

The Unity of Science

Mayr (1985a, p. 52) observes that 'evolutionary biology, with its interest in historical processes, is in some respects as closely allied to the humanities as it is to the exact sciences.' Thus greater direct inspiration for economics may be derived from modern biology. This is partly because of the way in which biology addresses diversity, complexity and change, but also to do with the claim that biology may encompass a wider set of principles than physics. In short, biology embraces life.

Following such a trail, a number of writers have developed schemata for the unity of science as a whole, including both its natural and its social branches. In general terms, of course, this is an old idea. But what marks out the new attempts at unity is the incorporation of the principles of hierarchy and emergence, as described above (Laszlo, 1987; Jantsch, 1980).

Accordingly, a unified science in these terms preserves a substantial amount of methodological and conceptual autonomy for each level.

Although there may be unifying metaprinciples, many methodological prescriptions may be unique to a given level. Notably, even the boldest attempts to preserve methodological diversity and pluralism – many gathered under the fashionable label of 'postmodernism' – have to posit the metaprinciple of plurality itself; any discourse of diversity is itself unifying. A recognition of this fact goes along with the pluralist aim of maintaining the necessary degree of overall coherence while nevertheless preserving different kinds of concepts and theories with respect to each analytical level.

Hence unity in these terms is not equivalent to the old idea of unification by reductionism – where one set of concepts and theories dominate all. Neither are phenomena to be broken down analytically into atomistic units, to make up a complete mechanistic system such as in the dream of Laplace – where the entire universe is explained in such terms. A complete mechanical reduction is not only unobtainable in practice; attempts to work extensively and exclusively in such a manner neglect the very life, spontaneity and complexity of nature, and of (social) systems containing living things.

The principles of hierarchy and emergence combine to prevent the reduction of all this complexity to common, simple units and theoretical laws. Each level in the hierarchy has its own autonomy, and thereby its own principles of explanation and its own units of analysis. However, to preserve overall coherence this autonomy cannot be absolute. Phenomena at one level are underlain by phenomena at the level below and affected by those at the level above. Hence explanations at each level have to be eventually compatible with those on other tiers.

Paul Oppenheim and Hilary Putnam (1968) have put forward a sketch of a future, unified science, discussing six 'reductive levels': social groups, multicellular living things, cells, molecules, atoms, and elementary particles. More recently, addressing some additional methodological questions and taking heed of some of the developments in the philosophy of biology discussed above, Nancy Maull contrasts two approaches to the unity of science. On the one hand, there is the limited and traditional approach of 'derivational reduction'. On the other, there is an 'interlevel theory' which 'by establishing, explaining, and warranting the connections between different levels' (Maull, 1977, p. 158) bridges different tiers in the hierarchy.

In an equally ambitious work, Laszlo (1987) portends the unification of science within an evolutionary framework. He addresses ideas about dissipative structures and 'self-organization' in complex systems (G. Nicolis and Prigogine, 1977; Prigogine and Stengers, 1984) and concerning autopoietic systems which 'can maintain themselves in time only if they evolve the capacity to replicate or reproduce their structure' (Laszlo, 1987, p. 38).[11] Laszlo's work offers some useful suggestions for economic theory, some of which are taken up in this present book.

An important feature of the hierarchically ordered view of reality is that different levels are both divided and interconnected. It is important to neglect neither the interconnectedness nor the division of the hierarchy. Marshall Sahlins's (1977) spirited critique of sociobiology is an important example of an error of the former kind. His reaction against biology leads him to build Chinese Walls, completely detaching the realm of the social and cultural from the realm of the natural upon which it depends. This is a common trait in modern social science, and it is eloquently rebutted by Paul Hirst and Penny Woolley (1982).

Eric A. Smith rightly notes the thrust of Sahlins's position: 'In the extreme form of cultural determinism espoused by Sahlins . . . cultural systems have their own internal logic, which dominate any individual motives (fitness-maximizing or not) and replace the trajectory of natural selection with that of cultural teleology' (1987, p. 234). Sahlins's reaction against biology thus becomes a cultural reductionism.

In a similar critique, David Depew and Bruce Weber (1985a, p. 239) note Sahlins's attempt 'to draw a line between the natural and the cultural.' They comments on Sahlins's over-reaction against sociobiology in the following terms: 'It is only against the vision of a fully reduced nature, all of whose dimensions are controlled by events at a lowest level, that we need to preserve our intuitions about the uniqueness of human culture by withdrawing from nature.' In contrast, they propose a 'fully articulated, nonreductionistic, hierarchically structured naturalism' in which some elements of sociobiology could possibly have a place (ibid.).

Notably, an anti-reductionism of a hierarchically structured kind may be able to accommodate some highly limited notion of genetic causation at the social level, without reducing social explanations wholly or largely to lower-level, biological causes. The ontology of the structured hierarchy thus promotes the connectedness of multiple methods, without denying the methodologies of the social and the life sciences some respective autonomy.

To repeat: as well as its interconnectedness, it is important not to ignore the divided character of the hierarchy, and the autonomy of its different levels. The latter error is committed by Dawkins (1976) and E. O. Wilson (1975) in attempting to explain all social behaviour in biological terms.[12] Generally, such atomistic reductionism is inadequate in that it tries to explain separate levels in terms of one.

However, some presentations of holism are likewise reductionist, by suggesting that we can somehow study wholes directly without considering the workings of their constituent parts. Such a version of holism is another kind of reductionism, and simply the obverse of the mistaken, atomistic view that systems can be completely understood simply by addressing the interactions between their constituent parts. The term 'holism' can only be acceptable if it is defined in a non-reductionist way, accepting the relative autonomy of the parts as well as the wholes.

Conclusion

In attempting to ape nineteenth-century physics, economics has become progressively more reductionist and formalistic. Yet modern insights from both biology and chaos theory suggest that the reductionist research programme is both flawed and misconceived. A complete reductive analysis is unlikely to be achieved, even on the basis of the oversimplified core assumptions of neoclassical theory. Furthermore, even if such an analysis were achieved it would be of little analytical and practical use; this partly because of the non-linearities and the degree of complexity involved, and partly because of the kind of crude assumptions employed to enact the reductionist programme.

The science of biology has had to face up to the problem of the analysis of complex systems, and it seems to offer a tentative way out. Not only have many biologists adopted a non-atomistic ontology and rejected reductionism, they have also inspired methods and approaches which may prove fruitful for economists.

In addition, Whitehead's philosophical work seems highly appropriate in dealing with the common problems of complexity in both these sciences. Whitehead (1926, p. 163) wrote: 'In so far as there are internal relations, everything must depend upon everything else. But if this be the case, we cannot know about anything till we equally well know everything else.' His solution to this problem was to propose a nested hierarchy of sets of internal relations. Each layer in this hierarchy relates to a particular set of characteristics, thus defining the units at any given level. The hierarchy has the feature that the layers relating to wider and more general phenomena are more stable than the narrower and more specific ones.

Such a hierarchy within an overall system allows for the possibility of theoretical abstraction, disregarding certain aspects of the phenomena at hand, to focus on the main causal linkages (Whitehead, 1926, 1929a, 1929b, 1938). 'Nature, for Whitehead, is then such a co-ordinated system of subordinate societies of different grades of complexity or levels' (Mays, 1959, p. 88).

It is with this hierarchical view that we proceed to the next chapter. It will be argued that it is of relevance, for instance, to the establishing of the autonomy of the macroeconomic level of analysis, and also has application to the theory of technological change. In general, the ideas advanced here seem to provide a way of escaping from the intractable difficulties of reductionism in both biology and economics.

16
Bringing Life Back into Economics

The preceding chapter has established both the impossibility and the undesirability of complete reductionism. Nevertheless, units of analysis are necessary; there must be relatively invariant categories upon which analysis may proceed. In this chapter the idea of institutions – rather than atomistic individuals – as units of analysis is established. This core proposition is the hallmark, even a passable defining characteristic, of the 'old' institutional economics, from Thorstein Veblen and John Commons to the present day.[1] There follow some brief suggestive remarks on institutional and technological evolution. Finally we proceed to establish an independent role for macroeconomic analysis which is denied by the reductionism of much modern economic theory.

Institutions as Units of Analysis

Among the preliminary tasks of scientific analysis are taxonomy and classification, involving the assignment of sameness and difference. Classification, by bringing together entities in discrete groups, must refer to common qualities.[2] For classification to be enduring, it must be assumed that the common qualities themselves must be invariant. As Philip Mirowski (1989b) points out, a kind of 'conservation principle' is required. However: 'No posited invariance holds without exceptions and qualifications. We live in a world of broken symmetries and partial invariances' (ibid., p. 397). As Georgescu-Roegen (1971) has insisted, operational concepts have a contradictory or dialectical quality; they uneasily encompass their opposites.

The structured hierarchy of theories and concepts incorporates a web of partial invariances at each level. The problem, then, is to develop meaningful and operational principles of invariance on which analysis can be founded. In social science, the institutionalist tradition has a tentative answer to this problem, locating invariances in the (imperfect) self-reinforcing mechanisms of (partially) stable social institutions: 'such as the institutions of accounting conventions (say, Werner Sombart or David Ellerman) or in the legal definition of property rights (John R. Commons), or else in money itself (Knapp and the German Historicist School)' (Mirowski, 1989b, p. 400).

In other words, the relatively invariant unit is the social institution. We may define institutions in broad terms. They refer to the commonly held patterns of behaviour and habits of thought, of a routinized and durable nature, that are associated with people interacting in groups or larger collectives. Institutions enable ordered thought and action by imposing form and consistency on the activities of human beings.

As we have seen in chapter 9, Veblen suggested that habits and institutions play an evolutionary role similar to that of the gene in the natural world. He observed that institutions have a stable and inert quality, and tend to sustain and thus 'pass on' their important characteristics through time. Institutions are seen as both outgrowths and reinforcers of the routinized thought processes that are shared by a number of persons in a given society.

The power and durability of institutions and routines are manifest in a number of ways. In particular, with the benefit of modern developments in modern anthropology and psychology it can be seen that institutions play an essential role in providing a cognitive framework for interpreting sense-data and in providing intellectual habits or routines for transforming information into useful knowledge (Hodgson, 1988).

Let us consider the institutional dimension of information in more detail. Contrary to many assertions, neither genetic 'information' nor the 'information' stored in the memory of a computer is the same as the kind of information that is processed by, and transmitted between, humans. Following Charles Sanders Peirce (1932, pp. 156–73), semiotic theory makes a distinction between an 'icon', an 'index' and a 'symbol' (Fitzgerald, 1966; Greenlee, 1975). Unlike an icon or an index, a symbol represents an entity by virtue of habitual and established rules and conventions, usually involving the complex association of many ideas. For instance, the meanings of 'man' are obtained only by relating it to alternative and distinct concepts such as 'woman', 'child', 'animal', and so on. The information held and transmitted in the form of a symbol is thus embedded in a network of interconnected meanings, related to and reproduced by social structures. Genetic or computer information does not have this quality; it is at most indexical. In contrast, human information is structured and cultural; it is entwined with institutions.[3]

The cultural and cognitive functions of institutions have been investigated by anthropologists such as Mary Douglas (1970, 1973, 1987) and Barbara Lloyd (1972). Reference to the cognitive functions of institutions and routines is important in understanding their relative stability and capacity to replicate. Indeed, the strong, mutually reinforcing interaction between social institutions and individual cognition provides some significant stability in socioeconomic systems, partly by buffering and constraining the diverse and variable actions of many agents. Processes similar to what Veblen (1899, pp. 15–16; 1904, pp. 214ff.) described as 'emulation', or what Boyd and Richerson (1980, 1985) have modelled as 'conformism', can be important in removing internal variation and stabilizing individual behaviour in social institutions. For these and other reasons, institutions become 'locked in' to relatively stable and constrained paths of development.[4]

Hence the institution is 'a socially constructed invariant' (Mirowski, 1987b, p. 1034n), and institutions can be taken as the units and entities of analysis. This contrasts with the idea of the individual as the irreducible unit of analysis in neoclassical economics, and applies to both microeconomics and macroeconomics. Accordingly, theories based on aggregates become plausible when based on corresponding social institutions. Money is a legitimate unit of account because money itself is an institutionally sanctioned medium; aggregate consumption functions should relate to a set of persons with strong institutional and cultural links; and so on. Again this contrasts with the approach based on reasoning from axioms based on the supposed universals of individual behaviour. The approach based on institutional specifics rather than ahistorical universals is characteristic of institutional economics, and has parallels in some of the economics of the Marxian and Post Keynesian schools.

This does not mean, of course, that institutions are regarded as immutable. Institutions themselves may change, and they have nothing like the degree of permanence of the gene. What is important is to stress the *relative* invariance and self-reinforcing character of institutions: to see socioeconomic development as periods of institutional continuity punctuated by periods of crisis and more rapid development.

Overlapping Hierarchies

Arguably, hierarchy is ubiquitous. Just as within institutions routines are hierarchically ordered, habits are so arranged in regard to an individual. Notably, economic agents inhabit multiple and parallel hierarchies; they may react to one institution with the dispositions provided by another. We should not assume, therefore, that each hierarchy is itself disconnected and freestanding. As Arthur Koestler (1967, p. 387) puts it: 'Hierarchies can be regarded as "vertically" arborizing structures whose branches interlock with those of other hierarchies at a multiplicity of levels and form "horizontal" networks; arborization and reticulation are complementary principles in the architecture of organisms and societies.' There is not one hierarchy in regard to each institution but several. Formal institutions have an obvious hierarchy in terms of their legal precedence or position in a chain of command. Thus a legislative assembly may be deemed to have sovereignty; and the head office of a corporation has powers over its branches or plants. Nevertheless, the formal hierarchy never corresponds to the pattern of control in the real world. Overlapping with it is a web of informal institutions and routines, embedded in the social culture. Thus there are compelling informal links between many persons at the pinnacles of power, and likewise strong community bonds between actors with less status or influence.

Additionally, the information that is processed and transmitted by institutions itself has its own internal hierarchy of meaning. Thus, at the apex, there is information about information, overriding instructions or rules, and so on. Lower-level information is often more detailed and specific.

Not only is there an explicit structure for information in itself, but once it becomes knowledge it is subject to different degrees of tacitness or codifiability, as pointed out by Nelson (1980) and others. Non-codifiable, 'unteachable' or 'tacit' knowledge (Michael Polanyi, 1957, 1967) is partly embodied in informal routines and habits, and cannot readily be reduced to or transmitted in a codified form.

There is an important dissimilarity here with biology, where attention is focused at 'information' transmission at the level of the gene.[5] In contrast, the hierarchy of knowledge in socioeconomic systems involves information transmission at several different levels, incorporating many varied types of information – including both the codifiable and non-codifiable – and with many different modes of interaction and effects.

Notably, non-codifiable knowledge is more difficult to augment or change, involving relatively long periods of 'learning by doing' and so on. In contrast, while codifiable knowledge may sometimes be complex and difficult to acquire, it can often be altered or augmented more readily. Furthermore, short-run disturbances in the course of economic development are more likely to emanate from changes in codifiable knowledge, simply because it can be communicated more easily.

Hence the immediate sensitivity of the economy to changes in prices or other indicators, and the greater responsiveness of the modernized sectors of the economy to R&D initiatives and technological diffusion, in contrast to the sluggishness of the more traditional industries. In short, informational feedback loops are likely to be more immediate and significant in regard to codifiable rather than non-codifiable knowledge.

Other forms of codifiable knowledge concern the political system, formal institutions and so on. Here the transmission of codifiable information can correspond to a change in the rules, or to signals concerning economic and other policies which lead to shifts in the expectations of entrepreneurs and other agents. Thus, in the manner that John Maynard Keynes described in chapter 12 of the *General Theory*, the state of long-term expectation is vulnerable to changes in 'the news'.

In sum, the closer to the codifiable end of the knowledge hierarchy, the greater the degree of adaptability and change in the content of that knowledge. Consequently, changes in technological knowledge, or prices, or information concerning governments and laws, are likely to account for the more dramatic changes to the pace and direction of socioeconomic development. In contrast, more gradual and enduring change is likely to emanate from the non-codifiable end of the spectrum: in changes to deeply embedded habits and routines.

When it comes to the institutional hierarchies – or even the ecological hierarchies in nature – as opposed to the hierarchies of information and knowledge, it is probably more difficult to make changes, whatever the intentions of the agents involved. Thus, for example, it may be easier for most of the population to change the type or pattern of their employment than for a nation to alter the fundamental thrust of its foreign policy. This is because, in the latter case, change is much more constrained, subject to innumerable counterbalancing wills, acting and blocking each other with unintended consequences, and in regard to more numerous and more enduring signals and assurances of stability. Thus historians may explain the development of national foreign policy or the pace of industrial progress by reference to the accretions not merely of months or years, but of centuries.

For the aforementioned reasons a socioeconomic system combines elements of stability with instability. In regard to aspects of the system which are highly dependent on codifiable information, concerning, for example, prices or other economic indicators, activity will be vulnerable to volatile expectations and waves of speculation. In contrast, its structures and social relations will be much less vulnerable to immediate shocks and short-term changes, and severe social and political disruption may be experienced before fundamental shifts occur.

Some Remarks on Institutional Evolution

Considering these overlapping hierarchies of formal and informal institutions, it is also likely that the capacity to adapt to change, and in contrast to retain habits and routines, is different at different levels. Habitual actions such as driving a car do not need to be relearned after a break of several months. If the contrary was true, too much time would be wasted in relearning each skill anew after a lapse in its use. There are good reasons to presume that this capacity to retain habits for some time is part of our biological evolution, as a degree of durability in this regard would clearly be advantageous for an organism. Furthermore, behavioural patterns of greater flexibility at a more conscious level may also be advantageous from the point of view of biological evolution, such as in response to danger or threat.

Michael Hannan and John Freeman (1989, pp. 66–90) argue that social selection processes favour organizations which have high levels of reliability of performance and accountability. These in turn depend on the capacity to reproduce structure with high fidelity. New organizations tend to have a lower fidelity in reproducing structure. Fidelity of reproduction is seen to increase with age.[6]

However, concerning social institutions, we have to treat the biological analogy with care. 'Institutional mutation' (Harris, 1934) is not the same as genetic mutation, and we cannot automatically assume that a Darwinian process of natural selection is at work. The latter involves the gradual accumulation and selection of small mutations over long periods of time, whereas in the case of institutions adaptation is much more rapid with much less opportunity for any efficiency-breeding selection to work. As Philippe van Parijs (1981, pp. 88–9) observes: 'if the pressures of selection are negligible compared to counteracting pressures of variation, there can be no evolutionary attractor' in the socioeconomic domain.

Likewise, James March and Johan Olsen (1984, p. 737) point out that if evolution is to lead through a selection process to improvements or greater efficiency in some sense, then the environment must be sufficiently stable for selection to take place. Improvement must be accomplished before any disruptive environmental change occurs. In the economic context, however, improvements may not become established before there is such a disturbance in the rapidly changing environment.

Another major difference between biological and economic evolution is that habits and routines, which are taken as analogous to the genes in the economic sphere, are much more likely to change than the biological genes. Furthermore, biological genes are transmitted through sexual reproduction, whereas in economies habits and routines can be acquired and spread around without transfer of people. Word of mouth, informal networks and imitation are thus very important in modern economies (Czepiel, 1975; Hippel, 1987, 1988; Martilla, 1971; McKelvey, 1982).

By such means the lines of descent of both technological artifacts and institutional structures may merge. This is unlike the evolution of species of organic life which is in the form of a branching tree, whose branches, once separated, do not recombine (Kroeber, 1948, p. 260; Basalla, 1989, pp. 137–9).

While institutional variation and differentiation occurs much more rapidly and extensively than mutation in the biological world, nevertheless, the observed inertia of cultural and institutional evolution suggests that there are strong stabilizing forces at work. Thus it is more reasonable to conjecture that relatively stable, chreodic-type development is more evocative of institutional evolution than the more traditional and gradualist Darwinian picture of sharpened adaptation in face of a ceaseless and formidable struggle for survival. As we have already noted, Devendra Sahal (1985) and Norman Clark and Calestous Juma (1987) see the chreod as an analogy for the pattern of techno-logical development in an industrial economy. A technological 'para-digm' provides a general direction and channel for relatively stable development.

Christopher Freeman and Carlota Perez (1988, pp. 45–7) propose a hierarchical taxonomy of types and levels of innovation, from 'incre-mental innovations', often arising from 'learning by doing', to more major and longlasting changes in 'techno-economic paradigm'.[7] This parallels Joel Mokyr's (1990a, 1990b) similarly useful distinction between 'microinventions' and 'macroinventions', regarded as com-plementary aspects of technological development, analogous to micromutations and macromutations in biology. The idea of 'national systems of innovation' also refers to some of the more enduring and global characteristics of technology systems.[8] Once again it is argued that there will be more rigidity at the higher, paradigmatic level than at the level relating to incremental innovation. All these ideas suggest some degree of invariance at the system level, despite fluctuations at the micro level or in the external environment (Saviotti, 1986).

If institutional and industrial development are typically chreodic then the policy conclusions are quite different from the more promin-ent attempts to bring the evolutionary analogy into social science in the past. In contrast to the theories of Spencer in the nineteenth century, and Friedman, Hayek and Williamson in the twentieth, an evolutionary paradigm is not a basis for the policy outlook of Dr Pangloss. As selective processes will not ensure a rigorous drive towards greater efficiency, and chreodic development will exhibit a path of develop-ment more determined by its past than by its adaptation to the present, there are no grounds for proclaiming that evolution will produce the best of all possible worlds.

Neither can the manifest stability of the chreod be relied on forever. As shown by the work of Conrad Waddington and René Thom, devel-opment along a stable path can sometimes lead to catastrophe.[9] In-stitutions change, and even gradual change can eventually put such a strain on a system that there can be outbreaks of conflict or crisis, leading to a radical change in actions and attitudes. Thus there is always the possibility of a breakdown of regularity. In any social sys-tem there is an interplay between routinized behaviour and the vari-able or volatile decisions of other agents and their outcomes.

This non-deterministic view stresses both the weight of routine and habit in the formation of behaviour and the importance of some elements of strategic deliberation and their possibly disruptive effects on stability. With these ingredients it is possible to envisage processes whereby for long periods the reigning habits of thought and action are cumulatively reinforced and stabilized. But this very process can lead to sudden and rapid change. The very ossification of society could lead to the decimation of the economic system by more vigorous competition from outside, or there could be an internal reaction leading to a newly modernized order.

In policy terms, although the existence of chreodic-type development implies that small, marginal adjustments towards a more optimal path of development are generally ineffective, it does leave open the possibility of the planned transition from one chreodic path to another. Indeed, such a transition may be necessary if the chreodic path is approaching a 'catastrophe'. A feasible transition can be instigated either at the early stage of development of a chreodic path, close to the point of bifurcation, or even later with a sufficiently large investment in resources.

Organicism and Macroeconomics

The preceding chapter has helped to establish the legitimacy of higher levels of economic analysis above that of the individual, particularly at the macroeconomic level. In fact, organicist thinking played an important part in the original development of macroeconomics, from Marx onwards. Some remarks about the historical relevance of organicist modes of thought for macroeconomics follow.

A focus on organic wholes, and levels of analysis higher than the individual or the firm, is reflected in both the second and the third volumes of Marx's *Capital*. In this work Marx aimed eventually to lay bare 'the process of capitalist production as a whole'. He thereby prefigured many of the developments in twentieth-century macroeconomics, such as business cycle theory and growth theory. Furthermore, we should not forget that it was through the development of the ideas in Marx, not Marshall, that Michal Kalecki was able to lay down the essentials of the theory of effective demand simultaneously with, and independently of, Keynes.

The organicist and 'holist' strains of thought in American institutionalism have been established in chapter 1. Institutionalists typically stress the interconnectedness of economic phenomena. As discussed earlier, and further below, Thorstein Veblen and John Commons saw organic institutions or 'transactions', rather than atomistic individuals, as the basic units of economic analysis.

Another important link between institutionalism and the development of Keynesianism was the innovation of national income accounting, in which the work of the American institutionalist Wesley Mitchell played a vital part. Being traditionally linked with organicist or holistic views, institutionalism thereby developed and sanctioned the conceptualization and measurement of economic aggregates. The theoretical and empirical work involved here was of major importance in the development of twentieth-century economics.

Through the development of national income accounting the work of Mitchell and his colleagues influenced and inspired the macroeconomics of Keynes (Mirowski, 1989b, p. 307). With the innovatory macroeconomic concepts in Keynes's *General Theory*, the legitimacy of dealing with aggregates was established. Crucial theoretical developments in early postwar Keynesian economics, such as James Duesenberry's (1949) 'habit persistence' theory of the consumption function, were influenced by institutionalists such as Veblen (Dorfman, 1958, p. 9). It was with institutionalism as a midwife that Keynesian macroeconomics was born.

The degree to which Keynes's economics expresses an organicist ontology is open to dispute. What is clear, however, is that this radical philosophical message did not become prominent in the mainstream versions of Keynesianism which emerged after Keynes's death. The postwar consensus in economic theory amounted to a combination of neoclassical microeconomics with a bowdlerized textbook Keynesianism, still based on the newly developed principles of national income accounting.

It was left to a nagging minority to complain that neoclassical microeconomics was incompatible with much of Keynesian macroeconomic theory. In particular, standard Walrasian general equilibrium analysis predicted a full employment equilibrium, whereas textbook Keynesianism did not. Keynesians accepted the possibility of such an involuntary surplus of labour, thereby conflicting with Robbins's very definition of the subject in terms of 'scarce means'.

An even smaller minority complained about the reliance on aggregate national income data. Even before the publication of the *General Theory*, Hayek addressed economic aggregates, such as the total quantity of money, the general level of prices and the total amount of production, and argued that

> none of these magnitudes *as such* ever exerts an influence on the decisions of individuals; yet it is on the assumption of a knowledge of the decisions of individuals that the main propositions of non-monetary economic theory are based. It is to this 'individualistic' method that we owe whatever understanding of economic phenomena we possess. (Hayek, 1931, p. 4)

This questionable denial of the impact of aggregate data on individual decision-making became a rallying cry in the Austrian attack on Keynesianism.[10] Correctly noting the incompatibility of such aggregative methods with strict methodological individualism, the economists of the Austrian School endangered their own popularity in the immediate postwar period by challenging one of the major achievements of applied economics. Yet while they confronted one of the most successful and practical developments in that science, they were correct to note its incongruity with the ubiquitous and enduring individualism of mainstream microeconomic theory.

Despite discrepancies such as this, the awkward consensus survived the criticism, at least until the 1970s. Eventually, however, something had to give: either neoclassical microeconomics with its individualistic outlook and its atomistic ontology, or the accepted versions of Keynesianism. Partly due to changes in the political climate favouring individualistic ideas, and partly because of the apparent headway made in the 1970s by monetarists against Keynesians in the debate over the causes and cures of inflation, it was the neoclassical economists that triumphed after the consensus had collapsed.

It was in this context that the alleged 'adhocery' of Keynesian macroeconomics was widely rejected, and the attempt to base macroeconomics on 'sound microfoundations' was given renewed vigour. As noted in chapter 15 above, however, by the end of the 1980s leading microfoundations theorists were accepting that the project faced intractable problems. So can macroeconomics be rescued today?

The Autonomy of Macroeconomics

One thing that is remarkable about modern, complex economic systems is their enduring stability and resilience over long periods of time, despite the multitude of decisions and actions, and the plethora of variety at the microeconomic level. We may conjecture that for years or sometimes even decades, socioeconomic systems become locked in to a fixed overall pattern of dynamic development. While there will be *parametric* change in economic variables such as output and employment, there may be years or decades of overall and relative *structural* stability. Such structural stability, based on a set of dominant socioeconomic relations, creates the possibility of macroeconomic analysis and modelling.

General support for such a notion can be found in the modern theory of non-linear systems. As Jay Forrester (1987, p. 108) argues:

> A rich representation of nonlinearities leads to a model that is relatively insensitive to parameter values. Being insensitive to parameter values is also a characteristic of most social systems. ... In fact, the operating point of a system tends to move along the changing slopes of its nonlinearities until it finds an operating region that is determined more by the structure of the system than by plausible differences in parameter values. In a high-order nonlinear system, one can move many parameters within a plausible range with little effect on essential behaviour.

The modern theory of complex systems has led to the idea of autopoiesis. An autopoietic system is not in a state of equilibrium, at least in the normal senses of that term. Precisely because it is far from a thermodynamic or mechanical equilibrium, such an open system must absorb energy from its environment. Autopoietic systems 'can maintain themselves in time only if they evolve the capacity to replicate or reproduce their structure' (Laszlo, 1987, p. 38). Like living animals and plants, such systems maintain an autonomy and continuity of pattern 'despite the endless turnover of their constituents' (Zeleny, 1987, p. 393). Clearly, economic systems may well exhibit autopoietic self-replication and growth.

It is important to note that, just as the features of a plant may change during its growth, autopoietic development in economic systems does not, within limits, exclude changes in technology and tastes. The structural stability implied is not rigid; it is sufficient to provide coherence and a consistent mode of self-organization. A socioeconomic system in an autopoietic phase will be one that is exhibiting particular patterns of growth and development. The growth rate and economic fluctuations will be within a broad range. Socioeconomic structures and institutions will be subject to piecemeal rather than fundamental change.

In contrast, there may be apparent randomness at the micro level, with substantial variety in the structure and behaviour of individual units. However, the interactions between these elements help to generate a degree of (impermanent) stability and coherence at the macro level. This idea of the generation of macro-order out of micro-chaos was advanced a early as the latter part of the nineteenth century by Charles Sanders Peirce. For him, chance begets order (Peirce, 1934, p. 226).

Such an argument is also reminiscent of the 'principle of *stratified determinism*' adduced by Paul Weiss (1969), that is, the 'principle of *determinacy in the gross despite demonstrable indeterminacy in the small*' (emphasis in the original). Today, however, with the insights of chaos theory it has to be accepted that even apparent indeterminacy may have deterministic roots. Thus, paraphrasing Weiss, an autopoietic system exhibits a high degree of order at the macro level, in contrast to variety and chaos at the micro level. At the higher and more complex level, spanning many territories and units, the behaviour of institutions is more stable, and more determined or weighed down by cumulative interactions in the system and the constraints of its past. Variations are buffered out and rendered inconsequential.

Through this feature of 'self-organization', as the work of Ilya Prigogine and his collaborators shows, order can result from chaos. Indeed, although individual variations are rendered inconsequential in systems in this state, the degree of homoeostatic self-regulation vitally *depends upon* extensive diversity and chaos at the micro level.

Without the latter, the system as a whole would be more vulnerable to aggregative and cumulative feedback effects and prone to instability itself.

This is essentially the point about population thinking, rather than typological thinking, which has been raised in chapters 3, 4 and elsewhere in this book. Higher levels of analysis and corresponding aggregative measures are established, but with a crucial recognition of the inherent variety at that level. In reacting against aggregation, Hayek and other critics of macroeconomic theory seem to be recoiling against typological thinking. However, while establishing the importance of population thinking, it is possible both to incorporate higher levels of analysis and to recognize the variety of the system that fuels the evolutionary process. It is the simultaneous attention to population thinking and to higher levels of analysis above the individual that is crucial for the reinvigoration of modern economics.

We now return to the earlier point about institutions as units of analysis. The macroeconomic system may be treated as a legitimate unit and level of analysis only if it has its own intrinsic set of institutional structures. To be regarded as an autopoietic or self-organizing system, these constituent institutions and structures must be partially autonomous and strongly self-reinforcing. The national economic systems of most developed industrial countries satisfy this latter criterion.

One important unifying component of a national economic system is its culture. Through a common culture, agents form compatible perceptions and complex modes of communication and interaction. They establish norms and codes. On the basis of these typically self-reinforcing norms of perception and behaviour, the economy can exhibit some structural stability for long periods of time.

However, no complex system is an undifferentiated whole, and cumulative reinforcement of a number of multiple and parallel institutions can eventually lead to conflict and disruption. Institutions change, and even gradual change can eventually put such a strain on a system that there can be outbreaks of conflict or crisis, leading to changes in actions and attitudes. As noted in a preceding chapter, the processes underlying institutional change can be likened to strata shifting slowly at different rates, but occasionally causing seismic disturbance and discontinuities.

Thus there is always the possibility of the breakdown of regularity: 'there will be moments of crisis situations or structural breaks when existing conventions or social practices are disrupted' (Lawson, 1985, p. 920). In any social system there is an interplay between routinized behaviour and the variable or volatile decisions of other agents. While the underlying culture may exhibit little change, some of the established norms and conventions may 'change violently as the result of sudden fluctuations of opinion' (Keynes, 1936, p. 154). As Nicholas

Georgescu-Roegen (1971, p. 127) has argued in general terms, the history 'of an individual or of a society, seems to be the result of two factors: a hysteresis process and the emergence of novelty'.

This is the socioeconomic equivalent of 'punctuated equilibria' in biology.[11] The use of the word 'equilibria' by these biologists should not mislead. In this context the term is different from that found in mechanics and orthodox economics, in that to some degree it encompasses mutation and change within the same evolutionary track. Furthermore, the punctuations refer to abrupt speciation and are just as important as the equilibria. As Stephen Jay Gould (1982b) makes clear, the concept of punctuated equilibrium is tied up with the idea of a hierarchy of evolutionary processes, where exogenous shocks lead to a temporary breakdown in the articulation of levels and to rapid changes in speciation.

Accordingly, in the socioeconomic sphere the shifting strata of institutional change may lead to crisis. Outcomes of conflicts between several simultaneously locked-in processes can give rise to something like this notion of discontinuous development (Arthur, 1990, p. 85). Similar emphasis should also be given to major disruptions such as revolutions or wars. In such a manner the idea of 'punctuated equilibria' has been applied to the economic and technological development of capitalist countries (Mokyr, 1990a, 1990b, 1991).

It has been argued above that the 'natural selection' of institutions is not like that in the biotic world, partly because of the way in which institutions become locked in by conformist and other self-reinforcing mechanisms. Consequently, during periods of stable development the sources of variety become progressively exhausted; there is nothing in economics that is equivalent to the novelty generating process of sexual recombination. Accordingly, the periods of disruption, whether they are endogenously or exogenously determined, generate bursts of novelty and innovation, and lay the basis for periods of faster growth.[12]

The intermediate periods of structural stability make macroeconomic modelling and estimation feasible; the periods of crisis confound secure prediction, particularly regarding the more volatile variables. As John Maynard Keynes (1936, 1937) argued, it is not only difficult or impossible to make reliable predictions during a period of high turbulence in the economy, but the timing of major structural changes and disruptive events cannot be forecast with any assurance.

Nevertheless, the macroeconomist must make do. Empirical work should involve the search for regularities and tendencies as part of the process of establishing plausible causal linkages. As Tony Lawson (1989, p. 65) asserts, 'to the extent that any manifest phenomenon appears to reveal some degree of uniformity, generality, or persistency, albeit by no means complete in such respects, it would seem to provide a prima facie case for supposing that some enduring generative mechanisms are at work.' Lawson argues that such an approach is compatible both with philosophical realism and the methodological essentials of the macroeconomic work of Post Keynesians such as Nicholas Kaldor. It is also notable that it is consistent with the autonomous and non-reductionist status of macroeconomic theory proposed in this chapter.

In Defence of the Ad Hoc

The old charge against the type of macroeconomics associated with the Keynesians is that it is 'ad hoc'. Such is the rallying cry of the reductionist, dismissing all theoretical formulations based on aggregated terms, and condemning all such constructions because of the absence of secure microfoundations. Such a charge, however, is dubious and misconceived.

In fact, all attempts to find secure microfoundations must inevitably involve gross simplifications and ad hoc assumptions of another kind. As Lawson (1989) points out, neoclassical general equilibrium theory involves a number of arbitrary assumptions or 'axioms'. Some of these axioms, like 'people have preferences', are 'relatively contentless'. Others are added largely to make the mathematics tractable, such as the ceremonial assumption of a production function in a Cobb-Douglas form.

However, both types of assumption are restrictive and ad hoc. The 'people have preferences' assumption, for instance, is normally interpreted in such a way that it is inconsistent with the arguably more realistic idea of lexicographic choice (Earl, 1983). As noted in the preceding chapter, most existing general equilibrium theory goes even further by assuming that all individuals are identical. Hence another ad hoc, restrictive and unrealistic assumption is made. Again, heroic assumptions about the well-behaved and stable character of the 'production function' show adhocness in a most fanciful and confident mood.

There is also the problem of explaining why reduction should stop short at the level of the individual. For the thoroughgoing reductionist to stop short the process of reduction at any level other than the most elemental subatomic particle currently known to science requires some explanation. Furthermore, because the most elemental level is never actually reached, a degree of adhocness is inevitable, thus committing the very same crime with which Keynesians and others have been charged.

In general, as Larry Laudan (1977, pp. 114–18) has argued, adhocness in scientific theories cannot be entirely avoided. Most major and prestigious theories, including Newton's and Darwin's, are ad hoc. Furthermore, he insists, adhocness with theories is generally a cognitive virtue rather than a vice, because it becomes a pragmatic lever in the process of problem solving.

The ontological ideas discussed above, particularly the Whiteheadian view that reality is hierarchically ordered, sustain a methodology which endorses a kind of adhocness in relation to each level in the system. Because each level has a degree of autonomy, assumptions cannot be justified in reductionist terms, that is by basing them entirely upon the characteristics of entities discerned at a lower level. However, because the levels are connected, assumptions made in regard to a particular level cannot be arbitrary, and attempts must be made to render them consistent with other assumptions or results, at lower, higher, or equivalent levels.

Conclusion

As made clear at the start, this work has not constructed a new economic theory to replace the neoclassical mainstream. It has involved little more than an attempt to learn from the past history of economics, leading to the compilation of new signposts and directions. Nevertheless, it has highlighted the crucial problems of methodological individualism and reductionism in mainstream economics. With use of the biological analogy, an approach has been developed which establishes the legitimacy of higher levels of analysis, including the macroeconomic level, without individualistic reductionism.

Above all, economics and biology both address complex systems, with abundant path-dependent developments. The reductionist methods and equilibrium orientated theories of neoclassical economics are sorely deficient in such a context. To repeat the words of Frank Hahn which headed part I of this volume, we must be less concerned with 'grand unifying theory' and 'the pleasures of theorems and proof. Instead the uncertain embrace of history and sociology and biology.'

Hence there should be no expectation of the kind of formalistic theory that has dominated economics in the latter half of the twentieth century. Careful economic history, informed by a perceptive framework of analysis, along with the careful and critical reinstatement of some of the past and present theory which has been brushed aside in the tirades against 'Keynesianism', should instead become the norm.

But the lessons from the past must be learned. It is necessary for all economists to address again the now-unfashionable study of the history of their own subject. The Keynesians lost in the theoretical battles of the 1970s partly because they paid insufficient attention to theoretical fundamentals. They were thus unable to counter the reductionist charge of lacking 'sound microfoundations'. The rather vague collection of ideas under the 'Post Keynesian' label suffers a similar fate. While applied theory may be the best theory, there is still no way of displacing bad theory except by better theory. And even applied theory depends on a set of philosophical and theoretical presuppositions.

Nothing is more central to this issue than the mechanistic paradigm at the core of neoclassical economics.

Nevertheless, the questions involved are not simply theoretical. The history of mechanistic and equilibrium modelling in economics has sustained a view that the economic system may reach 'optima' which ignore the coupling of economic and biotic systems and have little or no regard to the limited natural resources on this planet.[13] In mainstream economic models, the factors to be maximized are individual utilities, not the needs of the biotic system. Consequently, economic policy has ignored the ecological requirements and biotic constraints. However, unless these are recognized, there is a strong danger the planet will be irrevocably damaged. Mainstream economists are becoming more aware of these serious problems, but without a recognition that the mechanistic and utilitarian foundations of economic theory must be replaced.

It is upon these reforming convictions that we should turn to the biological metaphor to help us build an alternative economics. Alfred Marshall tried this more than a hundred years ago, referring episodically to an inadequate and Spencerian biology. Thorstein Veblen was more consistent in his appeal to that science, but both the incompleteness of his own theoretical system and the relative underdevelopment of biology in his time meant that the cue was not followed by his disciples. Biology has flowered since the passing of these two great economic theorists; it is now set to overwhelm the prestige that physics has enjoyed for three centuries, and it is earmarked as the leading science of the twenty-first century. Economics is all the poorer if we ignore its intellectual riches. And the world itself may be impoverished by rapacious economic activity if we continue to disregard the biotic foundations of economic life.

Notes

Chapter 1   A Brief Diagnosis

1   For a brief but useful specification of the 'hard core' and 'protective belt' of neoclassical economics, each with its respective 'heuristics', see Lavoie (1992, pp. 76–8). An earlier Lakatosian depiction of the 'neo-Walrasian' research programme is found in Weintraub (1985, p. 109). For a short definition of neoclassical economics see Hodgson (1988, p. xiv).

2   For further discussions of the impact of chaos theory on economics see Baumol and Benhabib (1989), Coricelli and Dosi (1988), Dopfer (1988), Grandmont (1987), Kelsey (1988), Mirowski (1990a), Radzicki (1990), and Rosser (1990).

3   Of course, there is always room for dispute over what is functional and what is not. But this does not mean that we should make the mistake of assuming that *all* developments are functional. In a rather chilling example, Michael Harner (1977) argues that Aztec human sacrifices and the subsequent eating of limbs can be explained in terms of the need for otherwise deficient protein at the time. This explanation is countered by Stephen Jay Gould and Richard Lewontin (1979) in a brilliant critique of adaptationism and functionalism. They argue that sacrifice and cannibalism did not necessarily have adaptive value; they did not need to be *for* anything.

4   Some of the words and sentiments above are taken from 'A Plea for a Pluralistic and Rigorous Economics', organized by Uskali Mäki, Donald McCloskey and the present author, signed by 44 leading economists – including four Nobel Laureates – and published in the May 1992 edition of the *American Economic Review*.

5   See, for instance, Aronson (1984), Bhaskar (1975, 1979, 1986, 1991), Chalmers (1985), Harré (1986), Kanth (1991), Leplin (1984), Manicas (1987), Sayer (1984). Two realists who have concentrated on the philosophy of economics are Lawson (1987, 1989, 1990) and Mäki (1989, 1991).

6   The philosophical realist Roy Bhaskar (1991) has similarly criticized the pragmatism of Richard Rorty (1979, 1982). Bhaskar sees Rorty as defining being in terms of knowledge, thereby denying the precedence

of ontology. Rorty's pragmatism helps us understand the historicity of scientific and other knowledge, but not the reality of its objects. Bhaskar's critique is well taken, but this would not seem to rule out a synthesis of philosophical realism with elements of pragmatism.

7 The mature writings of the realist philosopher Karl Popper (e.g. 1972) are also influenced by Peirce.

8 The comparative philosophical value of Peirce and Dewey, and their respective degrees of influence on Veblen and Commons, is a matter of controversy. On this see Mirowski (1987b) and Bush (1989).

9 On the influence of Darwinism on institutional economics see chapter 9 below. On the relationship between the pragmatist philosophers and evolutionary theory see Philip Wiener (1949) and Cynthia Russett (1976). David Hull (1973, 1974), however, rightly argues that most nineteenth-century philosophers of science, including Peirce, had a flawed and incomplete understanding of Darwinism, and under-estimated its intellectual stature. Thus Peirce (1934, p. 196) writes that: 'The *Origin of Species* of Darwin merely extends politico-economic views of progress to the entire realm of animal and vegetable life.' This sentence tersely expresses a typical nineteenth-century miscon-ception of Darwinism (see Bowler, 1988) by simultaneously stress-ing progress and ignoring natural selection. (Note also that Friedrich Hayek, 1982, vol. 1, p. 153, quotes without reflection this very same passage in a clumsy attempt to depict Darwinism merely as a con-tinuation of preceding theory. For further criticisms of Hayek in this vein see chapter 11 below.)

10 Organicist views are sometimes described as 'holistic' by later insti-tutionalist writers (Wilber and Harrison, 1978). Allan Gruchy (1947, p. 4), for instance, insists that the whole is not only greater than the sum of its parts, 'but that the parts are so related that their function-ing is conditioned by their interrelations'. Such a view is perfectly compatible with organicism. However, Gruchy's (1947, p. vii) defini-tion of holism is less satisfactory. For him, holism involves 'studying the economic system as an evolving, unified whole or synthesis, in the light of which the system's parts take on their full meaning'. This view is inadequate unless it is added that it is also necessary to ex-amine the parts in order to understand the whole. Without such an addendum 'holism' itself becomes one-sided and perhaps even reductionist: in social analysis a mirror image of methodological individualism. The problems and ambiguities in the term 'holism' suggest that organicism might be a better touchstone for institution-alist methodology.

11 Writers supporting the view that Keynes's thought has an organicist quality include Brown-Collier (1985), Brown-Collier and Bausor (1988), Carabelli (1985, pp. 164–8, and 1988, 1991), Dow (1985, 1990), Fitzgibbons (1988, pp. 18–21), Hamouda and Smithin (1988), Lawson (1985, pp. 923–4), O'Donnell (1989, pp. 127–36, 177–8) and Rotheim (1989–90). But Bateman (1989) and Davis (1989, 1989–90) take a dif-ferent view.

12　The principal architect of modern systems theory was the biologist Ludwig Bertalanffy (1952, 1971). Other biologists, such as Paul Weiss (1973; Weiss et al. 1971), made major additional contributions.

13　In a lively essay on Hobson, John King (1988, pp. 127–8) notes these influences, as well as the impact of Hobson on Vladimir Ilyich Lenin, John R. Commons and Wesley Clair Mitchell. In addition, Hobson (1936) wrote a book on Veblen.

14　These issues are discussed in more detail in chapters 14, 15 and 16 below.

15　Although the influence of this article on sections of this chapter should be noted, Mirowski somewhat overstates his case, particularly by forcing an excessively wide gulf between Dewey and Peirce. Note also the critical response of Paul Dale Bush (1989) to some of Mirowski's arguments. However, Mirowski is right to suggest that too much of mid twentieth-century American institutional economics is of a positivist kind. Even sympathizers such as Gunnar Myrdal (1958, p. 254) saw traditional American institutional economics as marked by a 'naive empiricism'.

　　Furthermore, Mirowski's misgivings about the substance and utility of the so-called 'Veblenian dichotomy' (Waller, 1982) – between institutions and technology, and between so-called 'ceremonial' and 'instrumental' institutions – are shared by the present author. In the first instance, their Veblenian pedigree is open to doubt. Even sophisticated attempts to develop these ideas – such as Bush (1986) – retain a number of problems, fundamentally in terms of the precise definitional and operational distinctions between the 'ceremonial' and the 'instrumental'. As in Samuels (1977), the basis of these dichotomies may be questioned. Notably, in his conclusion, Mirowski points to the possible revival of institutionalism, based in part on the recent comeback of pragmatism in modern American philosophy. If so, this makes an examination of such fundamental concepts and distinctions all the more apposite.

16　In this context note Tony Lawson's (1987, p. 952) point that:

> It is noticeable . . . that economists who are concerned with realism of analysis, and who focus explicitly on the knowledge that individuals possess, tend to emphasize almost exclusively the fact of *uncertainty* surrounding economic activity. Now it is the case, of course, that uncertainty is a pervasive fact of human agency. Nevertheless, an over-preoccupation with emphasizing and describing it can mask the fact that certainty is a pervasive feature of human agency.

Lawson goes on to relate belief and certainty with rule following and convention, in a manner reminiscent of Peirce.

17　Alan Dyer (1986, p. 26) sees in Koestler's book *The Act of Creation* ideas which are similar to those of Peirce on scientific creativity and the role of 'abduction'.

18 This example was put to the author in a personal communication from Frank Hahn.

19 Peirce's view of the limitations of experiment for scientific progress differs from the later and more optimistic emphasis on experimentalism found in the works of Dewey. Dewey's belief that science is largely a matter of experimentation and procedures is false and misleading, and contrasts somewhat with the Peircean emphasis on abduction (see below) as the source of creativity. In line with Peirce, however, several authors have argued that experiment plays a limited role in science. Note, for instance, Gerald Holton's (1974) and Michael Polanyi's (1957, pp. 9–15) refutation of the myth that the Michelson-Morley experiment was the instigation for Einstein to formulate the theory of relativity.

20 Although a sharper definition is discussed in Dyer (1986), some of Peirce's attempts to define abduction are unsatisfactory, for example: 'Abduction consists in studying facts and devising a theory to explain them' (Peirce, 1934, p. 90). This vague formulation would not exclude inductivism, thereby resting on the unsatisfactory empiricist notion that facts can be observed through atheoretical eyes. In contrast, all descriptions of facts are theory-laden, and dependent on the theories and conceptual frameworks of the observer. Peirce can also be criticized for his attempt 'to construe the clarity (or content) of a statement in terms of its observable consequences' (Scheffler, 1974, p. 204), which would also seem to sustain an empiricist view of knowledge.

21 In their critical discussion of attempts to develop artificial intelligence, Hubert Dreyfus and Stuart Dreyfus (1986) also emphasize intuition. They argue that the human mind depends less on analytic skills, with fixed and codifiable rules, and more on intuition and tacit knowledge. The Peircean emphasis on intuition and metaphor also suggests why the artificial intelligence research programme is very unlikely to lead to an adequate simulation of human intelligence, at least in its creative aspects.

Chapter 2   On Mechanistic and Biological Metaphors

1 See also the evolutionary epistemology of Donald Campbell (1987) and others.

2 See Ghiselin (1969, p. 16), La Vergata (1985, p. 939), Manier (1978) and R. M. Young (1985a).

3 Michael Ruse (1971, pp. 317–18) has attempted to translate the metaphorical term 'struggle for life' into non-teleological terms which are capable of fully expressing the senses in which Darwin used the phrase. The result should impress all those still holding to the view that metaphor in science is mere literary ornament: 'struggle for life' = 'organisms (or groups of organisms) respond in certain kinds of ways and they so respond in order to survive long enough to reproduce – in so doing they usually bring about the deaths of other organisms,

or at least, the failures of others to reproduce, and if they fail to do so, then their own deaths probably follow.'

4   See, for instance, Deutsch (1951), Georgescu-Roegen (1966, 1971, 1976, 1978, 1979, 1990), Gowdy (1985, 1987), Kornai (1971), Lowe (1951), Mirowski (1988a, 1989b), Norgaard (1987, 1989), Sebba (1953), Thoben (1982), Veblen (1919).

5   As well as Boulding (1970), for the relevance of the Heisenberg principle to economics see also Georgescu-Roegen (1971), Thoben (1982) and Weisskopf (1979).

6   Interesting alternative, or perhaps complementary, approaches can be found. János Kornai (1983) discusses the analogy between medical science and economics. Bart Nooteboom (1993) applies the metaphor of the linguistics of Ferdinand de Saussure to the theory of industrial organization, marketing, and transaction cost economics. The resulting analysis has a strong organicist quality.

7   For discussions of Social Darwinism, including the matter of the difficulty of its definition, see Bannister (1979), Bellomy (1984), Burrow (1966), Hofstadter (1959), Jones (1980), La Vergata (1985, pp. 958–62) and Sanderson (1990). For other evaluations of evolutionary ideas in social science see Campbell (1975), Corning (1983), Durham (1990), Gerard et al. (1956), Hallpike (1986), Hill (1978), Hirst (1976), Lewontin (1968), Parsons (1966), Pulliam and Dunford (1980), Sahlins (1977), Sahlins and Service (1960), Schmid and Wuketits (1987), Service (1968, 1975), Van Parijs (1981), White (1959).

8   Such prejudices must be tempered by the belief of a realist in the ultimate continuity and wholeness of the physical and the living worlds. Accordingly, there cannot be a complete division between the two, and in some ways physical and biological principles must be entwined. This is happening with attempts to synthesize evolutionary theory with the entropy law. Such a synthesis itself transcends Cartesian dualism, and embraces organicist modes of thought. See Brooks and Wiley (1988), Brooks et al. (1989), Collier (1986), Coveney and Highfield (1990), Georgescu-Roegen (1971), Weber et al. (1989).

9   See C. M. A. Clark (1988, 1991), O'Brien (1975, chs 1–2). Lippi (1979) has found similar traces on 'naturalism' in Marx's labour theory of value.

10   Note also Alfred Lotka's (1956, pp. 395, 415–16) reference to Veblen, as a rare period example of an economist being quoted by a leading biologist.

11   See Dupré (1987), Kitcher (1985, ch. 7), Maynard Smith (1978b, 1982), Oster and Wilson (1978, pp. 293–9), E. O. Wilson (1975). The importation of ideas and techniques from neoclassical economics has not been without some resistance from biology (E. Allen et al., 1976). However, sociobiologists such as George Oster and Edward Wilson (1978, p. 293) are strongly in support of transactions of this kind.

12   On this school of 'economic imperialism', desiring to invade biology with neoclassical weapons, see Becker (1974, 1976b), Hirshleifer (1977, 1978, 1982, 1985, 1987a) and Tullock (1979, 1987). See also Radnitzky

and Bernholz (1987) and the critique in Udéhn (1992). Much earlier, Hendrik Houthakker had bemoaned the lack of contact between economics and biology, but, anticipating Becker, Hirshleifer and Tullock, saw rectification in terms of 'extending economic analysis to biological phenomena' (Houthakker, 1956, p. 187) rather than the other way round. Institutionalists such as Morris Copeland (1958, pp. 58–9) saw economics as 'a branch of zoology' but in a different spirit, and outside the confines of neoclassical theory.

13 For a comparison of the views of Veblen and Kropotkin on human evolution see Dugger (1984).

14 The title of Reinheimer's (1913) work is *Evolution by Co-operation: A Study in Bioeconomics.* This, incidentally, is the first ever appearance of the term 'bioeconomics'. Despite the claims of the Becker-Hirshleifer-Tullock school, today the term is more often associated with the very different economics of Georgescu-Roegen (1971). See also Adler-Karlsson (1977), C. W. Clark (1976), Dragan and Demetrescu (1986), Gowdy (1987).

Ironically, the populist book by M. L. Rothschild, *Bionomics: The Inevitability of Capitalism* (1992), unknowingly turns Reinheimer's argument upside down. With Rothschild's biological justifications of market competition, the wheel has turned full circle. The subtitle has been changed to *Economy as Ecosystem* in later editions, stressing Rothschild's apposite critique of mechanistic thinking in orthodox economics. Nevertheless, the individualistic and pro-market bias remains.

15 See, for example, Allee (1951), Augros and Stanciu (1987, 1991), Benedict (1934), Harman (1991), Mead (1937), Montagu (1952), Wheeler (1930, 1939).

16 Durham (1991, ch. 4) has a detailed analysis of the limitations of the concepts of culture found in sociobiology. For an insightful discussion in relation to economics see Witt (1991b). For other critiques of sociobiology see Campbell (1972, 1975), Caplan (1978), Hayek (1982), Quadagno (1979), Sahlins (1977), Rose, Kamin and Lewontin (1984).

17 For critiques of 'economic imperialism' see, for example, Gowdy (1985, 1987), Harcourt (1979) and Norgaard (1989). Norgaard (1985, 1987, 1989) in particular has made a strong case for methodological pluralism, particularly in regard to environmental economics, contrary to the monopolistic doctrine of the 'economic imperialists'.

18 Gould (1987, p. 18) argues that biological evolution 'is a bad analogue for cultural change', giving three reasons: (1) cultural evolution can be much faster than biological evolution, (2) cultural evolution is Lamarckian, unlike biological evolution, and (3) biological evolution presents constant divergence of lineages, without subsequent joining of branches, whereas in human history transmission across lineages is a major source of cultural change.

However, none of these arguments is decisive, and Gould's rejection of the biological analogy could be primarily motivated by his concern that 'comparisons between biological evolution and human cultural or technological change have done vastly more harm than good.' Yet past harm does not rule out greater good in the future, and despite his own warning, Gould proceeds to compare the evolution of the 'QWERTY' typewriter keyboard with the evolution of biological entities such as the panda's thumb.

For very briefly elaborated and unclear reasons, De Bresson (1987) also argues against the adoption of an evolutionary framework for the economics of technological change. In his case an aversion to all use of analogy seems to be at root.

19   It should not be assumed, however, that all evolutionary processes in biology are irreversible. See Cook, Mani and Varley (1986) and Mani (1991) on the case of melanism in the peppered moth. Dosi and Metcalfe (1991) give an extended discussion of irreversibility in economics.

20   In this vein the entropy law has been applied to economics by Nicholas Georgescu-Roegen (1971, 1976) and his followers (Dragan and Demetrescu, 1986; Rifkin, 1980). However, this idea has proved to be controversial in theoretical terms (Khalil, 1990a, 1991; Lozada, 1991).

21   For recent applications of broadly evolutionary ideas to economics and to the theory of technical change, see Basalla (1989), Boulding (1981), Chase (1985), N. G. Clark (1988, 1990), Clark and Juma (1987), Cohen (1984), Coombs et al. (1992), Day (1984, 1987a, 1987b), Dopfer and Raible (1990), Dosi et al. (1988), Fao (1982), Foster (1987), Freeman (1990b), Freeman and Soete (1987, 1990), Futia (1980), Gomulka (1990), Goodwin (1986), Guha (1981), Hanusch (1988), Hayek (1988), Heertje and Perlman (1990), Hirshleifer (1982), Hodgson and Screpanti (1991), Iwai (1984a, 1984b), Jimenez Montano and Ebeling (1980), Kay (1982), Marquand (1989), Mokyr (1990a, 1990b, 1991), Morroni (1992), Nelson (1987), Nelson and Winter (1982), Pantzar (1991), Petit and Tahar (1989), Sahal (1981), Saviotti and Metcalfe (1984, 1991), Silverberg et al. (1988), Simon (1990), Witt (1991a, 1991c, forthcoming).

22   There was a preceding phase of 'evolutionary' thinking in anthropology in the 1950s and 1960s, of which one of the more sophisticated attempts was the work of Marshall Sahlins and Elman Service (1960). However, many of the works of this period have more to do with grand schemes of development rather than the careful appropriation of ideas from biology. Hence Marion Blute (1979) has argued that up to the late 1970s the strict application of evolutionary biology to anthropology was previously 'untried'.

23   With one exception (1988) Hayek's major works on socioeconomic evolution all originally appeared before 1980. Kenneth Boulding (1981) and Richard Nelson and Sidney Winter (1982) published their works on evolutionary economics after that date. There is no chapter devoted to Georgescu-Roegen (1971) because his work is concerned primarily with the entropy law, and less with evolutionary selection. Furthermore, a full discussion of this rich and complex *magnum opus* is beyond the scope of the present work. The conceptions of the relationship between economics and biology presented by Becker (1974, 1976b)

and Hirshleifer (1977, 1978, 1982, 1985) are of lesser significance, and have been briefly examined in this chapter. The uses and abuses of evolutionary ideas by other thinkers, such as Armen Alchian (1950), Milton Friedman (1953) and Oliver Williamson (1975) are mentioned again later. The influence of evolutionary thinking, however, has spread wider in economics, and can be detected, for example, in the works of Richard Cyert and James March (1963) and Thomas Schelling (1978). Others, like Trygve Haavelmo (1954) use the term 'evolution' in a loose sense.

Chapter 3   Economic Evolution:
A Preliminary Taxonomy

1   For discussions of the uses and evolution of the term 'evolution' in biology and social sciences see Bowler (1975, 1989a), Gould (1977, pp. 28–32, and 1978, p. 34), Lewontin (1968), Richards (1992), Schmid and Wuketits (1987), Van Parijs (1981), R. Williams (1976).

2   The general idea of using the distinction between ontogeny and phylogeny to taxonomize economic theories was suggested to the author by Pavel Pelikan, although the precise taxonomic classification of the economists here was done by the author. He is also grateful to Hilary Rose and Steven Rose for discussions on this point.

   A similar distinction between 'developmental' and 'selectional' theories is made by Sober (1985), just as Blute (1979) makes an equivalent distinction between 'development' and 'evolution'. In both cases, 'development' refers to the ontogeny of single social systems or organizations through their lifespan. Sober's idea of 'selectional', like Blute's 'evolutionary' theories, are concerned with descent with modification in populations across generations. A similar contrast is drawn by W. McKelvey (1982, pp. 226–9). Faber and Proops (1990, 1991) have the equivalent idea in mind when they use the (slightly misleading) distinguishing terms of 'phenotypic' and 'genotypic' evolution. (These terms mask the fact that phylogeny involves the evolution of phenotypes as well as of genotypes.)

   Nevertheless, all the above are similar to the distinction made here between, respectively, ontogenetic and phylogenetic theories. A precedent for the use of these biological terms to describe different types of evolutionary economic theory may be found in Morris Copeland's (1958, pp. 64, 67) discussion of Veblen's economics. (See chapter 9 below.)

3   See the discussion of Marx in chapter 5 and the Veblenian critique of Marx discussed in chapter 9.

4   Smith's and other Scottish School ideas of evolution, as well as the influence of Smith on Darwin, are discussed in more detail in chapter 4.

5   Scott Moss (1990c) has reproduced some of the Nelson–Winter simulations and shown once more that their equilibriating properties depend on restrictive assumptions.

For Moss, however, this seems to be a negative rather than a positive result. He is keen to demonstrate 'that evolution and equilibrium are by no means incompatible. Rules of thumb reflecting bounded rationality can result in competitive equilibrium. The approach to equilibrium is quite unlike the convergent series one expects from analytic dynamic models. Moreover, equilibrium results from the evolutionary algorithm only when all agents act as if they have nothing more to learn' (Moss, 1990a, p. 16). But this is precisely an evolutionary equilibrium which denies novelty and creativity. Moss has modelled phylogenetic evolution of the consummatory type.

6   On punctuated equilibria in biology see Eldredge (1985b) and Eldredge and Gould (1977). On their relevance to economics see Arthur (1990), Awan (1986), Hodgson (1991c) and Mokyr (1990a, 1990b, 1991).

7   Methodological individualism is discussed further in Hodgson (1988, ch. 3) and chapter 11 below. Its relationship with individual selection and evolution is also examined in Hodgson (1991a) and Sober (1981).

8   Variety is sometimes equated with the variance of a given characteristic (Metcalfe and Gibbons, 1986; Nelson and Winter, 1982, p. 243). Otherwise, it involves the number of distinguishable elements in a set (Saviotti, 1991), but this raises the taxonomic problem of the criteria of selection (Ashby, 1956; Espejo and Howard, 1982).

9   See Mayr (1963, 1976, pp. 26–9, 1982, pp. 45–7, 1985a, p. 56, 1985b, pp. 766, 769), Metcalfe (1988), Metcalfe and Gibbons (1989), Sober (1985, p. 880) and the discussions of the relevance of the concept in later chapters of the present work.

10 In their discussion of 'evolutionary drive', Peter Allen and J. M. McGlade (1987b) show how evolution creates diversity and diversity drives evolution.

11 Joseph Steindl's (1952) theory of capitalist development involves conceptions of profitability and competitiveness based on differences in unit costs between firms in the same industry. Likewise, J. Downie's (1955) study starts from the premise of the permanent coexistence of firms of different efficiency in the same industry. More recently, Giovanni F. Chiaromonte and Giovanni Dosi (1992), Gunnar Eliasson (1984, 1991) and Richard Nelson (1991) also emphasize firm heterogeneity in their analyses of competition and economic growth. Population thinking is exemplified in evolutionary modelling of the Nelson and Winter (1982) type. Also Pier Paolo Saviotti (1988, 1991) argues that an increasing variety of products and services is an important feature of economic development.

12 The likelihood of genetic drift is greater in small populations. In his 'neutral model', the biologist Motoo Kimura (1983) sees drift as the major process of evolutionary change, rather than natural selection.

13 Simon (1990) develops an interesting model of the evolution of altruism where imitative behaviour is central.

14 For example, Faber and Proops (1991, p. 80).

15 Notwithstanding this propensity definition of fitness, the concept still remains highly problematic, as Alexander Rosenberg (1985, ch. 6)

makes clear. Kenneth Waters (1986) makes a plausible argument that the idea of 'survival of the fittest' can be abandoned. According to Waters (1986, p. 222): 'the significance of Darwin's theory did not stem from the belief that natural selection was everywhere occurring, but from the idea that natural selection could explain the adaptation that appeared everywhere.'

Christian Knudsen has remarked in personal conversation that the concept of fitness enjoys a similar status in biology to that of rationality in mainstream economics. Both concepts are at the Lakatosian hard core of their respective discipline, and are tenaciously defended by adherents. It is purported that both concepts help to explain a great deal – but by their very wideness they explain or describe very little.

16 The biologist Ronald Fisher (1930, pp. 39–40) notes an important difference between the concept of fitness in biology and fundamental concepts in physics: 'Fitness, although measured by a uniform method, is qualitatively different for every different organism, whereas entropy, like temperature, is taken to have the same meaning for all physical systems.'

17 Multiple levels of selection are discussed in chapters 12 and 15 below.

Chapter 4   Political Economy and the Darwinian Revolution

1 However, Hayek's own account of the intellectual influences on Darwin is defective, as noted below.

2 Note that Hayek seems to suggest here that Darwin was simply taking a relay baton from the past: applying an idea rather than inventing it. Hayek repeats his underestimation of Darwin's own contribution in several places. Hence his overestimation of the influence of the Scottish School in the Darwinian revolution is combined with a diminution of the scale and significance of that revolution itself. See the two chapters on Hayek below.

3 Without any mention of Malthus, the Mandeville–Scottish School influence on Darwin is repeated by Hayek (1967, pp. 111, 119; 1978, p. 265; 1982, vol. 1, p. 22; 1982, vol. 3, p. 154; 1988, pp. 24, 145–6; 1991a, pp. 96–7), i.e. in at least five separate works spanning more than 20 years of his most mature period of intellectual development. It is only in a relatively obscure article, appearing originally in 1931 in German and in 1936 in French, and for the first time in 1985 in English, that Hayek (in 1991a, p. 262) briefly and without further discussion, and without either endorsement or denial, quotes another author's view that 'Darwin was inspired by Malthus.'

4 Unlike Schumpeter, who similarly neglected Malthus, Hayek did have access to Darwin's notebooks. Notably, Hayek's view of evolution is orientated more to harmony and equilibrium – as in the cases of

Adam Smith and Herbert Spencer – than to the relentless discord to be found in the works of Malthus and Darwin. Hayek is really a utopian who believes in the perfectibility of society, but this time not through the concord of common ownership but on the bedrock of markets and private property. See the discussions of Spencer, Schumpeter and Hayek in later chapters.

5   Continuing his distorted account of these events, even after Darwin's notebooks have appeared, Hayek (1988, p. 24) writes: 'As we learn from his notebooks, Darwin was reading Adam Smith just when, in 1838, he was formulating his own theory.' Likewise, he proposes that recent examinations of Darwin's notebooks 'suggest that his reading of Adam Smith in the crucial year 1838 led Darwin to his decisive breakthrough' (p. 146). Even with the benefit of recent research, Malthus and other key influences receive no mention.

6   In giving the credit solely to Mandeville and the Scottish School, Hayek (1988, p. 146) cites Gruber (1974) and Vorzimmer (1977), giving the impression that these sources support his account. However, for Gruber (1974, p. 7) a crucial entry in the notebooks marks the point of Darwin's 'Malthusian insight' when he 'recognized the force of the idea of evolution through natural selection'. Likewise, for Vorzimmer (1969, p. 539) the 'great watershed' in the development of Darwin's theory came with the reading of Malthus, particularly in regard to 'the great pressures bearing upon each *individual* being and the resultant struggle among offspring of the same parents'. Vorzimmer's work on the notebooks does not seem to have changed his mind on this point.

7   See, for instance, Gruber (1985), Herbert (1971, 1977), Jones (1986), Kohn (1980, 1985), Ospovat (1979), Richardson (1981), Schweber (1977, 1980). A good recent overview and assessment on the question of the influence of Malthus is provided by Jones (1989).

8   See Schweber (1977) p. 286, and 1980, pp. 260–1, 270–1.

9   Babbage (1846, p. 176n) adduced this principle from 'personal examination of a number of manufactories and workshops devoted to different purposes' in consequence of his work on his inspired but ill-fated mechanical computer (Berg, 1987; Hyman, 1982). He subsequently found that it had also been anticipated by Melchiorre Gioia in his *Nuovo Prospetto delle Scienze Economiche* of 1815. However, as Ugo Pagano (1991, p. 317) points out, 'there is a difference between the two formulations: whereas Babbage refers to the advantage of the division of labour for a cost-minimising "master manufacturer", Gioia considers the same advantage for a rational society taken as a whole.' Pagano's stimulating and extensive discussion of these ideas in the context of the theory of the firm is highly recommended.

10 Mandeville did believe that government should maintain the buoyancy of demand by promoting the production of armaments and other services, and he advocated the 'skilful management of the dextrous politician' in economic affairs. However, it has been convincingly argued by Nathan Rosenberg (1963) that Mandeville opposed

substantial economic intervention or regulation, other than the slow and piecemeal elaboration, by trial and error, of the legal and institutional framework most conducive to the expansion of trade. For a further discussion of this point see Hayek (1978, pp. 258–60), who also emphasizes Mandeville's role as a precursor of both Hume and Smith.

11 Smith's anti-interventionist views are often exaggerated. He admitted an economic, as well as a political and juridical role for government. As Albert Hirschman (1977, p. 104) puts it: 'It appears that Smith advocated less a state with minimal functions than one whose capacity for folly would have some ceiling.' For a related discussion of Smith see Forbes (1976).

12 There are several possible reasons for Schumpeter's denial. For instance, it offers evidence, but only of a prima facie character, that Schumpeter's understanding of Darwinism was deficient. However, Schumpeter did not have access to Darwin's notebooks and the evidence therein of a substantial Malthusian influence.

13 The huge range of issues and hypotheses involved has been measured out by La Vergata (1985, pp. 953–8) and by L. Jones (1989).

14 La Vergata (1985, p. 922) also wonders 'whether this emphasis on manuscripts and on the young Darwin may lend itself to operations similar to those that took place on the young Marx and the 1844 manuscripts'.

15 Related ideas have found ample expression in literature. Consider the words of John Milton from his *Areopagitica*:

> He that can apprehend and consider vice with all her baits and seeming pleasures, and yet abstain, and yet distinguish, and yet prefer that which is truly better, he is the true wayfaring Christian. I cannot praise a fugitive and cloistered virtue, unexercised and unbreathed, that never sallies out and seeks her adversary, but slinks out of the race, where the immortal garland is to be run for, not without dust and heat. Assuredly we bring not innocence into the world, we bring impurity much rather: that which purifies us is trial, and trial is by what is contrary.

A beautiful modern example, on the theme of suffering and death, is in the poem 'A Kumquat for John Keats', by the North of England poet Tony Harrison, epitomized in the lines:

> Then it's the kumquat fruit expresses best
> how days have darkness round them like a rind,
> life has a skin of death that keeps its zest.

(Selected Poems, Penguin, 1984)

Within economics, note in particular the discussions of human restlessness and desires for excitement in the work of Tibor Scitovsky (1976, 1986). Scitovsky's arguments that such desires undermine equilibrium, and make the attainment of any lasting optimum impossible, are strongly redolent of Malthus. See also my discussion of the 'impurity principle' (Hodgson, 1984, chs 6–7, and 1988, pp. 167–71, 254–62).

16 See Young (1969) for a discussion of this point. In the second edition of the *Essay*, Malthus dropped the references to Godwin and Condorcet from the title and also removed some of the chapters on natural theology.

17 For such reasons, Malthus's views were subsequently an important infusion for Keynes's (1936, pp. 362–4) theory of unemployment, in which self-righting and optimizing characteristics of the labour market are not assumed. In addition, as Alexander Field (quoted in Hirschman, 1981, p. 302) has pointed out, while Malthus endorsed the idea of the global benefits of the pursuit of self-interest, he systematically added the reservation that an individual should so act only 'while he adheres to the rules of justice' (Malthus, 1820, pp. 3, 518). In contrast, according to Field, Smith added such a qualification only once in the *Wealth of Nations*.

18 Paley's influence at Cambridge survived at least until the 1920s. Indeed, Keynes (1933, p. 108) saw Paley as 'for a generation or more an intellectual influence on Cambridge only second to Newton. Perhaps in a sense *he* was the *first* of the Cambridge economists.' The economist Mary Paley – Paley's great-granddaughter – married Alfred Marshall.

19 As quoted in Kohn (1980, p. 141) and Jones (1989, p. 412). Compare with the later version in Darwin's *Origin of Species*: 'The face of nature may be compared to a yielding surface, with ten thousand sharp wedges packed close together and driven inwards by incessant blows, sometimes one wedge being struck, and then another with greater force' (1859, p. 67).

20 Note the similarities between Malthus's anti-perfectionist views and those of American pragmatists such as Charles Peirce, William James and John Dewey; they were generally hostile to all absolutist social rationalizations.

21 Notably, Hansson and Stuart's (1990) 'Malthusian' model of 'selection of preferences' focuses on a 'very long run equilibrium' outcome. Hence, for reasons given here, it is not strictly Malthusian in character.

22 Of course, equilibrium thinking eventually dominated neoclassical economics. The inadequacies of a concept of competition based on the idea of equilibrium have been stressed by economists of the modern Austrian School, and by McNulty (1968).

Chapter 5 Revolutionary Evolution: Karl Marx and Frederick Engels

1 It is a myth, moreover, that I among others have repeated in the belief that it was true. Penance should follow a reading of Fay (1978) and Colp (1982) where the record is eventually put straight.

2 Writing much later, John Maynard Keynes is similarly critical of the use of evolutionary theory by supporters of *laissez-faire*:

The economists were teaching that wealth, commerce and machinery were the children of free competition ... But the Darwinians could go one better than that – free competition had built man. The human eye was no longer the demonstration of design, miraculously contriving all things for the best; it was the supreme achievement of chance, operating under the conditions of free competition and *laissez faire*. The principle of the survival of the fittest could be regarded as a vast generalisation of the Ricardian economics. Socialistic interferences became, in the light of this grander synthesis, not merely inexpedient, but impious, as calculated to retard the onward movement of the mighty process by which we ourselves had risen like Aphrodite out of the primeval slime of ocean. (Keynes, 1931, p. 276)

3 Marx and Engels were not alone in their revulsion against Malthus. See Fonseca (1991, ch. 13) for a discussion of the manner in which the parson was widely misunderstood and reviled. For example, Henry George (1879) focused on the apologetic and reactionary interpretations of Malthus, rebutting them with the assertion that nature could not be blamed for man's failure to distribute its bounty fairly. George's intellectual influence was, of course, enormous. Indeed, Wallace informed Darwin in 1881 that George's *Progress and Poverty* had convinced him that Malthus's doctrine could not be applied to human evolution.

4 As Gould (1978, p. 211) suggests, Haeckel was probably the source of some of Engels's (1964, pp. 172–86) major ideas in his celebrated essay 'The Part Played by Labour in the Transition from Ape to Man'.

5 If the reader questions how such hackles can be raised by Haeckel, then inspect the highly racist picture from the 1874 edition of his *Anthropogenie*, reproduced in Gould (1978, p. 215). For a discussion of Haeckel's Social Darwinism and his influence in Germany see Corsi and Weindling (1985).

6 See Hodgson (1984, and 1988, pp. 252–74) for a further discussion of this issue.

7 As evolutionary ideas became more prominent in social science in the late 1800s, there were several unsuccessful attempts to reconcile Darwinism and Marxism, by prominent theorists and popularizers such as Karl Kautsky, Georgy Plekhanov and August Bebel. See Bannister (1979, pp. 131–5), Bellomy (1984, pp. 43–8), Garranta (1973), Runkle (1961) and chapter 9 below. For a critical evaluation of a strain in modern biology which is purportedly Marxian-inspired see Kassiola (1990).

Chapter 6 Herbert Spencer: The Lost Satellite

1 See Bowler (1983, 1988) and Mayr (1980). Part of the hostility to Darwinism in the years around 1900 arose because it had seemingly failed to give a plausible explanation of the presumed variation of offspring and the selection of species. Such an explanation was an outcome of the later synthesis between Darwinism and Mendelian genetics.

2   This is, of course, one of the least damaging effects. The current rift between sociology and economics is so deleterious that it could be remarked that many of the more important questions in social theory have become lost in the abyss that separates the two disciplines.

3   Against Toulmin and Mayr, several other analysts have argued that Darwin allowed some of his formulations to drift with the progressionist current (Ospovat, 1981; Ruse, 1988, p. 103). Richards (1988, 1992) goes even further, arguing that Darwin was a committed progressionist, despite all the caution and qualification in his writings. However, if for Darwin progressionism was a prejudice, for Spencer it was an explicit and guiding principle.

4   Curiously, however, Wallace believed that some superior intelligence had guided the evolution of humans, accounting for their greater mental capacities and free will. Wallace also deviated here from the Malthusian doctrine and embraced the notion of the perfectibility of humankind. This optimistic ideal helped to endear him to socialist views. Darwin was troubled by his friend's exclusion of humanity from the theory of natural selection and wrote to Wallace in 1869: 'I hope that you have not murdered too completely your own and my child' (Wallace, 1916, p. 197). For a discussion of Darwin's contrasting atheism and materialism see Gould (1978, pp. 21–7) and Desmond and Moore (1991).

5   Republished in Spencer (1892).

6   For useful accounts of von Baer's theory see Ospovat (1976) and Mayr (1982).

7   Apart from the problem of defining complexity, its association with evolutionary adaptability is not self-evidently a universal principle. For instance, Holling (1986) argues that as a system becomes more complex and more connected it may reach a threshold beyond which it is more vulnerable to external shocks and potentially unstable. In this case there are 'accidents waiting to happen'. Likewise, Kay (1982, p. 75) sees synergetic linking in organizations as having beneficial effects, but often reducing organizational flexibility. Modern work in the theory of chaos and antichaos suggests that evolving systems embody a combination of both 'frozen' and 'liquid' networks and relations (Kauffman, 1991).

8   For this reason, as noted in a preceding chapter, the inspiration that Darwin drew from the concept of the division of labour was possibly as much from Charles Babbage as from Bernard Mandeville or Adam Smith. Unlike the Mandeville–Smith idea, for Babbage the division of labour is built on the preexistence of a variety in skills.

9   However, Norman Clark (1991, p. 99) has argued that 'information-intensive systems tend to grow in *complexity* as they evolve'. This would bolster the Spencerian proposition that increasing complexity is likely in human systems.

10   This point has been argued and illustrated extensively in the works of Stephen Jay Gould (1978, 1980a, 1989).

11   For a general discussion of the distinctive reaction of the American pragmatists to the rise of evolutionary theory see Wiener (1949).

12   It is shown in later chapters that this 'reversed Haeckel's Law' also applies to the theory of socioeconomic evolution developed by Friedrich Hayek.

13   Note, for example, the early criticisms of James Ward, to which Spencer attempted to reply in an appendix to the sixth edition of his *First Principles*. Spencer's riposte was not successful, and his fundamental principles became the object of criticism by a number of subsequent authors. On this issue see Peel (1971) and Wiltshire (1978). A bibliography of early critical writings on Spencer is found in Rumney (1934, pp. 325–51).

14   Nevertheless, the evolution of so-called 'altruistic' behaviour is still explicable in neo-Darwinian terms. On this see E. O. Wilson (1975) and Dawkins (1976, 1982), as well as the work of Axelrod (1984) on 'the evolution of cooperation'.

15   Maureen McKelvey (1992) argues convincingly that the misrepresentation of evolution to be 'survival of the fittest' rather than 'success in reproduction' inflates the importance of males over females in the evolutionary process. Furthermore, it flaunts the typically male notions of toughness and conflict, rather than the roles of caring for and nurturing the young offspring, roles traditionally associated with women.

16   See Brooks and Wiley (1988), Brooks et al. (1989), Collier (1986), Coveney and Highfield (1990), Georgescu-Roegen (1971), Weber et al. (1989).

Chapter 7   The Mecca of Alfred Marshall

1   His concerns about increasing returns are divulged in appendix H of the *Principles*. Marshall's reluctance to ignore reality should be an example to our relatively blinkered profession today. For discussions of Marshall's treatment of time and increasing returns see Currie and Steedman (1990, ch. 2), Loasby (1978), Schumpeter (1954, p. 995), Shackle (1972, pp. 244, 286–96), Thomas (1991, pp. 4–5) and, of course, the famous article by Sraffa (1926).

2   Marshall then refers to the theorists Haeckel and Schäffle, but it should be noted that the latter at least was strongly influenced by Spencer (Bellomy, 1984, p. 41). For a discussion of the work of Schäffle and other German-speaking social theorists towards the end of the nineteenth century see Weingart (1990). The general influence of German-speaking theorists on Marshall is examined in Streissler (1990).

3   The neglect of the Spencerian influence on Marshall can be judged by an examination of the proceedings of the various centenary conferences for Marshall's *Principles*, held in 1990. The author has yet to come across an extended discussion of the Marshall–Spencer relationship in this literature. Even when mentioned, as for example in McWilliams Tullberg (1990), it is a matter of few words. Apart from Niman (1991)

and Thomas (1991) the general question of the inspiration that Marshall drew from biology has been relatively unexplored. Reisman (1987), however, makes frequent mention of the influence of Spencer.

4   For a further discussion of 'institutionalist signposts' in Marshall's work see Jensen (1990).

5   Darwin's own motto was similar: *'natura non facit saltum.'* This was apparently, in turn, borrowed from Linnaeus.

6   Not only does Marshall argue that skills are developed by use, but also, in the subsequent chapter, he sides with Charles Babbage (1846, pp. 175–6), in contrast to Adam Smith, in presuming that the division of labour must itself be founded on differences of skill (Marshall, 1949, p. 220).

7   Marshall (1949, p. 1) suggested that 'character is being formed' during employment and that 'each new step upwards is to be regarded as the development of new activities giving rise to new wants' (ibid., p. 76). Marshall's assumption here that tastes and preferences may alter through time clearly differs from modern neoclassical orthodoxy (Chasse, 1984; Hodgson, 1988; Parsons, 1937, ch. 4). However, this did not become the basis of a theory of phylogenetic change, where there is something analogous to the 'natural selection' of attributes, or of 'genetic drift' or whatever.

8   However, Samuelson was able to borrow appropriate materials that had been developed in the early editions of Alfred Lotka's *Elements of Mathematical Biology*. Herbert Simon (1959b) noted how Samuelson had appropriated analytical ideas concerning the use of differential equations, the stability of equilibria and comparative statics from Lotka's work. However, these have little to do with biology *per se*. They are mechanistic notions, common to physics, and have nothing to do with richer biological notions such as population thinking and time irreversibility which have been highlighted here.

Chapter 8   Carl Menger and the Evolution of Money

1   Timothy Congdon (1981) explicitly endorses Knapp's view. However, in contrast to Congdon and other supporters of the state monopoly of money such as Milton Friedman, Knapp rejects the quantity theory of money as an explanation of the price level. Knapp sees it as being determined by 'real' phenomena such as the level of wages, which 'constituted a first step towards the later theories of Keynes and his school' (Schefold, 1987, p. 54). For a comparative discussion of 'monetary nominalism' see Frankel (1977).

2   It is notable that the Mengerian account of the emergence of money is repeated by Ludwig von Mises (1980, pp. 42–6) and others of the later Austrian School.

3   Apparently the first use of the term 'genetic' was in its German form of *genetisch* in the eighteenth century. It was imported into English by Thomas Carlyle well before it was taken up by modern biologists (Hayek, 1988, p. 147).

4 Accordingly, the American institutionalist Walton Hamilton (1919, p. 15) saw the 'genetic' approach as implying 'that the thing is "becoming"' and as involving 'not a historical account but a method of analysis' explaining 'what a thing is in terms of how it came to be'. This is clearly in accord with Menger's usage, and not the one of modern biology. It may also suggest a hitherto undetected degree of resonance between the work of Menger and that of the institutionalists.

5 For a more extensive discussion of the concept of causality in Menger's 'invisible hand' explanation of money see Mäki (1991), and for a more general discussion of 'invisible hand explanations' see Ullmann-Margalit (1978).

6 Note, for instance, Viktor Vanberg's (1989, p. 340) useful summary of the steps involved in Menger's theory of the emergence of money. Significantly, Vanberg writes of the 'discovery' of the monetary unit, rather than of its selection from a set of competitive rival units.

7 It is not implied here that Menger believed that markets reached optimal outcomes. In addition, Menger was not as opposed to state intervention as some later members of the Austrian School (Prisching, 1989; Vanberg, 1986, p. 99).

8 See, for instance, Black (1970), Dowd (1989), Fama (1980), Glasner (1989), Goodhart (1987), Hayek (1976), Hoover (1988), Selgin (1988), Wärneryd (1989, 1990), White (1986, 1987), Wray (1990), Yeager (1987, 1989). It should be noted, however, that Menger's theory is not always used to bolster non-interventionism. It is sometimes used as part of a critique of some specific proposals to limit the role of the state in the monetary system. Observe, for instance, the criticisms of the Greenfield and Yeager (1983, 1986) 'cashless competitive payments system' by Mott (1989), Selgin and White (1987) and White (1984b, 1989). Selgin, White and Mott all make some appeal to Menger's conception of money to rebut the Greenfield–Yeager idea that the government should define the unit of value but should be forbidden to issue money itself. However, Yeager (1989) disputes the relevance, but not the validity, of the Mengerian story in this context.

9 In his discussion of coinage debasement, von Mises (1980, p. 79) writes that: 'Not every kind of money has been accepted at sight, but only those with a good reputation for weight and fitness.' The question, then, is how such fitness is maintained.

10 Babbage's concept of quality variation is related to his concept of the division of labour. As noted in a preceding chapter, the idea of the division of labour in the works of Mandeville and Smith does not proceed from the assumption of the initial diversity of talent or skill. It assumes that such variations arise from learning in the process of production itself. Variety is thus a result of the division of labour, not its starting point. In contrast, for Babbage (1846, pp. 175–6), prior variations in skill are the economic foundation upon which the division of labour is built. Menger (1981, pp. 71–4) also differs from Smith, in seeing the division of labour as principally the consequence of the decentralization, growth and increasing complexity of knowledge.

11   Alec Nove (1980, 1983) has also emphasized the problem of quality variation in his discussion of the limits and possibilities of socialist planning. However, in noting that 'a kilowatt-hour is a kilowatt-hour is a kilowatt-hour' he argues that commodities such as electricity which are least susceptible to such variation are the best candidates for planned production by the state. Unlike Babbage, therefore, Nove thus suggests that state intervention is *less* appropriate in cases of variable quality. What Nove ignores, however, is the problem of quality verification that is highlighted by Babbage. Consideration of all the relevant issues in the cases where there is significant potential quality variation suggests a market solution, but one which is highly regulated by the state.

12   Strictly, this is not the exact law associated with Sir Thomas Gresham (*c.*1519–1579), which is taken to apply to the case where 'by legal enactment a government assigns the same nominal value to two or more forms of circulatory medium whose intrinsic values differ' (Harris, 1987, p. 565). Understandably, agents prefer to make payments with the less costly or inferior form, and 'bad money drives out good.' This argument relates to the existence of a single state authority sanctioning and assigning invariant value to a debaseable currency unit. (Hayek's (1967, pp. 318–20) brief discussion of Gresham's Law is regrettably vague on this point.) The idea discussed in the present chapter is of differences arising within a class of commodities of the same perceived type. The taxonomic designation of the group of commodities, e.g. various degrees and types of impure gold, could arise from common perception rather than by the assignation of the state.

13   We may hypothesize that changes in language occur through something analogous to the 'genetic drift': the accumulation of small and possibly random changes in one general direction over time. Interestingly, as in biology, such 'genetic drift' is a source of change other than through evolutionary selection.

14   However, there may even be a case for some limited institutional regulation of language, as in France, and spelling reforms, as in the Netherlands. There is no reason to presume that self-regulating linguistic evolution always leads to satisfactory outcomes.

15   Veblen's critical attitude to Menger is evidenced in Veblen (1919, pp. 72–3). See also the very interesting comparison of Menger and Commons in Vanberg (1989).

Chapter 9   *Thorstein Veblen and Post-Darwinian Economics*

1   A sympathetic and knowledgeable adversary such as Frank Knight (1935a, p. 209) responded to Veblen's assertion that he had applied Darwinian principles to economics with the riposte: 'I cannot find

anything in particular that he could reasonably have meant by this claim.' More recently, Lamar Jones (1986) argued that Veblen's attachment to Darwinism involved 'a case of mistaken identity'. Both standpoints are rebutted by the argument in this chapter.

2   See Dorfman (1934, p. 46), Edgell (1975), Edgell and Tilman (1989), Eff (1989), Murphree (1959), Peel (1971, p. 198). For a good general discussion of the origins of American institutionalism see Mayhew (1987b).

3   By the end of the nineteenth century the influence of Darwinism had entered a period of decline, mainly because it was not able to explain all the mechanisms in the processes of variation and natural selection (Bowler, 1983; Mayr, 1980; Provine, 1985). Such mechanisms did not become apparent until after the recognition and development of the work of Gregor Mendel in genetics. Subsequently, in the 1930s and 1940s, a group of modern Darwinians (principally Theodosius Dobzhansky, Ronald Fisher, John B. S. Haldane, Julian Huxley, Ernst Mayr, George Gaylord Simpson, G. Ledyard Stebbins, Bernhard Rensch and Sewall Wright) accomplished a synthesis between theoretical work on natural selection and genetics. Thus the gene became fully incorporated into the theory of evolution, giving a plausible explanation of the presumed variation of offspring and the selection of species (Eldredge, 1985b, p. v; Mayr, 1978, pp. 51–2; Stebbins, 1982, pp. 46–7). The neo-Darwinian 'evolutionary synthesis' gave the Darwinian idea of natural selection a renewed vitality which has continued to this day.

4   Note the famous definition of the institution by the later institutionalist writer, Walton Hamilton (1963, p. 84): 'It connotes a way of thought or action of some prevalence and permanence, which is embedded in the habits of a group or the customs of a people. . . . Institutions fix the confines of and impose form upon the activities of human beings.' This may be preferred to Veblen's rather mentalistic definition because of its inclusion of human action as well as thought.

Nevertheless, in the writings of the American pragmatists who influenced Veblen, there is a close connection between habits of thought and action. For instance, Charles Sanders Peirce (1878, p. 294; 1934, p. 255–6) wrote: 'The essence of belief is the establishment of habit; and different beliefs are distinguished by the different modes of action to which they give rise . . . the whole function of thought is to produce habits of action.' This identification of belief with habit, which is manifest in action, is a cornerstone of Peirce's pragmatism, and to some extent explains Veblen's terminology. This notion of belief as a potentiality for action was taken up by later pragmatists such as John Dewey (1929, p. 138): 'ideas are statements not of what is or has been – but of acts to be performed.'

5   See, for example, Veblen (1919, pp. 192n, 402–5).

6   Alan Dyer (1986, pp. 31–8) argues convincingly that in deriving the idea of creative 'idle curiosity', Veblen was influenced by Peirce's

notion of 'musement'. Note that a similar idea was also put forward by John A. Hobson – the closest contemporary English thinker to the American institutionalists – in a work published in the same year as Veblen's *Instinct of Workmanship*. Hobson (1914, pp. 240–1, 336) saw the role of human error and playful inventiveness as decisive in creating mutations in behavioural patterns, and thereby they were a source of continuous evolutionary innovation. Interestingly, he gave more stress to the function of the 'freedom of the human will' than Veblen in this context. However, Hobson did not go so far as Veblen to incorporate this idea into an evolutionary theory of the phylogenetic type.

7   It has been suggested by Lamar Jones (1986, p. 1053) that for Veblen part of the appeal of Darwin's ideas is due to the fact that they were perceived to undermine the oppressive intolerance of contemporary religion by promoting a naturalistic or materialistic world-view. The truth or untruth of this is not easily established, but Jones fails to note the additional and manifest significance of Veblen's interpretation of Darwinism based on 'cumulative causation', as elaborated here.

8   It should be noted that in some passages Marshall (1949, pp. 1, 76) also accepted that individual wants are moulded by circumstances. For discussions of this see Parsons (1937, ch. 4), Chasse (1984). But this is not the Marshall that is formalized into theorems, nor represented in the textbooks.

9   For discussions of the genesis of cumulative process models see Kapp (1976, p. 218) and Humphrey (1990). In Myrdal (1978) there is a note of his own conversion to institutionalism.

10   For a discussion of different interpretations of Veblen's theory of institutional change, see Tilman (1987).

11   Forest Hill (1958, p. 139) elaborates Veblen's critique of Marx with the following words:

> In Veblen's opinion, Marx uncritically adopted natural rights and natural law preconceptions and a hedonistic psychology of rational self-interest. On these bases Marx elaborated his labor theory of value, with labor as the source and measure of value, and the corollary doctrines of labor's right to its full product, of surplus value, and exploitation of labor. He attributed rational self-interest not only to individuals but to entire classes, thereby explaining their asserted solidarity and motivation in class struggle. Veblen rejected the concept of rational class interest and the labor theory of value, along with its corollaries and natural rights basis.

12   The fact that the Veblenian cumulative process of evolutionary change of, say, consumer tastes is phylogenetic, and not ontogenetic, was perhaps first noted by Copeland (1958, pp. 64, 67).

13   Dosi's (1988b) rich discussion of technological innovation has a strong Veblenian tone. Recent prominent discussions of technological evolution which briefly acknowledge Veblen include Clark and Juma (1987) and David (1985).

14 See the discussions in Rutherford (1983) and Biddle (1990).

15 It is probably thus in part an accident that the strong revival in evolutionary theorizing in economics since the 1970s is frequently described as 'Schumpeterian', rather than 'institutionalist' or 'Veblenian'.

16 Ayres (1932) wrote a popular and 'racy' book on that champion of Darwinism and scourge of the creationists, Thomas Henry Huxley. Yet this book is more concerned with Huxley's scientific campaign to establish the fact of human descent from the apes, rather than the precise mechanisms of natural selection. Furthermore, Huxley had private misgivings about the theory of natural selection (Kottler, 1985).

17 Recognition of the enabling function of constraints and institutions is important for biological as well as social science. To impress its general relevance for evolutionary processes note the following quotation from two theoretical biologists:

> It is common to think of constraints in a negative fashion – as preventing things from happening, and thereby reducing the variety found in nature. But if the process of producing variation is open-ended, the introduction of constraints can channel the variation, and by directing it, produce much further or deeper exploration in a given direction than would otherwise be possible. Constraints can thus play a creative and, in one sense, ultimately progressive role. This is a deep truth, not only about evolution, but about problem-solving and exploration in general. (Wimsatt and Schank, 1988, p. 235)

Chapter 10   *Joseph Schumpeter and the Evolutionary Process*

1 See, for example, Dosi et al. (1988), Futia (1980), Hanusch (1988), Heertje and Perlman (1990), Iwai (1984a, 1984b), Nelson and Winter (1982), Silverberg et al. (1988).

2 Note also the misleading statement by Heertje and Perlman (1990, p. 3) that 'the concept of Walrasian equilibrium does not have a place in Schumpeterian dynamics.' However, both the Heertje and Perlman (1990) and the Hanusch (1988) volumes contain essays which contest such views, contrary to the apparent sentiments of their editors.

3 Clark and Juma (1987, p. 58) wrongly go on to describe Schumpeter's picture of capitalism as being in a *'far from equilibrium'* state, with an obvious allusion to the works of Nicolis and Prigogine (1977), Prigogine (1980) and Prigogine and Stengers (1984). In these terms, however, the Schumpeterian model is not one 'far from equilibrium' but one which is 'near to equilibrium', as the following textual analysis will suggest. Furthermore, the Prigogine et al. concept of being 'far from equilibrium' specifically refers to an *open* system, not one which, in Schumpeter's words, evokes 'development from within'.

4 For a further discussion of the dynamic aspects of Walras's work see Morishima (1977).

5   Freeman (1990a, pp. 31ff.) goes on to argue that Schumpeter's theory can be augmented by Carlota Perez's (1983, 1985) idea of a 'techno-economic paradigm' involving the pervasive changes in technology that underlie 'successive industrial revolutions'. This, it is argued, can help to account for the temporal 'clusters of innovations' in the Schumpeterian approach, as identified, for instance, by Mensch (1979).

6   See Fritz Machlup (1978, pp. 454, 472), Mark Blaug (1980, p. 49) and Bertram Schefold (1986, p. 97). Note, however, that while Schumpeter believed in the reduction of explanations to individual terms, he criticized Keynes for introducing and failing to explain individual expectations in his theory: 'An expectation acquires explanatory value only if we are made to understand *why* people expect *what* they expect. Otherwise expectation is a mere *deus ex machina* that conceals problems instead of solving them' (Schumpeter, 1951, p. 154). However, this actually threatens methodological individualism by suggesting that individual expectations must in turn be explained in terms of 'the cyclical situations that give rise to them' (ibid.). If the individual, in turn, has to be explained, then explanation can never come to rest with individuals. To be consistent, either Schumpeter should also berate Walras for his neoclassical *deus ex machina* of individual preference functions and abandon methodological individualism, or he should withdraw this criticism of Keynes. Lars Udéhn (1987, p. 10) notes that for Schumpeter methodological individualism was applicable to some branches of social science but not, for instance, to history. However, the imperative of methodological individualism that 'all social phenomena (their structure and change) are explicable only in terms of individuals – their properties, goals, and beliefs' (Elster, 1983, p. 453) is universal, and cannot be applied in one case and not in another.

7   It should also be noted that 'by 1921 Schumpeter . . . considered socialism a viable and rational economic system' (Chaloupek, 1990, p. 672) and he retained a similar view for the remainder of his life. Consequently, he did not seem to adopt the Austrian critique by Ludwig von Mises and Friedrich Hayek of the Walrasian theoretical foundations of the models of socialism proposed by Oskar Lange, Fred Taylor and others in the 1930s (Lavoie, 1985; Vaughn, 1980). Assimilation of this critique would have undermined both his reluctant belief in the viability of socialism and his strong attachment to Walrasian theory.

8   Peter Kalmbach and Heinz Kurz (1986) examine various discussions of possible effects of technological change, such as rising unemployment or falling wages, noting that Schumpeter (1934, p. 250) invoked a Say's Law argument to suggest that 'total real demand for labour cannot in general permanently fall' with the introduction of mechanization.

9   The attitude of Schumpeter himself to the American institutionalists is recorded as follows: 'Institutionalism is nothing but the methodological errors of German historians, combined with the great and lasting contribution made to our sciences. It is only error and not achievement. This, of course, is the one dark spot in the American atmosphere' (1991, p. 292). However, Schumpeter does not make clear what

those 'methodological errors' are, neither does he acknowledge Veblen's (1919, pp. 58, 252–78) criticisms of Schmoller and the German Historical School. Note, for instance, the following remarks by Veblen:

> no economics is farther from being an evolutionary science than the received economics of the Historical School ... they have contented themselves with an enumeration of data and a narrative account of industrial development, and have not presumed to offer a theory of anything or to elaborate their results into a consistent body of knowledge. Any evolutionary science, on the other hand, is a close-knit body of theory. It is a theory of process, of an unfolding sequence. (Veblen, 1919, p. 58)

One of the good points of Seckler's (1975) otherwise flawed work is his demonstration (ch. 2) of the incorrectness of the view – perpetrated by Hayek and Robbins as well as Schumpeter – that institutionalism is simply an extension of German historicism (Bush, 1981, p. 143).

Chapter 11   *The Evolution of Friedrich Hayek*

1   Late on, Hayek (1988, p. 26) does indeed mention the distinction between ontogeny and phylogeny. This is with a view to associating ontogeny, in contrast with phylogeny, with false and 'historicist' notions of economic development. This is misleading because all organisms are open systems, and all ontogenetic development is context dependent. With an unpredictable environment, and like phylogeny, ontogeny is neither predictable nor 'historicist'.

2   Some sociobiologists, such as Alexander Alland (1967), go even further, promoting the unacceptable notion that culture is merely a kind of biological adaptation.

3   The idea of acquired character inheritance in socioeconomic evolution is somewhat tardily recognized by Hayek (1982, vol. 3, p. 156). We must wait even later, and after the influence of Sir Karl Popper (1972), for an explicit description of the socioeconomic evolution as being Lamarckian rather than Darwinian (Hayek, 1988, p. 25).

4   Against Hayek's mistaken view concerning the simplicity of the theory of natural selection, it should be noted, for instance, that Charles Darwin and Alfred Russell Wallace argued at length over the details of the theory long after the publication of the *Origin*. Even 'Darwin's bulldog', Thomas Henry Huxley, had reservations about the theory, particularly over the problem of the origin and persistence of sterility (Kottler, 1985). It was thus hardly a 'simple' theory, even to those who invented and popularized it.

5   Pollock's quotation, with similar claims by Hayek, is repeated in Hayek (1982, vol. 1, p. 153). At the risk of protesting a little too much, in this same place Hayek (pp. 152–3) cites no less than 14 sources, all in apparent support of Hayek's claim that there were many 'Darwinians before Darwin' (p. 23). Unfortunately, five of these references are pre-1900 and thus stem from a period when Darwin's theory was neither

fully understood nor universally accepted. Another four stem from 1900 to 1930 when things were only slightly better.

In parading such inappropriate references, Hayek does not seem aware that it is only in the twentieth century that the distinctiveness of Darwin's theory has been widely understood and appreciated. One of the remaining and most recent references by Hayek is to the work by Bentley Glass et al., *Forerunners of Darwin*. Yet Hayek fails to caution us with the words of Glass in the preface of this book, that certain of the alleged forerunners 'were hardly evolutionists: others, in their own eyes, not evolutionists at all. Some, who lived in the period after 1859, even hated the Darwinian teaching and fought it vehemently' (Glass, 1959, p. vi).

6   Although Herbert Spencer does receive a few brief and rare mentions in Hayek's writings, there is no discussion of his evolutionary theory, or of that of other nineteenth-century theorists of social evolution such as Ernst Haeckel, Lewis Henry Morgan, Albert Schäffle, William Graham Sumner and Edward Tylor. For rather inadequate comparisons of Hayek's work with Sumner or Spencer see Gray (1984) and Paul (1988).

7   Hayek's faulty account of the influences of and upon Darwin is paralleled by his inadequate examination of other evolutionary thinkers in social science. His failure to give Herbert Spencer and William Graham Sumner anything more than a passing mention is particularly notable (Paul, 1988). Furthermore, his dismissals of the American institutionalists are brief and inaccurate (Leathers, 1990, pp. 164–5). Among other things, they are placed in the camp of the German historicists, ignoring not only the criticisms of that very school by Thorstein Veblen (1919, pp. 58, 252–78) but also the sustained appeal to Darwinian evolutionary theory in the economic thought of the latter theorist.

8   Mayr (1985b, p. 769) goes on to explain that these earlier 'evolutionary' theories concerned eliminations of 'degradations of type', now referred to as 'stabilizing selection'. These ideas evinced typological essentialism, not the 'population thinking' at the core of Darwin's theory: 'Essentialism always had great difficulty in coping with the phenomenon of variation. One of its collateral concepts was that any deviation from the type that was too drastic would be eliminated. But such a process is not natural selection in the Darwinian sense, a force that would permit directional change and an improvement of adaptation.'

9   For an excellent elaboration of this point see Hirst and Woolley (1982). Even the aggressive attack on genetic determinism by Rose et al. (1984) admits the probability that genes have some influence on our behaviour, even if the significance of this for social and economic policy is denied.

10   For mentions of evolutionary selection see Hayek (1967, pp. 32, 67, 71, 111; 1982, vol. 1, pp. 9, 23; 1982, vol. 3, pp. 155, 158, 202; 1988, pp. 16, 20, 24, 26).

11 In this passage Hayek suggests that we can recognize a rule simply through the identification and description of its phenomenal form. However, this suggests an empiricist route to the knowledge of rules, and ignores the fact that no rule can be known or described independently of concepts and other rules. As Hayek himself writes: 'Rules which we cannot state thus do not govern only our actions. They also govern our perceptions, and particularly our perceptions of other people's actions' (1967, p. 45). Thus there is a difference between rules governing perception and rules governing action which is noted (pp. 56–7), but not brought out adequately, in his work.

12 See, for instance, Hayek (1967, pp. 46–8; 1982, vol. 3, pp. 155–7; 1988, pp. 21, 24).

13 However, the possibility of the existence of cultural traditions among birds and mammals is recognized by Hayek (1988, pp. 16–17). Contrary to Hayek's earlier anti-scientism, this usefully erodes a significant conceptual barrier between the social and the natural world, and suggests that some careful 'imitation' of the life sciences by economics might not be so bad after all.

14 In chapter 14 below a tentative solution to this problem is suggested where choice has a real, but constrained, role.

15 Recent attempts not only to combine but also to maintain the autonomy and reality of both structure and choice are provided by Anthony Giddens (1984) and Viktor Vanberg (1988). Although Vanberg's work expresses formal adherence to methodological individualism, while Giddens's does not, it is notable that the gap between them is not as great as it may appear at first sight. Lars Udéhn (1987) argues convincingly that many verbal attachments to methodological individualism are more formal than real, and that the prescriptions of strict methodological individualist analysis cannot be fully implemented in practice. Recoiling against mechanistic versions of such a doctrine, G. B. Madison (1990, p. 91) asserts that Hayek 'decidedly rejects the notion held by some methodological individualists that the only acceptable account of social phenomena is an analytic-reductive-empiricist one which is formulated entirely in terms of facts about individuals.' However, this raises the question of the nature and viability of the kind of methodological individualism that may be left after the reductive and mechanistic varieties are exorcized.

16 Vanberg's important critique of Hayek's ideas is discussed further in the next chapter.

Chapter 12   *Friedrich Hayek and Spontaneous Order*

1 There is a further distinction in Hayek's (1982, vol. 3, p. 140) work between an order and an organization. The state, for example, is an obvious example of the latter. Viktor Vanberg takes up this distinction in an interesting comparison of the theories of Carl Menger and

John Commons; he thus sees 'some kind of deliberate co-ordination of individual actions' as 'the essential definitional attribute of what is commonly called an organization' (1989, p. 342). However, as argued elsewhere, the spontaneity of many real-world institutions, in particular the market, is often overestimated (Hodgson, 1988, pp. 173–6).

2   In one passage, however, Dawkins accepts the possibility of an autonomous level of cultural evolution. He argues that because a bit of cultural information can 'make copies of itself' (1976, p. 208), through imitation and learning, it is a viable unit of selection in addition to the gene. This seems to undermine the kind of genetic reductionism which is more prominent elsewhere in his writings, and perhaps points to a 'dual inheritance' model of the Boyd and Richerson (1985) kind.

3   Faced with arguments such as this, Wynne-Edwards (1978) subsequently accepted that he had failed to specify an adequate mechanism of group selection. More recently, however, Wynne-Edwards (1986, pp. 316–26) has adopted D. S. Wilson's (1975, 1977, 1980) theoretical justification of the phenomenon, as discussed in the appendix to this chapter.

4   Sober (1985, p. 880) makes the important point, relating to the discussion of 'population thinking' in earlier chapters, that 'group selection hypotheses are examples of population thinking *par excellence.*'

5   See also the interesting discussion by Masahiko Aoki (1990) of the collective nature of employee knowledge in the firm. Since 'learning and communication of employees take place only within the organizational framework, their knowledge, as well as their capacities to communicate with each other are not individually portable' (p. 45).

6   However, as noted above, Boyd and Richerson's individualism does not imply a rejection of group selection. For related quantitative models involving the interaction of genetic and cultural evolution see Cavalli-Sforza and Feldman (1981), Pulliam and Dunford (1980) and Werren and Pulliam (1981).

7   See the discussion of the differences between genetic, computer and human 'information' in chapter 16 below.

8   Robert Sugden (1989, p. 86) writes that 'the market itself is in important respects a spontaneous order' and he considers 'the possibility that the institution of property itself may ultimately be a form of spontaneous order'. But by extending the concept of spontaneous order to these elemental institutions, Sugden is leaving open the question of the nature of the selection process between different spontaneous orders. He does not describe the structural context in which such selection between (say) market and non-market orders takes place. A similar problem arises in a work by Douglass North (1978, p. 970) where he suggests that the United States has adopted political regulation of economic transactions rather than pure markets because of the relative price of these two options. In response, Philip Mirowski (1981, p. 609) points out that this leaves unresolved the issue of 'what structures organize this "meta-market" to allow us to buy more or less market organization'.

9 As Vanberg (1986, p. 99) and M. Prisching (1989) both note, and contrary to many other members of the Austrian School, Carl Menger did not take the suitability of 'organic' institutions such as the market for granted (*Problems*, 1883, see Menger, 1963).

10 For similar and related points see Commons (1934, p. 713), Dosi (1988a), Hodgson (1988, ch. 8), Lowry (1976), Polanyi (1944), Samuels (1966), and even Robbins (1952). It is also striking that modern experimental economists, in simulating a market, have found that they have had also to face the unavoidable problem of setting up its institutional structure. As Vernon Smith (1982, p. 923) writes: 'it is not possible to design a resource allocation experiment without designing an institution in all its detail.'

11 See Hayek (1967, p. 77; 1978, p. 250; 1982, vol. 1, p. 23; 1982, vol. 3, p. 158).

12 Paul makes the even more general point that the survival of liberalism must involve the ditching of all evolutionist baggage. Clearly she would prefer the evolutionism, rather than the liberalism, to be thrown away. However, the understanding on which her hostility to evolutionism is based is defective. For instance, she does not note the arguments by modern evolutionary thinkers (such as Gould, 1978, 1980a, 1989, and Gould and Lewontin, 1979) who reject the idea that what happens to evolve is necessarily superior or just or even fitter than what does not. Her poor knowledge of the development of evolutionary theory is exemplified by her suggestion that 'Under the pressure of Darwinian influences, Spencer came to concede that the "survival of the fittest" could play a role' (Paul, 1988, p. 271). In fact it was Darwin who was persuaded, against his initial judgement, to adopt the 'survival of the fittest' phrase which Spencer had first coined. Nevertheless, while there are several flaws in both her account of evolution and her understanding of Spencer, she is right to point out the tension between the Hayekian concept of a spontaneous order and a specifically Darwinian theory of evolution. In contrast, the allegation of general incompatibility between liberalism and some version of evolutionism remains unproven and unconvincing.

13 See, for instance, Bertalanffy (1952, 1969, 1971), Emery (1981), Laszlo (1972), Miller (1978), Weiss (1969, 1973), Weiss et al. (1971).

14 See Brooks and Wiley (1988), Benseler et al. (1980), Jantsch (1975, 1980), Laszlo (1987), Nicolis and Prigogine (1977), Prigogine (1976, 1980, 1987), Prigogine and Stengers (1984), Salthe (1985), Varela et al. (1974), Wicken (1987), Zeleny (1980, 1981, 1987).

15 The application of the idea of a dissipative structure to socioeconomic systems has been criticized by Peter Gould (1987) with a reply by Peter Allen (1987).

16 See the discussion of Hayek's aversion to Malthus in chapter 4 above.

17 In contrast, John Commons (1950, p. 29) rejected fixed constitutions as reflecting the 'individualistic devices of our founding fathers'. Charles Leathers has made a useful comparison of the theories of Commons and Hayek, noting that:

By interpreting the evolutionary changes in customs as a process of natural selection, Hayek was able to develop his concept of spontaneous orders and, hence, an argument against activist government. By interpreting the same evolutionary process as involving artificial selection guided by human purpose, Commons developed a much more activist view of government as a generally positive form of collective action that creates a workable mutuality which is sustainable even as economic and political conditions change.' (Leathers, 1989, p. 378)

18   For a further discussion of this concept of 'insufficient variety' and the related 'impurity principle' see Hodgson (1984, pp. 108, 238; 1988, pp. 257–8, 262–7, 303–4). The 'insufficient variety' idea was originally developed by Raul Espejo and Nigel Howard (1982).

19   Those who disbelieve are invited to go see it exemplified in the USA: a vast and wonderful country of over nine million square kilometres and around a quarter of a billion inhabitants, with immense natural beauty yet arguably containing less internal cultural or structural variety than in a single major country of Europe. There is talk of the American dream, but it begins to lose its meaning as the immigrant's nightmare of past totalitarianism in Europe fades from the collective memory.

20   Jim Tomlinson (1990, p. 49) points out that even collectivist regimes have been associated with huge increases in population. Yet Hayek uses population growth as his main measure of evolutionary progress. Hayek never attempts to deal with this striking contradiction.

21   See, for instance, Aganbegyan (1988), Hodgson (1984), Nove (1980, 1983).

22   Another definition of group selection is found in a work by Brandon (1982) but this is criticized by Sober (1984a, p. 229n). However, these relatively slight differences need not concern us here because they do not affect the conclusions of the present argument.

23   Subsequently, Maynard Smith (1987a, pp. 130–1) has asserted that 'the argument between Wynne-Edwards and others about "group selection" was ultimately empirical: are populations sufficiently isolated, and free of intragroup selection, to evolve complete group adaptations?' However, see the critique of Maynard Smith by Sober (1987), and the further reply by Maynard Smith (1987b).

Chapter 13   *Optimization and Evolution*

1   On adaptationism see Gould (1980a, 1983, 1989), Gould and Lewontin (1979), Lewontin (1978, 1979, 1980).

2   The evidence relating participatory structures to greater productivity seems to be even stronger than the evidence on a correlation between participation and job satisfaction. See, for example, Blumberg (1968), Espinosa and Zimbalist (1978), Hodgson (1982, 1984), D. C. Jones and Svejnar (1982), Mygind (1987), Stephen (1982). Aoki (1988, 1990) gives theoretical reasons why the Japanese type of participatory firm may be more efficient than strictly hierarchical units.

3 Williamson (1985, pp. 269–70) devotes only a few words to a very partial glimpse at the relevant literature.

4 In the nineteenth century the physicist Joseph Bertrand (1883) discovered that if out-of-equilibrium trading is incorporated into a Walrasian model, then it can lead to indeterminate and path-dependent results that are inconsistent with Walras's general approach. Likewise, in a prescient essay, Nicholas Kaldor (1934) saw the possibility of path dependency in economic models. See also M. S. Farrell (1970), F. M. Fisher (1983), Arthur (1989), Pelikan (1988), Roland (1990).

5 See the many examples discussed in Gould (1980a, 1987, 1989) and Gould and Lewontin (1979).

6 With variations, this idea is proposed in McNeill (1980), Mumford (1934), Nef (1950), M. R. Smith (1985) and J. M. Winter (1975) among others.

7 See, for instance, Arthur (1983, 1988, 1989, 1990), Cowan (1991), David (1985), Farrell and Saloner (1985, 1986), Gould (1987), Haltiwanger and Waldman (1991), Katz and Shapiro (1985, 1986).

8 In a study of Italian cooperatives, S. Gherardi and A. Masiero (1990) argue that the development of a close-knit system of intra-organizational trust relations and networking activities has been crucial to their success.

9 Although such a proposition is a hallmark of the 'dialectical biology' of Richard Levins and Richard Lewontin (1985) it is also now widely accepted by mainstream biologists.

10 For a discussion of the fallacy of composition see Hodgson (1987).

Chapter 14   *Evolution, Indeterminacy and Intention*

1 Note in particular the preceding discussion of this issue in chapters 11 and 12 on Hayek's theory.

2 For a moving account of Kammerer's work and tragic life see Koestler (1971).

3 This is a flaw in Robert Frank's (1988) ingenious attempt to bring the emotions within the compass of both self-interest and rational choice. Frank argues that emotions like love, sympathy and hate can be 'rational' in that they serve to substantiate commitments, and to make them appear credible to others. According to Frank the 'best' strategy may be to follow the emotions, which arise through cultural or genetic evolution, or both. Hence emotions may serve 'rational' ends.

But there is a dilemma in Frank's argument. On the one hand, if emotions dispose us to act in certain ways then we cannot be said to exercise real choice. In contrast, if we do have the choice to resist our emotions then their role in bolstering our commitments is severely undermined. Furthermore, Frank seems unaware that his adherence to a reductionist biology of the Wilson–Trivers–Dawkins type conflicts with any kind of rationality that is bound up with purposefulness and real choice.

Above all, Frank's attempt to incorporate the emotions fails because he is trying to force them into a hedonistic and utilitarian framework, in which there can be no other underlying emotion other than the Benthamite calculus of pleasure and pain.

4   However, Thorp's argument does not entertain the possibility that the firing of the neurons may not be a case of indeterminacy but deterministic chaos. Indeed, chaos theory might put a new perspective on these controversies.

5   As argued in chapter 9, Veblen was more strongly attached to a traditional notion of causality, and it was precisely on the grounds of the minute examination of the supposed sequence of cause and effect that he admired Charles Darwin's work. Veblen was taught by Peirce, but the teacher failed to remove the faith of the pupil in the pervasive nineteenth-century idea of efficient causality, although there are several other Peircean aspects to Veblen's thought.

6   Knight (1933, p. 221) saw reason to contend that ' "mind" may in some inscrutable way originate action,' i.e. as an 'uncaused cause'. For a discussion of Knight on this issue see Lawson (1988). Mirowski (1989a) makes some more general, but controversial, remarks on the impact of quantum theory on economics.

7   The work of Anthony Giddens (1984) in sociology is particularly close to this viewpoint. Note also the case studies by Richard Whittington (1989) of the varied strategic behaviour of firms enduring a common recession, and the remarks about firm discretionary behaviour made by Richard Nelson (1991).

8   However, some recent work by biologists on learning processes goes against the idea of a hermetic division between physiology and the sphere of learning. J. H. Gould and Marler (1987) suggest that some instinctive and genetically inherited routines are necessary for learning to take place, so that the individual may be more able to select the appropriate cues from the multitude of stimuli reaching the brain.

Furthermore, in a major philosophical work, George Lakoff (1987) argues, against Cartesian dualism, that reason has a bodily basis.

9   For relevant critical discussions of this Cartesian view see Capra (1982), Koestler (1967, 1980) and Hodgson (1988), as well as chapter 1 of the present volume.

10 Among others, Marshall (1949) and Wicksteed (1910) have insisted that habits must directly or indirectly emanate from deliberate choice. Likewise, Hirshleifer (1985, p. 61) asserts that habit 'is surely a way of economizing on scarce reasoning ability', as if every phenomenon has to be placed into the Robbinsian conceptual mould. In some cases, neoclassical theorists have tried to model habitual behaviour, particularly in relation to the theory of the consumption function (Alessie and Kapteyn, 1991; Blanciforti and Green, 1983; Muellbauer, 1988; Pollak, 1970; Spinnewijn, 1981; Thaler and Shefrin, 1981; Winston, 1980). These models often include decision-making processes at more than one level. In such models, habitual acts are regulated by

a secondary preference function, but they are also governed by a primary preference function to which habitual preferences gradually adjust through time. While such a two-level approach removes the implication that habits are activated in the same manner as higher-level decisions, low-level choices over habitual acts are still made as if with a full calculation of benefits and costs.

11 While it is possible to admit some autonomy for the physical, biological and social levels, it would be unwarranted to render each as absolute and self-contained. For an interesting discussion of this in the context of Marxian theory see Sebastiano Timpanaro (1975). The social theorists Paul Hirst and Penny Woolley (1982, p. 24) have argued forcefully that social relations should not 'be rigidly differentiated from biological or psychological phenomena'. Note also the statement by the biologist Theodosius Dobzhansky (1955, p. 20): 'Human evolution is wholly intelligible only as an outcome of the interaction of biological and social facts.'

12 This is similar to Georgescu-Roegen's (1971, p. 127) proposition that history is the outcome of two conflicting factors: hysteresis and novelty. See also Donald Campbell's (1965) discussion of 'vicarious selection'.

13 Veblen (1914, p. 31) wrote: 'all instinctive action is teleological. It involves holding to a purpose.' By 'instinct' here he referred in part to 'habits' (ibid., p. 2).

14 David Hull (1988b, pp. 468–74) argues that the assumption of intentional behaviour in humans or animals in no way invalidates the idea that natural selection is operating.

15 The earlier idea of James Baldwin was based on his anti-mechanistic theory of 'organic selection'. He suggests that a deliberately chosen behaviour pattern could influence the evolution of a species. An organism could adapt itself to a new situation, but instead of the adaptation being directly inherited, the species would be given time through the development of appropriate habits during which random variation could produce truly hereditable equivalent genotypes, which would then be favoured by selection. Directed habit is thus seen as the guiding force of evolution, through its supposed ability to sustain a trend of bodily development which is then endorsed by selection.

This is different from Waddington's theory of 'genetic assimilation', because in the latter there is selection within a population for genes in response to the environment, whereas in the Baldwin effect the organism breeds in the environment until such a time as a mutation produces a gene which would produce the appropriate phenotypic modifications. (For discussions see: Bowler, 1983, pp. 81, 131–2; Hardy, 1965, pp. 161–70; Koestler and Smythies, 1969, p. 386; Piaget, 1979, pp. 14–21; Waddington, 1969, 1976.)

16 See also the critique of dualism by Sheila Dow (1990).

17 For further discussion of novelty in regard to technological change see Farmer and Matthews (1991).

Chapter 15   The Problem of Reductionism in Biology and Economics

1 Arguably, notable exceptions are Karl Marx, John Maynard Keynes, John Hobson, and the American institutionalists. For a relevant debate on Keynes see, for example, Winslow (1986, 1989), O'Donnell (1989, pp. 127–36, 177–8) and Davis (1989, 1989–90). On Hobson see Freeden (1990). On Keynes and the institutionalists see Gruchy (1948).

2 Note, for example, the neoclassical analyses of the family by Gary Becker (1976a); of the firm by Alchian and Demsetz (1972) and Oliver Williamson (1975, 1985); and of government by Anthony Downs (1957) and James Buchanan and Gordon Tullock (1962).

3 The crisis in economic theory afflicts heterodox as well as orthodox traditions but for reasons of brevity the other schools of thought are not discussed in detail here.

4 As a result of the dominance of the physicalist view, until quite recently 'there was an almost total neglect of specific biological phenomena in the literature of the philosophy of science' (Mayr, 1985a, p. 45).

5 See, for example, Hull (1976), Maull (1977), Nagel (1961, pp. 428–46), A. Rosenberg (1985), Ruse (1976), Schaffner (1976), Wimsatt (1976). Mani (1991, p. 53) plausibly suggests that because of the strong conservatism of the fundamental biotic structures at the molecular and genetic level, and by contrast the extreme diversity at the species level, 'molecular biology alone cannot provide all the answers to biological evolution.'

6 After attack from Dawkins, the notion of group selection has been refined and defended by a number of authors, particularly Sober (1984a). See Brandon and Burian (1984), Hodgson (1991a) and chapter 12 above for discussions and references.

7 See, in particular, Eldredge (1985a), Gould (1982b).

8 On entropy and evolution see Brooks and Wiley (1988), Brooks et al. (1989), Collier (1986), Coveney and Highfield (1990), Georgescu-Roegen (1971), B. H. Weber et al. (1989). Norman Clark (1991, p. 102) argues that 'there is a *prima facie* case for regarding the evolution of economic systems as an entropic phenomenon but with information rather than energy providing the main propagating role.' Although tantalising, this suggestion must overcome the difficult problem of the definition of 'information' and the distinction between different types of information or knowledge.

9 Recall William Wordsworth's lines in his poem *The Tables Turned*:

> Sweet is the lore which Nature brings;
> Our meddling intellect
> Mishapes the beauteous form of things:–
> We murder to dissect.

10 Notably, however, the self-organizing processes do not need to involve the true equivalent of 'natural selection'.

11 For discussions of autopoietic systems, and in some cases their relevance for socioeconomic systems, see Benseler et al. (1980), Jessop (1990), Luhmann (1986), Maturana (1975), Teubner (1988), Varela (1981), Varela et al. (1974), Zeleny (1980, 1981, 1987).

12 In the final chapter of his bestselling book, Richard Dawkins (1976) admits the possibility of cultural as well as genetic transmission in human societies, with his idea of the 'meme'. He also suggests that cultural evolution may not necessarily involve the maximization of genetic fitness. However, these arguments seem to undermine the kind of genetic reductionism which is much more prominent elsewhere in his writings. Perhaps it is for this reason that he takes the extreme and controversial view that the role of culture in the non-human domain is insignificant, dismissing cases of cultural evolution in animal communities as 'just interesting oddities' (p. 204).

Chapter 16 Bringing Life Back into Economics

1 As yet, the 'old' institutionalists have failed to provide a clear and widely accepted definition of their own school of thought. However, the 'old' institutionalism, of which the present work is a variant, arguably has the following characteristics:

  1 The 'old' institutionalism eschews atomism and reductionism in economic analysis, typically positing holistic or organicist alternatives.

  2 The 'old' institutionalism sees individuals as situated in and moulded by an evolving social culture, so that their preferences and purposes can be in a process of continuous adaptation or change.

  3 Instead of an exclusive focus on individuals as units of analysis, the 'old' institutionalism regards institutions as additional or even alternative analytical units.

  4 Rather than an exclusive concern with equilibrium, the 'old' institutionalism focuses on processes of cumulative causation.

2 Classification must transcend the old dilemma of nominalism versus essentialism. Mary Douglas (1987, p. 397) rightly remarks that 'it is naive to think of the quality of sameness, which characterizes members of a class, as if it were a quality inherent in things or as a power of recognition inherent in the mind.' The latter nominalism implies that the human mind can be treated as unitary and self-contained, the former essentialism implies an atomist ontology of things in themselves.

3 Note the preceding critical discussion of the concept of culture found in Boyd and Richerson (1985) and in the works of Hayek, in chapter 12 above. Note also that Boulding (1981) sees the concept of

'information' as a central organizing principle of his general evolutionary theory, which spans both the biotic and socioeconomic domains. There is, however, no distinction made between genetic information and the kind of information communicated by humans. The argument in this paragraph suggests that Boulding's presentation is undiscriminating and over-simplified.

4   An important set of psychological arguments for the stability of institutions is provided by Ronald Heiner (1983, 1986, 1988, 1989a, 1989b).

5   This ignores the real possibility that some animal species have a culture. If so, their evolution can be incorporated in some kind of 'dual inheritance' model, as developed by Boyd and Richerson (1985) and others.

6   Accordingly, Abernathy (1978) argues that the firm's technology becomes progressively less fluid over time.

7   See also Nelson and Winter (1977, 1982) and Georghiou et al. (1986) on 'technological regimes', Andersen (1991) and Dosi (1982) on 'technological paradigms', Dahmén (1989) on 'development blocks', and Sahal (1981) on 'technological guideposts'. The general idea of 'technological regimes' or 'technological styles' is related to the controversial theory of long waves (C. Freeman, 1983; Tylecote, 1992) and is also related to the work of the French *régulation* school (Boyer and Mistral, 1978).

8   See Lundvall (1988), McKelvey (1991), Nelson (forthcoming).

9   René Thom, the founder of catastrophe theory in mathematical topology, was influenced by Waddington when he extended such ideas to morphogenesis (Thom, 1975). Waddington 'anticipated important parts of Thom's biological thought, and was the first scientist of great stature to acclaim catastrophe theory' (Woodcock and Davis, 1980, p. 21).

10   Note that Keynes, in his (1936, ch. 12) argument concerning 'conventions', does indeed imply that individuals are influenced by aggregate data. Institutionalists, with an even greater emphasis on conventions and norms, would take a similar view.

11   For the modern version of this theory see Eldredge and Gould (1972, 1977) and Gould (1982b). For a discussion of the surrounding controversy in biology see Somit and Peterson (1989). Among the forerunners of this idea were Henri Bergson in *Creative Evolution*, 1907 (see Bergson, 1944, p. 71), writing that 'new species come into being all at once by the simultaneous appearance of several new characters ... Species pass through alternate periods of stability and transformation'. Also Richard Goldschmidt (1940) saw the occasional possibility of macromutations creating 'hopeful monsters'.

12   For the development and discussion of this idea, with econometric tests, see Hodgson (1989a, 1991e).

13   For innovative analyses of the problems of limited resources and economy-environment interactions see Perrings (1987), as well as the classic work of Georgescu-Roegen (1971).

Bibliography

Abernathy, W. (1978) *The Productivity Dilemma* (Baltimore: Johns Hopkins University Press).

Ackoff, R. L. and Emery, F. E. (1972) *On Purposeful Systems* (London: Tavistock).

Adams, J. (ed.) (1980) *Institutional Economics: Essays in Honor of Allan G. Gruchy* (Boston: Martinus Nijhoff).

Adler-Karlsson, G. (1977) 'Bioeconomics: A Coming Subject', in Steppacher et al. (1977), pp. 85–92.

Aganbegyan, A. (1988) *The Challenge: Economics of Perestroika* (London: Hutchinson).

Akerlof, G. A. (1970) 'The Market for "Lemons": Quality Uncertainty and the Market Mechanism', *Quarterly Journal of Economics*, **84**(3), Aug. pp. 488–500. Reprinted in Akerlof (1984).

Akerlof, G. A. (1984) *An Economic Theorist's Book of Tales* (Cambridge: Cambridge University Press).

Akerlof, G. A. (1991) 'Procrastination and Obedience', *American Economic Review (Papers and Proceedings)*, **81**(2), May, pp. 1–19.

Akerlof, G. A. and Yellen, J. L. (1985) 'A Near-Rational Model of the Business Cycle With Wage and Price Inertia', *Quarterly Journal of Economics*, **100**(supplement), pp. 823–38.

Albeda, R., Gunn, C. and Waller, W. (eds) (1987) *Alternatives to Economic Orthodoxy* (Armonk, NY: M. E. Sharpe).

Alchian, A. A. (1950) 'Uncertainty, Evolution and Economic Theory', *Journal of Political Economy*, **58**, June, pp. 211–22.

Alchian, A. A. (1953) 'Comment', *American Economic Review*, **43**(3), Sept., pp. 600–3.

Alchian, A. A. and Demsetz, H. (1972) 'Production, Information Costs, and Economic Organization', *American Economic Review*, **62**(4), Dec., pp. 777–95. Reprinted in Putterman (1986).

Aldrich, H. E. (1979) *Organizations and Environments* (Englewood Cliffs, NJ: Prentice-Hall).

Alessie, R. and Kapteyn, A. (1991) 'Habit Formation, Interdependent Preferences and Demographic Effects in the Almost Ideal Demand System', *Economic Journal*, **101**(3), May, pp. 404–19.

Alexander, R. M. (1982) *Optima for Animals* (London: Edward Arnold).

Alland Jr, A. (1967) *Evolution and Human Behavior* (New York: Natural History Press).

Allee, W. C. (1951) *Cooperation Among Animals: With Human Implications* (New York: Henry Schuman).

Allen, E. et al. (35 authors comprising the Sociobiology Study Group of Science for the People) (1976) 'Sociobiology – Another Biological Determinism', *Bioscience*, **26**(3), pp. 182–6.

Allen, P. M. (1987) 'Comments on the Paper of P. Gould', *European Journal of Operational Research*, **30**(2), June, p. 222.

Allen, P. M. (1988) 'Evolution, Innovation and Economics', in Dosi et al. (1988), pp. 95–119.

Allen, P. M. and Lesser, M. (1991) 'Evolutionary Human Systems: Learning, Ignorance and Subjectivity', in Saviotti and Metcalfe (1991), pp. 160–71.

Allen, P. M. and McGlade, J. M. (1987a) 'Modelling Complex Human Systems: A Fisheries Example', *European Journal of Operational Research*, **30**(2), pp. 147–67.

Allen, P. M. and McGlade, J. M. (1987b) 'Evolutionary Drive: The Effects of Microscopic Diversity, Error-Making and Noise', *Foundations of Physics*, **17**(7), pp. 723–38.

Amariglio, J. (1990) 'Economics as a Postmodernist Discourse', in Samuels (1990), pp. 15–46.

Andersen, E. S. (1991) 'Techno-Economic Paradigms as Typical Interfaces between Producers and Users', *Journal of Evolutionary Economics*, **1**(2), pp. 119–44.

Anderson, P. W., Arrow, K. J. and Pines, D. (eds) (1988) *The Economy as an Evolving Complex System* (Reading, MA: Addison-Wesley).

Ando, A., Fisher, F. M. and Simon, H. A. (1963) *Essays on the Structure of Social Science Models* (Cambridge, MA: MIT Press).

Aoki, M. (1988) *Information, Incentives and Bargaining in the Japanese Economy* (Cambridge: Cambridge University Press).

Aoki, M. (1990) 'The Participatory Generation of Information Rents and the Theory of the Firm', in Aoki et al. (1990), pp. 26–51.

Aoki, M., Gustafsson, B. and Williamson, O. E. (eds) (1990) *The Firm as a Nexus of Treaties* (London: Sage).

Apel, K.-O. (1981) *Charles S. Peirce: From Pragmatism to Pragmaticism* (Amherst, MA: University of Massachusetts Press).

Arcangeli, F., David, P. and Dosi, G. (eds) (1988) *The Diffusion of Innovation* (Oxford: Oxford University Press).

Armstrong, W. E. (1958) 'Utility and the Ordinalist Fallacy', *Review of Economic Studies*, **25**(2), June, pp. 172–81.

Arnold, A. J. and Fristrup, K. (1982) 'The Theory of Evolution by Natural Selection: A Hierarchical Expansion', *Paleobiology*, **8**, pp. 113–29. Reprinted in Brandon and Burian (1984).

Aronson, J. (1984) *A Realist Philosophy of Science* (Basingstoke: Macmillan).

Arrow, K. J. (1962) 'The Economic Implications of Learning by Doing', *Review of Economic Studies*, **29**, pp. 155–73.

Arrow, K. J. (1968) 'Mathematical Models in the Social Sciences', in Brodbeck (1968), pp. 635–67.

Arrow, K. J. (1974) *The Limits of Organization* (New York: Norton).

Arrow, K. J. (1982) 'Risk Perception in Psychology and Economics', *Economic Inquiry*, **20**(1), Jan., pp. 1–9.

Arrow, K. J. (1986) 'Rationality of Self and Others in an Economic System', *Journal of Business*, **59**(4.2), Oct., pp. S385–99. Reprinted in Hogarth and Reder (1987).

Arrow, K. J. (1987) 'Oral History I: An Interview', in G. R. Feiwel (ed.) *Arrow and the Ascent of Modern Economic Theory* (Basingstoke: Macmillan), pp. 191–242.

Arthur, W. B. (1983) 'Competing Technologies and Lock In by Historical Events', International Institute for Applied Systems Analysis, Paper WP–83–90, Laxenburg, Austria. Revised version 1985, Center for Economic Policy Research, Stanford University, Paper 43.

Arthur, W. B. (1988) 'Self-Reinforcing Mechanisms in Economics', in Anderson et al. (1988), pp. 9–31.

Arthur, W. B. (1989) 'Competing Technologies, Increasing Returns, and Lock-in by Historical Events', *Economic Journal*, **99**(1), March, pp. 116–31. Reprinted in Freeman (1990a).

Arthur, W. B. (1990) 'Positive Feedbacks in the Economy', *Scientific American*, **262**(2), Feb., pp. 80–5.

Arthur, W. B. (1991) 'Designing Economic Agents that Act Like Human Agents: A Behavioral Approach to Bounded Rationality', *American Economic Review (Papers and Proceedings)*, **81**(2), May, pp. 353–9.

Arthur, W. B., Ermoliev, Y. M. and Kaniovski, Y. M. (1987) 'Path-Dependent Processes and the Emergence of Macro-Structure', *European Journal of Operational Research*, **30**(2), June, pp. 294–303.

Ashby, W. R. (1956) *An Introduction to Cybernetics* (New York: Wiley).

Asquith, P. D. and Giere, R. N. (eds) (1981) *Philosophy of Science Association 1980*, vol. 2 (East Lansing, MI: Philosophy of Science Association).

Asquith, P. D. and Nickles, T. (eds) (1982) *Philosophy of Science Association 1982*, vol. 1 (East Lansing, MI: Philosophy of Science Association).

Augros, R. and Stanciu, G. (1987) *The New Biology: Discovering the Wisdom in Nature* (Boston: Shambhala).

Augros, R. and Stanciu, G. (1991) 'Competition and the Enculturation of Science', *World Futures*, **31**(2–4), pp. 85–94.

Awan, A. A. (1986) 'Marshallian and Schumpeterian Theories of Economic Evolution: Gradualism versus Punctualism', *Atlantic Economic Journal*, **14**, pp. 37–49.

Axelrod, R. M. (1984) *The Evolution of Cooperation* (New York: Basic Books).

Axelrod, R. M. (1986) 'An Evolutionary Approach to Norms', *American Political Science Review*, **80**(4), Dec., pp. 1095–111.

Axelrod, R. M. and Dion, D. (1988) 'The Further Evolution of Cooperation', *Science*, no. 242, 9th Dec., pp. 1385–90.

Ayala, F. J. (1985) 'Reduction in Biology: A Recent Challenge', in Depew and Weber (1985b), pp. 65–79.

Ayala, F. J. (1988) 'Can "Progress" be Defined as a Biological Concept?', in Nitecki (1988), pp. 75–96.

Ayala, F. J. and Dobzhansky, T. (eds) (1974) *Studies in the Philosophy of Biology* (Berkeley and Los Angeles: University of California Press).

Ayer, A. J. (1954), 'Freedom and Necessity', in A. J. Ayer, *Philosophical Essays* (London: Macmillan).

Ayres, C. E. (1932) *Huxley* (New York: Norton).

Ayres, C. E. (1944) *The Theory of Economic Progress*, 1st edn (Chapel Hill, North Carolina: University of North Carolina Press).

Ayres, C. E. (1958) 'Veblen's Theory of Instincts Reconsidered', in Dowd (1958), pp. 25–37.

Babbage, C. (1846) *On the Economy of Machinery and Manufactures*, (1st edn 1832), 4th edn (London: John Murray).

Bannister, R. C. (1979) *Social Darwinism; Science and Myth in Anglo-American Social Thought* (Philadelphia: Temple University Press).

Baranzini, M. and Scazzieri, R. (eds) (1990) *The Economic Theory of Structure and Change* (Cambridge: Cambridge University Press).

Barber, W. J. (ed.) (1991) *Perspectives in the History of Economic Thought, vol. 6: Themes in Keynesian Criticism and Supplementary Modern Topics* (Aldershot: Edward Elgar).

Barkow, J. H. (1978) 'Culture and Sociobiology', *American Anthropologist*, **80**(2), June, pp. 5–20.

Barkow, J. H. (1989) *Darwin, Sex, and Status: Biological Approaches to Mind and Culture* (Toronto: University of Toronto Press).

Barringer, H. R., Blanksten, G. I. and Mack, R. W. (eds) (1965) *Social Change in Developing Areas: A Reinterpretation of Evolutionary Theory* (Cambridge, MA: Schenkman).

Barry, B. M. (1970) *Sociologists, Economists and Democracy* (London: Collier-Macmillan).

Barry, N. (1979) *Hayek's Social and Economic Philosophy* (London: Macmillan).

Basalla, G. (1989) *The Evolution of Technology* (Cambridge: Cambridge University Press).

Bateman, B. W. (1989) '"Human Logic" and Keynes's Economics: A Comment', *Eastern Economic Journal*, **15**(1), Jan.–Mar., pp. 63–7.

Bateman, B. W. and Davis, J. B. (eds) (1991) *Keynes and Philosophy: Essays on the Origin of Keynes's Thought* (Aldershot: Edward Elgar).

Batten, D., Casti, J. L. and Johansson, B. (eds) (1987) *Economic Evolution and Structural Adjustment* (Berlin: Springer-Verlag).

Baumol, W. J. and Benhabib, J. (1989) 'Chaos, Significance, Mechanism, and Economic Applications', *Journal of Economic Perspectives*, **3**(1), Winter, pp. 77–105.

Baumrin, B. (ed.) (1963) *Philosophy of Science: The Delaware Seminar* (New York: Interscience).

Bay, C. (1958) *The Structure of Freedom* (Stanford: Stanford University Press).

Bechtel, W. (ed.) (1986) *Integrating Scientific Disciplines* (Dordrecht: Martinus-Nijhoff).

Becker, G. S. (1962) 'Irrational Behavior and Economic Theory', *Journal of Political Economy*, **70**(1), pp. 1–13.

Becker, G. S. (1974) 'A Theory of Social Interactions', *Journal of Political Economy*, **82**(6), Nov.–Dec., pp. 1063–93.

Becker, G. S. (1976a) *The Economic Approach to Human Behavior* (Chicago: University of Chicago Press).

Becker, G. S. (1976b) 'Altruism, Egoism, and Genetic Fitness: Economics and Sociobiology', *Journal of Economic Literature*, **14**(2), Dec., pp. 817–26.

Bell, D. and Kristol, I. (eds) (1981) *The Crisis in Economic Theory* (New York: Basic Books).

Bellomy, D. C. (1984) 'Social Darwinism Revisited', *Perspectives in American History*, New Series, **1**, pp. 1–129.

Benedict, R. (1934) *Patterns of Culture* (New York: New American Library).

Benseler, F., Hejl, P. M. and Koeck, W. K. (eds) (1980) *Autopoiesis, Communication and Society* (Frankfurt: Campus).

Berg, M. (1980) *The Machinery Question and the Making of Political Economy, 1815–1848* (Cambridge: Cambridge University Press).

Berg, M. (1987) 'Babbage, Charles', in Eatwell, et al. (1987), vol. 2, pp. 166–7.

Berg, M. (1991) 'On the Origins of Capitalist Hierarchy', in Gustafsson (1991), pp. 173–94.

Bergson, H. (1944) *Creative Evolution*, trans. A. Mitchell from the French edn of 1907 (New York: Random House).

Bernstein, R. (1983) *Beyond Objectivism and Relativism* (Philadelphia: University of Pennsylvania Press).

Bertalanffy, L. von (1952) *Problems of Life: An Evaluation of Modern Biological Thought* (New York: Wiley).

Bertalanffy, L. von (1969) 'Chance or Law', in Koestler and Smythies (1969), pp. 56–84.

Bertalanffy, L. von (1971) *General System Theory: Foundation Development Applications* (London: Allen Lane).

Bertrand, J. (1883) 'Théorie mathématique de la richesse sociale, par L. Walras', *Journal des savants*, pp. 499–508.

Best, M. H. (1982) 'The Political Economy of Socially Irrational Products', *Cambridge Journal of Economics*, **6**(1), Mar., pp. 53–64.

Bhaskar, R. (1975) *A Realist Theory of Science* (Leeds: Leeds Books). 2nd edn 1978 (Brighton: Harvester).

Bhaskar, R. (1979) *The Possibility of Naturalism: A Philosophic Critique of the Contemporary Human Sciences* (Brighton: Harvester).

Bhaskar, R. (1986) *Scientific Realism and Human Emancipation* (London: Verso).

Bhaskar, R. (1991) *Philosophy and the Idea of Freedom* (Oxford: Blackwell).

Bianchi, M. (1990) 'The Unsatisfactoriness of Satisficing: From Bounded Rationality to Innovative Rationality', *Review of Political Economy*, **2**(2), July, pp. 149–67.

Bianchi, M. (forthcoming) 'How to Learn Sociality: True and False Solutions to Mandeville's Problem', *History of Political Economy*.

Biddle, J. E. (1990) 'Purpose and Evolution in Commons's Institutionalism', *History of Political Economy*, **22**(1), Spring, pp. 19–47.

Binger, B. R. and Hoffman, E. (1989) 'Institutional Persistence and Change: The Question of Efficiency', *Journal of Institutional and Theoretical Economics*, **145**(1), Mar., pp. 67–84.

Black, F. (1970) 'Banking and Interest Rates in a World without Money: The Effects of Uncontrolled Banking', *Journal of Bank Research*, **1**, pp. 9–20.

Black, M. (1962) *Models and Metaphors: Studies in Language and Philosophy* (Ithaca: Cornell University Press).

Blanciforti, L. and Green, R. (1983) 'An Almost Ideal System Incorporating Habits: An Analysis of Expenditures on Food and Aggregate Commodity Groups', *Review of Economics and Statistics*, **65**, pp. 511–15.

Blatt, J. M. (1983) 'How Economists Misuse Mathematics', in Eichner (1983), pp. 166–86.

Blaug, M. (1980) *The Methodology of Economics: Or How Economists Explain* (Cambridge: Cambridge University Press).

Blaug, M. (1991) 'Introduction', to M. Blaug (ed.) *Historiography of Economics* (Aldershot: Edward Elgar).

Blum, H. F. (1951) *Time's Arrow and Evolution* (Princeton: Princeton University Press).

Blumberg, P. (1968) *Industrial Democracy: The Sociology of Participation* (London: Constable).

Blute, M. (1979) 'Sociocultural Evolutionism: An Untried Theory', *Behavioral Science Research*, **24**, pp. 46–59.

Boettke, P. (1989) 'Evolution and Economics: Austrians as Institutionalists', *Research in the History of Economic Thought and Methodology*, vol. 6, pp. 73–89.

Bohm, D. (1980) *Wholeness and the Implicate Order* (London: Routledge and Kegan Paul).

Böhm, S. (1989) 'Hayek on Knowledge, Equilibrium and Prices: Context and Impact', *Wirtschaftspolitische Blatter*, **36**(2), pp. 201–13.

Böhm, S. (1990) 'The Austrian Tradition: Schumpeter and Mises', in Hennings and Samuels (1990), pp. 201–41.

Boland, L. A. (1982) *The Foundations of Economic Method* (London: George Allen and Unwin).

Boler, J. F. (1963) *Charles Peirce and Scholastic Realism: A Study of Peirce's Relation to John Duns Scotus* (Seattle: University of Washington Press).

Boulding, K. E. (1970) *Economics as a Science* (New York: McGraw-Hill).

Boulding, K. E. (1981) *Evolutionary Economics* (Beverly Hills, CA: Sage Publications).

Boulding, K. E. (1987) 'The Epistemology of Complex Systems', *European Journal of Operational Research*, **30**(2), June, pp. 110–16.

Boulding, K. E. (1991) 'What is Evolutionary Economics?', *Journal of Evolutionary Economics*, **1**(1), Jan., pp. 9–17.

Bowler, P. J. (1975) 'The Changing Meaning of "Evolution"', *Journal of the History of Ideas*, **36**(1), Jan.–Mar., pp. 95–114.

Bowler, P. J. (1983) *The Eclipse of Darwinism: Anti-Darwinian Evolution Theories in the Decades around 1900* (Baltimore: Johns Hopkins University Press).

Bowler, P. J. (1988) *The Non-Darwinian Revolution: Reinterpreting a Historical Myth* (Baltimore: Johns Hopkins University Press).

Bowler, P. J. (1989a) *Evolution: The History of an Idea* (Berkeley: University of California Press).

Bowler, P. J. (1989b) *The Mendelian Revolution: The Emergence of Hereditarian Concepts in Modern Science and Society* (London: Athlone Press).

Boyd, R. and Richerson, P. J. (1980) 'Sociobiology, Culture and Economic Theory', *Journal of Economic Behavior and Organization*, 1(1), Mar., pp. 97–121.

Boyd, R. and Richerson, P. J. (1985) *Culture and the Evolutionary Process* (Chicago: University of Chicago Press).

Boyer, R. and Mistral, J. (1978) *Accumulation, inflation et crises* (Paris: Universitaire de France).

Brandon, R. N. (1978) 'Adaptation and Evolutionary Theory', *Studies in History and Philosophy of Science*, 9, pp. 181–206. Reprinted in Sober (1984b).

Brandon, R. N. (1981) 'A Structural Description of Evolutionary Theory', in Asquith and Giere (1981), pp. 427–39.

Brandon, R. N. (1982) 'The Levels of Selection', in Asquith and Nickles (1982), pp. 315–22. Reprinted in Brandon and Burian (1984).

Brandon, R. N. and Burian, R. M. (eds) (1984) *Genes, Organisms, Populations: Controversies over the Units of Selection* (Cambridge, MA: MIT Press).

Bray, M. (1982) 'Learning, Estimation and the Stability of Rational Expectations', *Journal of Economic Theory*, 26, pp. 318–39.

Brodbeck, M. (ed.) (1968) *Readings in the Philosophy of the Social Sciences* (New York: Macmillan).

Brooks, D. R. and Wiley, E. O. (1988) *Evolution as Entropy: Toward a Unified Theory of Biology*, 2nd edn (Chicago: University of Chicago Press).

Brooks, D. R., Collier, J., Maurer, B. A., Smith, J. D. H., Wiley, E. O. (1989) 'Entropy and Information in Evolving Biological Systems', *Biology and Philosophy*, 4(4), Oct., pp. 407–32.

Brown, D. (1991) 'An Institutionalist Look at Postmodernism', *Journal of Economic Issues*, 25(4), Dec., pp. 1089–104.

Brown, T. (1981) *The Mechanical Philosophy and Animal Oeconomy* (New York: Arno).

Brown-Collier, E. K. (1985) 'Keynes' View of an Organic Universe: The Implications', *Review of Social Economy*, 43(1), pp. 14–23.

Brown-Collier, E. K. and Bausor, R. (1988) 'The Epistemological Foundations of the *General Theory*', *Scottish Journal of Political Economy*, 35(3), Aug., pp. 227–41.

Buchanan, J. M. (1982) 'The Domain of Subjective Economics: Between Predictive Science and Moral Philosophy', in Kirzner (1982), pp. 7–20.

Buchanan, J. M. (1991) 'Economics in the Post-Socialist Century', *The Economic Journal*, 101(1), Jan., pp. 15–21.

Buchanan, J. M. and Tullock, G. (1962) *The Calculus of Consent* (Ann Arbor: University of Michigan Press).

Buchanan, J. M. and Vanberg, V. J. (1991) 'The Market as a Creative Process', *Economics and Philosophy*, 7(2), Oct., pp. 167–86.

Bunge, M. A. (ed.) (1973) *The Methodological Unity of Science* (Dordrecht: Reidel).

Burkhardt Jr, R. W. (1977) *The Spirit of System: Lamarck and Evolutionary Biology* (Cambridge, MA: Harvard University Press).

Burrow, J. W. (1966) *Evolution and Society: A Study of Victorian Social Theory* (Cambridge: Cambridge University Press).

Bush, P. D. (1981) '"Radical Individualism" vs. Institutionalism, I', *American Journal of Economics and Sociology*, **40**(2), Apr., pp. 139–48.

Bush, P. D. (1986) 'On the Concept of Ceremonial Encapsulation', *Review of Institutional Thought*, **3**, Dec., pp. 25–45.

Bush, P. D. (1989) 'Institutionalist Methodology and Hermeneutics: A Comment on Mirowski', *Journal of Economic Issues*, **23**(4), Dec., pp. 1159–72.

Butler, S. (1877) *Life and Habit* (London: Trubner).

Caldwell, B. J. (ed.) (1984) *Appraisal and Criticism in Economics: A Book of Readings* (Boston: Allen and Unwin).

Camic, C. (1986) 'The Matter of Habit', *American Journal of Sociology*, **91**(5), pp. 1039–87.

Campbell, D. T. (1965) 'Variation and Selective Retention in Sociocultural Evolution', in Barringer et al. (1965), pp. 19–49. Reprinted in *General Systems*, **14**, pp. 69–85.

Campbell, D. T. (1972) 'On the Genetics of Altruism and the Counter-Hedonic Components in Human Culture', *Journal of Social Issues*, **28**, pp. 21–37.

Campbell, D. T. (1974) '"Downward Causation" in Hierarchically Organized Biological Systems', in Ayala and Dobzhansky (1974), pp. 179–86.

Campbell, D. T. (1975) 'On the Conflicts between Biological and Social Evolution and between Psychology and Moral Tradition', *American Psychologist*, **30**, pp. 1103–26.

Campbell, D. T. (1987) 'Blind Variation and Selective Retention as in Other Knowledge Processes', in Radnitzky and Bartley (1987), pp. 91–114.

Campbell, J. H. (1985) 'An Organizational Interpretation of Evolution', in Depew and Weber (1985b), pp. 133–67.

Campbell, L. and Garnett, W. (1882) *The Life of James Clerk Maxwell* (London: Macmillan).

Capek, M. (1961) *The Philosophical Impact of Contemporary Physics* (Princeton, NJ: Van Nostrand).

Caplan, A. L. (ed.) (1978) *The Sociobiology Debate: Readings on Ethical and Scientific Issues* (New York: Harper and Row).

Capra, F. (1975) *The Tao of Physics: An Exploration of the Parallels Between Modern Physics and Eastern Mysticism* (London: Wildwood House).

Capra, F. (1982) *The Turning Point: Science, Society and the Rising Culture* (London: Wildwood House).

Carabelli, A. M. (1985) 'Keynes on Cause, Chance and Probability', in Lawson and Pesaran (1985), pp. 151–80.

Carabelli, A. M. (1988) *On Keynes's Method* (London: Macmillan).

Carabelli, A. M. (1991) 'The Methodology of the Critique of Classical Theory: Keynes on Organic Interdependence', in Bateman and Davis (1991), pp. 104–25.

Carlsson, B. (ed.) (1989) *Industrial Dynamics: Technological Organization and Structural Changes in Industries and Firms* (Boston: Kluwer).

Carneiro, R. L. (1968) 'Spencer, Herbert', in Sills (1968), vol. 15, pp. 121–8.

Casti, J. L. (1991) 'Money is Funny, or Why Finance is Too Complex for Physics', in R. O'Brien (ed.) *Finance and the International Economy: 5* (Oxford: Oxford University Press), pp. 148–61.

Cavalli-Sforza, L. L. and Feldman, M. W. (1981) *Cultural Transmission and Evolution: A Quantitative Approach* (Princeton, NJ: Princeton University Press).

Chalmers, A. F. (1985) *What is This Thing Called Science?* (Milton Keynes: Open University Press).

Chaloupek, G. K. (1990) 'The Austrian Debate on Economic Calculation in a Socialist Economy', *History of Political Economy*, **22**(4), Winter, pp. 659–75.

Chase, R. X. (1985) 'A Theory of Socioeconomic Change: Entropic Processes, Technology, and Evolutionary Development', *Journal of Economic Issues*, **19**(4), Dec., pp. 797–823.

Chasse, J. D. (1984) 'Marshall, the Human Agent and Economic Growth: Wants and Activities Revisited', *History of Political Economy*, **16**(3), Fall, pp. 381–404.

Checkland, S. G. (1975) *Scottish Banking: A History 1695–1793* (Glasgow: Collins).

Chiaromonte, F. and Dosi, G. (1992) 'The Microfoundations of Competitiveness and their Macroeconomic Implications', in Foray and Freeman (1992).

Clark, C. M. A. (1988) 'Natural Law Influences on Adam Smith', *Quaderni di Storia del Economia Politica*, **6**, pp. 59–83.

Clark, C. M. A. (1990) 'Adam Smith and Society as an Evolutionary Process', *Journal of Economic Issues*, **24**(3), Sept., pp. 825–44.

Clark, C. M. A. (1991) 'Naturalism and Economic Theory: The Use of "State of Nature" Explanations in the History of Economic Thought', in Barber (1991), pp. 134–46.

Clark, C. W. (1976) *Mathematical Bioeconomics: The Optimal Use of Renewable Resources* (New York: Wiley).

Clark, C. W. (1987) 'Bioeconomics', in Eatwell, et al. (1987), vol. 1, pp. 245–6.

Clark, N. G. (1988) 'Some New Approaches to Evolutionary Economics', *Journal of Economic Issues*, **22**(2), June, pp. 511–31.

Clark, N. G. (1990) 'Evolution, Complex Systems and Technological Change', *Review of Political Economy*, **2**(1), Mar., pp. 26–42.

Clark, N. G. (1991) 'Organization and Information in the Evolution of Economic Systems', in Saviotti and Metcalfe (1991), pp. 88–107.

Clark, N. G. and Juma, C. (1987) *Long-Run Economics: An Evolutionary Approach to Economic Growth* (London: Pinter).

Clark, N. G. and Juma, C. (1988) 'Evolutionary Theories in Economic Thought', in Dosi et al. (1988), pp. 197–218.

Clark, W. and Munn, R. (eds) (1986) *Sustainable Development of the Biosphere* (Cambridge: Cambridge University Press).

Clutton-Brock, T. H. and Harvey, P. H. (eds) (1978) *Readings in Sociobiology* (Reading: W. H. Freeman).

Coase, R. H. (1937) 'The Nature of the Firm', *Economica*, **4**(4), Nov., pp. 386–405. Reprinted in Putterman (1986).

Cohen, A. (1984) 'Technological Change as Historical Process', *Journal of Economic History*, **44**, pp. 775–99.

Cohen, R. S. and Wartofsky, M. W. (eds) (1965) *Boston Studies in the Philosophy of Science* (New York: Humanities Press).

Cohen, R. S. et al. (eds) (1976) *Philosophy of Science Association 1974*, (Dordrecht: Reidel).

Cohen, W. M. and Levinthal, D. A. (1989) 'Innovation and Learning: The Two Faces of R&D', *Economic Journal*, **99**(3), Sept., pp. 569–96.

Cohn, S. (1990) 'The Political Economy of Nuclear Power (1945–1990): The Rise and Fall of an Official Technology', *Journal of Economic Issues*, **24**(3), Sept., pp. 781–811.

Colander, D. (1990) 'Form and Content in Appraising Recent Economic Developments', *Methodus*, **2**(2), Dec., pp. 16–22.

Coleman, W. and Limoges, C. (eds) (1980) *Studies in the History of Biology*, vol. 4 (Baltimore: Johns Hopkins University Press).

Collard, D., Dimsdale, W. H., Helm, D. R., Gilbert, C. L., Scott, M. F. G. and Sen, A. K. (eds) (1985) *Economic Theory and Hicksian Themes* (Oxford: Oxford University Press).

Collier, J. (1986) 'Entropy and Evolution', *Biology and Philosophy*, **1**(1), Jan., pp. 5–24.

Colonna, M. (1990) 'Hayek on Money and Equilibrium', *Contributions to Political Economy*, **9**, pp. 43–68.

Colp, R. (1974) 'The Contacts between Karl Marx and Charles Darwin', *Journal of the History of Ideas*, **35**(2), Apr.–June, pp. 329–38.

Colp, R. (1982) 'The Myth of the Marx-Darwin Letter', *History of Political Economy*, **14**(4), Winter, pp. 416–82.

Commons, J. R. (1934) *Institutional Economics – Its Place in Political Economy* (New York: Macmillan). Reprinted 1990 with a new introduction by M. Rutherford (New Brunswick: Transaction).

Commons, J. R. (1950) *The Economics of Collective Action* (New York: Macmillan).

Compte, A. (1853) *The Positive Philosophy of Auguste Compte*, 2 vols, transl. Harriet Martineau (London: Chapman).

Congdon, T. (1981) 'Is the Provision of a Sound Currency a Necessary Function of the State?', *National Westminister Bank Quarterly Review*, Aug., pp. 2–21.

Conlisk, J. (1980) 'Costly Optimizers versus Cheap Imitators', *Journal of Economic Behavior and Organization*, **1**(3), Sept., pp. 275–93.

Cook, L. M., Mani, G. S. and Varley, M. E. (1986) 'Postindustrial Melanism in the Peppered Moth', *Science*, no. 231, pp. 611–13.

Cook, L. M., Mani, G. S. and Wynnes, G. (1985) 'Evolution in Reverse: Clean Air and the Peppered Moth', *Biological Journal of the Linnaean Society*, **13**, pp. 179–98.

Coombs, R., Saviotti, P. and Walsh, V. (1987) *Economics and Technological Change* (Basingstoke: Macmillan).

Coombs, R., Saviotti, P. and Walsh, V. (eds) (1992) *Technological Change and Corporate Strategy: Economic and Sociological Perspectives* (London: Academic Press).

Cooper, W. S. (1989) 'How Evolutionary Biology Challenges the Classical Theory of Rational Choice', *Biology and Philosophy*, 4(4), Oct., pp. 457–81.

Copeland, M. A. (1958) 'On the Scope and Method of Economics' in Dowd (1958), pp. 57–75.

Coricelli, F. and Dosi, G. (1988) 'Coordination and Order in Economic Change and the Interpretative Power of Economic Theory', in Dosi et al. (1988), pp. 124–47.

Corning, P. A. (1983) *The Synergism Hypothesis: A Theory of Progressive Evolution* (New York: McGraw-Hill).

Corsi, P. and Weindling, P. J. (1985) 'Darwinism in Germany, France, and Italy', in Kohn (1985), pp. 683–729.

Coveney, P. and Highfield, R. (1990) *The Arrow of Time: A Voyage through Science to Solve Time's Greatest Mystery* (London: W. H. Allen).

Cowan, R. (1991) 'Tortoises and Hares: Choice among Technologies of Unknown Merit', *Economic Journal*, 101(4), July, pp. 801–14.

Crick, F. (1966) *Of Molecules and Men* (Seattle: University of Washington Press).

Crutchfield, J. P., Farmer, J. D. and Huberman, B. A. (1982) 'Fluctuations and Simple Chaotic Dynamics', *Physics Reports*, 92, pp. 45–82.

Crutchfield, J. P., Farmer, J. D., Packard, N. H., Shaw, R. S. (1986) 'Chaos', *Scientific American*, 255(6), Dec., pp. 38–49.

Currie, M. and Steedman, I. (1990) *Wrestling With Time: Problems in Economic Theory* (Manchester: Manchester University Press).

Cvitanovic, P. (ed.) (1984) *Universality in Chaos* (Bristol: Adam Hilger).

Cyert, R. M. and March, J. G. (1963) *A Behavioral Theory of the Firm* (Engelwood Cliffs, NJ: Prentice-Hall).

Czepiel, J. A. (1975) 'Patterns of Interorganizational Communications and the Diffusion of a Major Technological Innovation in a Competitive Industrial Community', *Academy of Management Journal*, 18, pp. 6–24.

Dahmén, E. (1984) 'Schumpeterian Dynamics: Some Methodological Notes', *Journal of Economic Behavior and Organization*, 5(1), Mar., pp. 23–34.

Dahmén, E. (1989) ' "Development Blocks" in Industrial Economics', in Carlsson (1989), pp. 109–21.

Darwin, C. (1859) *The Origin of Species by Means of Natural Selection*, 1st edn (London: Watts).

Darwin, C. (1904) *The Descent of Man*, 2nd edn (New York: Hill).

Dasgupta, P. and Stoneman, P. L. (eds) (1987) *Economic Policy and Technological Performance* (Cambridge: Cambridge University Press).

David, P. A. (1975) *Technical Choice, Innovation, and Economic Growth* (Cambridge: Cambridge University Press).

David, P. A. (1985) 'Clio and the Economics of QWERTY', *American Economic Review (Papers and Proceedings)*, 75(2), May, pp. 332–7. Reprinted in Freeman (1990b).

David, P. A. (1986) 'Understanding the Economics of QWERTY: The Necessity of History', in Parker (1986), pp. 30–49.

David, P. A. (1987) 'Some New Standards for the Economics of Standardization in the Information Age', in Dasgupta and Stoneman (1987), pp. 206–39.

Davidson, D. (1980) *Essays on Action and Events* (Oxford: Oxford University Press).

Davis, J. B. (1989) 'Keynes on Atomism and Organicism', *Economic Journal*, **99**(4), Dec., pp. 1159–72.

Davis, J. B. (1989–90) 'Keynes and Organicism', *Journal of Post Keynesian Economics*, **12**(2), Winter, pp. 308–15.

Dawkins, R. (1976) *The Selfish Gene* (Oxford: Oxford University Press).

Dawkins, R. (1982) *The Extended Phenotype: The Gene as the Unit of Selection* (Oxford: Oxford University Press).

Dawkins, R. (1986) *The Blind Watchmaker* (Harlow: Longman).

Dawkins, R. (1989) *The Selfish Gene*, 2nd edn (Oxford: Oxford University Press).

Dawkins, R. and Ridley, M. (eds) (1986) *Oxford Surveys in Evolutionary Biology*, vol. 2 (Oxford: Oxford University Press).

Day, R. H. (1984) 'Disequilibrium Economic Dynamics: A Post-Schumpeterian Approach', *Journal of Economic Behavior and Organization*, **5**(1), Mar., pp. 57–76. Reprinted in Day and Eliasson (1986).

Day, R. H. (1987a) 'The Evolving Economy', *European Journal of Operational Research*, **30**(2), June, pp. 251–7.

Day, R. H. (1987b) 'The General Theory of Disequilibrium Economics and of Economic Evolution', in Batten et al. (1987), pp. 46–63.

Day, R. H. and Eliasson, G. (eds) (1986) *The Dynamics of Market Economies* (Amsterdam: North-Holland).

Day, R. H. and Groves, T. (eds) (1975) *Adaptive Economic Models* (New York: Academic Press).

De Bresson, C. (1987) 'The Evolutionary Paradigm and the Economics of Technological Change', *Journal of Economic Issues*, **21**(2), June, pp. 751–61.

De Uriarte, B. (1990) 'On the Free Will of Rational Agents in Neoclassical Economics', *Journal of Post Keynesian Economics*, **12**(4), Summer, pp. 605–17.

Debreu, G. (1959) *Theory of Value: An Axiomatic Analysis of General Equilibrium* (New Haven: Yale University Press).

Debreu, G. (1991) 'The Mathematization of Economic Theory', *American Economic Review*, **81**(1), Jan., pp. 1–7.

Degler, C. N. (1990) *In Search of Human Nature: The Decline and Revival of Darwinism in American Social Thought* (Oxford: Oxford University Press).

Depew, D. J. and Weber, B. H. (1985a) 'Innovation and Tradition in Evolutionary Theory: An Interpretive Afterword', in Depew and Weber (1985b), pp. 227–60.

Depew, D. J. and Weber, B. H. (eds) (1985b) *Evolution at the Crossroads: The New Biology and the New Philosophy of Science* (Cambridge, MA: MIT Press).

Desmond, A. (1990) *The Politics of Evolution: Morphology, Medicine and Reform in Radical London* (Chicago: University of Chicago Press).

Desmond, A. and Moore, J. R. (1991) *Darwin* (London: Michael Joseph).

Deutsch, K. W. (1951) 'Mechanism, Organism and Society: Some Models in Natural and Social Science', *Philosophy of Science*, **18**(3), pp. 230–52.

Dewey, J. (1929) *The Quest for Certainty: A Study of the Relation of Knowledge and Action* (New York: Minton, Balch).

Dewey, J. (1938) *Logic: The Theory of Enquiry* (New York: Holt).

Dewey, J. and Tufts, J. (1908) *Ethics* (New York: Henry Holt).

Dobzhansky, T. (1955) *Evolution, Genetics and Man* (London: Wiley).

Dobzhansky, T. (1968) 'On Some Fundamental Concepts of Darwinian Biology', in Dobzhansky et al. (1968), pp. 1–34.

Dobzhansky, T. (1970) *Genetics and the Evolutionary Process* (New York: Columbia University Press).

Dobzhansky, T. (1980) 'The Birth of the Genetic Theory of Evolution in the Soviet Union in the 1920s', in Mayr and Provine (1980), pp. 229–42.

Dobzhansky, T., Hecht, M. K. and Steere, W. C. (eds) (1968) *Evolutionary Biology* (Amsterdam: North Holland).

Dobzhansky, T., Ayala, F. J., Stebbins, G. L. and Valentine, J. W. (1977) *Evolution* (San Francisco: Freeman).

Docherty, J., Graham, E. and Malek, M. (eds) (1991) *Postmodernism in the Social Sciences* (London: Macmillan).

Dopfer, K. (1988) 'Classical Mechanics with an Ethical Dimension: Professor Tinbergen's Economics', *Journal of Economic Issues*, **22**(3), Sept., pp. 675–706.

Dopfer, K. and Raible, K.-F. (eds) (1990) *The Evolution of Economic Systems: Essays in Honour of Ota Sik* (London: Macmillan).

Dorfman, J. (1934) *Thorstein Veblen and his America* (New York: Viking Press).

Dorfman, J. (1958) 'The Source of Veblen's Thought', in Dowd (1958), pp. 1–12.

Dorfman, J. (1964) 'Introductory Note', to 1964 edn of Veblen (1914).

Dorn, J. A. and Schwartz, A. J. (eds) (1987) *The Search for Stable Money* (Chicago: University of Chicago Press).

Dosi, G. (1982), 'Technological Paradigms and Technological Trajectories', *Research Policy*, **11**, pp. 147–62.

Dosi, G. (1984) *Technical Change and Industrial Transformation: The Theory and an Application to the Semiconductor Industry* (London: Macmillan).

Dosi, G. (1988a) 'Institutions and Markets in a Dynamic World', *The Manchester School*, **56**(2), June, pp. 119–46.

Dosi, G. (1988b) 'The Sources, Procedures, and Microeconomic Effects of Innovation', *Journal of Economic Literature*, **26**(3), Sept., pp. 1120–71. Reprinted in Freeman (1990b).

Dosi, G. (1990a) 'Economic Change and its Interpretation, or, Is There a "Schumpeterian Approach"?', in Heertje and Perlman (1990), pp. 335–41.

Dosi, G. (1990b) 'Finance, Innovation and Industrial Change', *Journal of Economic Behavior and Organization*, **13**(3), Sept., pp. 299–319.

Dosi, G. (1991) 'Some Thoughts on the Promises, Challenges and Dangers of an "Evolutionary Perspective" in Economics', *Journal of Evolutionary Economics*, **1**(1), Jan., pp. 1–3.

Dosi, G. and Metcalfe, J. S. (1991) 'On Some Notions of Irreversibility in Economics', in Saviotti and Metcalfe (1991), pp. 133–59.

Dosi, G., Freeman, C., Nelson, R., Silverberg, G. and Soete, L. (eds) (1988) *Technical Change and Economic Theory* (London: Pinter).

Douglas, M. (1970) *Natural Symbols* (London: Barrie and Jenkins).

Douglas, M. (ed.) (1973) *Rules and Meanings* (Harmondsworth: Penguin).

Douglas, M. (1987) *How Institutions Think* (London: Routledge and Kegan Paul).

Dow, G. K. (1987) 'The Function of Authority in Transaction Cost Economics', *Journal of Economic Behavior and Organization*, 8(1), Mar., pp. 13–38.

Dow, S. C. (1985) *Macroeconomic Thought: A Methodological Approach* (Oxford: Blackwell).

Dow, S. C. (1990) 'Beyond Dualism', *Cambridge Journal of Economics*, 14(2), June, pp. 143–57.

Dow, S. C. (1991a) 'Postmodernism in Economics', in Docherty et al. (1991).

Dow, S. C. (1991b) 'Are there any Signs of Postmodernism with Economics?', *Methodus*, 3(1), June, pp. 81–5.

Dowd, D. F. (ed.) (1958) *Thorstein Veblen: A Critical Appraisal* (Ithaca, NY: Cornell University Press).

Dowd, K. (1989) *The State and the Monetary System* (Hemel Hempstead: Philip Allan).

Downie, J. (1955) *The Competitive Process* (London: Duckworth).

Downs, A. (1957) *An Economic Theory of Democracy* (New York: Harper).

Dragan, J. C. and Demetrescu, M. C. (1986) *Entropy and Bioeconomics: The New Paradigm of Nicholas Georgescu-Roegen* (Milan: Nagard).

Dreyfus, H. L. and Dreyfus, S. E. (1986) *Mind Over Machine: The Power of Human Intuition and Expertise in the Era of the Computer* (New York: Free Press).

Drucker, P. F. (1955) *The Practice of Management* (London: Heinemann).

Duesenberry, J. S. (1949) *Income, Saving and the Theory of Consumer Behavior* (Cambridge, MA: Harvard University Press).

Dugger, W. M. (1984) 'Veblen and Kropotkin on Human Evolution', *Journal of Economic Issues*, 18(4), Dec., pp. 971–85.

Dunbar, M. S. (1960) 'The Evolution of Stability in Marine Environments: Natural Selection at the Level of the Ecosystem', *American Naturalist*, 94, pp. 129–36.

Dupré, J. A. (ed.) (1987) *The Latest on the Best: Essays on Evolution and Optimality* (Cambridge, MA: MIT Press).

Durham, W. H. (1990) 'Advances in Evolutionary Theory', *Annual Review of Anthropology*, 19, pp. 187–210.

Durham, W. H. (1991) *Coevolution: Genes, Culture, and Human Diversity* (Stanford: Stanford University Press).

Durkheim, E. and Mauss, M. (1963) *Primitive Classification* (London: Cohen and West).

Dyer, A. W. (1984) 'The Habit of Work: A Theoretical Exploration', *Journal of Economic Issues*, 18(2), June, pp. 557–64.

Dyer, A. W. (1986) 'Veblen on Scientific Creativity', *Journal of Economic Issues*, 20(1), Mar., pp. 21–41.

Dyke, C. (1985) 'Complexity and Closure', in Depew and Weber (1985b), pp. 97–131.

Earl, P. E. (1983) *The Economic Imagination: Towards a Behavioural Analysis of Choice* (Brighton: Wheatsheaf).

Earl, P. E. (ed.) (1988) *Psychological Economics: Development, Tensions, Prospects* (Boston: Kluwer).

Eaton, B. C. (1984) Review of *An Evolutionary Theory of Economic Change* by R. R. Nelson and S. G. Winter, *Canadian Journal of Economics*, 17(4), Nov., pp. 868–71.

Eatwell, J., Milgate, M. and Newman, P. (eds) (1987) *The New Palgrave Dictionary of Economics*, 4 vols (London: Macmillan).

Ebling, F. J. and Stoddart, D. M. (eds) (1978) *Population Control by Social Behaviour* (London: Institute of Biology).

Edgell, S. (1975) 'Thorstein Veblen's Theory of Evolutionary Change', *American Journal of Economics and Sociology*, 34, July, pp. 267–80.

Edgell, S. and Tilman, R. (1989) 'The Intellectual Antecedents of Thorstein Veblen: A Reappraisal', *Journal of Economic Issues*, 23(4), Dec., pp. 1003–26.

Edwards, K. J. R. (1977) *Evolution in Modern Biology* (London: Edward Arnold).

Eff, E. A. (1989) 'History of Thought as Ceremonial Genealogy: The Neglected Influence of Herbert Spencer on Thorstein Veblen', *Journal of Economic Issues*, 23(3), Sept., pp. 689–716.

Eggertsson, T. (1990) *Economic Behavior and Institutions* (Cambridge: Cambridge University Press).

Ehrlich, P. R. (1989) 'The Limits to Substitution: Meta-Resource Depletion and a New Economic-Ecological Paradigm', *Ecological Economics*, 1(1), Feb., pp. 9–16.

Eichner, A. S. (ed.) (1983) *Why Economics is Not Yet a Science* (Armonk, NY: Sharpe).

Eiseley, L. (1958) *Darwin's Century* (New York: Doubleday).

Eisenstadt, S. N. (1968) 'Social Evolution', in Sills (1968), vol. 5, pp. 228–34.

Eldredge, N. (1985a) *Unfinished Synthesis: Biological Hierarchies and Modern Evolutionary Thought* (Oxford: Oxford University Press).

Eldredge, N. (1985b) *Time Frames: Rethinking of Darwinian Evolution and the Theory of Punctuated Equilibria* (New York: Simon and Schuster).

Eldredge, N. and Gould, S. J. (1972) 'Punctuated Equilibria: An Alternative to Phyletic Gradualism', in Schopf (1972), pp. 82–115.

Eldredge, N. and Gould, S. J. (1977) 'Punctuated Equilibria: The Tempo and Mode of Evolution Reconsidered', *Paleobiology*, 3, pp. 115–51.

Eliasson, G. (1984) 'Microheterogeneity of Firms and the Stability of Industrial Growth', *Journal of Economic Behavior and Organization*, 5(3–4), Sept.–Dec., pp. 249–74.

Eliasson, G. (1991) 'Deregulation, Innovative Entry and Structural Diversity as a Source of Stable and Rapid Economic Growth', *Journal of Evolutionary Economics*, 1(1), Jan., pp. 49–63.

Elliot, J. E. (1980) 'Marx and Schumpeter on Capitalism's Creative Destruction: A Comparative Restatement', *Quarterly Journal of Economics*, 95(1), Aug., pp. 45–68. Reprinted in Freeman (1990b).

Elliot, J. E. (1983) 'Schumpeter and the Theory of Capitalist Economic Development', *Journal of Economic Behavior and Organization*, 4(4), Dec., pp. 277–308.

Elliot, J. E. (1985) 'Schumpeter's Theory of Economic Development and Social Change: Exposition and Assessment', *International Journal of Social Economics*, 12(6–7), pp. 6–33.

Elster, J. (1982), 'Marxism, Functionalism and Game Theory', *Theory and Society*, 11(4), pp. 453–82.

Elster, J. (1983) *Explaining Technical Change* (Cambridge: Cambridge University Press).

Elster, J. (1985) *Making Sense of Marx* (Cambridge: Cambridge University Press).

Emery, F. E. (ed.) (1981) *Systems Thinking*, 2 vols (Harmondsworth: Penguin).

Engels, F. (1964) *Dialectics of Nature* (London: Lawrence and Wishart).

Enke, S. (1951) 'On Maximizing Profits: A Distinction between Chamberlin and Robinson', *American Economic Review*, 41(3), Sept., pp. 566–78.

Enke, S. (1953) 'Comment', *American Economic Review*, 43(3), Sept., p. 603.

Espejo, R. and Howard, N. (1982) 'What is Requisite Variety? A Re-examination of the Foundation of Beer's Method', *University of Aston Management Centre Working Paper no. 242*, Sept.

Espinosa, J. G. and Zimbalist, A. S. (1978) *Economic Democracy: Workers' Participation in Chilean Industry, 1970–1973* (New York: Academic Press).

Everett, M. J. and Minkler, A. P. (1991) 'Evolution and Organizational Choice in 19th Century Britain', Department of Economics, University of Connecticut, mimeo.

Faber, M. and Proops, J. L. R. (1990) *Evolution, Time, Production and the Environment* (Berlin: Springer).

Faber, M. and Proops, J. L. R. (1991) 'Evolution in Biology, Physics and Economics: A Conceptual Analysis', in Saviotti and Metcalfe (1991), pp. 58–87.

Faber, M., Proops, J. L. R., Ruth, M. and Michaelis, P. (1990) 'Economy–Environment Interactions in the Long-Run: A Neo-Austrian Approach', *Ecological Economics*, 2(1), Apr., pp. 27–55.

Fama, E. (1980) 'Banking in the Theory of Finance', *Journal of Monetary Economics*, 6(1), Jan., pp. 39–57.

Fao, B. (1982) 'Marshall Revisited in the Age of DNA', *Journal of Post Keynesian Economics*, 5(1), Fall, pp. 3–16.

Farkas, G. and England, P. (eds) (1988) *Industries, Firms, and Jobs: Sociological and Economic Approaches* (New York: Plenum Press).

Farmer, M. K. and Matthews, M. L. (1991) 'Cultural Difference and Subjective Rationality: Where Sociology Connects with the Economics of Technological Choice', in Hodgson and Screpanti (1991), pp. 103–16.

Farrell, J. R. and Saloner, G. (1985) 'Standardization, Compatibility and Innovation', *Rand Journal of Economics*, 16(1), Spring, pp. 70–83.

Farrell, J. R. and Saloner, G. (1986) 'Installed Base and Compatability: Innovation, Product Preannouncements, and Predation', *American Economic Review*, 76(5), Dec., pp. 940–55.

Farrell, M. J. (1970) 'Some Elementary Selection Processes in Economics', *Review of Economic Studies*, **37**, pp. 305–19.

Fay, M. A. (1978) 'Did Marx Offer to Dedicate *Capital* to Darwin?', *Journal of the History of Ideas*, **39**(1), Jan.–Mar., pp. 133–46.

Feigl, H., Scriven, M. and Maxwell, G. (eds) (1968) *Concepts, Theories, and the Mind–Body Problem, Minnesota Studies in the Philosophy of Science*, vol. 2 (Minneapolis: University of Minnesota Press).

Ferguson, A. (1767) *An Essay on the History of Civil Society*. Reprinted 1986 (Edinburgh: Edinburgh University Press).

Feyerabend, P. K. (1965) 'Reply to Criticism', in Cohen and Wartofsky (1965), pp. 223–61.

Field, A. J. (1979) 'On the Explanation of Rules Using Rational Choice Models', *Journal of Economic Issues*, **13**(1), Mar., pp. 49–72.

Field, A. J. (1981) 'The Problem with Neoclassical Institutional Economics: A Critique with Special Reference to the North/Thomas Model of Pre-1500 Europe', *Explorations in Economic History*, **18**(2), Apr., pp. 174–98.

Field, A. J. (1984) 'Microeconomics, Norms and Rationality', *Economic Development and Cultural Change*, **32**(4), July, pp. 683–711.

Fisher, F. M. (1983) *Disequilibrium Foundations of Equilibrium Economics* (Cambridge: Cambridge University Press).

Fisher, R. A. (1930) *The Genetic Theory of Natural Selection* (Oxford: Clarendon Press).

Fitzgerald, J. J. (1966) *Peirce's Theory of Signs as Foundation for Pragmatism* (The Hague: Mouton).

Fitzgibbons, A. (1988) *Keynes's Vision: A New Political Economy* (Oxford: Clarendon Press).

Flew, A. G. N. (1959) 'The Structure of Darwinism', *New Biology*, **28**, pp. 25–44.

Flew, A. G. N. (1963) 'The Structure of Malthus' Population Theory', in Baumrin (1963), vol. 1, pp. 283–307.

Flew, A. G. N. (1966) 'The Conception of Evolution: A Comment', *Philosophy*, **41**, pp. 70–5.

Flew, A. G. N. (1978) *A Rational Animal, and Other Philosophical Essays on the Nature of Man* (Oxford: Clarendon Press).

Foley, V. (1973) 'An Origin of the Tableau Oeconomique', *History of Political Economy*, **5**(2), Summer, pp. 121–50.

Foley, V. (1976) *The Social Physics of Adam Smith* (West Lafayette: Purdue University Press).

Fonseca, E. G. da (1991) *Beliefs in Action: Economic Philosophy and Social Change* (Cambridge: Cambridge University Press).

Foray, D. and Freeman, C. (eds) (1992) *Technology and Competitiveness* (London: Pinter).

Forbes, D. (1976) 'Sceptical Whiggism, Commerce and Liberty', in Skinner and Wilson (1976), pp. 194–201.

Forrester, J. W. (1987) 'Nonlinearity in High-Order Models of Social Systems', *European Journal of Operational Research*, **30**(2), June, pp. 104–9.

Forsyth, M. (1988) 'Hayek's Bizarre Liberalism: A Critique', *Political Studies*, **36**(2), June, pp. 235–50.

Foss, N. J. (1991) 'The Suppression of Evolutionary Approaches in Economics: The Case of Marshall and Monopolistic Competition', *Methodus*, 3(2), Dec., pp. 65–72.

Foster, J. (1987) *Evolutionary Macroeconomics* (London: George Allen and Unwin).

Foster, J. (1991) 'Econometric Methodology in an Environment of Evolutionary Change', in Saviotti and Metcalfe (1991), pp. 239–55.

Foster, R. (1986) *Innovation* (London: Macmillan).

Francis, A., Turk, J. and Willman, P. (eds) (1983) *Power, Efficiency and Institutions: A Critical Appraisal of the 'Markets and Hierarchies' Paradigm* (London: Heinemann).

Frank, R. H. (1988) *Passions Within Reason: The Strategic Role of the Emotions* (New York: Norton).

Frankel, S. H. (1977) *Money: Two Philosophies; The Conflict of Trust and Authority* (Oxford: Blackwell).

Freeden, M. (ed.) (1990) *Reappraising J. A. Hobson: Humanism and Welfare* (London: Unwin Hyman).

Freeman, C. (ed.) (1983) *Long Waves in the World Economy* (London: Butterworth).

Freeman, C. (1990a) 'Schumpeter's *Business Cycles* Revisited', in Heertje and Perlman (1990), pp. 17–38.

Freeman, C. (ed.) (1990b) *The Economics of Innovation* (Aldershot: Edward Elgar).

Freeman, C. and Perez, C. (1988) 'Structural Crises of Adjustment, Business Cycles and Investment Behaviour', in Dosi et al. (1988), pp. 38–66.

Freeman, C. and Soete, L. L. G. (eds) (1987) *Technical Change and Full Employment* (Oxford: Blackwell).

Freeman, C. and Soete, L. L. G. (eds) (1990) *New Explorations in the Economics of Technical Change* (London: Pinter).

Freeman, C., Clark, J. and Soete, L. L. G. (1982) *Unemployment and Technical Innovation: A Study of Long Waves in Economic Development* (London: Pinter).

Freeman, D. (1974) 'The Evolutionary Theories of Charles Darwin and Herbert Spencer', *Current Anthropology*, **15**, pp. 211–37.

Friedman, M. (1953) 'The Methodology of Positive Economics', in M. Friedman, *Essays in Positive Economics* (Chicago: University of Chicago Press), pp. 3–43. Reprinted in Caldwell (1984).

Friedman, M. (1991) 'Old Wine in New Bottles', *Economic Journal*, **101**(1), Jan., pp. 33–40.

Futia, C. A. (1980) 'Schumpeterian Competition', *Quarterly Journal of Economics*, **94**(2), June, pp. 677–95.

Futuyma, D. J. (1979) *Evolutionary Biology* (Sunderland, MA: Sinauer).

Gallagher, C. (1987) 'The Body versus the Social Body in the Works of Thomas Malthus and Henry Mayhew', in Gallagher and Laqueur (1987), pp. 83–106.

Gallagher, C. and Laqueur, T. (eds) (1987) *The Making of the Modern Body: Sexuality and Society in the Nineteenth Century* (Berkeley: University of California Press).

Garranta, V. (1973) 'Marx and Darwin', *New Left Review*, no. 82, Nov.–Dec., pp. 60–82.

Gee, J. M. A. (1983) 'Marshall's Views an "Short Period" Value Formation', *History of Political Economy*, 15(2), Summer, pp. 181–205.

George, H. (1879) *Progress and Poverty: An Inquiry into the Cause of Industrial Depression and Increase of Want with Increase of Wealth* (London: Kegan Paul).

Georgescu-Roegen, N. (1954) 'Choice, Expectations and Measurability', *Quarterly Journal of Economics*, 68(4), Nov., pp. 503–34.

Georgescu-Roegen, N. (1966) *Analytical Economics* (Cambridge, MA: Harvard University Press).

Georgescu-Roegen, N. (1971) *The Entropy Law and the Economic Process* (Cambridge, MA: Harvard University Press).

Georgescu-Roegen, N. (1976) *Energy and Economic Myths* (London: Pergamon).

Georgescu-Roegen, N. (1978) 'Mechanistic Dogma in Economics', *British Review of Economic Issues*, no. 2, May, pp. 1–10.

Georgescu-Roegen, N. (1979) 'Methods in Economic Science', *Journal of Economic Issues*, 13(2), June, pp. 317–28.

Georgescu-Roegen, N. (1990) 'Production Process and Dynamic Economics', in Baranzini and Scazzieri (1990), pp. 198–226.

Georghiou, L., Metcalfe, J. S., Evans, J., Ray, T. and Gibbons, M. (1986) *Post-Innovation Performance* (Basingstoke: Macmillan).

Gerard, R. W., Kluckhohn, C. and Rapoport, A. (1956) 'Biological and Cultural Evolution: Some Analogies and Explorations', *Behavioral Science*, 1, pp. 6–42.

Geyer, F. and Zouwen, J. van der (eds) (1986) *Sociocybernetic Paradoxes* (London: Sage).

Gherardi, S. and Masiero, A. (1990) 'Solidarity as a Networking Skill and a Trust Relation: Its Implications for Cooperative Development', *Economic and Industrial Democracy*, 11(4), Nov., pp. 553–74.

Ghiselin, M. T. (1969) *The Triumph of the Darwinian Method* (Berkeley: University of California Press).

Ghiselin, M. T. (1974) *The Economy of Nature and the Evolution of Sex* (Berkeley: University of California Press).

Ghiselin, M. T. (1975) 'The Rationale of Pangenesis', *Genetics*, 79(supplement), pp. 47–57.

Giddens, A. (1979) *Central Problems in Social Theory* (Berkeley and Los Angeles: University of California Press).

Giddens, A. (1984) *The Constitution of Society: Outline of the Theory of Structuration* (Cambridge: Polity Press).

Gilpin, M. E. (1975) *Group Selection in Predator–Prey Communities* (Princeton: Princeton University Press).

Glasner, D. (1989) *Free Banking and Monetary Reform* (Cambridge: Cambridge University Press).

Glass, B., Temkin, O. and Strauss Jr, W. L. (eds) (1959) *Forerunners of Darwin, 1745–1859* (Baltimore: Johns Hopkins University Press).

Gleick, J. (1988) *Chaos: Making a New Science* (London: Heinemann).

Goldberg, M. A. (1975) 'On the Inefficiency of Being Efficient', *Environment and Planning*, **7**(8), pp. 921–39.

Goldschmidt, R. B. (1940) *The Material Basis of Evolution* (New Haven: Yale University Press).

Gomulka, S. (1990) *The Theory of Technological Change and Economic Growth* (London: Routledge).

Goodenough, W. H. (1981) *Culture, Language and Society* (Menlo Park, CA: Benjamin/Cummings).

Goodhart, C. A. E. (1987) 'Why do Banks Need a Central Bank?', *Oxford Economic Papers*, **39**(1), Jan., pp. 75–89.

Goodwin, R. M. (1986) 'The Economy as an Evolutionary Pulsator', *Journal of Economic Behavior and Organization*, **7**(4), Dec., pp. 341–9.

Goodwin, R. M. (1990) 'Walras and Schumpeter: The Vision Reaffirmed', in Heertje and Perlman (1990), pp. 39–49.

Gordon, S. (1989) 'Darwin and Political Economy: The Connection Reconsidered', *Journal of the History of Biology*, **22**(3), Fall, pp. 437–59.

Gordon, S. (1991) *The History and Philosophy of Social Science* (London: Routledge).

Gordon, W. and Adams, J. (1989) *Economics as a Social Science: An Evolutionary Approach* (Riverdale, MD: Riverdale).

Gould, J. L. and Marler, P. (1987) 'Learning by Instinct', *Scientific American*, **256**(1), pp. 74–85.

Gould, P. (1987) 'A Critique of Dissipative Structures in the Human Realm', *European Journal of Operational Research*, **30**(2), June, pp. 211–21.

Gould, S. J. (1977) *Ontogeny and Phylogeny* (Cambridge, MA: Harvard University Press).

Gould, S. J. (1978) *Ever Since Darwin: Reflections in Natural History* (London: Burnett Books).

Gould, S. J. (1980a) *The Panda's Thumb: More Reflections in Natural History* (New York: Norton).

Gould, S. J. (1980b) 'G. G. Simpson, Paleontology, and the Modern Synthesis', in Mayr and Provine (1980), pp. 153–72.

Gould, S. J. (1980c) 'Is a New and General Theory of Evolution Emerging?', *Paleobiology*, **6**(1), pp. 119–30.

Gould, S. J. (1982a) 'Darwinism and the Expansion of Evolutionary Theory', *Science*, no. 216, Apr., pp. 380–7.

Gould, S. J. (1982b) 'The Meaning of Punctuated Equilibrium and its Role in Validating a Hierarchical Approach to Macroevolution', in Milkman (1982), pp. 83–104.

Gould, S. J. (1983) *Hen's Teeth and Horse's Toes: Further Reflections in Natural History* (New York: Norton).

Gould, S. J. (1985) 'The Paradox of the First Tier: An Agenda for Paleobiology', *Paleobiology*, **11**, pp. 2–12.

Gould, S. J. (1987) 'The Panda's Thumb of Technology', *Natural History*, **1**, Jan., pp. 14–23.

Gould, S. J. (1988) 'On Replacing the Idea of Progress with an Operational Notion of Directionality', in Nitecki (1988), pp. 319–38.

Gould, S. J. (1989) *Wonderful Life: The Burgess Shale and the Nature of History* (London: Hutchinson Radius).

Gould, S. J. and Lewontin, R. C. (1979) 'The Spandrels of San Marco and the Panglossian Paradigm: A Critique of the Adaptationist Programme', *Proceedings of the Royal Society of London*, series B, **205**, pp. 581–98. Reprinted in Sober (1984b).

Gould, S. J. and Vrba, E. S. (1982) 'Exaption – A Missing Term in the Science of Form', *Paleobiology*, **8**, pp. 4–15.

Gowdy, J. M. (1985) 'Evolutionary Theory and Economic Theory: Some Methodological Issues', *Review of Social Economy*, **43**, pp. 316–24.

Gowdy, J. M. (1987) 'Bio-economics: Social Economy versus the Chicago School', *International Journal of Social Economics*, **14**(1), pp. 32–42.

Gowdy, J. M. (1991) 'New Controversies in Evolutionary Biology: Lessons for Economists', *Methodus*, **3**(1), June, pp. 86–9.

Grandmont, J.-M. (ed.) (1987) *Nonlinear Economic Dynamics* (New York: Academic Press). Reprint of October 1986 issue of the *Journal of Economic Theory*.

Granovetter, M. (1979) 'The Idea of "Advancement" in Theories of Social Evolution and Development', *American Journal of Sociology*, **85**(3), Nov., pp. 489–515.

Granovetter, M. and Soong, R. (1986) 'Threshold Models of Interpersonal Effects in Consumer Demand', *Journal of Economic Behavior and Organization*, **7**(2), June, pp. 83–99.

Gray, J. (1984) *Hayek on Liberty* (Oxford: Blackwell).

Greenfield, R. L. and Yeager, L. B. (1983) 'A Laissez-Faire Approach to Monetary Stability', *Journal of Money, Credit and Banking*, **15**(3), Aug., pp. 302–15.

Greenfield, R. L. and Yeager, L. B. (1986) 'Competitive Payments Systems: Comment', *American Economic Review*, **76**(5), Dec., pp. 848–9.

Greenlee, D. (1975) *Peirce's Concept of Sign* (The Hague: Mouton).

Griffiths, P. E. (ed.) (1991) *Trees of Life: Essays in the Philosophy of Biology* (Boston: Kluwer).

Groenewegen, P. (1990) 'Marshall and Hegel', *Economie Appliquée*, **43**(1), pp. 63–84.

Grubel, H. G. and Boland, L. A. (1986) 'On the Efficient Use of Mathematics in Economics: Some Theory, Facts and Results of an Opinion Survey', *Kyklos*, **39**, fasc. 3, pp. 419–42.

Gruber, H. E. (1974) *Darwin on Man: A Psychological Study of Scientific Creativity, together with Darwin's Early and Unpublished Notebooks*, transcribed and annotated by P. H. Barret (New York: E. P. Dutton).

Gruber, H. E. (1985) 'Going to the Limit: Toward the Construction of Darwin's Theory (1832–1839)', in Kohn (1985), pp. 9–34.

Gruchy, A. G. (1947) *Modern Economic Thought: The American Contribution* (New York: Prentice Hall).

Gruchy, A. G. (1948) 'The Philosophical Basis of the New Keynesian Economics', *Ethics*, **58**(4), July, pp. 235–44.

Gruchy, A. G. (1949) 'J. M. Keynes' Concept of Economic Science', *Southern Economic Journal*, **15**(1), Jan., pp. 249–66.

Gruchy, A. G. (1987) *The Reconstruction of Economics: An Analysis of the Fundamentals of Institutional Economics* (New York: Greenwood Press).

Grunberg, E. (1978) '"Complexity" and "Open Systems" in Economic Discourse', *Journal of Economic Issues*, **12**(3), Sept., pp. 541–60.

Guha, A. (1981) *An Evolutionary View of Economic Growth* (Oxford: Clarendon Press).

Gustafsson, B. (ed.) (1991) *Power and Economic Institutions: Reinterpretations in Economic History* (Aldershot: Edward Elgar).

Haavelmo, T. (1954) *A Study in the Theory of Economic Evolution* (Amsterdam: North-Holland).

Hahn, F. H. (1980) 'General Equilibrium Theory', *The Public Interest*, special issue, pp. 123–38. Reprinted in Bell and Kristol (1981) and in Hahn (1984).

Hahn, F. H. (1984) *Equilibrium and Macroeconomics* (Oxford: Blackwell).

Hahn, F. H. (1991) 'The Next Hundred Years', *Economic Journal*, **101**(1), Jan., pp. 47–50.

Hahn, F. H. and Hollis, M. (eds) (1979) *Philosophy and Economic Theory* (Oxford: Oxford University Press).

Haines, V. A. (1988) 'Is Spencer's Theory an Evolutionary Theory?', *American Journal of Sociology*, **93**(5), Mar., pp. 1200–23.

Hall, P. (ed.) (1986) *Technology, Innovation and Economic Policy* (Oxford: Philip Allen).

Hallpike, C. R. (1986) *The Principles of Social Evolution* (Oxford: Clarendon Press).

Haltiwanger, J. and Waldman, M. (1985) 'Rational Expectations and the Limits of Rationality: An Analysis of Heterogeneity', *American Economic Review*, **75**(3), Sept., pp. 159–73.

Haltiwanger, J. and Waldman, M. (1991) 'Responders versus Non-Responders: A New Perspective on Heterogeneity', *Economic Journal*, **101**(5), Sept., pp. 1085–102.

Hamilton, D. B. (1991) *Evolutionary Economics: A Study in Change in Economic Thought*, 3rd edn (New Brunswick, NJ: Transaction).

Hamilton, W. H. (1919) 'The Institutional Approach to Economic Theory', *American Economic Review*, **9** (supplement), pp. 309–18. Reprinted in Albeda et al. (1987).

Hamilton, W. H. (1963) 'Institution', in E. R. A. Seligman and A. Johnson (eds) *Encyclopaedia of the Social Sciences*, vol. 7, pp. 84–9.

Hamouda, O. F. and Smithin, John N. (1988) 'Some Remarks on "Uncertainty and Economic Analysis"', *Economic Journal*, **98**(1), Mar., pp. 159–64.

Hamowy, R. (1987) *The Scottish Enlightenment and the Theory of Spontaneous Order* (Carbondale, Il: Southern Illinois Press).

Hannan, M. T. and Freeman, J. (1977) 'The Population Ecology of Organizations', *American Journal of Sociology*, **82**(4), pp. 929–64.

Hannan, M. T. and Freeman, J. (1989) *Organizational Ecology* (Cambridge, MA: Harvard University Press).

Hanson, N. R. (1958) *Patterns of Discovery: An Enquiry into the Conceptual Foundations of Science* (Cambridge: Cambridge University Press).

Hansson, I. and Stuart, C. (1990) 'Malthusian Selection of Preferences', *American Economic Review*, **80**(2), June, pp. 529–44.

Hanusch, H. (ed.) (1988) *Evolutionary Economics: Applications of Schumpeter's Ideas* (Cambridge: Cambridge University Press).

Harcourt, G. C. (1979) 'The Social Science Imperialists', *Politics*, **14**(2), Nov., pp. 243–51. Reprinted in G. C. Harcourt (1982) *The Social Science Imperialists* (London: Routledge and Kegan Paul).

Hardin, G. (1960) *Nature and Man's Fate* (London: Jonathan Cape).

Hardy, A. C. (1965) *The Living Stream: A Restatement of Evolution Theory and its Relation to the Spirit of Man* (London: Collins).

Harman, G. (1965) 'The Inference to the Best Explanation', *Philosophical Review*, **74**(1), pp. 88–95.

Harman, G. (1973) *Thought* (Princeton: Princeton University Press).

Harman, W. W. (1991) 'The Emerging "Wholeness" Worldview and its Probable Impact on Cooperation', *World Futures*, **31**(2–4), pp. 73–83.

Harner, M. (1977) 'The Ecological Basis for Aztec Sacrifice', *American Ethnologist*, **4**, pp. 117–35.

Harré, R. (1986) *Varieties of Realism* (Oxford: Blackwell).

Harris, A. L. (1934) 'Economic Evolution: Dialectical and Darwinian', *Journal of Political Economy*, **42**(1), Feb., pp. 34–79.

Harris, C. A. (1987) 'Gresham's Law', in Eatwell et al. (1987), vol. 2, p. 565.

Harris, M. (1968) *The Rise of Anthropological Theory: A History of Theories of Culture* (New York: Crowell).

Harris, M. (1971) *Culture, Man and Nature* (New York: Crowell).

Hartz, L. (1955) *The Liberal Tradition in America: An Interpretation of American Political Thought since the Revolution* (New York: Harcourt, Brace, World).

Hausman, D. (ed.) (1984) *The Philosophy of Economics* (Cambridge: Cambridge University Press).

Hayek, F. A. (1931) *Prices and Production* (London: Routledge and Kegan Paul).

Hayek, F. A. (1933), 'The Trend of Economic Thinking', *Economica*, **1**(2), May, pp. 121–37. Reprinted in Hayek (1991a).

Hayek, F. A. (ed.) (1935) *Collectivist Economic Planning* (London: Routledge and Kegan Paul).

Hayek, F. A. (1948) *Individualism and Economic Order* (Chicago: University of Chicago Press).

Hayek, F. A. (1952) *The Counter-Revolution of Science: Studies on the Abuse of Reason*, 1st edn. (Glencoe, II: Free Press).

Hayek, F. A. (1967) *Studies in Philosophy, Politics and Economics* (London: Routledge and Kegan Paul).

Hayek, F. A. (1976) *The Denationalisation of Money* (London: Institute of Economic Affairs). Revised and reprinted in Hayek (1991b).

Hayek, F. A. (1978) *New Studies in Philosophy, Politics, Economics and the History of Ideas* (London: Routledge and Kegan Paul).

Hayek, F. A. (1982) *Law, Legislation and Liberty*, 3-volume combined edn (London: Routledge and Kegan Paul).

Hayek, F. A. (1988) *The Fatal Conceit: The Errors of Socialism*, vol. 1 of *Collected Works of F. A. Hayek* (London: Routledge).

Hayek, F. A. (1991a) *The Trend of Economic Thinking: Essays on Political*

Economists and Economic History, vol. 3 of *Collected Works of F. A. Hayek* (London: Routledge).

Hayek, F. A. (1991b) *Economic Freedom* (Oxford: Blackwell).

Heertje, A. (1977) *Economics and Technical Change* (London: Weidenfeld and Nicholson).

Heertje, A. (1987) 'Schumpeter, Joseph Alois', in Eatwell et al. (1987), vol. 4, pp. 263–6.

Heertje, A. (1988) 'Schumpeter and Technical Change', in Hanusch (1988), pp. 71–89.

Heertje, A. and Perlman, M. (eds) (1990) *Evolving Technology and Market Structure: Studies in Schumpeterian Economics* (Ann Arbor: University of Michigan Press).

Heiner, R. A. (1983) 'The Origin of Predictable Behavior', *American Economic Review*, **73**(4), Dec., pp. 560–95.

Heiner, R. A. (1986) 'Uncertainty, Signal-Detection Experiments, and Modeling Behavior', in Langlois (1986), pp. 59–115.

Heiner, R. A. (1988) 'Imperfect Decisions and Routinized Production: Implications for Evolutionary Modeling and Inertial Technical Change', in Dosi et al. (1988), pp. 148–69.

Heiner, R. A. (1989a) 'Imperfect Choice and Self-Stabilizing Rules', *Economics and Philosophy*, **5**(1), Apr., pp. 19–32.

Heiner, R. A. (1989b) 'The Origin of Predictable Dynamic Behavior', *Journal of Economic Behavior and Organization*, **12**(3), Sept., pp. 233–57.

Hennings, K. and Samuels, W. J. (eds) (1990) *Neoclassical Economic Theory, 1870 to 1930* (Boston: Kluwer).

Hennis, W. (1988) *Max Weber, Essays in Reconstruction* (London: George Allen and Unwin).

Herbert, S. (1971) 'Darwin, Malthus, and Selection', *Journal of the History of Biology*, **4**(1), Spring, pp. 209–17.

Herbert, S. (1977) 'The Place of Man in the Development of Darwin's Theory of Transmutation', *Journal of the History of Biology*, **11**, Fall, pp. 155–227.

Hesse, M. B. (1966) *Models and Analogies in Science* (Notre Dame: University of Notre Dame Press).

Hesse, M. B. (1980) *Revolutions and Reconstructions in the Philosophy of Science* (Brighton: Harvester Press).

Hey, J. D. (ed.) (1989) *Current Issues in Microeconomics* (Basingstoke: Macmillan).

Heyer, P. (1982) *Nature, Human Nature, and Society: Marx, Darwin, Biology and the Human Sciences* (Westport, CT: Greenwood Press).

Hill, F. G. (1958) 'Veblen and Marx', in Dowd (1958), pp. 129–49.

Hill, J. (1978) 'The Origin of Sociocultural Evolution', *Journal of Social and Biological Structures*, **1**, 377–86.

Himmelfarb, G. (1959) *Darwin and the Darwinian Revolution* (London: Chatto and Windus).

Himmelstrand, U. (ed.) (1992) *Interfaces in Economic and Social Analysis* (London: Routledge).

Hindess, B. (1989) *Political Choice and Social Structure* (Aldershot: Edward Elgar).

Hippel, E. von (1987) 'Cooperation Between Rivals: Informal Know-How Trading', *Research Policy*, **16**, pp. 291–302.

Hippel, E. von (1988) *The Sources of Innovation* (Oxford: Oxford University Press).

Hirschman, A. O. (1976) 'On Hegel, Imperialism, and Structural Stagnation', *Journal of Development Economics*, 3(1), Mar., pp. 1–8. Reprinted in Hirschman (1981).

Hirschman, A. O. (1977) *The Passions and the Interests: Political Arguments for Capitalism Before Its Triumph* (Princeton: Princeton University Press).

Hirschman, A. O. (1981) *Essays in Trespassing: Economics to Politics and Beyond* (Cambridge: Cambridge University Press).

Hirschman, A. O. (1982) 'Rival Interpretations of Market Society: Civilizing, Destructive, or Feeble?', *Journal of Economic Literature*, 20(4), pp. 1463–84. Reprinted in Hirschman (1986).

Hirschman, A. O. (1985) 'Against Parsimony: Three Ways of Complicating Some Categories of Economic Discourse', *Economics and Philosophy*, 1(1), Mar., pp. 7–21.

Hirschman, A. O. (1986) *Rival Views of Market Society and Other Essays* (New York: Viking).

Hirshleifer, J. (1977) 'Economics from a Biological Viewpoint', *Journal of Law and Economics*, 20(1), Apr., pp. 1–52.

Hirshleifer, J. (1978) 'Natural Economy versus Political Economy', *Journal of Social and Biological Structures*, 1, pp. 319–37.

Hirshleifer, J. (1982) 'Evolutionary Models in Economics and Law: Cooperation versus Conflict Strategies', in R. O. Zerbe Jr and P. H. Rubin (eds) *Research in Law and Economics*, 4, pp. 1–60.

Hirshleifer, J. (1985) 'The Expanding Domain of Economics', *American Economic Review*, 75(6), Dec., pp. 53–68.

Hirshleifer, J. (1987a) 'On the Emotions as Guarantors of Threats and Promises', in Dupré (1987), pp. 307–26.

Hirshleifer, J. (1987b) *Economic Behavior in Adversity* (Chicago: University of Chicago Press).

Hirst, P. Q. (1976) *Social Evolution and Sociological Categories* (London: Allen and Unwin).

Hirst, P. Q. and Woolley, P. (1982) *Social Relations and Human Attributes* (London: Tavistock).

Hobson, J. A. (1914) *Work and Wealth* (London: Macmillan).

Hobson, J. A. (1926) *The Evolution of Modern Capitalism: A Study of Machine Production*, revised edn (London: Walter Scott; New York: Charles Scribner's).

Hobson, J. A. (1929) *Wealth and Life: A Study in Values* (London: Macmillan).

Hobson, J. A. (1936) *Veblen* (London: Chapman and Hall).

Hodge, M. J. S. (1985) 'Darwin as a Lifelong Generation Theorist', in Kohn (1985), pp. 207–43.

Hodge, M. J. S. and Kohn, D. (1985) 'The Immediate Origins of Natural Selection', in Kohn (1985), pp. 185–206.

Hodgson, G. M. (1982) 'Theoretical and Policy Implications of Variable Productivity', *Cambridge Journal of Economics*, 6(3), Sept., pp. 213–29. Reprinted in Hodgson (1991b).

Hodgson, G. M. (1984) *The Democratic Economy: A New Look at Planning, Markets and Power* (Harmondsworth: Penguin).

Hodgson, G. M. (1987) 'Economics and Systems Theory', *Journal of Economic Studies*, **14**(4), Dec., pp. 65–86. Reprinted in Hodgson (1991b).

Hodgson, G. M. (1988) *Economics and Institutions: A Manifesto for a Modern Institutional Economics* (Cambridge: Polity Press; Philadelphia: University of Pennsylvania Press).

Hodgson, G. M. (1989a) 'Institutional Rigidities and Economic Growth', *Cambridge Journal of Economics*, **13**(1), Mar., pp. 79–101. Reprinted in Lawson et al. (1989) and Hodgson (1991b).

Hodgson, G. M. (1989b) 'Institutional Economic Theory: The Old versus the New', *Review of Political Economy*, **1**(3), Nov., pp. 249–69. Reprinted in Hodgson (1991b).

Hodgson, G. M. (1989c) 'Post-Keynesianism and Institutionalism: The Missing Link', in Pheby (1989), pp. 94–123. Reprinted in Hodgson (1991b).

Hodgson, G. M. (1991a) 'Hayek's Theory of Cultural Evolution: An Evaluation in the Light of Vanberg's Critique', *Economics and Philosophy*, **7**(1), Apr., pp. 67–82.

Hodgson, G. M. (1991b) *After Marx and Sraffa* (Basingstoke: Macmillan).

Hodgson, G. M. (1991c) 'Economic Evolution: Intervention Contra Pangloss', *Journal of Economic Issues*, **25**(2), June, pp. 519–33.

Hodgson, G. M. (1991d) 'Evolution and Intention in Economic Theory', in Saviotti and Metcalfe (1991), pp. 108–32.

Hodgson, G. M. (1991e) 'Socio-political Disruption and Economic Development', in Hodgson and Screpanti (1991), pp. 153–71.

Hodgson, G. M. (1993) 'Institutional Economics: Surveying the "Old" and the "New"', *Metroeconomica*, **44**(1), pp. 1–28.

Hodgson, G. M. and Screpanti, E. (eds) (1991) *Rethinking Economics: Markets, Technology and Economic Evolution* (Aldershot: Edward Elgar).

Hofstadter, R. (1959) *Social Darwinism in American Thought*, revised edn (New York: Braziller).

Hogarth, R. M. and Reder, M. W. (eds) (1987) *Rational Choice: The Contrast between Economics and Psychology* (Chicago, University of Chicago Press).

Holling, C. S. (1986) 'The Resilience of Terrestrial Ecosystems', in Clark and Munn (1986).

Holling, C. S. (1987) 'Simplifying the Complex: The Paradigms of Ecological Function and Structure', *European Journal of Operational Research*, **30**(2), June, pp. 139–46.

Holton, G. (1974) *Thematic Origins of Scientific Thought: Kepler to Einstein*, 2nd edn (Cambridge, MA: Harvard University Press).

Holton, R. J. (1985) *The Transition from Feudalism to Capitalism* (London: Routledge and Kegan Paul).

Hoover, K. D. (1988) 'Money, Prices and Finance in the New Monetary Economics', *Oxford Economic Papers*, **40**, pp. 150–67.

Horvat, B. (1975) 'An Institutional Model of a Self-Managed Socialist Economy' in B. Horvat, M. Markovic and R. Supek (eds) *Self-Governing Socialism* (White Plains, NY: International Arts and Sciences Press).

Houthakker, H. S. (1956) 'Economics and Biology: Specialization and Speciation', *Kyklos*, **9**, pp. 180–200.

Hrebeniak, L. G. and Joyce, W. F. (1985) 'Organisational Adaptation: Strategic Choice and Environmental Determinism', *Administrative Science Quarterly*, **30**(3), Sept., pp. 336–49.

Hull, D. L. (1973) *Darwin and his Critics: The Reception of Darwin's Theory of Evolution by the Scientific Community* (Cambridge, MA: Harvard University Press).

Hull, D. L. (1974) *Philosophy of Biological Science* (Englewood Cliffs: Prentice Hall).

Hull, D. L. (1976) 'Informal Aspects of Theory Reduction', in Cohen et al. (1976), pp. 653–70. Reprinted in Sober (1984b).

Hull, D. L. (1980) 'Individuality and Selection', *Annual Review of Ecology and Systematics*, **11**, pp. 311–32.

Hull, D. L. (1981) 'Units of Evolution: A Metaphysical Essay', in Jensen and Harré (1981), pp. 23–44). Reprinted in Brandon and Burian (1984).

Hull, D. L. (1985) 'Darwinism as a Historical Entity: A Historiographic Proposal', in Kohn (1985), pp. 773–812.

Hull, D. L. (1988a) 'A Mechanism and its Metaphysics: An Evolutionary Account of the Social and Conceptual Development of Science', *Biology and Philosophy*, **3**(2), Apr., pp. 123–55.

Hull, D. L. (1988b) *Science as Progress* (Chicago: University of Chicago Press).

Hull, D. L. (1988c) 'Progress in Ideas of Progress', in Nitecki (1988), pp. 27–48.

Hume, D. (1886) *Philosophical Works*, 4 vols, ed. T. H. Green and T. H. Grose (London: Longmans, Green).

Humphrey, T. M. (1990) 'Cumulative Process Models from Thornton to Wicksell', in Moggridge (1990), pp. 40–52.

Hyman, A. (1982) *Charles Babbage, Pioneer of the Computer* (Oxford: Oxford University Press).

Hymans, S. H. (ed.) (1982) *Economics and the World Around It* (Ann Arbor, MI: University of Michigan Press).

Ingrao, B. and Israel, G. (1985) 'General Economic Equilibrium: A History of Ineffectual Paradigmatic Shifts', *Fundamenta Scientiae*, **6**, pp. 1–45, 89–125.

Ingrao, B. and Israel, G. (1990) *The Invisible Hand: Economic Equilibrium in the History of Science* (Cambridge, MA: MIT Press).

Iwai, K. (1984a) 'Schumpeterian Dynamics, Part I: An Evolutionary Model of Innovation and Imitation', *Journal of Economic Behavior and Organization*, **5**(2), June, pp. 159–90.

Iwai, K. (1984b) 'Schumpeterian Dynamics, Part II: Technological Progress, Firm Growth and "Economic Selection"', *Journal of Economic Behavior and Organization*, **5**(3–4), Sept.–Dec., pp. 321–51.

Jacobs, J. (1986) 'Teleology and Reductionism in Biology', *Biology and Philosophy*, **1**(3), July, pp. 389–99.

James, W. (1880) 'Great Men, Great Thoughts, and the Environment', *Atlantic Monthly*, **46**, pp. 441–59. Reprinted in James (1897).

James, W. (1897) *The Will to Believe* (New York: Harcourt, Brace).

Jantsch, E. (1975) *Design for Evolution: Self-Organization and Planning in the Life of Human Systems* (New York: Braziller).

Jantsch, E. (1980) *The Self-Organizing Universe: Scientific and Human Implications of the Emerging Paradigm of Evolution* (Oxford and New York: Pergamon Press).

Jantsch, E. and Waddington, C. H. (eds) (1976) *Evolution and Consciousness: Human Systems in Transition* (Reading, MA: Addison-Wesley).

Jensen, H. E. (1990) 'Are There Institutionalist Signposts in the Economics of Alfred Marshall?', *Journal of Economic Issues*, **24**(2), June, pp. 405–13.

Jensen, M. C. and Meckling, W. H. (1979) 'Rights and Production Functions: An Application to Labor-Managed Firms and Codetermination', *Journal of Business*, **52**(4), Oct., pp. 469–506.

Jensen, U. L. and Harré, R. (1981) *The Philosophy of Evolution* (Brighton: Harvester Press).

Jessop, J. A. (1990) *State Theory: Putting the Capitalist State in its Place* (Oxford: Blackwell).

Jimenez Montano, M. A. and Ebeling, W. (1980) 'A Stochastic Evolutionary Model of Technological Change', *Collective Phenomena*, **3**, pp. 107–14.

Jones, D. C. and Svejnar, J. (eds) (1982) *Participatory and Self-Managed Firms* (Lexington, MA: Heath).

Jones, G. (1980) *Social Darwinism and English Thought* (Brighton: Harvester; Atlantic Highlands, NJ: Humanities Press).

Jones, L. B. (1986) 'The Institutionalists and "On the Origin of Species": A Case of Mistaken Identity', *Southern Economic Journal*, **52**(4), Apr., pp. 1043–55.

Jones, L. B. (1989) 'Schumpeter versus Darwin: In re Malthus', *Southern Economic Journal*, **56**(2), Oct., pp. 410–22.

Jones, R. A. (1976) 'The Origin and Development of Media of Exchange', *Journal of Political Economy*, **84**(4), part 1, Aug., pp. 757–75.

Kaldor, N. (1934) 'A Classificatory Note on the Determinateness of Equilibrium', *Review of Economic Studies*, **1**(1), Feb., pp. 122–36. Reprinted in Targetti and Thirlwall (1989).

Kaldor, N. (1972) 'The Irrelevance of Equilibrium Economics', *Economic Journal*, **82**(4), Dec., pp. 1237–55. Reprinted in Kaldor (1978) and Targetti and Thirlwall (1989).

Kaldor, N. (1978) *Further Essays on Economic Theory*, vol. 5 of *Collected Economic Essays* (London: Duckworth).

Kalmbach, P. and Kurz, H. D. (1986) 'Economic Dynamics and Innovation: Ricardo, Marx and Schumpeter on Technological Change and Unemployment', in Wagener and Drukker (1986), pp. 71–92.

Kamien, M. I. and Schwartz, N. L. (1981) *Market Structure and Innovation* (Cambridge: Cambridge University Press).

Kammerer, P. (1924) Article in *New York Evening Post*, 23 February, quoted in Koestler (1971), p. 133.

Kanth, R. K. (1991) 'Economic Theory and Realism: Outlines of a Reconstruction', *Methodus*, **3**(2), Dec., pp. 37–45.

Kaplan, D. and Manners, R. A. (1972) *Culture Theory* (Englewood Cliffs, NJ: Prentice Hall).

Kapp, K. W. (1976) 'The Nature and Significance of Institutional Economics', *Kyklos*, **29**, pp. 209–32. Reprinted in Samuels (1988), vol. 1.

Kassiola, J. (1990) 'Can Marxism Help Biology?', *Philosophy of the Social Sciences*, **20**(4), Dec., pp. 467–82.

Katz, M. L. and Shapiro, C. (1985) 'Network Externalities, Competition, and Compatibility', *American Economic Review*, **75**(3), June, pp. 424–40.

Katz, M. L. and Shapiro, C. (1986) 'Technology Adoption in the Presence of Network Externalities', *Journal of Political Economy*, **94**(4), Aug., pp. 822–41.

Katzner, D. W. (1991) 'Aggregation and the Analysis of Markets', *Review of Political Economy*, **3**(2), April, pp. 220–31.

Kauffman, S. A. (1969) 'Metabolic Stability and Epigenesis in Randomly Constructed Genetic Nets', *Journal of Theoretical Biology*, **22**, pp. 437–67.

Kauffman, S. A. (1985) 'Self-organization, Selective Adaptation and its Limits: A New Pattern of Inference in Evolution and Development', in Depew and Weber (1985b), pp. 169–207.

Kauffman, S. A. (1986) 'A Framework to Think about Evolving Genetic Regulatory Systems', in Bechtel (1986), pp. 165–84.

Kauffman, S. A. (1988) 'The Evolution of Economic Webs', in Anderson et al. (1988), pp. 125–46.

Kauffman, S. A. (1991) 'Antichaos and Adaptation', *Scientific American*, **265**(2), Aug., pp. 64–70.

Kay, N. M. (1982) *The Evolving Firm: Strategy and Structure in Industrial Organization* (Basingstoke: Macmillan).

Keesing, R. (1974) 'Theories of Culture', *Annual Review of Anthropology*, **3**, pp. 73–9.

Keizer, W. (1989) 'Recent Reinterpretations of the Socialist Calculation Debate', *Journal of Economic Studies*, **16**(2), pp. 63–83.

Kell, D. B. and Welch, G. R. (1991) 'No Turning Back', *Times Higher Education Supplement*, 9 August, p. 15.

Kelsey, D. (1988) 'The Economics of Chaos or the Chaos of Economics', *Oxford Economic Papers*, **40**(1), Mar., pp. 1–31.

Keynes, J. M. (1924) 'Alfred Marshall', *Economic Journal*, **34**(3), Sept., pp. 311–72. Reprinted in Pigou (1925) and Keynes (1933).

Keynes, J. M. (1931) *Essays in Persuasion* (London: Macmillan).

Keynes, J. M. (1933) *Essays in Biography* (London: Macmillan).

Keynes, J. M. (1936) *The General Theory of Employment, Interest and Money* (London: Macmillan).

Keynes, J. M. (1937) 'The General Theory of Employment', *Quarterly Journal of Economics*, **51**, pp. 209–23. Reprinted in Keynes (1973).

Keynes, J. M. (1973) *The Collected Writings of John Maynard Keynes*, vol. 14: *The General Theory and After: Defence and Development* (London: Macmillan).

Khalil, E. L. (1990a) 'Entropy Law and Exhaustion of Natural Resources: Is Nicholas Georgescu-Roegen's Paradigm Defensible?', *Ecological Economics*, **2**(2), June, pp. 163–78.

Khalil, E. L. (1990b) 'Natural Complex vs. Natural System', *Journal of Social and Biological Structures*, **13**(1), pp. 11–31.

Khalil, E. L. (1991) 'Entropy and Nicholas Georgescu-Roegen's Paradigm: A Reply', *Ecological Economics*, **3**(1), Apr., pp. 161–3.

Khalil, E. L. (1992) 'Neoclassical Economics and Neo-Darwinism', in Nell et al. (1992), pp. 22–72.

Kimura, M. (1983) *The Neutral Theory of Molecular Evolution* (Cambridge: Cambridge University Press).

Kindleberger, C. P. (1983) 'Standards, as Public, Collective and Private Goods', *Kyklos*, **36**, pp. 377–96.

King, J. E. (1988) *Economic Exiles* (London: Macmillan).

King, R. G. (1983) 'On the Economics of Private Money', *Journal of Monetary Economics*, **12**(1), Jan., pp. 127–58.

Kirman, A. P. (1989) 'The Intrinsic Limits of Modern Economic Theory: The Emperor Has No Clothes', *Economic Journal (Conference Papers)*, **99**, pp. 126–39.

Kirzner, I. M. (ed.) (1982) *Method, Process and Austrian Economics* (Lexington, MA: Heath).

Kitcher, P. (1985) *Vaulting Ambition: Sociobiology and the Quest for Human Nature* (Cambridge, MA: MIT Press).

Kitcher, P. (1987) 'Why Not the Best?', in Dupré (1987), pp. 77–102.

Knapp, G. F. (1924) *The State Theory of Money* (London: Macmillan).

Knight, F. H. (1933) *Risk, Uncertainty and Profit*, 2nd edn (London: London School of Economics).

Knight, F. H. (1935a) 'Intellectual Confusion on Morals and Economics', *International Journal of Ethics*, **45**(1), Jan., pp. 200–20.

Knight, F. H. (1935b) *The Ethics of Competition and Other Essays* (New York: Harper).

Koestler, A. (1964) *The Act of Creation* (London: Hutchinson).

Koestler, A. (1967) *The Ghost in the Machine* (London: Hutchinson).

Koestler, A. (1971) *The Case of the Midwife Toad* (London: Hutchinson).

Koestler, A. (1978) *Janus – A Summing Up* (London: Hutchinson).

Koestler, A. (1980) *Bricks to Babel* (London: Hutchinson).

Koestler, A. and Smythies, J. R. (eds) (1969) *Beyond Reductionism: New Perspectives in the Life Sciences* (London: Hutchinson).

Kohn, D. (1980) 'Theories to Work By: Rejected Theories, Reproduction, and Darwin's Path to Natural Selection', in Coleman and Limoges (1980), pp. 67–170.

Kohn, D. (ed.) (1985) *The Darwinian Heritage* (Princeton: Princeton University Press).

Koopmans, T. C. (1957) *Three Essays on the State of Economic Science* (New York: McGraw Hill).

Koot, G. M. (1987) *English Historical Economics 1870–1926: The Rise of Economic History and Neomercantilism* (Cambridge: Cambridge University Press).

Kornai, J. (1971) *Anti-Equilibrium: On Economic Systems Theory and the Tasks of Research* (Amsterdam: North-Holland).

Kornai, J. (1983) 'The Health of Nations: Reflections on the Analogy between the Medical Science and Economics', *Kyklos*, **36**, fasc. 2, pp. 191–212.

Kottler, M. J. (1985) 'Charles Darwin and Alfred Russell Wallace: Two Decades of Debate over Natural Selection', in Kohn (1985), pp. 367–432.

Kroeber, A. L. (1948) *Anthropology* (New York: Harcourt Brace Jovanovich).

Kropotkin, P. A. (1972) *Mutual Aid: A Factor of Evolution* (1st edn published 1902) (London: Allen Lane).

Krupp, S. R. (ed.) (1966) *Essays in Methodology* (Englewood Cliffs, NJ: Prentice Hall).

Kuhn, T. S. (1970) *The Structure of Scientific Revolutions*, 2nd edn (Chicago: University of Chicago Press).

Kukathas, C. (1989) *Hayek and Modern Liberalism* (Oxford: Clarendon Press).

Kuran, T. (1987) 'Preference Falsification, Policy Continuity, and Collective Conservatism', *Economic Journal*, 97(3), Sept., pp. 642–65.

Kuran, T. (1988) 'The Tenacious Past: Theories of Personal and Collective Conservatism', *Journal of Economic Behavior and Organization*, 10(2), June, pp. 143–71.

La Vergata, A. (1985) 'Images of Darwin: A Historiographic Overview', in Kohn (1985), pp. 901–72.

Lachmann, L. M. (1969) 'Methodological Individualism and the Market Economy', in Streissler (1969), pp. 89–103. Reprinted in Lachmann (1977).

Lachmann, L. M. (1977) *Capital, Expectations and the Market Process*, edited with an introduction by W. E. Grinder (Kansas City: Sheed Andrews and McMeel).

Lakatos, I. (1970) 'Falsification and the Methodology of Scientific Research Programmes', in Lakatos and Musgrave (1970), pp. 91–195.

Lakatos, I. and Musgrave, A. (eds) (1970) *Criticism and the Growth of Knowledge* (Cambridge: Cambridge University Press).

Lakoff, G. (1987) *Women, Fire and Other Dangerous Things: What Categories Reveal About the Mind* (Chicago: Chicago University Press).

Lakoff, G. and Johnson, M. (1980) *Metaphors We Live By* (Chicago: Chicago University Press).

Lamarck, J. B. de (1963) *Zoological Philosophy: An Exposition with Regard to the Natural History of Animals*, trans. H. Elliot from the 1st French edn of 1809 (New York: Hafner).

Langlois, R. N. (ed.) (1986) *Economics as a Process: Essays in the New Institutional Economics* (Cambridge: Cambridge University Press).

Langlois, R. N. (1988) 'Economic Change and the Boundaries of the Firm', *Journal of Institutional and Theoretical Economics*, 144(3), Sept., pp. 635–57.

Langlois, R. N. (1989) 'What Was Wrong with the Old Institutional Economics (and What is Still Wrong with the New)?', *Review of Political Economy*, 1(3), Nov., pp. 270–98.

Laszlo, E. (1972) *Introduction to Systems Philosophy: Toward a New Paradigm of Contemporary Thought* (New York: Harper and Row).

Laszlo, E. (1987) *Evolution: The Grand Synthesis* (Boston, MA: New Science Library – Shambhala).

Laudan, L. (1977) *Progress and its Problems: Towards a Theory of Scientific Growth* (London: Routledge and Kegan Paul).

Lavoie, D. (1985) *Rivalry and Central Planning: The Socialist Calculation Debate Reconsidered* (Cambridge: Cambridge University Press).

Lavoie, D. (ed.) (1991) *Economics and Hermeneutics* (London: Routledge).

Lavoie, D., Baetjer, H. and Tulloh, W. (1990) 'High-Tech Hayekians: Some Possible Research Topics in the Economics of Computation', *Market Process*, **8**(1), Spring, pp. 120–48.

Lavoie, M. (1992) 'Towards a New Research Programme for Post-Keynesianism and Neo-Ricardianism', *Review of Political Economy*, **4**(1), Jan., pp. 37–78.

Lawson, A. (1985) 'Uncertainty and Economic Analysis', *Economic Journal*, **95**(4), Dec., pp. 909–27.

Lawson, A. (1987) 'The Relative/Absolute Nature of Knowledge and Economic Analysis', *Economic Journal*, **97**(4), Dec., pp. 951–70.

Lawson, A. (1988) 'Probability and Uncertainty in Economic Analysis', *Journal of Post Keynesian Economics*, **11**(1), Fall, pp. 38–65.

Lawson, A. (1989) 'Abstraction, Tendencies and Stylised Facts: A Realist Approach to Economic Analysis', *Cambridge Journal of Economics*, **13**(1), Mar., pp. 59–78. Reprinted in Lawson et al. (1989).

Lawson, A. (1990) 'Realism, Closed Systems and Expectations', University of Cambridge, mimeo.

Lawson, A. and Pesaran, H. (eds) (1985) *Keynes' Economics: Methodological Issues* (London: Croom Helm).

Lawson, A., Palma, J. G. and Sender, J. (eds) (1989) *Kaldor's Political Economy* (London: Academic Press).

Leathers, C. G. (1989) 'New and Old Institutionalists on Legal Rules: Hayek and Commons', *Review of Political Economy*, **1**(3), Nov., pp. 361–80.

Leathers, C. G. (1990) 'Veblen and Hayek on Instincts and Evolution', *Journal of the History of Economic Thought*, **12**(2), June, pp. 162–78.

Leontief, W. (1982) Letter in *Science*, No. 217, 9 July, pp. 104–7.

Leplin, J. (ed.) (1984) *Scientific Realism* (Berkeley: University of California Press).

Levins, R. and Lewontin, R. (1985) *The Dialectical Biologist* (Cambridge, MA: Harvard University Press).

Lewontin, R. C. (1968) 'The Concept of Evolution', in Sills (1968), vol. 5, pp. 202–10.

Lewontin, R. C. (1970) 'The Units of Selection', *Annual Review of Ecology and Systematics*, **1**, pp. 1–18.

Lewontin, R. C. (1974) *The Genetic Basis of Evolutionary Change* (New York: Columbia University Press).

Lewontin, R. C. (1978) 'Adaptation', *Scientific American*, no. 239, pp. 212–30.

Lewontin, R. C. (1979) 'Sociobiology as an Adaptationist Program', *Behavioral Science*, **24**, pp. 5–14.

Lewontin, R. C. (1980) 'Adaptation', in *The Encyclopedia Einaudi* (Einaudi: Milan). Reprinted in Sober (1984b).

Lewontin, R. C. (1982) *Human Diversity* (New York: Scientific American Books).

Lichnerowicz, A. (ed.) (1981) *Analogie et connaissance* (Paris: Maloine).

Liebhafsky, H. H. (1986) 'Peirce on the Summum Bonnum and the Unlimited Community', *Journal of Economic Issues*, **20**(1), Mar., pp. 5–20.

Lippi, M. (1979) *Value and Naturalism in Marx* (London: NLB).

Lloyd, B. B. (1972) *Perception and Cognition: A Cross-Cultural Perspective*, Harmondsworth: Penguin.

Loasby, B. J. (1976) *Choice, Complexity and Ignorance: An Enquiry into Economic Theory and the Practice of Decision Making* (Cambridge: Cambridge University Press).

Loasby, B. J. (1978) 'Whatever Happened to Marshall's Theory of Value?', *Scottish Journal of Political Economy*, **25**(1), Feb., pp. 1–12. Reprinted in Loasby (1989).

Loasby, B. J. (1989) *The Mind and Method of the Economist: A Critical Appraisal of Major Economists in the Twentieth Century* (Aldershot: Edward Elgar).

Loasby, B. J. (1991) *Equilibrium and Evolution: An Exploration of Connecting Principles in Economics* (Manchester: Manchester University Press).

Loomes, G. (1989) 'Experimental Economics', in Hey (1989), pp. 152–78.

Lotka, A. J. (1956) *Elements of Mathematical Biology* (New York: Dover).

Lovelock, J. E. (1979) *Gaia – A New Look at Life on Earth* (Oxford: Oxford University Press).

Lowe, A. (1951) 'On the Mechanistic Approach in Economics', *Social Research*, **18**(4), Dec., pp. 403–34.

Lowry, S. T. (1976) 'Bargain and Contract Theory in Law and Economics', *Journal of Economic Issues*, **10**(1), Mar., pp. 1–22. Reprinted in Tool and Samuels (1989).

Lozada, G. A. (1991) 'A Defense of Nicholas Georgescu-Roegen's Paradigm', *Ecological Economics*, **3**(1), Apr., pp. 157–60.

Lucas Jr, R. E. (1972) 'Expectations and the Neutrality of Money', *Journal of Economic Theory*, **4**(2), Apr., pp. 102–24.

Lucas Jr, R. E. (1985) 'An Equilibrium Model of the Business Cycle', *Journal of Political Economy*, **83**, pp. 1113–44.

Lucas Jr, R. E. (1986) 'Adaptive Behavior and Economic Theory', *Journal of Business*, **59**, pp. 401–76. Reprinted in Hogarth and Reder (1987).

Luhmann, N. (1984) *Soziale System: Grundriss einer allgemeinen Theorie* (Frankfurt a. M.: Suhrkamp).

Luhmann, N. (1986) 'The Autopoiesis of Social Systems', in Geyer and Zouwen (1986).

Lukes, S. (1973) *Individualism* (Oxford: Blackwell).

Lumsden, C. J. and Wilson, E. O. (1981) *Genes, Mind and Culture: The Coevolutionary Process* (Cambridge MA: Harvard University Press).

Lundvall, B.-Å. (1988) 'Innovation as an Interactive Process: From User–Producer Interaction to the National System of Innovation', in Dosi et al. (1988), pp. 349–69.

McCloskey, D. N. (1985) *The Rhetoric of Economics* (Madison: University of Wisconsin Press).

McCloskey, D. N. (1991) 'Economic Science: A Search through the Hyperspace of Assumptions', *Methodus*, **3**(1), June, pp. 6–16.

Machlup, F. (1978) *Methodology of Economics and Other Social Sciences* (London: Academic Press).

McDougall, W. (1908) *An Introduction to Social Psychology* (London: Methuen).

McFarland, F. (1986) 'Clarence Ayres and his Gospel of Technology', *History of Political Economy*, **18**(4), Winter, pp. 593–613.

McKelvey, M. (1991) 'How do National Systems of Innovation Differ? A Critical Analysis of Porter, Freeman, Lundvall and Nelson', in Hodgson and Screpanti (1991), pp. 117–37.

McKelvey, M. (1992) 'How Evolution Became Male', *European Association for Evolutionary Political Economy Newsletter*, Jan.

McKelvey, W. (1982) *Organizational Systematics: Taxonomy, Evolution, Classification* (Berkeley, CA: University of California Press).

McMullin, E. (1984) 'A Case for Scientific Realism', in Leplin (1984), pp. 8–40.

McNeill, W. H. (1980) *The Pursuit of Power: Technology, Armed Force, and Society Since A.D. 1000* (Chicago: University of Chicago Press).

McNulty, P. J. (1968) 'Economic Theory and the Meaning of Competition', *Quarterly Journal of Economics*, **82**(4), Nov., pp. 649–56.

McWilliams Tullberg, R. (ed.) (1990) *Alfred Marshall in Retrospect* (Aldershot: Edward Elgar).

Madison, G. B. (1990) 'Between Theory and Practice: Hayek on the Logic of Cultural Dynamics', *Cultural Dynamics*, **3**(1), pp. 83–112.

Mäki, U. (1989) 'On the Problem of Realism in Economics', *Ricerche Economiche*, **43**(1–2), pp. 176–98.

Mäki, U. (1991) 'Practical Syllogism, Entrepreneurship, and the Invisible Hand', in Lavoie (1991), pp. 149–76.

Malthus, T. R. (1798) *An Essay on the Principle of Population, as it Affects the Future Improvement of Society, with Remarks on the Speculations of Mr. Godwin, M. Condorcet, and other Writers* (London: Johnson). Reprinted 1926 with notes by J. Bonar (London: Macmillan).

Malthus, T. R. (1820) *Principles of Political Economy* (London: John Murray).

Mandeville, B. (1970) *The Fable of the Bees*, edited with an introduction by P. Harth from the first complete edition of 1724 (Harmondsworth: Penguin).

Mani, G. S. (1991) 'Is There a General Theory of Biological Evolution?', in Saviotti and Metcalfe (1991), pp. 31–57.

Manicas, P. T. (1987) *A History and Philosophy of the Social Sciences* (Oxford: Blackwell).

Manier, E. (1978) *The Young Darwin and his Cultural Circle: A Study of Influences which helped Shape the Language and Logic of the First Drafts of the Theory of Natural Selection* (Dordrecht: Reidel).

March, J. G. (ed.) (1965) *Handbook of Organizations* (Chicago: Rand McNally).

March, J. G. and Olsen, J. P. (1984) 'The New Institutionalism: Organizational Factors in Political Life', *American Political Science Review*, **78**(3), Sept., pp. 734–49.

Marquand, J. (1989) *Autonomy and Change: The Sources of Economic Growth* (Hemel Hempstead: Harvester Wheatsheaf).

Marshall, A. (1897) 'The Old Generation of Economists and the New', *Quarterly Journal of Economics*, **11**, pp. 115–35.

Marshall, A. (1898) 'Distribution and Exchange', *Economic Journal*, 8(1), Mar., pp. 37–59. Excerpted in Pigou (1925).

Marshall, A. (1904) 'On a National Memorial to Herbert Spencer', *Daily Chronicle*, 23 Nov. Reprinted in Pigou (1925).

Marshall, A. (1919) *Industry and Trade* (London: Macmillan).

Marshall, A. (1923) *Money, Credit and Commerce* (London: Macmillan).

Marshall, A. (1949) *The Principles of Economics*, 8th (reset) edn (1st edn 1890) (London: Macmillan).

Marshall, A. (1961) *The Principles of Economics*, 9th (variorum) edn with annotations by C. W. Guillebaud (London: Macmillan).

Marshall, A. (1975) *The Early Economic Writings of Alfred Marshall, 1867–1890*, ed. J. K. Whitaker (London: Macmillan).

Martilla, J. A. (1971) 'Word-of-Mouth Communication in the Industrial Adoption Process', *Journal of Marketing Research*, 8, pp. 173–8.

Marx, K. (1973) *Grundrisse: Foundations of the Critique of Political Economy*, trans. M. Nicolaus (Harmondsworth: Pelican).

Marx, K. (1976) *Capital*, vol. 1, trans. B. Fowkes from the 4th German edn of 1890 (Harmondsworth: Pelican).

Marx, K. (1977) *Karl Marx: Selected Writings*, ed. D. McLellan (Oxford: Oxford University Press).

Marx, K. and Engels, F. (1953) *Marx and Engels on Malthus*, ed. R. L. Meek (London: Lawrence and Wishart).

März, E. (1991) *Joseph Schumpeter: Scholar, Teacher and Politician* (New Haven: Yale University Press).

Matson, F. W. (1964) *The Broken Image* (New York: Doubleday).

Matthews, R. C. O. (1985) 'Darwinism and Economic Change', in Collard et al. (1985), pp. 91–117.

Maturana, H. R. (1975) 'The Organisation of the Living: A Theory of the Living Organisation', *International Journal of Man–Machine Studies*, 7, pp. 313–32.

Maull, N. (1977) 'Unifying Science Without Reduction', *Studies in the History and Philosophy of Science*, 9, pp. 143–62. Reprinted in Sober (1984b).

Maxwell, J. C. (1882) 'Science and Free Will', quoted in Campbell and Garnett (1882), p. 443.

Mayhew, A. (1980) 'Atomistic and Cultural Analysis in Economic Anthropology: An Old Argument Repeated', in Adams (1980), pp. 72–81.

Mayhew, A. (1987a) 'Culture: Core Concept under Attack', *Journal of Economic Issues*, 21(2), June, pp. 587–603.

Mayhew, A. (1987b) 'The Beginnings of Institutionalism', *Journal of Economic Issues*, 21(3), Sept., pp. 971–98.

Mayhew, A. (1989) 'Contrasting Origins of the Two Institutionalisms: The Social Science Context', *Review of Political Economy*, 1(3), Nov., pp. 319–33.

Maynard Smith, J. (1964) 'Group Selection and Kin Selection', *Nature*, 201, pp. 1145–7.

Maynard Smith, J. (1972) *On Evolution* (Edinburgh: Edinburgh University Press).

Maynard Smith, J. (1975) *The Theory of Evolution* (Harmondsworth: Penguin).

Maynard Smith, J. (1976) 'Group Selection', *Quarterly Review of Biology*, **51**, pp. 277–83. Reprinted in Clutton-Brock and Harvey (1978) and Brandon and Burian (1984).

Maynard Smith, J. (1978a) *The Evolution of Sex* (London: Cambridge University Press).

Maynard Smith, J. (1978b) 'Optimization Theory in Evolution', *Annual Review of Ecology and Systematics*, **9**, pp. 31–56. Reprinted in Sober (1984b).

Maynard Smith, J. (1980) 'The Concepts of Sociobiology', in Stent (1980), pp. 21–30.

Maynard Smith, J. (1982) *Evolutionary Game Theory* (Cambridge: Cambridge University Press).

Maynard Smith, J. (1987a) 'How to Model Evolution', in Dupré (1987), pp. 119–31.

Maynard Smith, J. (1987b) 'Reply to Sober', in Dupré (1987), pp. 147–9.

Maynard Smith, J. (1988a) *Did Darwin Get it Right?* (New York: Chapman and Hall).

Maynard Smith, J. (1988b) 'Evolutionary Progress and Levels of Selection', in Nitecki (1988), pp. 219–30.

Mayr, E. (1942) *Systematics and the Origin of Species* (New York: Columbia University Press).

Mayr, E. (1961) 'Cause and Effect in Biology', *Science*, no. 134, pp. 1501–6.

Mayr, E. (1963) *Animal Species and Evolution* (Cambridge, MA: Harvard University Press).

Mayr, E. (1964) 'Introduction', in C. Darwin, *On the Origin of Species*, facsimile of the first edition (Cambridge, MA: Harvard University Press), pp. vii–xxvii.

Mayr, E. (1972) 'The Nature of the Darwinian Revolution', *Science*, no. 176, pp. 981–9.

Mayr, E. (1976) *Evolution and the Diversity of Life: Selected Essays* (Cambridge, MA: Harvard University Press).

Mayr, E. (1978) 'Evolution', *Scientific American*, **239**(3), Sept., pp. 46–55.

Mayr, E. (1980) 'Prologue: Some Thoughts on the History of the Evolutionary Synthesis', in Mayr and Provine (1980), pp. 1–48.

Mayr, E. (1982) *The Growth of Biological Thought: Diversity, Evolution, and Inheritance* (Cambridge, MA: Harvard University Press).

Mayr, E. (1985a) 'How Biology Differs from the Physical Sciences', in Depew and Weber (1985b), pp. 43–63.

Mayr, E. (1985b) 'Darwin's Five Theories of Evolution', in Kohn (1985), pp. 755–72.

Mayr, E. (1992) *One Long Argument: Charles Darwin and the Genesis of Modern Evolutionary Thought* (London: Allen Lane).

Mayr, E. and Provine, W. B. (eds) (1980) *The Evolutionary Synthesis: Perspectives on the Unification of Biology* (Cambridge, MA: Harvard University Press).

Mays, W. (1959) *The Philosophy of Whitehead* (London: George Allen and Unwin).

Mead, M. (1937) *Cooperation and Competition among Primitive Peoples* (New York: McGraw-Hill).

Medawar, P. (1967) *The Art of the Soluble* (Harmondsworth: Penguin).

Ménard, C. (1981) 'La Machine et le coeur', in Lichnerowicz (1981).

Ménard, C. (1990) 'The Lausanne Tradition: Walras and Pareto', in Hennings and Samuels (1990), pp. 95–136.

Menger, C. (1892) 'On the Origins of Money', *Economic Journal*, 2(2), June, pp. 239–55.

Menger, C. (1963) *Problems of Economics and Sociology*, trans. F. J. Nock from the German edn of 1883 with an introduction by Louis Schneider (Urbana, IL: University of Illinois Press).

Menger, C. (1981) *Principles of Economics*, ed. J. Dingwall and trans. B. F. Hoselitz from the German edn of 1871 (New York: New York University Press).

Mensch, G. (1979) *Stalemate in Technology: Innovations Overcome Depression* (New York: Ballinger).

Metcalfe, J. S. (1981) 'Impulse and Diffusion in the Study of Technical Change', *Futures*, 13(5), Oct., pp. 347–59. Reprinted in Freeman (1990b).

Metcalfe, J. S. (1986) 'Technological Innovation and the Competitive Process', in Hall (1986), pp. 35–64.

Metcalfe, J. S. (1988) 'Evolution and Economic Change', in Silberston (1988), pp. 54–85.

Metcalfe, J. S. and Boden, M. (1992) 'Strategy, Paradigm and Evolutionary Change', in Coombs et al. (1992).

Metcalfe, J. S. and Gibbons, M. (1986) 'Technological Variety and the Process of Competition', *Economie appliquée*, 39(3), pp. 493–520.

Metcalfe, J. S. and Gibbons, M. (1989) 'Technology, Variety and Organisation: A Systematic Perspectus on the Diffusion Process', in Rosenbloom and Burgelman (1989).

Milenkovitch, D. (1971) *Plan and Market in Yugoslav Economic Thought* (New Haven: Yale University Press).

Milkman, R. (ed.) (1982) *Perspectives on Evolution* (Sunderland, MA: Sinauer).

Millar, J. R. (1980) 'Institutionalism from a Natural Science Point of View: An Intellectual Profile of Morris A. Copeland', in Adams (1980), pp. 105–24.

Miller, D. (1989) 'The Fatalistic Conceit', *Critical Review*, 3(2), Spring, pp. 310–23.

Miller, J. G. (1978) *Living Systems* (New York: McGraw-Hill).

Mills, S. and Beatty, J. (1979) 'The Propensity Interpretation of Fitness', *Philosophy of Science*, 46(2), pp. 263–86. Reprinted in Sober (1984b).

Mini, P. V. (1974) *Philosophy and Economics: The Origins and Development of Economic Theory* (Gainesville: University of Florida Press).

Mirowski, P. (1981) 'Is There a Mathematical Neoinstitutional Economics?', *Journal of Economic Issues*, 15(3), pp. 593–613. Reprinted in Samuels (1988), vol. 2.

Mirowski, P. (1983) 'An Evolutionary Theory of Economic Change: A Review Article', *Journal of Economic Issues*, 17(3), Sept., pp. 757–68. Reprinted in Mirowski (1988c).

Mirowski, P. (1986a) 'Institutions as a Solution Concept in a Game Theory Context', in Mirowski (1986c), pp. 241–63.

Mirowski, P. (1986b) 'Mathematical Formalism and Economic Explanation', in Mirowski (1986c), pp. 179–240.

Mirowski, P. (ed.) (1986c) *The Reconstruction of Economic Theory* (Boston: Kluwer-Nijhoff).

Mirowski, P. (1987a) 'Shall I Compare Thee to a Minkowski–Ricardo–Leontief–Metzler Matrix of the Mosak–Hicks Type?: Or, Rhetoric, Mathematics, and the Nature of Neoclassical Economic Theory', *Economics and Philosophy*, **3**(1), Mar., pp. 67–96.

Mirowski, P. (1987b) 'The Philosophical Bases of Institutional Economics', *Journal of Economic Issues*, **21**(3), Sept., pp. 1001–38. Reprinted in Mirowski (1988a).

Mirowski, P. (1988a) *Against Mechanism: Protecting Economics from Science* (Totowa, NJ: Rowman and Littlefield).

Mirowski, P. (1988b) 'Energy and Energetics in Economic Theory: Review Essay', *Journal of Economic Issues*, **22**(3), Sept., pp. 811–30.

Mirowski, P. (1989a) 'The Probabilistic Counter-Revolution, or How Stochastic Concepts Came to Neoclassical Theory', *Oxford Economic Papers*, **41**(2), Apr., pp. 217–35.

Mirowski, P. (1989b) *More Heat than Light: Economics as Social Physics, Physics as Nature's Economics* (Cambridge: Cambridge University Press).

Mirowski, P. (1990a) 'From Mandelbrot to Chaos in Economic Theory', *Southern Economic Journal*, **57**(2), Oct., pp. 289–307.

Mirowski, P. (1990b) 'Learning the Meaning of the Dollar: Conservation Principles and the Social Theory of Value in Economic Theory', *Social Research*, **57**(3), Fall, pp. 689–717.

Mirowski, P. (1991) 'Postmodernism and the Social Theory of Value', *Journal of Post Keynesian Economics*, **13**(4), Summer, pp. 565–82.

Mises, L. von (1949) *Human Action: A Treatise on Economics* (London: William Hodge).

Mises, L. von (1957) *Theory and History: An Interpretation of Social and Economic Evolution* (New Haven: Yale University Press).

Mises, L. von (1960) *Epistemological Problems of Economics* (Van Nostrand: New York).

Mises, L. von (1978) *Notes and Recollections*, trans. H. F. Sennholz (South Holland, II: Libertarian Press).

Mises, L. von (1980) *The Theory of Money and Credit*, trans. H. E. Batson (Indianapolis: Liberty Classics).

Mitchell, W. C. (1937) *The Backward Art of Spending Money and Other Essays* (New York: McGraw-Hill).

Moggridge, D. E. (ed.) (1990) *Perspectives in the History of Economic Thought, vol. 4: Keynes, Macroeconomics and Method* (Aldershot: Edward Elgar).

Mokyr, J. (1990a) *The Lever of Riches: Technological Creativity and Economic Progress* (Oxford: Oxford University Press).

Mokyr, J. (1990b) 'Punctuated Equilibria and Technological Progress', *American Economic Review (Papers and Proceedings)*, **80**(2), May, pp. 350–4.

Mokyr, J. (1991) 'Evolutionary Biology, Technical Change and Economic History', *Bulletin of Economic Research*, **43**(2), Apr., pp. 127–49.

Monod, J. (1971) *Chance and Necessity* (New York: Knopf).

Montagu, M. F. A. (1952) *Darwin, Competition and Cooperation* (New York: Henry Schuman).

Moore, J. R. (ed.) (1990) *History, Humanity and Evolution: Essays for John C. Greene* (Cambridge: Cambridge University Press).

Moorehead, P. S. and Kaplan, M. M. (eds) (1967) *Mathematical Challenges to the Neo-Darwinian Interpretation of Evolution* (Philadelphia: Wistar Institute Press).

Morgan, L. H. (1877) *Ancient Society* (Chicago: Charles Kerr).

Morishima, M. (1977) *Walras' Economics: A Pure Theory of Capital and Money* (Cambridge: Cambridge University Press).

Morishima, M. and Catephores, G. (1988) 'Anti-Say's Law versus Say's Law: A Change in Paradigm', in Hanusch (1988), pp. 23–53.

Morroni, M. (1992) *Production Process and Technical Change* (Cambridge: Cambridge University Press).

Moss, S. J. (1984) 'The History of the Theory of the Firm from Marshall to Robinson and Chamberlin: The Source of Positivism in Economics', *Economica*, **51**, Aug., pp. 307–18.

Moss, S. J. (1990a) 'Equilibrium and Evolution in Modelling Competitive Behaviour: An Artificial Intelligence Approach' (unpublished mimeo).

Moss, S. J. (1990b) 'Control Metaphors in the Modelling of Decision-Making Behaviour' (unpublished mimeo).

Moss, S. J. (1990c) 'Equilibrium, Evolution and Learning', *Journal of Economic Behavior and Organization*, **13**(1), Mar., pp. 97–115.

Moss, S. J. (1990d) 'Winter's Fundamental Selection Theorem: A Disproof', *Quarterly Journal of Economics*, **105**(4), Nov., pp. 1071–4.

Mott, T. (1989) 'A Post Keynesian Perspective on a "Cashless Competitive Payments System"', *Journal of Post Keynesian Economics*, **11**(3), Spring, pp. 360–9.

Muellbauer, J. (1988) 'Habits, Rationality and Myopia in the Life-Cycle Consumption Model', *Annales d'economie et de statistique*, no. 9, pp. 47–70.

Mumford, L. (1934) *Technics and Civilization* (New York: Harcourt, Brace and World).

Murphree, I. L. (1959) 'Darwinism in Thorstein Veblen's Economics', *Social Research*, **26**(2), June, pp. 311–24.

Murray, J. D. (1989) *Mathematical Biology* (Berlin: Springer).

Mygind, N. (1987) 'Are Self-Managed Firms Efficient? The Experience of Danish Fully and Partly Self-Managed Firms', *Advances in the Economic Analysis of Participatory and Labor-Managed Firms*, **2**, pp. 243–323.

Myrdal, G. (1939) *Monetary Equilibrium* (London: Hodge).

Myrdal, G. (1944) *An American Dilemma: The Negro Problem and Modern Democracy* (New York: Harper and Row).

Myrdal, G. (1957) *Economic Theory and Underdeveloped Regions* (London: Duckworth).

Myrdal, G. (1958) *Value in Social Theory* (New York: Harper).

Myrdal, G. (1978) 'Institutional Economics', *Journal of Economic Issues*, **12**(4), Dec., pp. 771–84.

Nagel, E. (1961) *The Structure of Science* (Indianapolis: Hackett Publishing).

Neale, W. C. (1984) 'Technology as Social Process: A Commentary on Knowledge and Human Capital', *Journal of Economic Issues*, 18(2), June, pp. 573–80.

Nef, J. U. (1950) *War and Human Progress: An Essay on the Rise of Industrial Civilization* (Cambridge, MA: Harvard University Press).

Nell, E. J., Chatha, J. and Blackwell, R. (eds) (1992) *Social Forces and Economic Questions: Essays of the Worldly Philosopher, a Festschrift in Honor of Robert L. Heilbroner* (London: Macmillan).

Nelson, R. R. (1980) 'Production Sets, Technological Knowledge and R&D: Fragile and Overworked Constructs for Analysis of Productivity Growth?', *American Economic Review (Papers and Proceedings)*, **70**(2), May, pp. 62–7.

Nelson, R. R. (1981), 'Research on Productivity Growth and Productivity Differences: Dead Ends and New Departures', *Journal of Economic Literature*, **29**, Sept., pp. 1029–64.

Nelson, R. R. (1987) *Understanding Technical Change as an Evolutionary Process* (Amsterdam: North-Holland).

Nelson, R. R. (1991) *Why Do Firms Differ, and How Does it Matter?*, working paper no. 91–7, Consortium on Competitiveness and Cooperation, University of California, Berkeley, California.

Nelson, R. R. (ed.) (forthcoming), *National Innovation Systems: A Comparative Study* (Oxford: Clarendon Press).

Nelson, R. R. and Winter, S. G. (1974) 'Neoclassical vs. Evolutionary Theories of Economic Growth: Critique and Prospectus', *Economic Journal*, **84**(4), Dec., pp. 886–905. Reprinted in Freeman (1990B).

Nelson, R. R. and Winter, S. G. (1977) 'In Search of a Useful Theory of Innovation', *Research Policy*, **6**, pp. 36–76.

Nelson, R. R. and Winter, S. G. (1982) *An Evolutionary Theory of Economic Change* (Cambridge, MA: Harvard University Press).

Newman, P. (1960) 'The Erosion of Marshall's Theory of Value', *Quarterly Journal of Economics*, **74**(4), Nov., pp. 587–601. Reprinted in John Cunninghan Wood (ed.) (1982) *Alfred Marshall: Critical Assessments* (London: Croom Helm).

Nicholson, A. J. (1960) 'The Role of Population Dynamics in Natural Selection', in S. Tax (ed.) *Evolution after Darwin* (Chicago: University of Chicago Press), vol. 1, pp. 477–522.

Nickles, T. (ed.) (1980) *Scientific Discovery, vol. 2: Historical and Scientific Case Studies* (Dordrecht: Reidel).

Nicolis, G. and Prigogine, I. (1977) *Self-Organization in Non-equilibrium Systems: From Dissipative Structures to Order through Fluctuations* (New York: Wiley).

Nicolis, J. S. (1986) *Dynamics of Hierachical Systems: An Evolutionary Approach* (Berlin: Springer-Verlag).

Nicolis, J. S. (1987) 'A Study Program of Chaotic Dynamics Applied to Information Processing', in Prigogine and Sanglier (1987).

Niman, N. B. (1991) 'Biological Analogies in Marshall's Work', *Journal of the History of Economic Thought*, **13**(1), Spring, pp. 19–36.

Nitecki, M. H. (ed.) (1988) *Evolutionary Progress* (Chicago: University of Chicago Press).

Nooteboom, B. (1993) 'Agent, Context and Innovation: A Saussurian View of Markets', in W. Blaas and J. Foster (eds), *Mixed Economies in Europe: An Evolutionary Perspective on their Emergence, Transition and Regulation* (Aldershot: Edward Elgar).

Norgaard, R. B. (1985) 'Environmental Economics: An Evolutionary Critique and a Plea for Pluralism', *Journal of Environmental Economics and Management*, **12**, pp. 382–93.

Norgaard, R. B. (1987) 'Economics as Mechanics and the Demise of Biological Diversity', *Economic Modelling*, nos 1–2, Sept., pp. 107–21.

Norgaard, R. B. (1989) 'The Case for Methodological Pluralism', *Ecological Economics*, **1**(1), Feb., pp. 37–57.

North, D. C. (1978) 'Structure and Performance: The Task of Economic History', *Journal of Economic Literature*, **16**(3), Sept., pp. 963–78.

North, D. C. (1981) *Structure and Change in Economic History* (New York: Norton).

North, D. C. (1990) *Institutions, Institutional Change and Economic Performance* (Cambridge: Cambridge University Press).

North, D. C. and Thomas, R. (1973) *The Rise of the Western World* (Cambridge: Cambridge University Press).

Nove, A. (1980) 'The Soviet Economy: Problems and Prospects', *New Left Review*, no. 119, Jan.–Feb., pp. 3–19.

Nove, A. (1983) *The Economics of Feasible Socialism* (London: George Allen and Unwin).

Novick, D. (1954) 'Mathematics: Logic, Quantity and Method', *Review of Economics and Statistics*, **3b**(4), Nov., pp. 357–8.

Nozick, R. (1977) 'On Austrian Methodology', *Synthese*, **36**, pp. 353–92.

O'Brien, D. P. (1975) *The Classical Economists* (Oxford: Clarendon Press).

O'Donnell, R. M. (1989) *Keynes: Philosophy, Economics and Politics* (London: Macmillan).

O'Driscoll Jr, G. P. (1986) 'Money: Menger's Evolutionary Theory', *History of Political Economy*, **18**(4), Winter, pp. 601–16.

O'Driscoll, Jr, G. P. and Rizzo, M. J. (1985) *The Economics of Time and Ignorance* (Oxford: Blackwell).

Oakeshott, M. (1962) *Rationalism in Politics and Other Essays* (London: Methuen).

Oakley, A. (1990) *Schumpeter's Theory of Capitalist Motion: A Critical Exposition and Reassessment* (Aldershot: Edward Elgar).

Olson Jr, M. (1965) *The Logic of Collective Action* (Cambridge, MA: Harvard University Press).

Oppenheim, P. and Putnam, H. (1968) 'Unity of Science as a Working Hypothesis', in Feigl et al. (1968), pp. 3–36.

Orsenigo, L. (1989) *The Emergence of Biotechnology: Institutions and Markets in Industrial Innovation* (London: Pinter).

Ospovat, D. (1976) 'The Influence of Karl Ernst von Baer's Embryology, 1828–1859: A Reappraisal in the Light of Richard Owen's and William B. Carpenter's "Palaeontological Application of von Baer's Law"', *Journal of the History of Biology*, **9**, pp. 1–28.

Ospovat, D. (1979) 'Darwin After Malthus', *Journal of the History of Biology*, **12**(2), Fall, pp. 211–30.

Ospovat, D. (1981) *The Development of Darwin's Theory* (Cambridge: Cambridge University Press).

Oster, G. F. and Wilson, E. O. (1978) *Caste and Ecology in the Social Insects* (Princeton: Princeton University Press).

Oyama, S. (1991) 'Ontogeny and Phylogeny: A Case of Metarecapitulation?', in Griffiths (1991).

Pagano, U. (1991) 'Property Rights, Asset Specificity, and the Division of Labour under Alternative Capitalist Relations', *Cambridge Journal of Economics*, **15**(3), Sept., pp. 315–42.

Paley, W. (1785) *The Principles of Moral and Political Philosophy* (London: Faulder).

Pantzar, M. (1991) *A Replicative Perspective on Evolutionary Dynamics*, Research Report 37 (Helsinki: Labour Institute for Economic Research).

Pareto, V. (1971) *Manual of Political Economy*, trans. A. S. Schwier from the French edn of 1927, ed. A. S. Schwier and A. N. Page (New York: Augustus Kelley).

Parker, W. N. (ed.) (1986) *Economic History and the Modern Economist* (Oxford: Blackwell).

Parsons, T. (1932) 'Economics and Sociology: Marshall in Relation to the Thought of his Time', *Quarterly Journal of Economics*, **46**, pp. 316–47. Reprinted in J. C. Wood (ed.) (1982) *Alfred Marshall, Critical Assessments* (London: Croom Helm).

Parsons, T. (1937) *The Structure of Social Action*, 2 vols (New York: McGraw-Hill).

Parsons, T. (1966) *Societies: Evolutionary and Comparative Perspectives* (Englewood Cliffs, NJ: Prentice-Hall).

Pascal, B. (1932) *Pensées*, trans. W. F. Trotter from the French (London: Dent).

Pattee, H. H. (1973) *Hierarchy Theory: The Challenge of Complex Systems* (New York: Braziller).

Paul, E. F. (1988) 'Liberalism, Unintended Orders and Evolutionism', *Political Studies*, **36**(2), June, pp. 251–72.

Peel, J. D. Y. (1971) *Herbert Spencer: The Evolution of a Sociologist* (New York: Basic Books).

Peirce, C. S. (1878) 'How to Make Our Ideas Clear', *Popular Science Monthly*, **12**, Jan., pp. 286–302. Reprinted in Peirce (1923, 1934) and in J. Buchler (ed.) (1955) *Philosophical Writings of Peirce* (New York: Dover).

Peirce, C. S. (1923) *Chance, Love, and Logic*, ed. M. R. Cohen (New York: Harcourt, Brace).

Peirce, C. S. (1932) *Collected Papers of Charles Sanders Peirce, vol 2: Elements of Logic*, ed. C. Hartshorne and P. Weiss (Cambridge, MA: Harvard University Press).

Peirce, C. S. (1934) *Collected Papers of Charles Sanders Peirce, vol. 5: Pragmatism and Pragmaticism*, ed. C. Hartshorne and P. Weiss (Cambridge, MA: Harvard University Press).

Peirce, C. S. (1935) *Collected Papers of Charles Sanders Peirce, vol. 6: Scientific Metaphysics*, ed. C. Hartshorne and P. Weiss (Cambridge, MA: Harvard University Press).

Peirce, C. S. (1958) *Collected Papers of Charles Sanders Peirce, vol. 7: Science and Philosophy*, ed. A. W. Burks (Cambridge, MA: Harvard University Press).

Pelikan, P. (1988) 'Can the Innovation System of Capitalism be Outperformed?', in Dosi et al. (1988), pp. 370–98.

Penrose, E. T. (1952) 'Biological Analogies in the Theory of the Firm', *American Economic Review*, 42(4), Dec., pp. 804–19.

Penrose, E. T. (1953) 'Rejoinder', *American Economic Review*, 43(3), Sept., pp. 603–7.

Penrose, E. T. (1959) *The Theory of the Growth of the Firm* (Oxford: Blackwell).

Perez, C. (1983) 'Structural Change and the Assimilation of New Technologies in the Economic and Social System', *Futures*, 15(4), pp. 357–75.

Perez, C. (1985) 'Microelectronics, Long Waves, and World Structural Change: New Perspectives of Developing Countries', *World Development*, 13(3), pp. 441–63.

Perrin, R. G. (1976) 'Herbert Spencer's Four Theories of Social Evolution', *American Journal of Sociology*, 81, May, pp. 1339–59.

Perrings, C. (1987) *Economy and Environment: A Theoretical Essay on the Interdependence of Economic and Environmental Systems* (Cambridge: Cambridge University Press).

Petit, P. and Tahar, G. (1989) 'Dynamics of Technological Change and Schemes of Diffusion', *The Manchester School*, 57(4), Dec., pp. 370–86.

Pheby, J. (ed.) (1989) *New Directions in Post-Keynesian Economics* (Aldershot: Edward Elgar).

Piaget, J. (1979) *Behaviour and Evolution*, trans. D. Nicholson-Smith from the French edn of 1976 (London: Routledge and Kegan Paul).

Pigou, A. C. (1922) 'Empty Economic Boxes: A Reply', *Economic Journal*, 32(4), Dec., pp. 458–65.

Pigou, A. C. (ed.) (1925) *Memorials of Alfred Marshall* (London: Macmillan).

Pigou, A. C. (1928) 'An Analysis of Supply', *Economic Journal*, 38(3), Sept., pp. 238–57.

Polanyi, K. (1944) *The Great Transformation* (New York: Rinehart).

Polanyi, M. (1957) *Personal Knowledge: Towards a Post-Critical Philosophy* (London: Routledge and Kegan Paul).

Polanyi, M. (1967) *The Tacit Dimension* (London: Routledge and Kegan Paul).

Pollak, R. A. (1970) 'Habit Formation and Dynamic Demand Functions', *Journal of Political Economy*, 78, July–Aug., pp. 745–63.

Pollock, F. (1890) *Oxford Lectures and Other Discourses* (London: Macmillan).

Popper, K. R. (1945) *The Open Society and its Enemies*, 2 vols (London: Routledge and Kegan Paul).

Popper, K. R. (1960) *The Poverty of Historicism* (London: Routledge and Kegan Paul).

Popper, K. R. (1972) *Objective Knowledge: An Evolutionary Approach* (Oxford: Oxford University Press).

Popper, K. R. (1974) 'Scientific Reduction and the Essential Incompleteness of All Science', in Ayala and Dobzhansky (1974), pp. 259–84.

Popper, K. R. (1982a) *Quantum Theory and the Schism in Physics*, from the *Postscript to the Logic of Scientific Discovery*, ed. W. W. Bartley III (London: Unwin Hyman).

Popper, K. R. (1982b) *The Open Universe: An Argument for Indeterminism*, from the *Postscript to the Logic of Scientific Discovery*, ed. W. W. Bartley III (London: Hutchinson).

Popper, K. R. and Eccles, J. C. (1977) *The Self and its Brain* (Berlin: Springer International).

Prigogine, I. (1976), 'Order through Fluctuation: Self-Organization and Social System', in Jantsch and Waddington (1976), pp. 93–133.

Prigogine, I. (1980) *From Being to Becoming* (New York: Freeman).

Prigogine, I. (1987) 'Exploring Complexity', *European Journal of Operational Research*, **30**(2), June, pp. 97–103.

Prigogine, I. and Sanglier, M. (eds) (1987) *Laws of Nature and Human Conduct* (Brussels: Gordes).

Prigogine, I. and Stengers, I. (1984) *Order out of Chaos: Man's New Dialogue with Nature* (London: Heinemann).

Prisching, M. (1989) 'Evolution and Design of Social Institutions in Austrian Theory', *Journal of Economic Studies*, **16**(2), pp. 47–62.

Proops, J. L. R. (1989) 'Ecological Economics: Rationale and Problem Areas', *Ecological Economics*, **1**(1), Feb., pp. 59–76.

Provine, W. B. (1985) 'Adaptation and Mechanisms of Evolution after Darwin: A Study in Persistent Controversies', in Kohn (1985), pp. 825–66.

Provine, W. B. (1988) 'Progress in Evolution and Meaning in Life', in Nitecki (1988), pp. 49–74.

Pullen, J. M. (1981) 'Malthus's Theological Ideas and their Influence on his Principles of Population', *History of Political Economy*, **13**(1), Spring, pp. 39–54.

Pulliam, H. R. and Dunford, C. (1980) *Programmed to Learn: An Essay on the Evolution of Culture* (New York: Columbia University Press).

Putterman, L. (ed.) (1986) *The Economic Nature of the Firm: A Reader* (Cambridge: Cambridge University Press).

Quadagno, J. S. (1979) 'Paradigms in Evolutionary Theory: The Sociobiological Model of Natural Selection', *American Sociological Review*, **44**, pp. 100–9.

Quine, W. van O. (1953) *From a Logical Point of View* (Cambridge, MA: Harvard University Press).

Radner, R. (1968) 'Competitive Equilibrium under Uncertainty', *Econometrica*, **36**(1), Jan., pp. 31–58.

Radnitzky, G. and Bartley III, W. W. (eds) (1987) *Evolutionary Epistemology, Theory of Rationality, and the Sociology of Knowledge* (La Salle, Il: Open Court).

Radnitzky, G. and Bernholz, P. (1987) *Economic Imperialism* (New York: Paragon House).

Radzicki, M. J. (1990) 'Institutional Dynamics, Deterministic Chaos, and Self-Organizing Systems', *Journal of Economic Issues*, **24**(1), Mar., pp. 57–102.

Rahmeyer, F. (1989), 'The Evolutionary Approach to Innovation Activity', *Journal of Institutional and Theoretical Economics*, **145**(2), June, pp. 275–97.

Ramstad, Y. (1986) 'A Pragmatist's Quest for Holistic Knowledge: The Scientific Methodology of John R. Commons', *Journal of Economic Issues*, **20**(4), Dec., pp. 1067–106. Reprinted in Samuels (1988), vol. 2.

Rand, D. (1978) 'Exotic Phenomena in Games and Duopoly Models', *Journal of Mathematical Economics*, **5**, pp. 173–84.

Rapport, D. J. and Turner, J. E. (1977) 'Economic Models in Ecology', *Science*, **195**, pp. 367–73.

Reinheimer, H. (1913) *Evolution by Co-operation: A Study in Bioeconomics* (London: Kegan, Paul, Trench, Trubner).

Reisman, D. (1987) *Alfred Marshall: Progress and Politics* (London: Macmillan).

Renfrew, A. C. (1987) 'Problems in the Modelling of Socio-cultural Systems', *European Journal of Operational Research*, **30**(2), June, pp. 179–92.

Reynolds, V. (1980) *The Biology of Human Action*, 2 edn (Oxford: Freeman).

Richards, I. A. (1936) *The Philosophy of Rhetoric* (Oxford: Oxford University Press).

Richards, R. J. (1988) 'The Moral Foundations of the Idea of Evolutionary Progress: Darwin, Spencer, and the Neo-Darwinians', in Nitecki (1988), pp. 129–48.

Richards, R. J. (1992) *The Meaning of Evolution: The Morphological Construction and Ideological Reconstruction of Darwin's Theory* (Chicago: University of Chicago Press).

Richardson, R. A. (1981) 'Biogeography and the Genesis of Darwin's Ideas on Transmutation', *Journal of the History of Biology*, **14**(1), Spring, pp. 1–41.

Richardson, R. A. and Kane, T. C. (1988) 'Orthogenesis and Evolution in the 19th Century: The Idea of Progress in American Neo-Lamarckism', in Nitecki (1988), pp. 149–67.

Riesman, D. (1963) *Thorstein Veblen: A Critical Interpretation* (New York: Charles Scribner's).

Rifkin, J. (1980) *Entropy: A New World View* (New York: Viking Press).

Robbins, L. (1935) *An Essay on the Nature and Significance of Economic Science*, 2nd edn (London: Macmillan).

Robbins, L. (1952) *The Theory of Economic Policy* (London: Macmillan).

Robinson, J. (1974) *History versus Equilibrium* (London: Thames Papers in Political Economy).

Roemer, J. E. (1981) *Analytical Foundations of Marxian Economic Theory* (Cambridge: Cambridge University Press).

Roemer, J. E. (1988) *Free to Lose: An Introduction to Marxist Economic Philosophy* (Cambridge, MA: Harvard University Press).

Roland, G. (1990) 'Gorbachev and the Common European Home: The Convergence Debate Revisited?', *Kyklos*, **43**, fasc. 3, pp. 385–409.

Rorty, R. (1979) *Philosophy and the Mirror of Nature* (Princeton: Princeton University Press).

Rorty, R. (1982) *The Consequences of Pragmatism: Essays* (Minneapolis: University of Minnesota Press).

Rose, S., Kamin, L. J. and Lewontin, R. C. (1984) *Not in our Genes: Biology, Ideology and Human Nature* (Harmondsworth: Penguin).

Rosen, R. (1975) 'Biological Systems as Paradigms for Adaptation', in Day and Groves (1975), pp. 39–72.

Rosen, R. (1987) 'On Complex Systems', *European Journal of Operational Research*, **30**(2), June, pp. 129–34.

Rosenberg, A. (1976) 'On the Interanimation of Micro and Macroeconomics', *Philosophy of the Social Sciences*, **6**(1), pp. 35–53. Reprinted in Hausman (1984).

Rosenberg, A. (1985) *The Structure of Biological Science* (Cambridge: Cambridge University Press).

Rosenberg, N. (1963) 'Mandeville and Laissez-Faire', *Journal of the History of Ideas*, **24**, May-June, pp. 183–96.

Rosenberg, N. (1975) *Perspectives on Technology* (Cambridge: Cambridge University Press).

Rosenberg, N. (1976) 'On Technological Expectations', *Economic Journal*, **86**(3), Sept., pp. 523–35. Reprinted in Freeman (1990b).

Rosenberg, N. (1982) *Inside the Black Box: Technology and Economics* (Cambridge: Cambridge University Press).

Rosenberg, N. and Birdzell Jr, L. E. (1986) *How the West Grew Rich: The Economic Transformation of the Industrial World* (New York: Basic Books).

Rosenbloom, R. S. and Burgelman, R. (eds) (1989) *Research on Technological Innovation, Management and Policy*, vol. 4 (Greenwich, CT: JAI Press).

Rosser, J. B. (1990) 'Chaos Theory and the New Keynesian Economics', *Manchester School*, **58**(3), Sept., pp. 265–91.

Roth, A. E. (1988) 'Laboratory Experiments in Economics: A Methodological Overview', *Economic Journal*, **98**(4), Dec., pp. 974–1031.

Rotheim, R. J. (1989–90) 'Organicism and the Role of the Individual in Keynes' Thought', *Journal of Post Keynesian Economics*, **12**(2), Winter, pp. 317–26.

Rothschild, K. W. (1988) 'Discussion' [of Heertje (1988)], in Hanusch (1988), pp. 90–4.

Rothschild, M. L. (1992) *Bionomics: The Inevitability of Capitalism* (London: Futura).

Rotwein, E. (1966) 'Mathematical Economics: The Empirical View and an Appeal for Pluralism', in Krupp (1966), pp. 102–13.

Roughgarden, J. (1979) *Theory of Population Genetics and Evolutionary Ecology: An Introduction* (New York: Macmillan).

Rubin, P. H. and Zerbe, R. O. (eds) (1982) *Evolutionary Models in Economics and Law*, vols 1–4 (Greenwich, CT: JAI Press).

Rumney, J. (1934) *Herbert Spencer's Sociology* (London: Williams and Norgate).

Runde, J. H. (1988) 'Subjectivism, Psychology, and the Modern Austrians', in Earl (1988), pp. 101–20.

Runkle, G. (1961) 'Marxism and Charles Darwin', *Journal of Politics*, **23**, pp. 108–26.

Ruse, M. (1971) 'Natural Selection in the *Origin of Species*', *Studies in the History and Philosophy of Science*, **1**, pp. 311–51.

Ruse, M. (1974) 'Cultural Evolution', *Theory and Decision*, **5**, pp. 413–40.

Ruse, M. (1976) 'Reduction in Genetics' in Cohen et al. (1976), pp. 653–70. Reprinted in Sober (1984b).

Ruse, M. (1986) *Taking Darwin Seriously: A Naturalistic Approach to Philosophy* (Oxford: Blackwell).

Ruse, M. (1988) 'Molecules to Men: Evolutionary Biology and Thoughts of Progress', in Nitecki (1988), pp. 97–126.

Russett, C. E. (1976) *Darwin in America: The Intellectual Response 1865–1912* (San Francisco: W. H. Freeman).

Rutherford, M. (1981) 'Clarence Ayres and the Instrumentalist Theory of Value', *Journal of Economic Issues*, **15**(3), Sept., pp. 657–74. Reprinted in Samuels (1988), vol. 3.

Rutherford, M. (1983) 'J. R. Commons's Institutional Economics', *Journal of Economic Issues*, **17**(3), Sept., pp. 721–44. Reprinted in Samuels (1988), vol. 1.

Rutherford, M. (1984) 'Thorstein Veblen and the Processes of Institutional Change', *History of Political Economy*, **16**(3), Fall, pp. 331–48.

Rutherford, M. C. (1989a) 'Some Issues in the Comparison of Austrian and Institutional Economics', *Research in the History of Economic Thought and Methodology*, vol. 6, pp. 159–71.

Rutherford, M. C. (1989b) 'What is Wrong with the New Institutional Economics (And What is Still Wrong with the Old)?', *Review of Political Economy*, **1**(3), Nov., pp. 299–318.

Sabel, C. and Zeitlin, J. (1985) 'Historical Alternatives to Mass Production: Politics, Markets and Technology in Nineteenth Century Industrialization', *Past and Present*, no. 108, Aug., pp. 132–76.

Sahal, D. (1981) *Patterns of Technological Innovation* (Reading, MA: Addison Wesley).

Sahal, D. (1985) 'Technological Guideposts and Innovation Avenues', *Research Policy*, **14**(1), pp. 61–82. Reprinted in Freeman (1990b).

Sahlins, M. D. (1977) *The Use and Abuse of Biology: An Anthropological Critique of Sociobiology* (London: Tavistock).

Sahlins, M. D. and Service, E. R. (eds) (1960) *Evolution and Culture* (Ann Arbor: University of Michigan Press).

Salthe, S. N. (1985) *Evolving Hierarchical Systems* (New York: Columbia University Press).

Samuels, W. J. (1966) *The Classical Theory of Economic Policy* (Cleveland, Ohio: World Publishing).

Samuels, W. J. (1977) 'Technology *vis-à-vis* Institutions in the JEI: A Suggested Interpretation', *Journal of Economic Issues*, **11**(4), Dec., pp. 871–95. Reprinted in Samuels (1988), vol. 3.

Samuels, W. J. (ed.) (1988) *Institutional Economics*, 3 vols (Aldershot: Edward Elgar).

Samuels, W. J. (1989a) 'Determinate Solutions and Valuational Processes: Overcoming the Foreclosure of Process', *Journal of Post Keynesian Economics*, **11**(4), Summer, pp. 531–46.

Samuels, W. J. (1989b) 'Austrian and Institutional Economics: Some Common Elements', *Research in the History of Economic Thought and Methodology*, vol. 6, pp. 53–71.

Samuels, W. J. (ed.) (1990). *Economics as Discourse: An Analysis of the Language of Economists* (Boston: Kluwer).

Sanderson, S. K. (1990) *Social Evolutionism: A Critical History* (Oxford: Blackwell).

Santarelli, E. and Pesciarelli, E. (1990) 'The Emergence of a Vision: The Development of Schumpeter's Theory of Entrepreneurship', *History of Political Economy*, **22**(4), Winter, pp. 677–96.

Saviotti, P. P. (1986) 'Systems Theory and Technological Change', *Futures*, **18**, pp. 773–86.

Saviotti, P. P. (1988) 'Information, Variety and Entropy in Technoeconomic Development', *Research Policy*, **17**, pp. 89–103.

Saviotti, P. P. (1991) 'The Role of Variety in Economic and Technological Development', in Saviotti and Metcalfe (1991), pp. 172–208.

Saviotti, P. P. and Metcalfe, J. S. (1984) 'A Theoretical Approach to the Construction of Output Indicators', *Research Policy*, **13**, pp. 141–51.

Saviotti, P. P. and Metcalfe, J. S. (eds) (1991) *Evolutionary Theories of Economic and Technological Change: Present Status and Future Prospects* (Reading: Harwood Academic).

Sayer, A. (1984) *Method in Social Science: A Realist Approach* (London: Hutchinson).

Schaffer, M. E. (1989) 'Are Profit-Maximisers the Best Survivors?: A Darwinian Model of Economic Natural Selection', *Journal of Economic Behavior and Organization*, **12**(1), Mar., pp. 29–45.

Schaffner, K. F. (1976) 'Reduction in Biology: Prospects and Problems' in Cohen et al. (1976), pp. 613–32. Reprinted in Sober (1984b).

Schaffner, K. F. and Cohen, R. S. (eds) (1974) *Philosophy of Science Association 1972*, Boston Studies in the Philosophy of Science, vol. 20 (Dordrecht: Reidel).

Scheffler, I. (1974) *Four Pragmatists: A Critical Introduction to Peirce, James, Mead, and Dewey* (London: Routledge and Kegan Paul).

Schefold, B. (1986) 'Schumpeter as a Walrasian Austrian and Keynes as a Classical Marshallian', in Wagener and Drukker (1986), pp. 93–111.

Schefold, B. (1987) 'Knapp, Georg Friedrich', in Eatwell, et al. (1987), vol. 3, pp. 54–5.

Schelling, T. (1978) *Micromotives and Macrobehavior* (New York: Norton).

Scherer, F. M. (1984) *Innovation and Growth: Schumpeterian Perspectives* (Cambridge, MA: MIT Press).

Schieve, W. C. and Allen, P. M. (eds) (1982) *Self-Organization and Dissipative Structures: Applications in the Physical and Social Sciences* (Austin, TX: University of Texas Press).

Schilcher, F. von and Tennant, N. (1984) *Philosophy, Evolution and Human Nature* (London: Routledge and Kegan Paul).

Schmid, M. and Wuketits, F. M. (eds) (1987) *Evolutionary Theory in Social Science* (Dordrecht: Reidel).

Schofield, N. (1985) 'Anarchy, Altruism and Cooperation', *Social Choice and Welfare*, **2**, pp. 34–44.

Schopf, T. J. M. (ed.) (1972) *Models in Paleobiology* (San Francisco: Freeman, Cooper).

Schotter, A. (1981) *The Economic Theory of Social Institutions* (Cambridge: Cambridge University Press).

Schotter, A. (1990) *Free Market Economics: A Critical Appraisal*, 2nd edn (Oxford: Blackwell).

Schumpeter, J. A. (1908) *Das Wesen und der Hauptinhalt der theoretischen Nationalökonomie* (Leipzig: Duncker und Humbolt).

Schumpeter, J. A. (1934) *The Theory of Economic Development*, trans. R. Opie from the German edn of 1912 (Cambridge, MA: Harvard University Press).

Schumpeter, J. A. (1939) *Business Cycles: A Theoretical, Historical and Statistical Analysis of the Capitalist Process*, 2 vols (New York: McGraw-Hill).

Schumpeter, J. A. (1951) *Essays on Economic Topics* (Cambridge: Cambridge University Press).

Schumpeter, J. A. (1952) *Ten Great Economists: From Marx to Keynes* (London: George Allen and Unwin).

Schumpeter, J. A. (1954) *History of Economic Analysis* (New York: Oxford University Press).

Schumpeter, J. A. (1976) *Capitalism, Socialism and Democracy*, 5th edn (1st edn 1942) (London: George Allen and Unwin).

Schumpeter, J. A. (1991) *The Economics and Sociology of Capitalism*, ed. R. Swedberg (Princeton: Princeton University Press).

Schweber, S. S. (1977) 'The Origin of the *Origin* Revisited', *Journal of the History of Biology*, **10**(2), Fall, pp. 229–316.

Schweber, S. S. (1980) 'Darwin and the Political Economists: Divergence of Character', *Journal of the History of Biology*, **13**(2), Fall, pp. 195–289.

Schweber, S. S. (1985) 'The Wider British Context in Darwin's Theorizing', in Kohn (1985), pp. 35–69.

Scitovsky, T. (1976) *The Joyless Economy: An Enquiry into Human Satisfaction and Consumer Dissatisfaction* (Oxford: Clarendon Press).

Scitovsky, T. (1986) *Human Desire and Economic Satisfaction: Essays on the Frontiers of Economics* (Brighton: Wheatsheaf).

Scott, M. F. (1989) *A New View of Economic Growth* (Oxford: Clarendon Press).

Scriven, M. (1959) 'Explanation and Prediction in Evolutionary Theory', *Science*, **130**, no. 3377, 28 Aug., pp. 477–82.

Seal, W. B. (1990) 'Deindustrialisation and Business Organisation: An Institutionalist Critique of the Natural Selection Analogy', *Cambridge Journal of Economics*, **14**(3), Sept., pp. 267–75.

Sebba, G. (1953) 'The Development of the Concepts of Mechanism and Model in Physical Science and Economic Thought', *American Economic Review (Papers and Proceedings)*, **43**(2), May, pp. 259–68.

Seckler, D. (1975) *Thorstein Veblen and the Institutionalists: A Study in the Social Philosophy of Economics* (London: Macmillan).

Selgin, G. A. (1988) *The Theory of Free Banking* (Totawa, NJ: Rowman and Littlefield).

Selgin, G. A. and White, L. H. (1987) 'The Evolution of a Free Banking System', *Economic Inquiry*, **25**(3), July, pp. 439–57.

Sen, A. K. (1976–7) 'Rational Fools: A Critique of the Behavioral Foundations of Economic Theory', *Philosophy and Public Affairs*, 6, pp. 317–44.
Reprinted in Hahn and Hollis (1979).

Sen, A. K. (1989) 'Economic Methodology: Heterogeneity and Relevance',
Social Research, 56(2), Summer, pp. 299–329. Reprinted in *Methodus*, 3(1),
June 1991, pp. 67–80.

Service, E. R. (1960) 'The Law of Evolutionary Potential', in Sahlins and
Service (1960), pp. 93–122.

Service, E. R. (1968) 'Cultural Evolution', in Sills (1968), vol. 5, pp. 221–8.

Service, E. R. (1975) *Origins of the State and Civilization: The Process of Cultural
Evolution* (New York: Norton).

Shackle, G. L. S. (1967) *The Years of High Theory: Invention and Tradition in
Economic Thought 1926–1939* (Cambridge: Cambridge University Press).

Shackle, G. L. S. (1972) *Epistemics and Economics: A Critique of Economic
Doctrines* (Cambridge: Cambridge University Press).

Shackle, G. L. S. (1989) 'What Did the "General Theory" Do?', in Pheby
(1989), pp. 48–58.

Shaw, G. B. (1939) *Back to Methuselah* (Harmondsworth: Penguin).

Shepherd, W. G. (1984) '"Contestability" vs. Competition', *American
Economic Review*, 74(4), Sept., pp. 572–87.

Sherry, M. S. (1977) *Preparing for the Next War: American Plans for Postwar
Defense, 1941–45* (New Haven, CT: Yale University Press).

Shionoya, Y. (1986) 'The Science and Ideology of Schumpeter', *Revista
Internazionale di Scienze Economiche e Commerciale*, 33(8), pp. 729–62.

Shionoya, Y. (1990) 'The Origin of the Schumpeterian Research Program:
A Chapter Omitted from Schumpeter's *Theory of Economic Development*',
Journal of Institutional and Theoretical Economics, 146(2), June, pp. 314–27.

Shiraishi, T. and Tsuru, S. (eds) (1989) *Economic Institutions in a Dynamic
Society: Search for a New Frontier* (Basingstoke: Macmillan, with the International Economic Association).

Shove, G. F. (1942) 'The Place of Marshall's *Principles* in the Development
of Economic Theory', *Economic Journal*, 52(4), Dec., pp. 294–329. Reprinted in John Cunningham Wood (ed.) (1982) *Alfred Marshall: Critical
Assessments* (London: Croom Helm).

Silberston, A. (ed.) (1988) *Technology and Economic Progress* (Basingstoke:
Macmillan).

Sills, D. L. (ed.) (1968) *International Encyclopedia of the Social Sciences* (New
York: Macmillan).

Silverberg, G. (1987) 'Technical Progress, Capital Accumulation and Effective Demand: A Self-Organization Model', in Batten, Casti and Johansson
(1987), pp. 116–44.

Silverberg, G. (1988) 'Modelling Economic Dynamics and Technical Change:
Mathematical Approaches to Self-Organisation and Evolution', in Dosi
et al. (1988), pp. 531–59.

Silverberg, G., Dosi, G. and Orsenigo, L. (1988) 'Innovation, Diversity and
Diffusion: A Self-Organisation Model', *Economic Journal*, 98(4), Dec., pp.
1032–54. Reprinted in Freeman (1990b).

Simon, H. A. (1955) 'A Behavioral Model of Rational Choice', *Quarterly
Journal of Economics*, 69(1), Feb., pp. 99–118. Reprinted in Simon (1957).

Simon, H. A. (1957) *Models of Man: Social and Rational* (New York: Wiley).

Simon, H. A. (1959a) 'Theories of Decision-Making in Economic and Behavioral Sciences', *American Economic Review*, **49**(2), June, pp. 253–83.

Simon, H. A. (1956b) Review of *Elements of Mathematical Biology* by Alfred J. Lotka, *Econometrica*, **27**(3), July, pp. 493–5.

Simon, H. A. (1962) 'The Architecture of Complexity', *Proceedings of the American Philosophical Society*, **106**, Dec., pp. 467–82. Reprinted in Simon (1968).

Simon, H. A. (1968) *The Sciences of the Artificial* (Cambridge, MA: MIT Press).

Simon, H. A. (1976) *Administrative Behavior*, 3rd edn (Free Press: New York).

Simon, H. A. (1983) *Reason in Human Affairs* (Oxford: Blackwell; Stanford: Stanford University Press).

Simon, H. A. (1990) 'A Mechanism for Social Selection and Successful Altruism', *Science*, **250**, 21 Dec., pp. 1665–8.

Simon, H. A. (1991) 'Organizations and Markets', *Journal of Economic Perspectives*, **5**(2), Spring, pp. 25–44.

Simpson, G. G. (1964) *This View of Life: The World of an Evolutionist* (New York: Harcourt, Brace and World).

Singh, M. G. (ed.) (1987) *Systems and Control Encyclopedia. Theory, Technology, Applications* (Oxford: Pergamon Press).

Skinner, A. S. and Wilson, T. (eds) (1976) *Essays on Adam Smith* (Oxford: Oxford University Press).

Smith, A. (1976a) *The Theory of Moral Sentiments* (originally published 1759), ed. D. D. Raphael and A. L. MacFie (Oxford: Clarendon).

Smith, A. (1976b) *An Inquiry into the Nature and Causes of the Wealth of Nations*, 2 vols (originally published 1776), ed. R. H. Campbell and A. S. Skinner (London: Methuen).

Smith, A. (1980) 'The Principles which Lead and Direct Philosophical Enquiries: Illustrated by the History of Astronomy', in *Essays on Philosophical Subjects*, ed. W. P. D. Wightman (Oxford: Clarendon).

Smith, A. (1983) *Lectures on Rhetoric and Belles Lettres*, ed. J. C. Bryce and A. S. Skinner (Oxford: Clarendon).

Smith, E. A. (1987) 'Optimization Theory in Anthropology: Applications and Critiques', in Dupré (1987), pp. 201–49.

Smith, K. (1951) *The Malthusian Controversy* (London: Routledge and Kegan Paul).

Smith, M. R. (ed.) (1985) *Military Enterprise and Technological Change* (Cambridge, MA: MIT Press).

Smith, V. L. (1982) 'Microeconomic Systems as an Experimental Science', *American Economic Review*, **72**(5), Dec., pp. 923–55.

Smith, V. L. (1986) 'Experimental Models in the Political Economy of Exchange', *Science*, no. 234, pp. 167–72.

Sober, E. (1981) 'Holism, Individualism, and the Units of Selection', in Asquith and Giere (1981), pp. 93–121. Reprinted in Sober (1984b).

Sober, E. (1984a) *The Nature of Selection: Evolutionary Theory in Philosophical Focus* (Cambridge, MA: MIT Press).

Sober, E. (ed.) (1984b) *Conceptual Issues in Evolutionary Biology: An Anthology* (Cambridge, MA: MIT Press).

Sober, E. (1985) 'Darwin on Natural Selection: A Philosophical Perspective', in Kohn (1985), pp. 867–99.

Sober, E. (1987) 'Comments on Maynard Smith's "How to Model Evolution"', in Dupré (1987), pp. 133–45.

Sober, E. and Lewontin, R. C. (1982) 'Artifact, Cause, and Genic Selection', *Philosophy of Science*, 49(2), pp. 157–80. Reprinted in Sober (1984b).

Somit, A. and Peterson, S. A. (1989) 'The Punctuated Equilibrium Debate: Scientific Issues and Implications', *Journal of Social Biology and Structuration*, 12(2–3), pp. 105–301.

Sowell, T. (1967) 'The "Evolutionary" Economics of Thorstein Veblen', *Oxford Economic Papers*, 19(2), July, pp. 177–98.

Spencer, H. (1851) *Social Statics* (London: Chapman).

Spencer, H. (1855) *The Principles of Psychology* (London: Williams and Norgate).

Spencer, H. (1880) *The Study of Sociology* (London: Williams and Norgate).

Spencer, H. (1887) *The Factors of Organic Evolution* (London: Williams and Norgate).

Spencer, H. (1890) *First Principles*, 5th edn (London: Williams and Norgate).

Spencer, H. (1892) *Essays Scientific, Political and Speculative* (New York: Appleton).

Spencer, H. (1893) 'The Inadequacy of Natural Selection', *Contemporary Review*, 63, pp. 153–66, 439–56.

Spencer, H. (1894) *The Principles of Biology*, 2 vols (London: Williams and Norgate).

Spencer, H. (1904) *An Autobiography*, 2 vols (London: Williams and Norgate).

Spencer, H. (1969) *Principles of Sociology* originally published between 1876 and 1896, ed. S. Andreski (London: Macmillan).

Spinnewijn, F. (1981) 'Rational Habit Formation', *European Economic Review*, 15, pp. 91–109.

Sraffa, P. (1926) 'The Laws of Returns under Competitive Conditions', *Economic Journal*, 36(4), Dec., pp. 535–50.

Stanley, S. M. (1975) 'A Theory of Evolution above the Species Level', *Proceedings of the National Academy of Sciences, U.S.A.*, 72, pp. 646–50.

Stanley, S. M. (1980) *Macroevolution: Pattern and Process* (San Francisco: Freeman).

Stebbins, G. L. (1982) *Darwin to DNA, Molecules to Humanity* (San Francisco: Freeman).

Steindl, J. (1952) *Maturity and Stagnation in American Capitalism* (Oxford: Blackwell).

Stenseth, N. C. and Maynard Smith, J. (1984) 'Coevolution in Ecosystems: Red Queen Evolution or Stasis?', *Evolution*, 38, pp. 870–80.

Stent, G. S. (ed.) (1980) *Morality as a Biological Phenomenon* (Berkeley: University of California Press).

Stent, G. S. (1985) 'Hermeneutics and the Analysis of Complex Biological Systems', in Depew and Weber (1985b), pp. 209–25.

Stephen, F. H. (ed.) (1982) *The Performance of Labour-Managed Firms* (London: Macmillan).

Steppacher, R., Zogg-Walz, B. and Hatzfeldt, H. (eds) (1977) *Economics in Institutional Perspective* (Lexington, MA: Lexington Books).

Stewart, I. (1989) *Does God Play Dice? The Mathematics of Chaos* (Oxford: Blackwell).

Stiglitz, J. E. (1987) 'The Causes and Consequences of the Dependence of Quality on Price', *Journal of Economic Literature*, **25**(1), Mar., pp. 1–48.

Stiglitz, J. E. (1991) 'Symposium on Organizations and Economics', *Journal of Economic Perspectives*, **5**(2), Spring, pp. 15–24.

Stiglitz, J. E. and Mathewson, G. F. (eds) (1985) *New Developments in the Analysis of Market Structure* (Cambridge, MA: MIT Press).

Stinchcombe, A. L. (1965) 'Social Structure and Organizations', in March (1965), pp. 142–93.

Streissler, E. W. (ed.) (1969) *Roads to Freedom: Essays in Honour of Friedrich A. von Hayek* (London: Routledge and Kegan Paul).

Streissler, E. W. (1990) 'The Influence of German Economics on the Work of Menger and Marshall', *History of Political Economy*, **22**, annual supplement, pp. 31–68.

Sugden, R. (1986) *The Economics of Rights, Co-operation and Welfare* (Oxford: Blackwell).

Sugden, R. (1989) 'Spontaneous Order', *Journal of Economic Perspectives*, **3**(4), Fall, pp. 85–97.

Sugden, R. (1990) 'Convention, Creativity and Conflict', in Varoufakis and Young (1990), pp. 68–90.

Sugden, R. (1991) 'Rational Choice: A Survey of Contributions from Economics and Philosophy', *Economic Journal*, **101**(4), July, pp. 751–85.

Suranyi-Unger, T. (1931) *Economics in the Twentieth Century* (New York: Norton).

Swedberg, R. (1991) *Joseph A. Schumpeter: His Life and Work* (Cambridge: Polity Press).

Targetti, F. and Thirlwall, A. P. (eds) (1989) *The Essential Kaldor* (New York: Holmes and Meier).

Teilhard de Chardin, P. (1959) *The Phenomenon of Man* (New York: Harper).

Teubner, G. (ed.) (1988) *Autopoietic Law* (Berlin: De Gruyter).

Thaler, R. H. and Shefrin, H. M. (1981) 'An Economic Theory of Self-Control', *Journal of Political Economy*, **89**, 392–406.

Thoben, H. (1982) 'Mechanistic and Organistic Analogies in Economics Reconsidered', *Kyklos*, **35**, fasc. 2, pp. 292–306.

Thom, R. (1975) *Structural Stability and Morphogenesis: An Outline of a General Theory of Models* (Reading, MA: Benjamin).

Thomas, B. (1991) 'Alfred Marshall on Economic Biology', *Review of Political Economy*, **3**(1), Jan., pp. 1–14.

Thomas, H. T. and Logan, C. (1982) *Mondragon: An Economic Analysis* (London: George Allen and Unwin).

Thorp, J. (1980) *Free Will: A Defence against Neurophysiological Determinism* (London: Routledge and Kegan Paul).

Tilly, C. (1987) 'The Analysis of Popular Collective Action', *European Journal of Operational Research*, **30**(2), June, pp. 223–9.

Tilman, R. (1987) 'Some Recent Interpretations of Thorstein Veblen's Theory of Institutional Change', *Journal of Economic Issues*, **21**(2), June, pp. 683–90.

Timpanaro, S. (1975) *On Materialism* (London: NLB).

Tomlinson, J. (1990) *Hayek and the Market* (London: Pluto Press).

Tool, M. R. and Samuels, W. J. (eds) (1989) *State, Society and Corporate Power*, 2nd edn (New Brunswick: Transaction).

Toulmin, S. (1972) *Human Understanding*, vol. 1 (Princeton: Princeton University Press).

Trivers, R. L. (1985) *Social Evolution* (Menlo Park, CA: Benjamin-Cummings).

Tullock, G. (1979) 'Sociobiology and Economics', *Atlantic Economic Journal*, Sept., pp. 1–10.

Tullock, G. (1987) 'Biological Applications of Economics', in Eatwell et al. (1987), vol. 1, pp. 246–7.

Turner, J. H. (1985) *Herbert Spencer: A Renewed Appreciation* (Beverly Hills, CA: Sage).

Tylecote, A. (1992) *Long Waves in the World Economy: The Present Crisis in Historical Perspective* (London: Routledge).

Udéhn, L. (1987) *Methodological Individualism: A Critical Appraisal* (Uppsala: Uppsala University Reprographics Centre).

Udéhn, L. (1992) 'The Limits of Economic Imperialism', in Himmelstrand (1992), pp. 239–80.

Ullmann-Margalit, E. (1977) *The Emergence of Norms* (Oxford: Oxford University Press).

Ullmann-Margalit, E. (1978) 'Invisible Hand Explanations', *Synthese*, **39**, pp. 263–91.

Urena, E. M. (1977) 'Marx and Darwin', *History of Political Economy*, **9**(4), Winter, pp. 548–59.

Ursprung, H. W. (1988) 'Evolution and the Economic Approach to Human Behavior', *Journal of Social and Biological Structure*, **11**, pp. 257–79.

Van Parijs, P. (1981) *Evolutionary Explanations in the Social Sciences: An Emerging Paradigm* (London: Tavistock).

Van Valen, L. M. (1973) 'A New Evolutionary Law', *Evolutionary Theory*, **1**, pp. 1–30.

Van Valen, L. M. (1975) 'Group Selection, Sex, and Fossils', *Evolution*, **29**, pp. 87–94.

Vanberg, V. J. (1986) 'Spontaneous Market Order and Social Rules: A Critique of F. A. Hayek's Theory of Cultural Evolution', *Economics and Philosophy*, **2**, June, pp. 75–100.

Vanberg, V. J. (1988) 'Rules and Choice in Economics and Sociology', *Jahrbuch für Neue Politische Ökonomie*, **7** (Tübingen: Mohr), pp. 1–22.

Vanberg, V. J. (1989) 'Carl Menger's Evolutionary and John R. Commons' Collective Action Approach to Institutions: A Comparison', *Review of Political Economy*, **1**(3), Nov., pp. 334–60.

Varela, F. J. (1981) *Principles of Biological Autonomy* (Amsterdam: North-Holland).

Varela, F. J., Maturana, H. R. and Uribe, R. (1974) 'Autopoiesis: The Organization of Living Systems, its Characterization and a Model', *BioSystems*, **5**, pp. 187–96.

Varoufakis, Y. (1990) 'Conflict in Equilibrium', in Varoufakis and Young (1990), pp. 39–67.

Varoufakis, Y. and Young, D. (eds) (1990) *Conflict in Economics* (Hemel Hempstead: Harvester Wheatsheaf).

Vaughn, K. I. (1980) 'Economic Calculation under Socialism: The Austrian Contribution', *Economic Inquiry*, **18**, pp. 535–54.

Veblen, T. B. (1899) *The Theory of the Leisure Class: An Economic Study of Institutions* (New York: Macmillan).

Veblen, T. B. (1904) *The Theory of Business Enterprise* (New York: Charles Scribners, reprinted Augustus Kelley).

Veblen, T. B. (1914) *The Instinct of Workmanship, and the State of the Industrial Arts* (New York: Augustus Kelley). Reprinted 1990 with a new introduction by M. G. Murphey and a 1964 introductory note by J. Dorfman (New Brunswick: Transaction).

Veblen, T. B. (1915) *Imperial Germany and the Industrial Revolution* (New York: Macmillan).

Veblen, T. B. (1919) *The Place of Science in Modern Civilisation and Other Essays* (New York: Huebsch). Reprinted 1990 with a new introduction by W. J. Samuels (New Brunswick: Transaction).

Veblen, T. B. (1921) *The Engineers and the Price System* (New York: Harcourt, Brace and World).

Veblen, T. B. (1934) *Essays on our Changing Order*, ed. L. Ardzrooni (New York: The Viking Press).

Veblen, T. B. (1936) *What Veblen Taught*, ed. W. C. Mitchell (New York: Augustus Kelley).

Voltaire, F. M. A. (1949) *Candide*. In *The Portable Voltaire*, ed. Ben Ray Redman (New York: Viking Press).

Von Neumann, J. and Morgenstern, O. (1944) *The Theory of Games and Economic Behavior* (Princeton: Princeton University Press).

Vorzimmer, P. J. (1969) 'Darwin, Malthus, and the Theory of Natural Selection', *Journal of the History of Ideas*, **30**, pp. 527–42.

Vorzimmer, P. J. (1977) *Charles Darwin: The Years of Controversy; The Origin of Species and its Critics, 1859–1882* (Philadelphia: Temple University Press).

Vrba, E. S. and Eldredge, N. (1984) 'Individuals, Hierarchies and Processes: Towards a More Complete Evolutionary Theory', *Paleobiology*, **10**, pp. 146–71.

Vrba, E. S. and Gould, S. J. (1986) 'The Hierarchical Expansion of Sorting and Selection: Sorting and Selection Cannot be Equated', *Paleobiology*, **12**, pp. 217–28.

Waddington, C. H. (1953) 'Genetic Assimilation of an Acquired Character', *Evolution*, **7**, pp. 118–26.

Waddington, C. H. (1957) *The Strategy of the Genes* (London: George Allen and Unwin).

Waddington, C. H. (1969) 'The Theory of Evolution Today', in Koestler and Smythies (1969), pp. 357–74.

Waddington, C. H. (ed.) (1972) *Towards a Theoretical Biology*, 4 vols (Edinburgh: Edinburgh University Press).

Waddington, C. H. (1975) *The Evolution of an Evolutionist* (Ithaca: Cornell University Press).

Waddington, C. H. (1976) 'Evolution in the Sub-human World', in Jantsch and Waddington (1976), pp. 11–15.

Wade, M. J. (1976) 'Group Selection among Laboratory Populations of *Tribolium*', *Proceedings of the National Academy of Sciences, USA*, **73**, pp. 4604–7.

Wade, M. J. (1977) 'An Experimental Study of Group Selection', *Evolution*, **31**, pp. 134–53.

Wade, M. J. (1978) 'A Critical Review of the Models of Group Selection', *Quarterly Review of Biology*, **53**, pp. 101–14. Reprinted in Brandon and Burian (1984).

Wade, M. J. (1979) 'The Evolution of Social Interactions by Family Selection', *American Naturalist*, **113**, pp. 399–417.

Wagener, H.-J. and Drukker, J. W. (eds) (1986) *The Economic Law of Motion of Modern Society: A Marx–Keynes–Schumpeter Centennial* (Cambridge: Cambridge University Press).

Walker, D. A. (1977) 'Thorstein Veblen's Economic System', *Economic Inquiry*, **15**(2), Apr., pp. 213–37. Reprinted in Samuels (1988), vol. 1.

Walker, D. A. (1986) 'Walras's Theory of the Entrepreneur', *De Economist*, **134**, pp. 1–24.

Wallace, A. R. (1905) *My Life: A Record of Events and Opinions*, 2 vols (London: Chapman and Hall).

Wallace, A. R. (1916) *Alfred Russell Wallace: Letters and Reminiscences*, ed. J. Marchant (New York: Harper).

Waller Jr, W. J. (1982) 'The Evolution of the Veblenian Dichotomy', *Journal of Economic Issues*, **16**(3), Sept., pp. 757–71. Reprinted in Albeda et al. (1987).

Waller Jr, W. J. (1988) 'Habit in Economic Analysis', *Journal of Economic Issues*, **22**(1), Mar., pp. 113–26.

Walras, L. (1954) *Elements of Pure Economics, or The Theory of Social Wealth* (1st edn 1874), trans. W. Jaffé from the French edn of 1926 (New York: Augustus Kelley).

Ward, L. F. (1893) *The Psychic Factors of Civilization* (Boston).

Wärneryd, K. (1989), 'Legal Restrictions and the Evolution of Media of Exchange', *Journal of Institutional and Theoretical Economics*, **145**(4), Dec., pp. 613–26.

Wärneryd, K. (1990), 'Legal Restrictions and Monetary Evolution', *Journal of Economic Behavior and Organization*, **13**(1), Mar., pp. 117–24.

Waters, C. K. (1986) 'Natural Selection without Survival of the Fittest', *Biology and Philosophy*, **1**(2), Apr., pp. 207–25.

Watson, A. J. and Lovelock, J. E. (1983) 'Biological Homoeostasis of the Global Environment: the Parable of Daisyworld, *Tellus*, **35**(B), pp. 284–9.

Weber, B. H., Depew, D. J., Dyke, C., Salthe, S. N., Schneider, E. D., Ulanowicz, R. E. and Wicken, J. S. (1989) 'Evolution in Thermodynamic Perspective: An Ecological Approach', *Biology and Philosophy*, 4(4), Oct., pp. 373–405.

Weber, M. (1978) *The Protestant Ethic and the Spirit of Capitalism* (1st edn. 1904–5) (London: Allen and Unwin).

Weeks, J. (1989) *A Critique of Neoclassical Macroeconomics* (Basingstoke: Macmillan).

Weinberg, S. (1974) 'Unified Theories of Elementary-Particle Interaction', *Scientific American*, 231(1), July, pp. 50–9.

Weinel, I. and Crossland, P. D. (1989) 'The Scientific Foundations of Technical Progress', *Journal of Economic Issues*, 23(3), Sept., pp. 795–808.

Weingart, P. (1990) 'Biology as Social Theory – The Bifurcation of Social Biology and Sociology in Germany ca. 1890', University of Bielefeld, mimeo.

Weintraub, E. R. (1979) *Microfoundations* (Cambridge: Cambridge University Press).

Weintraub, E. R. (1985) *General Equilibrium Analysis: Studies in Appraisal* (Cambridge: Cambridge University Press).

Weismann, A. (1893) *The Germ-Plasm: A Theory of Heredity*, trans. W. N. Parker and H. R. Ronnfeldt (London: Walter Scott).

Weiss, P. A. (1969) 'The Living System: Determinism Stratified', in Koestler and Smythies (1969), pp. 3–42.

Weiss, P. A. (1973) *The Science of Life* (Mt Kisco, NY: Futura).

Weiss, P. A. et al. (1971) *Hierarchically Organized Systems in Theory and Practice* (New York: Hafner).

Weisskopf, W. A. (1979) 'The Method is the Ideology: From a Newtonian to a Heisenbergian Paradigm in Economics', *Journal of Economic Issues*, 8(4), Dec., pp. 869–84.

Werren, J. H. and Pulliam, H. R. (1981) 'An Intergenerational Model of the Cultural Evolution of Helping Behavior', *Human Ecology*, 9, pp. 465–83.

West, B. J. and Salk, J. (1987) 'Complexity, Organization and Uncertainty', *European Journal of Operational Research*, 30(2), June, pp. 117–28.

Wheeler, W. M. (1930) *Social Life Among the Insects* (New York: Harcourt).

Wheeler, W. M. (1939) *Essays in Philosophical Biology* (Cambridge, MA: Harvard University Press).

Whitaker, J. K. (1977) 'Some Neglected Aspects of Alfred Marshall's Economic and Social Thought', *History of Political Economy*, 9(2), Summer, pp. 161–97.

Whitaker, J. K. (1990a) 'What Happened to the Second Volume of the Principles? The Thorny Path to Marshall's Last Books', in Whitaker (1990b), pp. 193–222.

Whitaker, J. K. (ed.) (1990b) *Centenary Essays on Alfred Marshall* (Cambridge: Cambridge University Press).

White, L. A. (1959) *The Evolution of Culture* (New York: McGraw-Hill).

White, L. H. (1984a) *Free Banking In Britain* (Cambridge: Cambridge University Press).

White, L. H. (1984b) 'Competitive Payments Systems and the Unit of Account', *American Economic Review*, **74**(3), Sept., pp. 699–712.

White, L. H. (1986) 'Competitive Payment Systems: Reply', *American Economic Review*, **76**(4), Dec., pp. 850–3.

White, L. H. (1987) 'Accounting for Non-Interest-Bearing Currency: A Critique of the Legal Restrictions Theory of Money', *Journal of Money, Credit and Banking*, **19**(4), Nov., pp. 448–56.

White, L. H. (1989) 'Alternative Perspectives on a Cashless Competitive Payments System', *Journal of Post Keynesian Economics*, **11**(3), Spring, pp. 378–84.

Whitehead, A. N. (1926) *Science and the Modern World* (Cambridge: Cambridge University Press).

Whitehead, A. N. (1929a) *Process and Reality: An Essay in Cosmology* (Cambridge: Cambridge University Press).

Whitehead, A. N. (1929b) *The Function of Reason* (Princeton: Princeton University Press).

Whitehead, A. N. (1938) *Modes of Thought* (Cambridge: Cambridge University Press).

Whittington, R. C. (1989) *Corporate Strategies in Recession and Recovery: Social Structure and Strategic Choice* (London: Unwin Hyman).

Wicken, J. S. (1987) *Evolution, Thermodynamics, and Information: Extending the Darwinian Paradigm* (Oxford: Oxford University Press).

Wicksteed, P. H. (1910) *The Commonsense of Political Economy*, ed. L. Robbins (London: Routledge).

Wiener, P. P. (1949) *Evolution and the Founders of Pragmatism* (Cambridge, MA: Harvard University Press).

Wilber, C. K. and Harrison, R. S. (1978) 'The Methodological Basis of Institutional Economics: Pattern Model, Storytelling, and Holism', *Journal of Economic Issues*, **12**(1), Mar., pp. 61–89. Reprinted in Samuels (1988), vol. 2.

Wiley, E. O. (1988) 'Evolution, Progress and Entropy', in Nitecki (1988), pp. 275–91.

Williams, G. C. (1966) *Adaptation and Natural Selection* (Princeton, NJ: Princeton University Press).

Williams, G. C. (1975) *Sex and Evolution* (Princeton, NJ: Princeton University Press).

Williams, G. C. (1986) 'A Defence of Reductionism in Evolutionary Biology', in Dawkins and Ridley (1986), pp. 1–27.

Williams, M. B. (1973a) 'Falsifiable Predictions of Evolutionary Theory', *Philosophy of Science*, **40**, pp. 518–37.

Williams, M. B. (1973b) 'The Logical Status of Natural Selection and Other Evolutionary Controversies', in Bunge (1973), pp. 84–102. Reprinted in Sober (1984b).

Williams, R. (1976) *Keywords: A Vocabulary of Culture and Society* (Glasgow: Fontana).

Williamson, O. E. (1975) *Markets and Hierarchies: Analysis and Anti-Trust Implications: A Study in the Economics of Internal Organization* (New York: Free Press).

Williamson, O. E. (1985) *The Economic Institutions of Capitalism: Firms, Markets, Relational Contracting* (London: Macmillan).

Williamson, O. E. (1988) 'The Economics and Sociology of Organization', in Farkas and England (1988), pp. 159–85.

Wilson, D. S. (1975) 'A General Theory of Group Selection', *Proceedings of the National Academy of Sciences, USA*, **72**, pp. 143–6.

Wilson, D. S. (1977) 'Structured Demes and the Evolution of Group Advantageous Traits', *American Naturalist*, **111**, pp. 157–85.

Wilson, D. S. (1980) *The Natural Selection of Populations and Communities* (Menlo Park, CA: Benjamin/Cummings).

Wilson, D. S. (1983) 'The Group Selection Controversy: History and Current Status', *Annual Review of Ecology and Systematics*, **14**, pp. 159–88.

Wilson, D. S. and Sober, E. (1989) 'Reviving the Superorganism', *Journal of Theoretical Biology*, **136**, pp. 337–56.

Wilson, E. O. (1975) *Sociobiology* (Cambridge, MA: Harvard University Press).

Wilson, E. O. (1978) *On Human Nature* (Cambridge, MA: Harvard University Press).

Wiltshire, D. (1978) *The Social and Political Thought of Herbert Spencer* (Oxford: Oxford University Press).

Wimsatt, W. C. (1974) 'Complexity and Organization', in Schaffner and Cohen (1974), pp. 67–86.

Wimsatt, W. C. (1976) 'Reductive Explanation: A Functional Account' in Cohen et al. (1976), pp. 671–710. Reprinted in Sober (1984b).

Wimsatt, W. C. (1980) 'Reductionist Research Strategies and their Biases in the Units of Selection Controversy', in Nickles (1980), pp. 213–59. Extracted in Brandon and Burian (1984) and reprinted in Sober (1984b).

Wimsatt, W. C. (1981) 'The Units of Selection and the Structure of the Multi-level Genome', in Asquith and Giere (1981), pp. 122–83.

Wimsatt, W. C. and Schank, J. C. (1988) 'Two Constraints on the Evolution of Complex Adaptations and the Means of their Avoidance', in Nitecki (1988), pp. 231–73.

Winslow, E. A. (1986) ' "Human Logic" and Keynes's Economics', *Eastern Economic Journal*, **12**, Oct.–Dec., pp. 413–30.

Winslow, E. A. (1989) 'Organic Interdependence, Uncertainty and Economic Analysis', *Economic Journal*, **99**(4), Dec., pp. 1173–82.

Winston, G. C. (1980) 'Addiction and Backsliding: A Theory of Compulsive Consumption', *Journal of Economic Behavior and Organization*, **1**(3), Sept., pp. 295–324.

Winter, J. M. (ed.) (1975) *War and Economic Development* (Cambridge, MA: Harvard University Press).

Winter Jr, S. G. (1964) 'Economic "Natural Selection" and the Theory of the Firm', *Yale Economic Essays*, **4**(1), pp. 225–72.

Winter Jr, S. G. (1971) 'Satisficing, Selection, and the Innovating Remnant', *Quarterly Journal of Economics*, **85**(2), May, pp. 237–61.

Winter Jr, S. G. (1975) 'Optimization and Evolution in the Theory of the Firm', in Day and Groves (1975), pp. 73–118.

Winter Jr, S. G. (1982) 'An Essay on the Theory of Production', in Hymans (1982), pp. 55–91.

Wisman, J. D. (1989) 'Economic Knowledge, Evolutionary Epistemology, and Human Interests', *Journal of Economic Issues*, **23**(2), June, pp. 647–56.

Witt, U. (1985), 'Coordination of Individual Economic Activities as an Evolving Process of Self-Organization', *Economie appliquée*, **37**(4), pp. 569–95.

Witt, U. (1986a) 'Evolution and Stability of Cooperation without Enforceable Contracts', *Kyklos*, **39**, pp. 245–66.

Witt, U. (1986b), 'Firms' Market Behavior under Imperfect Information and Economic Natural Selection', *Journal of Economic Behavior and Organization*, **7**(3), Sept., pp. 265–90.

Witt, U. (1989) 'The Evolution of Economic Institutions as a Propagation Process', *Public Choice*, **62**, pp. 155–72.

Witt, U. (1991a) 'Reflections on the Present State of Evolutionary Economic Theory', in Hodgson and Screpanti (1991), pp. 83–102.

Witt, U. (1991b) 'Economics, Sociobiology, and Behavioral Psychology on Preferences', *Journal of Economic Psychology*, **12**, pp. 557–73.

Witt, U. (ed.) (1991c) *Explaining Process and Change: Approaches to Evolutionary Economics* (Ann Arbor: Michigan University Press).

Witt, U. (forthcoming) *Individualistic Foundations of Evolutionary Economics* (Cambridge: Cambridge University Press).

Woo, H. K. H. (1986) *What's Wrong with Formalization in Economics?* (Newark, CA: Victoria Press).

Woo, H. K. H. (1990) 'Scientific Reduction, Reductionism and Metaphysical Reduction – A Broad View of Economic Methodology', *Methodus*, **2**(2), Dec., pp. 61–8.

Woodcock, A. and Davis, M. (1980) *Catastrophe Theory* (New York: Avon).

Worster, D. (1977) *Nature's Economy: A History of Ecological Ideas* (Garden City: Doubleday).

Wray, L. R. (1990) *Money and Credit in Capitalist Economies: The Endogenous Money Approach* (Aldershot: Edward Elgar).

Wright, S. (1931) 'Evolution in Mendelian Populations', *Genetics*, **16**, pp. 97–159.

Wright, S. (1956) 'Modes of Selection', *American Naturalist*, **90**, pp. 5–24.

Wright, S. (1959) 'Physiological Genetics, Ecology of Populations, and Natural Selection', *Perspectives on Biological Medicine*, **3**, pp. 107–51.

Wright, S. (1967) 'Comments', in Moorhead and Kaplan (1967), pp. 117–20.

Wright, S. (1978) *Evolution and the Genetics of Populations: A Treatise*, 4 vols (Chicago: University of Chicago Press).

Wynarczyk, P. (1992) 'Comparing Alleged Incommensurables: Institutional and Austrian Economics as Rivals and Possible Complements?', *Review of Political Economy*, **4**(1), Jan., pp. 18–36.

Wynne-Edwards, V. C. (1962) *Animal Dispersion in Relation to Social Behaviour* (Edinburgh: Oliver and Boyd).

Wynne-Edwards, V. C. (1978) 'Intrinsic Population Control: An Introduction', in Ebling and Stoddart (1978).

Wynne-Edwards, V. C. (1986) *Evolution through Group Selection* (Oxford: Blackwell).

Yeager, L. B. (1987) 'Stable Money and Free-Market Currencies', in Dorn and Schwartz (1987).

Yeager, L. B. (1989) 'A Competitive Payments System: Some Objections Considered', *Journal of Post Keynesian Economics*, 11(3), Spring, pp. 370–7.

Young, A. A. (1928) 'Increasing Returns and Economic Progress', *Economic Journal*, 38(4), Dec., pp. 527–42.

Young, H. D. (1968) *Fundamentals of Optics and Modern Physics* (New York: McGraw-Hill).

Young, R. M. (1969) 'Malthus and the Evolutionists: The Common Context of Biological and Social Theory', *Past and Present*, no. 43, May, pp. 109–41.

Young, R. M. (1971) 'Evolutionary Biology: Then and Now', *Social Studies*, 1, pp. 177–206.

Young, R. M. (1985a) *Darwin's Metaphor: Nature's Place in Victorian Culture* (Cambridge: Cambridge University Press).

Young, R. M. (1985b) 'Darwinism *is* Social', in Kohn (1985), pp. 609–38.

Zeleny, M. (ed.) (1980) *Autopoiesis, Dissipative Structures, and Spontaneous Social Orders* (Boulder, CO: Westview Press).

Zeleny, M. (ed.) (1981) *Autopoiesis: A Theory of Living Systems* (New York: North-Holland).

Zeleny, M. (1987) 'Autopoiesis', in Singh (1987), pp. 393–400.

Ziman, J. M. (1978) *Reliable Knowledge* (Cambridge: Cambridge University Press).

Index

376 Index